DISAPPEARING DESTINATIONS

DISAPPEARING DESTINATIONS

Climate Change and Future Challenges for Coastal Tourism

Edited by

Andrew Jones

University of Wales
Cardiff, UK

and

Michael Phillips

School of Built and Natural Environment
Swansea Metropolitan University
Swansea, Wales, UK

www.cabi.org

CABI is a trading name of CAB International

CABI Head Office
Nosworthy Way
Wallingford
Oxfordshire OX10 8DE
UK

Tel: +44 (0)1491 832111
Fax: +44 (0)1491 833508
E-mail: cabi@cabi.org
Website: www.cabi.org

CABI North American Office
875 Massachusetts Avenue
7th Floor
Cambridge, MA 02139
USA

Tel: +1 617 395 4056
Fax: +1 617 354 6875
E-mail: cabi-nao@cabi.org

A catalogue record for this book is available from the British Library, London, UK.

Library of Congress Cataloging-in-Publication Data
Disappearing destinations: climate change and future challenges for coastal tourism/edited by Andrew Jones and Michael Phillips.
    p. cm.
  Includes bibliographical references and index.
  ISBN 978-1-84593-548-1 (alk. paper)
  1. Marine ecotourism. 2. Coastal ecology. 3. Climatic changes. I. Jones, Andrew L., 1958. II. Phillips, Michael R., 1962- III. Title.
  G156.5.M36D57 2011
  338.4'79109146–dc22

                                                        2010009985

ISBN: 978 1 84593 548 1

Commissioning editor: Sarah Hulbert
Production editor: Shankari Wilford

Typeset by AMA Dataset, Preston, UK.
Printed and bound in the UK by CPI Antony Rowe Ltd, Chippenham, UK.

Contents

Contributors

Fátima Alves, CESAM – Centre for Environmental and Marine Studies, Department of Environment and Planning, University of Aveiro, 3810–193 Aveiro, Portugal. E-mail: malves@ua.pt

Giorgio Anfuso, Dpto de Ciencias de la Tierra, Facultad de Ciencias del Mar y Ambientales, Universidad de Cádiz, Polígono Río San Pedro s/n, 11510 Puerto Real (Cádiz), Spain. E-mail: giorgio.anfuso@uca.es

Lyn Bibbings, Oxford Brookes University, Business School, Oxford, UK; e-mail: ljbibbings@brookes.ac.uk

Paulo Borges, Department of Geosciences, University of the Azores, 9501-801 Ponta Delgada, Portugal. E-mail:pb@uac.pt

S.W. Boyd, Department of Hospitality and Tourism Management, University of Ulster, Cromore Road, Coleraine BT52 1SA, Northern Ireland, UK.

Peter Burns, University of Brighton, CENTOPS, Eastbourne, Sussex, UK. E-mail: P.M.Burns@brighton.ac.uk

Helena Calado, CIBIO – Research Centre in Biodiversity and Genetics Resources, Department of Biology/Geography Section, University of Azores, 9500-855 Ponta Delgada, Portugal. E-mail: geografia@uac.pt

J.A.G. Cooper, School of Environmental Sciences, University of Ulster, Cromore Road, Coleraine BT52 1SA, Northern Ireland, UK.

Philip Dearden, Marine Protected Areas Research Group, Department of Geography, University of Victoria , BC, Canada.

C. Michael Hall, Department of Management, University of Canterbury, Christchurch, New Zealand 8140. E-mail: michael.hall@canterbury.ac.nz

Zoe Hughes, Boston University, Department of Earth Sciences, 675 Commonwealth Ave, Boston, MA 02118, USA. E-mail: zoeh@bu.edu

Julia Jabour, Institute of Antarctic and Southern Ocean Studies, University of Tasmania, Private Bag 77, Hobart, Tasmania, 7001 Australia. E-mail: julia.jabour@utas.edu.au

Ian Jenkins, *STAR centre, Les Roches Gruyère University of Applied Science, Switzerland. E-mail: ian.jenkins@glion.edu*

Andrew Jones, *University of Wales, Cathays Park, Cardiff. E-mail: andrew.jones@wales.ac.uk*

Petch Manopawitr, *Marine Protected Areas Research Group, Department of Geography, University of Victoria, Canada, BC.*

Klaus J. Meyer-Arendt, *Department of Environmental Studies, University of West Florida, Pensacola, FL 3251, USA. E-mail: kjma@uwf.edu*

Alvaro Moreno, *International Centre for Integrated Assessment and Sustainable Development (ICIS), Maastricht University, PO Box 616, 6200MD, Maastricht, The Netherlands. E-mail: a.moreno@maastrichtuniversity.nl*

Driss Nachite, *UFR 'Sciences de la Mer', Laboratoire d'Océanographie Appliquée, Fac. Sciences, 93030 – Tetouan, Morocco.*

Kiat Ng, *CIBIO – Research Centre in Biodiversity and Genetics Resources, Department of Biology/Geography Section, University of Azores, 9500-855 Ponta Delgada, Portugal. E-mail: geografia@uac.pt*

Paul Osborne, *Faculty of Humanities, Swansea Metropolitan University, Swansea, Wales, UK. E-mail: paul.osborne@smu.ac.uk*

Michael Phillips, *School of Built and Natural Environment, Swansea Metropolitan University, Swansea, Wales, UK. E-mail: mike.phillips@smu.ac.uk*

Lisa Sousa, *CESAM – Centre for Environmental and Marine Studies, Department of Environment and Planning, University of Aveiro, 3810-193 Aveiro, Portugal.*

Stephen M. Turton, *JCU/CSIRO Tropical Landscapes Joint Venture & School of Earth & Environmental Sciences, James Cook University, Cairns, Australia. E-mail: steve.turton@jcu.edu.au*

Allan Williams, *School of Natural and Built Environment, Swansea Metropolitan University, Swansea, Wales, UK. E-mail: allan.williams@smu.ac.uk*

Robyn F. Wilson, *School of Earth & Environmental Sciences, James Cook University, Cairns, Australia.*

About the Authors

Editors

Andrew Jones is a Senior Lecturer at the University of Wales in Cardiff. He has professional experience in planning and tourism at international, regional and local levels and has been an enthusiastic contributor to the academic tourism community within the UK and Europe. In this respect, he has been an active practitioner, researcher and teacher in planning, conservation, regeneration and tourism planning since 1981. In his present post, he specializes in: Town and Country Planning; Cultural Regeneration; Tourism Development and Environmental Policy. He completed his PhD on research investigating the relationship and tensions between regeneration, the environment and sustainable tourism. His current research activities have consolidated this broad approach with a specific interest in two particular research areas. The first consolidates work over the last decade on waterfronts and coastal zone management, tourism and regeneration and the second, a more recent interest in the development of tourism micro-markets (focusing on cultural/rural community regeneration). These areas of research have enabled him to participate in a broad range of research networks and to become actively involved in his specific research community. With respect to this, Andrew has carried out numerous consultancy projects relating to tourism and leisure and has published a number of industry and academic articles, reports and conference papers. In recognition of his research to the industry he has been invited to international conferences in Europe, North America, Asia and Australasia.

Michael Phillips has a BSc in Civil Engineering, an MSc in Environmental Conservation Management and a PhD in Coastal Processes and Geomorphology. He is a member of the Institution of Environmental Sciences and Fellow of the Royal Geographical Society, where he is vice-chairman of the Coastal and Marine Working Group. Professor Phillips is Head of the School of Built and

Natural Environment at Swansea Metropolitan University and his research interests include coastal processes, morphological change and adaptation to climate change and sea level rise. He has been an invited speaker and presenter at many major international conferences and advisor and evaluator for various international coastal research projects. Consultancy includes beach replenishment issues and developing techniques to monitor underwater sediment movement to inform beach management. He is widely published and a member of the Climate Change Working Group of the Global Forum on Oceans, Coasts, and Islands, amongst others.

Contributors

Fátima Alves has a Degree in Urban and Regional Planning from the University of Aveiro, a Masters in Planning and Project for the Urban Environment from the University of Porto and a PhD in Environmental Sciences from the University of Aveiro. Currently, she is an invited Assistant Professor at the Department of Environment and Planning at the University of Aveiro and a researcher at the Centre for Environment and Sea Studies. She teaches Regional and Urban Planning, Environmental Engineering, Ocean Sciences, and the Joint European Masters in Environment Sciences (JEMES). Since 1993, she has collaborated with government, private sectors and universities in coastal zone planning, protected areas' spatial and management plans, as well as national and international projects (AIR'94; LIFE'96; LIFE'98; UNESCO'02; INTERREG III B; FCT; and CYTED'07). In 2006, she co-led the elaboration of the implementation of the EU Recommendation on Integrated Coastal Zone Management. Currently, she is a core member of the Portuguese Maritime Spatial Plan development.

Giorgio Anfuso has a PhD in Marine Sciences and is Professor of Coastal Geomorphology and Environmental Geology at the Faculty of Marine Sciences, University of Cádiz, Spain. His research specialisms include coastal processes, coastal evolution and morphological change, subjects on which he is widely published. Professor Anfuso has collaborated on several national and international projects on coastal zone characterization and management in different countries, especially Spain, Morocco, Italy, Colombia, etc.

Lyn Bibbings is a tourism academic with a practitioner background and she continues to combine her academic roles with responsibilities in the sector as a Director of Tourism South East, UK and as Chair of the Sub Regional Tourism committee for Buckinghamshire, Berkshire and Oxfordshire, UK. She is a management development consultant for FirstChoice, now TuiTravel, one of the world's largest travel firms. Lyn also Chairs, and is a Director of, the Association for Tourism in Higher Education and is a Director and Fellow of the Tourism Society. She has been the Liaison Officer for Tourism for the Higher Education Subject Network in the UK since its inception in 2000. She is a member of two committees of the Academy of Social Sciences: the committee of Learned Societies and the Events committee.

Paulo Borges holds a PhD in Geology (Coastal Geology) from the Geosciences Department of the University of the Azores. Prior to his PhD, Paulo Borges has been working as a researcher since 1992, and is currently an Auxiliary Researcher at the University of the Azores, and a collaborator at the Geology Centre of the University of Lisbon. He has carried out academic and applied research in coastal geology, mainly in the Azores archipelago, and published in several journals in these fields. His main scientific interests are sedimentology, geomorphology, coastal dynamics and coastal hazards, mainly on tsunamis, coastal storms, coastal flooding and coastal erosion. Based on his studies, particularly on the Azorean coastal hazards, he has recently started researching climate change impacts on the Azorean coastal zones. His scientific expertise and technical studies have been used and applied on the environmental planning and management of the Azorean coasts.

S.W. Boyd holds the Chair in Tourism in the Department of Hospitality and Tourism Management at the University of Ulster, Northern Ireland. He trained as a geographer, receiving his Bachelors degree from Queen's University, Belfast, his Masters from the University of Regina, Canada and his Doctorate from the University of Western Ontario, Canada, where he examined sustainability in Canada's National Parks as it related to policy, planning and management. He has published extensively in leading tourism journals on research areas as eclectic as heritage tourism, community involvement in tourism, tourism planning and development, the role of tourism in national parks and peripheral area settings, political and religious tourism, and the development of tourism trails.

Peter Burns joined the School of Service Management , University of Brighton, in 2000 as Professor of International Tourism and Development and founding Director of the Centre for Tourism Policy Studies (CENTOPS). Prior to this, he was Head of the Department of Leisure, Hospitality and Tourism at the University of Luton (RAE grade 4). Peter is the author of numerous papers on sustainable tourism and is the author of the internationally acclaimed publication *An Introduction to Tourism and Anthropology*, which has been translated into both Japanese and Portuguese.

Peter has two streams of current research. First, the roles and responsibilities throughout the tourism value chain in climate change. The approach thus far has been to identify a series of policy and business paradoxes. The findings have prompted the first of a series of online surveys to further investigate attitudes and values among various stakeholder groups.

The second stream, 'A Secret History of Holidays', uses private archive material and interviews to capture experiences and memories of the first generation of post-war tourists. Outputs include a short film, which was presented at the CENTOPS 2007 conference. This stream will be further developed by investigating various media public film archives including Screen Archive Southeast.

Helena Calado holds a Degree in Geography and Regional Planning from the New University of Lisbon in Portugal and a PhD in Land Use Planning and Management from the University of the Azores in Portugal. She is currently a researcher at the Research Centre in Biodiversity and Genetic Resources and

Professor at the Biology Department of the University of the Azores where she teaches Geography, Spatial Planning, Legislation and Environmental Management. Besides mentoring Masters students, she also manages a team of PhD students and researchers. With over 15 years of experience in land use planning and environmental impact assessments, she is currently focusing her research on coastal zone management plans, coastal hazards and mitigation measures, climate change impacts and implications, marine protected areas, and maritime spatial planning for small islands, particularly for the Azores. She has participated in numerous research projects, technical studies, and published numerous technical reports, in proceedings and in peer-reviewed academic journals and chapters.

Billiana Cicin-Sain is the author of over 100 publications in marine policy, with an emphasis on cross-cutting issues related to integrated ocean and coastal governance. Her 1998 book on *Integrated Coastal and Ocean Management: Concepts and Practices* has been used in academic and governmental training efforts around the world. Her 2000 book, *The Future of US Ocean Policy: Choices for the New Century*, which has been called 'the ultimate guide to the emerging debate on US ocean governance,' presented a blueprint for national ocean policy reform in the USA. *Integrated National and Regional Ocean Policies: Comparative Practices and Future Prospects* (forthcoming in 2010) will bring together analyses of the experiences of 15 nations and four regions of the world that have taken concrete steps toward cross-cutting integrated oceans governance.

J.A.G. Cooper is Professor of Coastal Studies at the University of Ulster, Northern Ireland, where he heads the coastal research group. He has a Bachelors degree in geology from Queen's University Belfast and Masters and PhD from the University of Natal in South Africa. He has over 20 years of research experience in coastal geomorphology and coastal zone management and is chair of the Northern Ireland Coastal and Marine Forum. He has published more than 200 articles in the field of coastal research and was lead author of the UK Marine Climate Change Impacts Partnership's report *Coastal Economies and People* in 2009.

Philip Dearden is Professor and Chair of Geography at the University of Victoria where he leads the Marine Protected Areas Research Group. His research interests range from seagrass ecology through to coral reef monitoring and diver surveys in South-east Asia. He is particularly interested in understanding MPA use patterns, zoning and developing incentive-based approaches to conservation and advises the World Bank, Asian Development Bank, UN, IUCN and national governments in Asia on marine protected area management. He has active MPA research projects in Mexico, Thailand, Cambodia and Comoros. He is the Leader of the national MPA Working Group for the Ocean Management Research Network and Co-Chair of Parks Canada's NMCA Marine Science Network.

C. Michael Hall is Professor in the Department of Management, University of Canterbury, Christchurch, New Zealand; Docent, Department of Geography, University of Oulu, Finland; and Visiting Professor, Linneaus University, Kalmar, Sweden. Co-editor of *Current Issues in Tourism*, he has published widely in tourism and mobility, regional development and tourism, environmental history and gastronomy. Current environmental change research focuses on issues associated with biosecurity and climate change, the role of tourism in biodiversity conservation, tourism's contribution to climate change especially in relation to marine and space tourism, social marketing, degrowth and sustainable consumption, and the development of steady-state/ecological economic approaches to sustainable approaches to tourism consumption and production.

Zoe Hughes is a coastal oceanographer who investigates the physical impacts of waves, currents and sea level rise on coastal geomorphology and hydrodynamics. She gained her PhD at the National Oceanography Centre, UK, examining wave–current interaction and bed morphology within a tidal inlet. After her PhD she moved to Boston University where her recent work involves collaborations with ecologists, undertaking interdisciplinary studies of feedbacks between hydrodynamics, sediment movement and the ecosystem. She is involved in a number of studies within coastal barrier and saltmarsh systems along the East and Gulf coasts of the USA from Maine to Louisiana.

Julia Jabour has been researching, writing and lecturing on matters to do with Antarctic law and policy for nearly 20 years at the University of Tasmania. She has visited Antarctica five times and has been on the Australian delegation to Antarctic Treaty Consultative Meetings. Julia has a BA degree majoring in politics, philosophy and sociology, and a Graduate Diploma (Honours) in Antarctic and Southern Ocean Studies. For her PhD she researched the changing nature of sovereignty in the Arctic and Antarctic in response to global environmental interdependence. Julia's research interests are eclectic and cover Antarctic tourism, international law, environmental law, threatened species conservation, international marine management and scientific ethics.

Ian Jenkins (BSc Econ, MPhil, PhD, University of Wales) has worked in the tourism and leisure industries for the last 20 years as a researcher, senior lecturer, consultant and director of several research units. This work has resulted in numerous publications including industry reports, conference papers, academic articles and book chapters; he has also been a peer reviewer for journal articles. Some of the research projects with which he has been involved have resulted in legislative change and improved industry standards. In addition, he has undertaken work for prestigious organizations such as UNESCO, British Council, British Standards Institute, Health and Safety Executive, VisitWales and CEN. His research and consultancy expertise ranges from niche tourism development through to risk management of adventure tourism products. Ian is currently Research Director of Les Roches Gruyère University of Applied Sciences, Switzerland together with being an external examiner for the University of Birmingham at both undergraduate and postgraduate level.

Petch Manopawitr is a Thai conservation scientist with extensive experience in the fields of conservation training, biodiversity research and protected area management. After his Masters degree from James Cook University, he joined the Wildlife Conservation Society, an international conservation organization, in 2001, as Training and Education Coordinator for the Thailand Program coordinating conservation training courses with local and international experts. He later become Deputy Director, implementing site-based conservation programmes. He has served as an Executive Committee member of the Bird Conservation Society of Thailand since 2002. He is a freelance environmental writer and has produced many reports and articles on conservation issues. From 2008–2009 he was a Fulbright's Humphrey Fellow based at Cornell University. Currently, he is based at the University of Victoria, Canada, as a PhD student, developing an integrated study on climate change and biodiversity conservation with emphasis on tropical marine ecosystems.

Klaus J. Meyer-Arendt, professor at the University of West Florida's Department of Environmental Studies, has a coastal background extending from Germany's Elbe estuary to Oregon, Louisiana and Florida. Combining his Louisiana State University academic training in cultural-historical geography and coastal geomorphology led him into coastal tourism and the environmental impacts of coastal resort development. He works primarily along the shores of the Gulf of Mexico (USA and Mexico) and the Caribbean Sea, where hurricane impacts and shoreline erosion have factored into his research. In 1994, Klaus was the recipient of a Fulbright/García Robles research award to Yucatán, Mexico, where his research focus was upon human modification of shorelines. Currently, his research is centred on human mortality associated with hurricanes, storm-surge measurement, and coastal tourism development along Mexico's Costa Maya.

Alvaro Moreno works at the International Centre for Integrated Assessment and Sustainable Development (ICIS/Maastricht University). His teaching activities focus on sustainable development and global environmental change. For the last 5 years he has been doing research on the relationship between weather and tourism and assessing the impacts of climate change on the sector, with special attention to the concept of vulnerability. He has collaborated with the UNWTO capacity-building programme in Mexico and participated as guest speaker in several different international conferences. Besides climate change, his PhD and research interests include the relationship between tourism and the environment and the role of tourism for poverty alleviation, international cooperation and development.

Driss Nachite has a PhD in Oceanography from the University of Bordeaux, France and a PhD in Geology from the University of Granada, Spain. He is now Professor of Oceanography and Integrated Coastal Zone Management, as well as Director of the Unit of Formation and Research in Marine Sciences, at the University Abdelmalek Essaadi in Tétouan, Morocco. During his career he has developed several research projects on coastal erosion and management for the littoral of Morocco, both on the Mediterranean and Atlantic sides, as well as for other African countries. Professor Driss has also collaborated on many research projects in Spain and across Europe.

Kiat Ng holds a Bachelor degree in Civil Engineering from McGill University in Canada and a Masters degree in Environmental Engineering from Stanford University in the USA. Since graduation, Kiat Ng has worked as an environmental engineer in environmental consulting firms in California. She has experiences in environmental, water resources and regulatory support projects. Currently, Kiat Ng is working as a researcher at the Research Centre in Biodiversity and Genetic Resources in the Azores in Portugal. Her research focuses on coastal zones, coastal hazards and mitigation measures, maritime spatial planning, as well as climate change impacts and implications for the Azores. She has also co-authored in peer-reviewed academic journals.

Paul Osborne is a qualified solicitor and Assistant Dean in the Faculty of Humanities, Swansea Metropolitan University (SMU). Paul's interest in climate change started whilst in practice in East Anglia and this led to his undertaking an LLM in Environmental Law at London University and work at FIELD (the Foundation for International Environmental Law and Development). Subsequently, Paul has worked as a lecturer at SMU, working specifically in the environmental law field at undergraduate and postgraduate levels. As well as law and climate change, Paul's research interests lie in the historical development of environmental protection legislation in England and Wales and contaminated land regimes (both nationally and internationally).

Lisa Sousa has a Degree and a Masters in Environmental Engineering from the University of Aveiro. Her Masters thesis is titled 'Marine Spatial Planning Methodologies: application to Aveiro's Lagoon'. She is currently working as a research grant holder in the Department of Environment and Planning at the University of Aveiro. Since 2008, she has collaborated in research projects on marine spatial planning methodologies. Presently, she is involved in the elaboration of the Portuguese Maritime Spatial Plan.

Stephen M. Turton is a professor in the School of Earth and Environmental Sciences at James Cook University in Cairns, Australia. His research interests include tropical climatology, rainforest ecology, urban ecology, recreation ecology and natural resource management. Steve has published over 100 scientific papers in these fields of study, comprising refereed journal articles, book chapters and research monographs. He is the co-editor of *Living in a Dynamic Tropical Forest Landscape* (2008: Wiley-Blackwell). His current research has a strong emphasis on sustainable use, planning and management of tropical forest landscapes in north Queensland, South-east Asia and Melanesia. He recently led the Sustainable Tourism Cooperative Research Centre's climate change destinations and adaptation special project. Steve is a former Councillor of the Institute of Australian Geographers and a member of the Wet Tropics Management Authority's Scientific Advisory Committee. He is also a Council member of the Association for Tropical Biology and Conservation.

Allan Williams has Geography and Geology degrees and, as a Commonwealth Scholar, a PhD in Coastal Geology. He is a Chartered Engineer, Chartered Scientist, Member of the Institution of Materials, Mining and Metallurgy, and a Winston Churchill Fellow. He has published more than 300 coastal research papers and technical reports, generated over £2 million in research grants and coordinated international research projects (e.g. 'DUNES' under the EC ELOISE programme). Previously he held chairs at the universities of Glamorgan and Bath Spa, and has been a Research Scholar at the International Hurricane

Research Center, Florida International University, Miami, Florida, USA and an Erskine Fellow, at the University of Canterbury, Christchurch, New Zealand as well as a research scientist at the universities of Massachusetts and Maryland, USA. He is a Professor in the School of Natural & Built Environment, Swansea Metropolitan University, Wales, UK.

Robyn F. Wilson is a postdoctoral research fellow in the School of Earth and Environmental Sciences at James Cook University in Cairns, Australia. Her research interests include rainforest ecology, recreation ecology and natural resource management. She has publications in wetland and rainforest ecology and is the co-editor of *The Impacts of Climate Change on Australian Tourism Destinations – Developing Adaptation and Response Strategies* and author of the *Cairns Case Study* (2009: CRC for Sustainable Tourism Pty Ltd). Her current research, as part of a national project in forest vulnerability assessment, is addressing adaptive capacity, barriers to adaptation and vulnerability of Australia's forests to climate change.

Preface

The growth of coastal tourism destinations and their relationship with the coastal environments in which they are located have become current and sometimes controversial topics of research, that are increasingly discussed internationally. In this respect, coastal destinations, beaches and beach resorts have become synonymous with tourism, tourism growth and economic success. With current predictions of climate change and sea level rise they are, however, becoming increasingly threatened by climate induced damage and economic uncertainty. In this context a fairly recent report by the UK-based Churchill Insurance Group highlighted that some of the world's most famous tourist attractions, such as Australia's Great Barrier Reef and Italy's Amalfi coast, could be closed to visitors within a few years because of worries about environmental damage and climate change. The report suggested that some destinations could be permanently closed to tourists by 2020 or face severe restrictions on visitor numbers and sharp increases in access costs. The report forecasted clear warnings, that within 20 to 40 years, destinations such as the Great Barrier Reef, Islands of the Caribbean, Pacific and Indian Ocean and swathes of America's Gulf Coast and Europe's Mediterranean Basin could experience severe damage, in turn forcing the closure or economic demise of many coastal tourism destinations.

Despite such predictions, tourism growth trends and consequent demands are showing continued signs of exponential growth, which will ultimately exacerbate current concerns regarding predicted climate threats and consequently the ultimate sustainability of such destinations. It is the consequences of such phenomena and dynamics that will impact upon the long term future of coastal tourism environments and, ultimately, their continued survival. It is, therefore, becoming increasingly vital to identify management strategies that protect coastal tourism infrastructure and resources, especially at destinations that are significantly reliant on the tourist industry for their economy and social structures. This includes destinations within both the developed and developing world, as coastal regions are places where destruction of both natural and tourist environments have no discrimination. This is exemplified, for example, by many coastal destinations around the world where direct and indirect pressures have led to unsustainable coastal development. As a result, political moves across continents – North America, Australasia, Asia and Europe – have now put coastal management strategies to tackle such challenges firmly on national and international agendas.

This book, and the chapters within, thus aim to discuss threats and consequences of climate predictions on coastal tourism destinations. In this context predicted changes and implications for management and policy at such destinations are globally assessed. From the analysis of specific tourism case studies, local impacts of climate change on coastal tourism infrastructures are evaluated and consequences for tourism development gauged. The validity and practicality of management options to tackle the complex nature and juxtaposition between tourism, climate change and coastal zone management are considered, including an evaluation of management responses and consequent policy choices. Whilst conclusions from the cases presented demonstrate that coastal protection measures should be linked to integrated processes, general results highlight that public perception and policy implementation often ignore such imperatives, often resulting in inappropriate or ill-informed management responses. More integrated management strategies are thus considered and advocated for managing coastal tourism destinations to offset pressures from predicted climate change. From an assessment of socio-economic, environmental and political standpoints, recommendations are made to ameliorate projected impacts on coastal tourism infrastructure. This in turn may go some way to better understand the uncertainties of climate threats and thus offer better sustainable options for many such destinations.

The book is divided into two key parts. Chapters 1 to 7 explore the theoretical and contextual frameworks of climate change processes and their general relationship with coastal tourism destinations. Such concepts for example evaluate the relationship and juxtaposition between climate change and tourism and explore emerging issues relating to the media, the law and risk assessments.

The following chapters 8 to 17 are more applied and draw upon a range of international case studies from leading academics, professionals and practitioners. These case studies illustrate contemporary issues in the development of coastal tourism destinations; perceived impacts of climate change; and review suggested or actioned ameliorative measures and evaluations of these. The case studies based on specific coastal tourism typologies, including established beach resorts, ecotourism destinations, island destinations and adventure/alternative coastal destinations, are drawn from key regions of the world including the Americas, Europe, Australasia and Asia.

Chapter 18 draws together the key themes and lessons that can be synthesized from such case examples and suggests possible frameworks for the most effective and feasible means of tackling the threats to tourism destinations from climate change.

Andrew Jones

Foreword

The oceans, comprising 72% of the Earth's surface, provide essential life-support functions without which life on Earth would not be possible. Oceans modulate short- and long-term climate and generate hazards such as storms, earthquakes and tsunamis. They support a wide array of human activities with significant economic and social value, while coastal areas are home to 50% of the world's population. The multitude of activities is placing increasing pressure on the integrity of coastal and marine ecosystems and many oceanic, coastal and island resources are threatened through overexploitation. Various reports have highlighted that oceans, coasts and islands are experiencing severe degradation due to overdevelopment along the coasts and increasing pollution from cities and farms amongst other factors. This situation is reaching a crisis state and in many places may lead to significant declines of wildlife and the irreversible collapse of ocean and coastal ecosystems. These problems are exacerbated by the effects of climate change. The 2007 report of the Intergovernmental Panel on Climate Change (IPCC) notes that climate change will have profound effects on marine ecosystems and coastal populations around the world, especially among the poorest peoples. It is expected that developing nations in Africa (which account for less than 3% of global carbon emissions) and Asia will be worst affected while the developed wealthy nations far from the equator will be least affected. Asia will be particularly vulnerable to the effects of climate change, especially in major population centres at low elevations such as Mumbai, Shanghai, Jakarta, Tokyo and Dhaka (Kullenberg et al., 2008). Therefore the impacts of climate change on developing nations, especially small island developing states (SIDS), will be significant, with implications ranging from changes in ocean chemistry and forecasted sea level rise to impacts on ecosystems, coastal infrastructure and human health. The need to address these issues is a vital first step in combating potentially severe effects of climate change. Capacity building is essential for achieving integrated management of oceans and coasts, especially in developing countries, SIDS and those with economies in transition. Moreover, coastal and marine areas should be managed with appropriate scientific inputs and participatory processes.

The travel and tourism industry is the fastest growing sector of the global economy, especially with regard to coastal and marine areas. Coastal tourism takes many forms and is a vital economic component for many countries. It frequently involves conflicts among stakeholders, as well as poses management challenges integrating physical and human environments. In addition, climate change now provides a significant future threat to tourism infrastructure and development, as well as the ecosystems on which some tourism activities depend. These problems are of considerable scientific interest and obvious economic importance. Currently, sea level rise and increased storminess seem certain consequences and these will lead to increased beach erosion, flooding, ecosystem destruction and coastal vulnerability. Higher global temperatures have been blamed for the loss of coral reefs, which is already affecting some ecotourism destinations. Such consequences will lead to additional loss of tourism income in an already challenged global economy. Tourism in developing countries will also create demands for fresh water to satisfy western markets, but there is concern over supply of this vital resource. Such development is therefore likely to exacerbate the availability of freshwater resources in many developing countries, posing serious issues of scarcity and national security. It is important to plan for such possibilities – risk assessments, vulnerability analyses and capacity building will help in developing adaptation strategies. These will be vital for improving the resilience of coastal communities, especially in SIDS.

This book clearly highlights such consequences for current and future coastal tourism alongside predicted threats and implications of climate change. It includes real issues facing tourism activities and addresses dilemmas from regional perspectives. Tourism issues in many coastal locations around the world are covered, including cases in North America, Asia, Africa, Europe and Antarctica, with a focus on specific tourism-related climate change problems. Chapters address vital issues in coastal adaptation, including the ability to absorb pressure under rapidly changing and stressful environmental circumstances and problems in maintaining coastal resources and ecosystems. Concerns such as future competitiveness, political and cultural dynamics, and absence of effective management policies are also examined. This book is, therefore, about integrating human activities with environmental change and facilitates and engages the debate for meeting climate change challenges to coastal tourism. The editors and authors are to be congratulated for bringing together in one volume an incisive discussion of the major issues facing coastal and ocean tourism in coastal areas around the world.

Biliana Cicin-Sain
Director, Gerard J. Mangone Center for Marine Policy
University of Delaware
and
Co-Chair and Head of Secretariat, Global Forum on Oceans, Coasts,
and Islands

Reference

Kullenberg, G., Mendler de Suarez, J., Wowk, K., McCole, K. and Cicin-Sain, B. (2008) *Policy Brief on Climate, Oceans, and Security.* Presented at the 4th Global Conference on Oceans, Coasts, and Islands, 7–11 April 2008, Hanoi, Vietnam. Available at: http://www.globaloceans.org/globaloceans/sites/udel.edu.globaloceans/files/Climate-and-Oceans-PB-April2.pdf   (accessed: June 2010).

Acknowledgements

We hope this book will provide a valuable new text for students, researchers, planners, environmentalists and tourism practitioners in understanding the growing complexities and dynamics between tourism coastal developments and the impacts of climate change.

Foremost, we would like to thank the support and contribution of the chapter authors, all twenty three of them, for this book. Their insights and professional contributions have been invaluable in both determining and understanding the nature of the problems confronting coastal tourism developments and the issues pertaining to climate change.

We would also like to thank the publishers, CABI, for their support and enthusiasm and especially Sarah Hulbert the commissioning editor who had the foresight and driving force to encourage us to consider embarking on this project after a chance meeting at a tourism conference in Portugal. Also thanks must go to Shankari Wilford the production editor who has kept the project on the straight and narrow over the last year.

Finally a special thanks must go to both our families and friends for without their support and perseverance in putting up with the inevitable work and time pressures associated with the production of such a volume, it would have been an impossible task. In this respect Andrew would like to give a personal big hug to his wife Louise and his son Alasdair who are more or less resigned to receive a signed copy of this book for Christmas this year. Mike would also like to give a special thanks to his wife....

Finally we hope you enjoy reading the diverse contributions from around the world and find the insights and conclusions discussed helpful in your own work environments and walks of life.

Andrew Jones and Michael Phillips

1 Introduction – Disappearing Destinations: Current Issues, Challenges and Polemics

ANDREW JONES AND MICHAEL PHILLIPS

The development of coastal tourism destinations form a major part of our understanding of the notions and concepts regarding the growth and definitions of modern day tourism. Indeed, within the context of symbiotic relationships the concept of tourism development along coastlines is one that has become synonymous with 'sun, sea and sand'. This relationship between climate and tourism growth has thus been one of the driving forces in the phenomena of emerging global tourism markets. Such destinations now form a well documented account of the historical development of modern day tourism and our basic understanding of it. However, one of the key issues confronting coastal environments is the continued growth of tourism development and the impact of such on coastal zones. In the mid-1990s, organizations such as the United Nations began to highlight such issues, particularly in developing tourist regions such as the Caribbean (UNEP, 1997). More recently the consequences of such development measured against predicted climate change on coastal belts and fringes has become a contemporary topic of debate (*Environmental Scientist*, 1999, 2000; Lohmann, 2002; Nature, 2002; Phillips and Jones, 2006).

A recent report by the consulting firm KPMG (2009) claims that tourism is among the industries least prepared and the most vulnerable to climate change. It suggests that the tourism industry has yet to come to terms with the risk and associated costs it is facing as threats from heat waves, droughts and rising sea levels are some factors that will directly impact the industry, especially in terms of social conflict and economic stability.

Indeed, the symbiotic relationship between coastal tourism destinations and amenable climates is one that in some respects has now become a paradox with climate now threatening to destroy the very nature of tourism that, in the past, it has so successfully encouraged. With respect to this, it is increasingly argued that some of these predictions, especially with respect to sea level rise, could have significant consequences for the future management of the coastal zone and tourism development within such zones. Authors such as Granja and Carvalho

(2000), Vilibic *et al.* (2000), Jensen *et al.* (2001), Phillips and Jones (2006) and Jones (2009) have already begun to highlight such issues. It has been suggested that concern particularly regarding erosion, poses a threat to all stakeholders, especially tourism infrastructure as the ever growing demand for recreational and tourism facilities along coastal fringes increases. This will also be further complicated by ever increasing concerns and debates over the continued need and merits for remedial actions to offset such problems and the need to protect such facilities. Who takes responsibility for the implementation and funding of such measures is also a key question (Basco, 1999; Wiegel, 2002; Argarwal and Shaw, 2007). Over the next decade this will increasingly have a significant impact on tourism, which, according to the United Nations World Tourism Organization (2009), continues to be the world's largest growth industry. A recent review by the United Nations Environment Programme (UNEP, 2009) in association with the French Government and the United Nations World Tourism Organization has also highlighted growing concerns between the need for better integrated coastal management and the need to adapt coastal tourism destinations for climate change. The media stunt of hosting an undersea cabinet meeting by the Maldives Government in autumn 2009 to emphasize climate change threats to the island nation is also a case in point.

Although climate change has been recognized for a number of years it is only recently through such august organizations as the Intergovernmental Panel on Climate Change (IPPC, 2007) and the Stern Review (MH Treasury-Cabinet Office, 2005) that it is believed to be affecting the planet in a potentially far reaching way. The IPCC has confirmed that the Earth's surface average temperature is increasing, leading to many potentially adverse impacts around the globe. For example, heat waves are becoming more frequent, glaciers and ice caps are melting at more rapid rates, and sea levels are predicted to rise leading to coastal flooding. Droughts and fires are happening more frequently, as well as unpredicted rains, heavy snowfalls and flooding (IPCC, 2007). Townsend's (2004) review of the potential fatal outcomes from inaction are also pertinent in this respect. The impacts on tourism are also predicted to be far reaching as Hall and Higham (2005) and Becken and Hay (2007) suggest in their recent assessments of climate change and its predicted impacts on tourism.

Although there has been much media attention since 2005, concerns are not just a contemporary phenomenon. There have been some earlier responses to predicted threats. In 1999 Viner and Agnew in association with WWF Tourism Issues paper (Viner and Agnew, 1999:2) recommended that:

> the tourism industry itself must take action to reduce its contribution to global greenhouse gas emissions. For example, in destinations, changes to energy supply should be introduced, creating a shift from fossil fuel to renewable sources of energy such as wind, biomass and solar power. This needs to be coupled with changes to planning procedures and laws, so that more opportunities for renewable energy sources can be developed. More stringent efficiency standards and a compulsory energy rating scheme could also be employed in buildings, such as hotels. Transport to, from, and around resorts and within destinations, is another key area where changes could be made.

Also, the United Nations has made some headway in the 15-plus years since it began addressing climate change. Nearly all countries are on record as taking the problem seriously, and the UN's 1997 Kyoto Protocol – though weaker than many had hoped – was ratified by countries that together represent the majority of people in the developed world – although only a third of global emissions (Henson, 2006).

More recently, however, in October 2007, the second International Conference on Climate Change took place in Davos, Switzerland. The conference agreed that the tourism sector must rapidly respond to climate change, within the evolving UN framework, and progressively reduce its Greenhouse Gas (GHG) contribution, especially if it is to grow in a sustainable manner. This, it suggested, will require action to: mitigate its GHG emissions, derived especially from transport and accommodation activities; adapt tourism businesses and destinations to changing climate conditions; apply existing and new technology to improve energy efficiency; and secure financial resources to help poor regions and developing countries (UNWTO, 2007). As a response to the United Nations Copenhagen Climate Change Conference in December 2009 there has been much speculation and debate concerning real outcomes and actions. It is still unclear how these will manifest themselves but it is quite clear that emergency actions will be required sooner than later and Copenhagen was not a positive start to this process.

In this respect, however, climate change is still increasingly seen as one of the major long-term threats facing nation states and for those reliant on tourism, their tourism industries. Predicted threats could potentially lead to the loss of many tourist destinations whose appeal depends on their natural environment, particularly coastlines. Many low-lying coastal regions are at risk from rising sea levels – as is already evident in examples such as Venice, highlighted in a recent UNESCO research assessment of impacts of climate change on world heritage (UNESCO, 2007). The report suggests that many of the world's greatest wonders may be under threat from climate change. It predicts that rising sea levels, increased flooding risks and depleted marine and land biodiversity could have disastrous effects on the 830 designated UNESCO world heritage sites.

The World Wide Fund for Nature (WWF, 1999, 2007) has also suggested that the tourism industry's heavy reliance on the local environment and climate to sell holidays means that it could face serious challenges as a result of climate change. Global and regional temperatures are rising. The hottest year of the last millennium was 1998 and the 1990s were the warmest decade. An increase in extreme weather events such as floods and storms is also expected. Such critical processes are predicted to have serious if not disastrous consequences for tourism destinations (WWF, 2007).

According to the WWF, climate change is also going to affect destinations in other ways. It is expected to increase the risk of illness in several parts of the world and this may lead to a 'falling-off' of tourism (WWF, 2007). Other social and economic impacts of climate change have been evaluated by the European Travel Commission. They claim that local service providers and tour operators will have to carry out assessments of the threat to their businesses from environmental changes and changes in tourism flows. In particular the cost of maintaining basic 'natural' resources for tourism, such as beaches and other coastal amenities, lakes and rivers will need to be addressed more seriously and effectively (European Travel Commission, 2007).

In Europe for example, research by Epaedia (2005), the European Union's Environmental Agency, also suggests that the biggest driver of development in the European coastal zone in recent years has been the demand for tourism. Its research states that Europe is still the world's largest holiday destination, with 60% of all international tourists and a continued growth of approximately 3.8% per annum. Evidence from Epaedia's research shows that the Mediterranean coasts of France, Spain and Italy are currently respectively receiving 75 million, 59 million and 40 million visitors a year, an increase of between 40% and 60% since 1990. Obvious concerns are raised regarding such growth and further concerns are now raised on growth along the eastern Mediterranean including the Greek islands, Cyprus and Malta (Epaedia, 2005). Using another Mediterranean example, the agency's research suggests that in French coastal regions alone tourism provides an estimated 43% of jobs, generating more revenue than fishing or shipping and that peak population densities on the Mediterranean coasts of France and Spain reach 2300 people/km^2, more than double the winter populations. Its estimates predict that a further 40% increase in peak populations is expected in the coming 20 years, thus emphasizing the critical economic, social and environment interrelationships at play within such destinations. Benoit and Comeau (2005) have also highlighted some of the key pressures on the coastal fringe. From their research for 'Plan Bleu', a UNEP/EU initiative, key pressures are identified with tourism being highlighted as one of the key coastal environment protagonists.

In the USA, Houston (2002) reported that travel and tourism had become the US's largest industry, employer and earner of foreign exchange and that beaches were the major factor in this tourism market. He further identified beach erosion as the number one concern of Americans who visit beaches. Research by the US Army Corps of Engineers (1994), illustrated that 33,000 km of shoreline within the USA were experiencing some kind of erosion and that 4300 km were critical. Their findings considered this a serious threat to tourism and therefore a major threat to the national economy. Earlier work by authors, such as Dharmaratne and Braithwaite (1998) in the Caribbean, has also stressed the importance of beaches to national economies. A more recent assessment of beaches to national economies has also been assessed by Williams and Micallef (2009).

In this context, climate models suggest a future warming of 0.2–0.3°C per decade with sea levels expected to rise at a rate of 4–10 cm per decade. An increase in extreme weather events such as floods and storms is also expected. A rise of 4–10 cm per decade does not seem like a rise that will adversely affect destinations but, as the IPCC predict, this will potentially cause major problems, particularly for coastal areas (IPCC, 2007).

A report by the UK-based Churchill Insurance Group (2006) highlighted that some of the world's most famous tourist attractions, such as Australia's Great Barrier Reef and Italy's Amalfi coast, could be closed to visitors within a few years because of worries about environmental damage and climate change.

The report suggested that some destinations could be permanently closed to tourists by 2020 or face severe restrictions on visitor numbers and sharp increases in admission prices. Evidence from the report goes on to warn that in 20 to 40 years' time the Great Barrier Reef could be severely damaged, forcing its closure, while other parts of Australia would be off-limits because of a rise in bushfires and insect-borne diseases. Other highlighted destinations at risk included the Taj coral reef in the Maldives, Goa in India, Florida's Everglades and Croatia's Dalmatian coastline (Smithers, 2006).

The report also suggests that coastal attractions are particularly vulnerable and comments that many resorts will run the risk of damage severe enough to put their long-term viability as destinations in doubt. One of Britain's leading climatologists, David Viner, senior research scientist at the University of East Anglia, has also supported such notions and has advocated that climate change will have a profound impact on tourism in the coming decades (Agnew and Viner, 2001; Viner, 2006). Becken and Hay's recent review of climate change and its impact on tourism destinations has also raised a keen and growing awareness of such issues (Becken and Hay, 2007).

Greenpeace (2007) issued a stark warning of this by illustrating a hypothetical future Spain if steps are not taken to stop the effects of climate change. The highly controversial warning was illustrated in a publication presented by the organization in Madrid in November 2007. Entitled 'Photoclima – Photoclimate,' it centres on six different themes depicted by six different places in Spain, showing the before and after effects of climate change. As an example, a few buildings and islets remain of La Manga del Mar Menor tourism resort as it is covered over by the Mediterranean Sea. (Due to ongoing litigation between Greenpeace and local tourism entrepreneurs, these illustrations cannot be published here. However they can be viewed at: www.greenpeace. org/espana/footer/search?q=photoclima. La Manga del Mar Menor: Spain before and predicted after shots of climate change: Illustration courtesy of GreenPeace (2007).)

From such evidence it seems increasingly apparent that coastal tourism and its relationship with the coastal zone are now significant topics of research, increasingly discussed within international policy contexts. In this respect, coastal destinations, beaches and beach resorts have become synonymous with tourism development and tourism growth. With current predictions of climate change and sea level rise they are clearly, however, becoming increasingly threatened by climate change and physical damage. Despite these threats, however, the ongoing exponential growth of tourism will continue to exacerbate these current impacts. It is the consequences of such phenomena that will ultimately impact upon the long term future of coastal tourism environments and, of course, their continued survival. With respect to such, it is becoming increasingly vital to identify management strategies that on the one hand recognize climatic threats and on the other, protect tourism infrastructure and coastal resources, especially in areas significantly reliant on the industry for their economy. This includes both the developed and developing world, as coastal regions are places where destruction of both natural and tourist environments have no discrimination. Within the USA and particularly Europe, coastal zone strategies to tackle such challenges are now firmly on the political agenda. Indeed, the European Commission in 1999 launched its own policy statements on integrated coastal zone management (ICZM) – Integrated Coastal Zone Management: a Strategy for Europe (European Commission, 1999) – whilst the USA has long had policies for regional coastal zone management, for instance the 1972 Coastal Zone Management Act (Office of Ocean and Coastal Resource Management/OCRM, 2004).

It is researchers such as Povh (2000) who have perhaps raised the most pertinent and significant stakes that still face the tourism industry today and for the future. Povh's assertions have predicted that three-quarters of the world's population will be living within 60 km of the shoreline by 2020, and as a consequence suggests there will be increased tensions between the demand for coastal leisure and tourism facilities and natural coastal environments and of course the unpredictable threats from climate change.

Clearly, in the first decade of this new millennium, two factors are clear: one suggests that tourism is having a major environmental impact on many coastal areas and the second suggests that potential threats from climate change are likely to create considerable adverse impacts unless managed effectively. Thus we find an increasingly clear juxtaposition and paradox emerging between, on the one hand, tourism itself, creating many undesirable impacts on the coastal zone and, on the other, climate change threatening to adversely impact on coastal tourism infrastructure, ultimately threatening the very nature, character and socio-economic well being of many tourist coastal destinations.

It is thus becoming clear that these processes are increasingly in conflict with one another and, consequently, the point at issue is one of how to balance the protection and management our coastal resources and to accommodate growing pressures for recreation and tourism developments. All this, of course, is set within the context of safeguarding and balancing the often crucial socio-economic development issues within such zones. Critical to this are escalating concerns for climate change and mounting pressure to take effective ameliorative actions such as hard and soft engineering responses and the need to advocate strategies for the effective and sustainable management of tourism infrastructure. Wider arguments relating to how such threats are recognized and accepted, who takes responsibility for enacting ameliorative measures and who ultimately pays the bill all contribute to the increasing complex debate on these emerging concerns.

This book will explore such issues and discuss the consequences of current and future tourism growth within coastal destinations and the threats and implications that are predicted from climate change. The book is thus divided into two areas. The first chapters concentrate on themes that highlight the current theoretical and conceptual issues that are currently in the policy and media arenas. For example, Chapters 1, 2, 3 and 4 will assess and evaluate contemporary relationships between climate change and tourism and the current policy and management concepts pertaining to these two dynamic, and increasingly interrelated, phenomena. Chapters 5, 6 and 7 discuss emerging strategic interrelated themes on risk assessment, legal implications and media attention now being discussed and debated at national and international levels. The second area of the book will present more specific global case examples illustrating the practical relationship between climate change and coastal tourism at local destinations. The case examples from Asia, Europe, North America, Australasia and Antarctica assess implications of current and predicted impact of climate change on coastal tourism destinations and discuss options for ameliorative management and policy measures that can be adopted to help offset predicted effects. In conclusion, from such case examples, local impacts of erosion on coastal tourism development are evaluated and consequences for tourism development outlined. The validity and practicality of management options to tackle the complex nature and juxtaposition between tourism, climate change and coastal zone management are explored and considered, including an evaluation of management responses and consequent policy choices. Conclusions from such local cases are evaluated and consider future options and choices for integrated coastal zone management solutions. Recommendations are made to ameliorate projected impacts on coastal tourism infrastructure by making choices that include both soft and hard remedial proactive measures and by addressing more lateral options regarding coastal destinations and their relationship with their natural hinterlands, which can often provide new opportunities for alternative sustainable tourism development.

References

Agnew, M.D. and Viner, D. (2001) Potential impacts of climate change on international tourism. *International Journal of Tourism and Hospitality Research* 3(1).

Argarwal, S. and Shaw, G. (2007) *Managing Coastal Tourism Resorts*. Clevedon, UK.

Basco, D.R. (1999) Misconceptions about seawall and beach interactions. In: Ozhan, E. (ed.) *Land–Ocean Interactions: Managing Coastal Ecosystems*. Proceedings of the Medcoast-EMECS Joint Conference, Vol. 3. Medcoast, Ankara, pp.1565–1578.

Becken, S. and Hay, J.E. (2007) *Tourism and Climate Change: Risks and Opportunities*. Channel View Publications, UK.

Benoit, G.E. and Comeau, A. (2005) *Sustainable Future for the Mediterranean: The Blue Plan's Environment and Development Outlook*. UNEP, Earthscan.

Churchill Insurance Group (2006) *Report into the Future of Travel*. The Centre for Future Studies, Churchill Insurance, London, UK.

Dharmaratne, G.S., and Braithwaite, A.E. (1998) Economic valuation of the coastline for tourism in Barbados. *Journal of Travel Research* 37(2), 138–144.

Environmental Scientist (1999) Living in the greenhouse. *Environmental Scientist* 8(1), 1–3.

Environmental Scientist (2000) The cost of climate change – UK report is a world first. *Environmental Scientist* 9(3), 1–2.

Epaedia (2010) www.eea.europa.eu/themes (Accessed: 1 January 2010).

European Commission (1999) *Towards a European Integrated Coastal Zone Management (ICZM) Strategy: General Principles and Policy Options*. Office for Official Publications of the European Communities, Luxembourg.

European Travel Commission (ETC) (2007) *Tourism Trends for Europe*. Bruges, Belgium.

Granja, H.M. and Carvalho, G.S. (2000) Inland Beach Migration (Beach Erosion) and the Coastal Zone Management (The Experience of the Northwest Coastal Zone of Portugal). Responsible Coastal Zone Management. *Periodicum Biologorum* 102(1), 413–424.

Greenpeace (2007) *Photoclima – Photoclimate – Spain*. Greenpeace, Madrid, Spain.

Hall, M. and Higham, J. (2005) *Aspects of Tourism: Tourism Recreation and Climate Change*. Channel View Publications, London, UK.

Henson, R. (2006) *The Rough Guide to Climate Change*. Rough Guides Limited, London.

HM Treasury – Cabinet Office (2005) *The Economics of Climate Change: Stern Review*. HM Treasury, HMSO, London, UK.

Houston, J.R. (2002) The Economic Value of Beaches – a 2002 Update. *Shore and Beach* 70(1), 9–12.

Intergovernmental Panel on Climate Change (IPCC) (2007) *Climate Change 2007, the Fourth IPCC Assessment Report*. UNEP, Cambridge University Press, UK.

Jensen, J., Bender, F. and Blasi, C. (2001) Analysis of the water levels along the German North Sea coastline. In: Ozhan, E. (ed.) *Medcoast 01: Proceedings of the fifth International Conference on the Mediterranean Coastal Environment*, vol. 3. Medcoast, Ankara, pp.1129–1140.

Jones, A.L. (2009) Climate change impacts on UK coastal tourism destinations. *Proceedings of Council for Australia Universities CAUTHE Annual Conference 2009 on See Change: Tourism and Hospitality in a Dynamic World*, 10–13 February, Fremantle, Australia.

KPMG (2009) *Climate Changes Your Business*. KPMG, UK.

Lohmann, M. (2002) Coastal resorts and climate change. In: Lockwood, A. and Medlick, S. (eds) *Tourism and Hospitality in the 21st Century*. Butterworth-Heinemann, Oxford, UK, pp.285–287.

Nature (2002) When doubt is a sure thing. News Feature. *Nature*, 1 August, Vol. 418, 476–478.

Phillips, M. and Jones, A. (2006) Erosion and tourism infrastructure in the coastal zone: problems, consequences and management. *Tourism Management* 27(3), 517–524.

Povh, D. (2000) Economic Instruments for Sustainable Development in the Mediterranean Region. Responsible Coastal Zone Management. *Periodicum Biologorum* 102(1), pp.407–412.

Smithers, R. (2006) Tourist hotspots at risk of closure. *The Guardian*, London, Friday 22 September.

Townsend, M. and Harris, P. (2004) Now the Pentagon Tells Bush: Climate Change Will Destroy Us, Secret Report Warns of Rioting and Nuclear War; Threat to the World is Greater than Terrorism. *The Observer*, 22 November, London.

UNEP (1997) *Coastal Tourism in the Wider Caribbean Region: Impacts and Best Management Practices*. CEP Technical Report No. 38. UNEP, Kingston, Jamaica.

UNEP (2009) *ICZM for Coastal Tourism Destinations Adapting to Climate*. UNEP, Cagliari, Italy.

UNESCO (2007) *Case Studies on Climate Change and World Heritage*. UNESCO, Venice, Italy.

United Nations World Tourism Organization (UNWTO) (2007) *Proceedings of 2nd International Conference on Climate Change and Tourism*, Davos, Switzerland, 1–3 October 2007.

United Nations World Tourism Organization (UNWTO) (2009) *UNWTO Tourism Highlights*, 2009 edn.

US Army Corps of Engineers (1994) *Shoreline protection and beach erosion control study. Phase 1: Cost comparison of shoreline protection projects of the US Corps of Engineers*. Water Resources Support Center, Washington, DC.

Viner, D. (ed.) (2006) Tourism and its interactions with climate change. *Journal of Sustainable Tourism* 14(4), 317–322.

Viner, D. and Agnew, M./World Wildlife Fund (WWF) (1999) *Climate Change and its Impacts on Tourism*. WWF, Norwich, UK, 2pp.

Wiegel, R.L. (2002) Seawalls, Seacliffs, Beachrock: What Beach Effects? Part 1. *Shore and Beach* 70(1), 17–27.

Williams, A. and Micallef, A. (2009) *Beach Management Principles and Practice.* Earthscan, London, UK.

World Wide Fund For Nature (2007) *Environmental Report 2007.* WWF, London, UK.

World Wildlife Fund (WWF) (1999) *Climate Change and its Impacts on Tourism.* Report prepared by David Viner and Maureen Agnew, WWF-UK, University of East Anglia, UK.

World Wildlife Fund (WWF) (2007) *Climate Solutions – WWF's Vision for 2050.* WWF International, Switzerland.

2 Climate Change and its Impacts on Tourism: Regional Assessments, Knowledge Gaps and Issues

C. Michael Hall

Although issues of the importance of climate for the development of tourism have been recognized since the onset of industrial tourism, the issue of the relationship between climate change and tourism is a much more recent phenomenon (Scott *et al.*, 2005). There are several reasons why this shift in focus has occurred (Hall, 2008a):

1. Because climate has a number of direct and indirect influences on tourist decision-making and the relative attractiveness of destinations, tourism is regarded as a potentially highly sensitive industrial sector with respect to climate change (Wilbanks *et al.*, 2007; UNWTO, UNEP and WMO, 2008). This situation is especially the case with small island developing states, which tend to have a high degree of economic dependence on tourism (Simpson *et al.*, 2008).
2. Policy discussions with respect to mitigating climate change, e.g. through the imposition of 'green taxes' on aviation, tourism businesses or tourists, or the development of carbon-trading schemes, clearly have implications for tourism flows and tourist behaviour (UNWTO, UNEP and WMO, 2008).
3. Tourism has itself become a more significant component of the reporting of the Intergovernmental Panel on Climate Change (IPCC) that was formed in 1988 under UN auspices to inform policy-makers and society with respect to knowledge on the causes and impacts of climate change. For example, the first IPCC assessment report did not even mention tourism, whereas the fourth assessment report published in 2007 has substantial reference to tourism and related subject areas (Wall, 1998; Hall, 2008a).
4. Most important of all, there is far greater public and media debate, and arguably concern with respect to the potential effects of climate change to which the academic community is responding and contributing, particular those that are engaged within the environmental and impact research tradition of tourism.

Research on tourism and climate change is broadly focused on three main areas. First, what are the emissions of tourism related activities and their contribution to climate change. Second, what are the effects of climate change on tourism. Third, how can the effects of climate change be mitigated or adapted to.

The Contribution of Tourism to Climate Change

Carbon dioxide (CO_2) is the most significant greenhouse gas (GHG), accounting for 77% of global anthropogenic (human-caused) global warming (Stern, 2006). CO_2 emissions from tourism have grown steadily since the 1950s to their current estimated level of about 5.0% of all anthropogenic emissions of CO_2. Globally, an average tourist trip lasts 4.15 days (average length for all international and domestic tourist trips) and generates average emissions of 0.25 t of CO_2 per traveller (Scott *et al.*, 2008a).

Transport generates the largest proportion of tourism related CO_2 emissions (75%), followed by accommodation (21%) and tourist activities (3%). In terms of radiative forcing, which is the change in the balance between radiation coming into the atmosphere and radiation going out, the contribution of transportation is significantly larger, ranging from 82% to 90%, with air transport alone accounting for 54% to 75% of the total change. Variation in emissions from different types of tourist trips is large. While the average trip generating 0.25 t of CO_2, as mentioned above, long-haul trips and high-end luxury cruises can generate up to 9 t CO_2 per person per trip (35 times the emissions caused by an average trip) (Scott *et al.*, 2008a).

The vast majority of trips produce low emissions, but a small share are highly emission-intense. For instance, a 14-day holiday from Europe to Thailand may cause emissions of 2.4 t of CO_2 per person and a typical fly and cruise trip from the Netherlands to Antarctica produces some 9 t CO_2 (Lamars and Amelung, 2007). Even holidays promoted as ecofriendly, such as dive holidays, will cause emissions in the range of 1.2–6.8 t CO_2 due to emissions from air, automobile and boat travel (Gössling *et al.*, 2007). Some trips, therefore, generate per person emissions in a single holiday that vastly exceed annual per capita emissions of the average world citizen (4.3 t CO_2), or even the higher average of an EU citizen (9 t CO_2). A small number of energy-intense trips are responsible for the majority of emissions. While air-based trips comprise 17% of all tourist trips, they cause about 40% of all tourism-related CO_2 emissions, and 54–75% of radiative forcing. For example, long-haul travel between the five world regions the UNWTO use for statistical aggregation purposes (Africa, Americas, Asia-Pacific, Europe and the Middle East) accounts for only 2.7% of all tourist trips, but contributes 17% of global tourist emissions. Similarly, long-haul (interregional) tourism from Europe represents 18% of all international trips, and 49% of all CO_2 emissions from travel (Scott *et al.*, 2008a).

Travel between and within the more economically developed regions of the world (Europe plus parts of the Americas and the Asia-Pacific) is the most significant contribution to emissions, comprising 67% of international trips worldwide and 50% of all passenger kilometres (pkm) travelled globally (Scott *et al.*, 2008a). The less developed countries contribute therefore only a relatively small amount of emissions as a result of long-haul tourism yet they are also the ones that are arguably not only the most susceptible to the physical effects of climate change because of their limited adaptive capacities, but, as discussed below, are also proportionately more economically dependent on tourism than most developed countries. Because of such issues there is enormous controversy about how international transport emissions can and should be incorporated into climate change mitigation and adaptation schemes, who should pay the associated costs, and how should future transport infrastructure be developed (Hall and Lew, 2009).

Focus on the Effects of Climate Change on Tourism

Along with alpine and winter tourism, tourism in coastal regions has arguably been the focus of much of the research on climate change and tourism relationships (Hall, 2008a). This situation is also reflected in much of the more general work on climate change where coastal areas are regarded as particularly vulnerable to the impacts of sea-level rise as well as high-magnitude storm events. For example, with respect to coastal systems and low-lying areas, the IPCC reported with 'very high confidence' that 'Coasts are experiencing the adverse consequences of hazards related to climate and sea level' and that 'Coasts will be exposed to increasing risks, including coastal erosion, over coming decades due to climate change and sea-level rise' (Nicholls *et al.*, 2007:317). Similarly, in the case of small islands, the IPCC reported with 'very high confidence' that 'Small islands, whether located in the tropics or higher latitudes, have characteristics which make them especially vulnerable to the effects of climate change, sea-level rise, and extreme events' and that 'Sea-level rise is expected to exacerbate inundation, storm surge, erosion and other coastal hazards, thus threatening vital infrastructure, settlements and facilities that support the livelihood of island communities' (Mimura *et al.*, 2007:689). Importantly, for tourism–climate change relationships, the IPCC also recognized that 'The impact of climate change on coasts is exacerbated by increasing human-induced pressures' (Nicholls *et al.*, 2007:317) including tourism because of the relative attractiveness of the coast in contemporary society.

Assessment of General Current and Future Threats

Although coastal regions are recognized as being extremely vulnerable to climate change there are substantial gaps in knowledge of the impact on coastal tourism both in general and with respect to specific locations. There are very few coastal areas around the world for which base-line conditions have been identified and that have received long-term monitoring in order to chart change over time. Those sites on which long-term research and monitoring has been conducted tend to be in developed countries and be very particular types of locations, such as within national parks (Hall and Lew, 2009). Furthermore, climate change research itself is often not integrated over various scales of analysis. Therefore, while there may be reasonable knowledge of the effects of climate change on coastal areas at a macro-scale, as in the case of IPCC reports, micro-scale, location-specific understandings and forecasts are far more difficult to predict. Table 2.1 identifies the relative level of tourism-specific climate change knowledge and estimated impact of climate change on tourism by region as of late 2008.

Knowledge gaps are enormous. In the case of Africa, Boko *et al.* (2007:450) emphasize that 'very few assessments of projected impacts on tourism and climate change are available' and states (Boko *et al.*, 2007:459):

> There is a need to enhance practical research regarding the vulnerability and impacts of climate change on tourism, as tourism is one of the most important and highly promising economic activities in Africa. Large gaps appear to exist in research on the impacts of climate variability and change on tourism and related matters, such as the impacts of climate change on coral reefs and how these impacts might affect ecotourism.

Tourism is similarly recognized by the IPCC as one of the most important economic sectors in Asia, although the lack of research is recognized (Cruz *et al.*, 2007). Even in the case of a developed region such as North America substantial knowledge gaps exist. For example, Field *et al.* (2007:634) note that, 'Although coastal zones are among the most important recreation resources in North America, the vulnerability of key tourism areas to sea-level rise has not been comprehensively assessed.'

The understanding of the impacts of climate change on coastal tourism is therefore operating in a relative vacuum. This situation has occurred in part because of a lack of specific focus on tourism in certain locations by researchers but also reflects a lack of appreciation of the nature of tourism as well. In particular, this relates to not only understanding the effects of climate change on a tourism destination but also the wider changes that are taking place in the tourism system. Figure 2.1 represents some of the issues with respect to coastal tourism.

Table 2.1. Relative level of tourism-specific climate change knowledge and estimated impact of climate change on tourism by region.

Region	Estimated impact of climate change on tourism	Relative level of tourism-specific climate change knowledge
Africa	Moderately–strongly negative	Extremely poor
Asia	Weakly–moderately negative	Extremely poor
Australia and New Zealand	Moderately–strongly negative	Poor–Moderate (high in Great Barrier Reef)
Europe	Weakly–moderately negative	Moderate (high in alpine areas)
Latin America	Weakly–moderately negative	Poor
North America	Weakly negative	Moderate (relatively high in coastal areas, high in ski areas)
Polar regions	Weakly negative–weakly positive	Poor
Small islands	Strongly negative	Moderate

From: Hall, 2008a derived from Hall and Higham, 2005; Gössling and Hall, 2006a; Parry *et al.*, 2007; Scott *et al.*, 2008a.

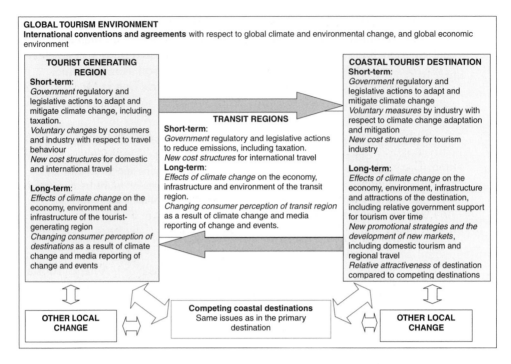

Fig. 2.1. System dimensions of tourism in coastal destinations and the impact of climate change (after Hall, 2005).

Tourism is affected by climate change because of the large number of tourism-dependent coastal economies as well as the increasing human induced pressures it brings to coastal areas (Hall, 2006a). Nicholls *et al.* (2007:331) in their summary of climate-related impacts in relation to recreation and tourism in coastal areas argued that a number of the physical effects of climate change would impact tourism. Strong impacts include:

- air and seawater temperature increase;
- extreme events (storms, waves);
- sea-level rise;
- erosion (sea level, storms, waves); and
- biological effects, such as ecosystem change and changes in species composition.

Extreme events, such as cyclones and hurricanes, for example, are regarded as significant because of both their impact on environment and infrastructure (Nurse and Moore, 2005) as well as a potentially negative contribution to destination image in both the short and long term depending on any change in frequency of such events (Hall, 2008b). Under climatic change more frequent high-magnitude events may mean there is less time for physical and human systems to recover, meaning that recovery may never be complete therefore resulting in long-term environmental deterioration (Hall, 2008a).

Given their contribution to biodiversity as well as economic importance via fishing and tourism, coral reefs have been a major focus of research interest in coastal destinations and have been identified as a coastal ecosystem in which the effects of environmental change has already been felt. In the western Indian Ocean region, a 30% loss of corals resulted in reduced tourism in Mombasa and Zanzibar, and caused financial losses of about US$12–18 million (Payet and Obura, 2004).

Australia's Great Barrier Reef in northern Queensland is one of the locations in which monitoring and research has been extensively conducted over time. The total direct and indirect contribution of the Great Barrier Reef Marine Park to the Great Barrier Reef Catchment Area was estimated to be just under A$3.6 billion in 2006–2007. The figure is larger for Queensland at just around A$4.0 billion. Australia-wide, the contribution is just over $5.4 billion. The estimated direct and indirect employment contributions of the park to the catchment area are 39,700 full time equivalents (FTE). The employment figures for Queensland and Australia are 43,700 and 53,800 respectively. Tourism accounts for 94% of the direct and indirect contribution (Access Economics, 2008). However, like many coral reefs around the world, the Great Barrier Reef is regarded as being particularly threatened by coral bleaching, which occurs as a result of a number of factors connected to anthropogenic induced climate change including:

- changes in water temperatures;
- increased solar irradiance (photosynthetically active radiation and ultra-violet band light); and
- ocean acidification and other changes in water chemistry.

The Great Barrier Reef has experienced eight mass bleaching events since 1979 (1980, 1982, 1987, 1992, 1994, 1998, 2002 and 2006). The most widespread and intense events occurred in the summers of 1998 and 2002, with about 42% and 54% of reefs affected respectively, and with approximately 5% of reefs in the Great Barrier Reef being severely damaged (Berkelmans *et al.*, 2004). In addition, climate-related changes to coral reef ecosystems can also be affected by other human impacts such as overfishing, and increased sedimentation as a result of silt run-off from coastal agriculture or urbanization, as well as diseases and changes in salinity (Hoegh-Guldberg, 2004; Bruno and McGinley, 2008).

Sea level rise is also significant because of the impacts it can have on many low-lying resort and second-home areas. One of the most well recognized locations in which tourism will be affected by climate change is the Maldives, which has over 80% of its land area less than 1 m above mean sea level. Tourism is the mainstay of the Maldivian economy with 70% of visitors coming primarily for beach holidays. In 2001 the Government of the Maldives reported that 50% of all inhabited islands and 45% of its tourist resorts face varying degrees of beach erosion and it was expected that even a 1 m rise in sea level would cause the loss of the entire land area of the Maldives (Government of the Maldives, 2001). The main impacts of climate change and associated sea level rise to the tourism industry, and in particular to the tourist resort islands of the Maldives are:

- Impacts on marine dive sites due to reef degradation as a result of elevated sea surface temperature.
- Decrease in value of the tourism product due to changes to the beach as a result of increase in sea level and wave action.
- Damage to tourist infrastructure due to coastal erosion and inundation.
- Changes to the image of the Maldives as a tourist destination due to alteration of climate and weather patterns.

Other effects on climate change, such as rising water tables (as a result of sea level rise) and saltwater intrusion (sea level rise, runoff change), are forecast to have a negligible impact or the level of impact is not yet established (Nicholls *et al.*, 2007).

Undoubtedly, climate change will have substantial physical effects on the tourism environment. With respect to small islands, Mimura *et al.* (2007:689) concluded that there was a high degree of confidence that the effects of climate change on tourism are likely to be direct and indirect, and largely negative:

> Tourism is the major contributor to GDP and employment in many small islands. Sea-level rise and increased sea water temperature will cause accelerated beach erosion, degradation of coral reefs, and bleaching. In addition, a loss of cultural heritage from inundation and flooding reduces the amenity value for coastal users. Whereas a warmer climate could reduce the number of people visiting small islands in low latitudes, it could have the reverse effect in mid- and high-latitude islands. However, water shortages and increased incidence of vectorborne diseases may also deter tourists.

Some time of climate change-related change may also have impacts on specific forms of tourism. For example, loss of biodiversity as a result of climate change is regarded as having substantial significance for nature-based tourism in marine and coastal environments (Uyarra *et al.*, 2005; Hall, 2006b). This can include changes to ecosystems, as in the case of coral reefs noted above, or the loss of iconic or charismatic marine species that are a focal point of ecotourism interest at destinations, such as marine mammals (seals, whales, dolphins), birds (penguins, albatross, gannets), fish (marlin, shark) or marine reptiles (marine iguanas, turtles).

Nevertheless, as Fig. 2.1 indicates, the impacts of climate change on a coastal tourism destination are not just in terms of environmental change. Just as importantly there is a need to consider the effects of economic and social change. In order to manage climate change, for example, there are proposals for various tax and economic schemes. Regulatory initiatives developed to mitigate climate change will have significant impacts on transport systems and thus the mobility of tourists. The potential for increased costs for the consumer arising from mitigation practices in the jurisdiction of the generating region, will have implications for the comparative price advantage of the coastal destination at an international scale as well as for domestic tourism travel. One possible effect is that those destinations which are the most peripheral and least accessible to markets, which typically are most in need of development initiatives, are therefore potentially the most impacted in relative terms by the costs of mitigation strategies based on distance travelled, size of emissions or energy consumed (Hall and Lew, 2009).

Such an observation is important in understanding the potential impacts of international and national climate change mitigation regimes on tourism flows and
destinations (Gössling *et al.*, 2008), as while preferred environmental attributes
are significant in destination choice (Gössling and Hall, 2006a; Scott *et al.*,
2008a; United Nations Framework Convention on Climate Change (UNFCCC),
2008), changes in price structure resulting from climate policy developments,
such as a post-Kyoto Protocol greenhouse gas (GHG) emissions reduction framework that includes bunker fuels, environmental taxes on arrival or departure and
regional environmental taxes, may be the most immediate and significant impact
for tourism development (Gössling *et al.*, 2009a). Importantly, for understanding
the system effects of mitigation strategies on coastal destinations, it should also
be stressed that the price competitiveness of a destination will be influenced by
the mitigation policies adopted in tourist-generating regions and/or in transit
regions. Therefore, the relative price attractiveness of a destination needs to be
understood in relation to its source markets, the actions of competitors, as well as
the policies in place at the destination itself. In such a situation it is therefore possible to envisage scenarios where some destinations may not implement an
emissions reduction framework in order to retain cost leadership.

In addition to the system-wide complications provided by the implementation of any emissions reduction framework or broader environmental regulations that affect tourism, the determination of future tourism scenarios is
complicated by the difficulties of assessing future changes in tourist behaviour.
Wilbanks *et al.*'s (2007) assessment on industry, settlement and society probably provided the most substantial assessment of the impact of climate change
on tourism within the IPCC context. Tourism is identified as a 'climate-sensitive
human activity', with the authors concluding that vulnerabilities of industries to
climate change are 'generally greater in certain high-risk locations, particularly
coastal and riverine areas, and areas whose economies are closely linked with
climate sensitive resources, such as agricultural and forest product industries,
water demands and tourism; these vulnerabilities tend to be localised but are
often large and growing' (Wilbanks *et al.*, 2007:359). However, one of the greatest problems with assessing the impacts of climate change on tourism is that
both direct and indirect effects will vary greatly with location (Gössling and
Hall, 2006b).

Direct effects include the role that climate variables, such as temperature,
sunshine hours, precipitation, humidity and storm frequency and intensity play
with respect to tourist decision-making over the short term, as in the case of
selection of daily activities when on holiday, as well as the long term, with respect
to the issue of destination choice. Another direct effect is the extent to which
particular environments, such as many coastal resorts, also gain some of their
appeal from their climatic variables, such as the opportunity to promote hot or
warm weather. Indirect effects of climate change such as heat waves, fires, disease outbreaks, and landscape change, can also have substantial effects on tourism activities, perceptions of a location, and the capacity of firms to do business.
Nevertheless, as noted above, these will need to be ongoing occurrences or
extremely high magnitude events to cause long-term change in tourist decision-
making. This is because there is a co-evolutionary relationship between markets

and destinations in the tourism system. In other words, changes at a destination will lead to adaptive change in the market and vice versa. Radical reordering of a tourism system can occur but for that to happen a critical 'tipping point' must be reached at which stage the system will undergo a reordering in which some destinations will win, some will lose, and some will stay the same. However, our current level of knowledge is such that we do not know what those critical points will be, especially as they do not remain constant in such a dynamic social and economic system as tourism. As Rosenzweig *et al.* (2007:111) identified, 'as a result of the complex nature of the interactions that exist between tourism, the climate system, the environment and society, it is difficult to isolate the direct observed impacts of climate change upon tourism activity. There is sparse literature about this relationship at any scale'.

Climate change is likely to have a long term effect on domestic and international tourist flows and tourist behaviours throughout the tourism system. This means that it will influence all stages of the travel experience prior to travel, en route, and at the destination as well as in future choice of destination (Hall and Lew, 2009). Higher temperatures are likely to change summer and winter destination preferences globally (Hall and Higham, 2005; Deutsche Bank Research, 2008; Scott *et al.*, 2008a), either through direct effects on tourism, such as availability of a tourism resource, for example snow in alpine areas, or in terms of making competing destinations more or less attractive in terms of their climatic comfort. Changes in temperatures may also lead to new patterns of seasonality as a result of shifts in travel preferences in generating areas as well as product change in destinations. Although the capacity of potential tourists to accurately judge the implications of increases in average temperatures or climate overall for a destination is quite questionable (Gössling *et al.*, 2006). For example, Scott *et al.* (2008b) examined tourist perceptions of optimal climatic conditions (for temperature, sunshine, wind) and the relative importance of four climatic parameters (temperature, precipitation, sunshine, wind) in three major tourism environments (beach-coastal, urban, mountains) via a survey of university students (n = 831) in Canada, New Zealand and Sweden. They found significant variation in the perceived optimum climatic conditions for the three major tourism environments, differences in the relative importance of the four climatic parameters in the three tourism environments, and similarities as well as differences in the climatic preferences of respondents from the different countries.

Despite the complexities of tourist preferences for climate, there has been a strong dependence on deterministic models of tourist–climate relationships in trying to forecast future preferences under different climate change scenarios. For example, the Tourism Comfort Index of Amelung and Viner (2006) indicates improved conditions for tourism in northern Europe, while econometric modelling by Hamilton *et al.* (2005) (the only tourist study included in the influential Stern (2006) report) suggested that an arbitrary climate change scenario of 1°C would lead to a gradual shift of tourist destinations further north and up mountains, thereby affecting the preferences of European summer tourists (Alcamo *et al.*, 2007). Nevertheless, Gössling and Hall (2006b, c, d) have argued that there are a number of major weaknesses with respect to current models in predicting changes in travel flows as a result of climate change (see also Scott *et al.*, 2008b) and have urged substantial caution in utilizing the results of deterministic approaches to climate change adaptation (Table 2.2). However, despite some of the difficulties in identifying future flows of tourists it is still possible to identify some of the locations that may be most at risk as a result of environmental change. The next section therefore briefly identifies some of the most at risk coastal tourism destinations.

Assessment of 'Disappearing Destinations': Identifying the Most Vulnerable Destinations

The capacity for countries and destinations to respond to the impacts of climate change on tourism is a combination of a number of factors, including:

- direct climatic effects, including high-magnitude events such as storms, floods and droughts;
- effects of regulatory attempts to mitigate climate change, which increase the price of travel;
- destination substitution effects resulting from climatic or regulatory factors. This includes price substitution whereby a destination that provides similar benefits for customers becomes relatively cheaper, and activity and environmental substitution effects whereby because of the impacts of climate change the capacity to engage in an activity and/or experience a specific environment is greater elsewhere; and
- the actual capacities each destination has to adapt to the effects of climate change.

A further key element in the threat of climate change on tourism is the extent to which a country is economically dependent on tourism. Clearly, almost by definition, a destination will have a degree of dependence on tourism. However, its

Table 2.2. Major weaknesses of current models in predicting travel flows under climate change forecasts.

- Validity and structure of statistical databases, including international and domestic statistics
- Assumption of temperature assumed as the most important weather parameter
- Importance of other weather parameters (rain, storms, humidity, hours of sunshine, air pollution) largely unknown
- Role of weather extremes unknown
- Role of information in decision-making unclear
- Role of non-climatic parameters in influencing travel flows unclear (e.g. perception of security and political instability, risk perceptions, destination perception)
- Existence of fuzzy-variables problematic (terrorism, war, epidemics, natural disasters)
- Assumed linearity of change in behaviour unrealistic
- Future costs of transport and availability of tourism infrastructure uncertain
- Future levels of personal disposable income (economic budget) and availability of leisure time (time budget) that are allocated to travel uncertain

From: Gössling and Hall, 2006b, c, d; Hall, 2008a.

capacity to adapt to climate change will depend on a range of other factors, including the overall capacity of the local and national economy to respond to change, the national innovation system, and a range of environmental health factors. Countries and destinations that are already under significant environmental, social and/or economic stress will clearly find it harder to adapt than those which are not. Given such a situation it should therefore not be surprising that the IPCC report (Nicholls *et al.*, 2007) concluded with a high degree of confidence that adaptation for the coasts of developing countries will be more challenging than for coasts of developed countries, due to constraints on adaptive capacity.

Many of the less developed countries (LDCs) that have strongly developed tourism industries are therefore greatly at risk from the effects of climate change (Gössling *et al.*, 2008). Scott *et al.* (2008a) estimated that that the total number of international arrivals to LDCs corresponds to approximately 0.9% of all international tourist trips made in 2005. However, as trips from tourist generating areas in the industrialized countries to the least developed countries are usually long-haul, the share of distances travelled and emissions associated with these trips is higher, amounting to 4.7% of the transport volume (by passenger kilometre) and 4.6% of the CO_2 emissions caused by international tourist air transport (Scott *et al.*, 2008a). This highlights that there may be a general trade-off between tourism's development benefits in the LDCs and its contribution to climate change (Gössling *et al.*, 2009a).

Table 2.3 details the developing economies for which visitor expenditure represents 10% or more of GDP. Vulnerability is also assessed by whether the country's tourism industry is substantially dependent on ecotourism or being a long-haul destination as well as having tourism in coastal areas. Of the four developing economies for which visitor expenditure is greater than 50% of GDP, all are islands and three are long-haul destinations. All of the ten countries for which visitor expenditure is between 25% and 50% of GDP are islands and long-haul destinations. Of the 21 countries for which visitor expenditure is between 10% and 25% of GDP, only Zimbabwe is not either a coastal destination or an island developing economy. Although not included in the table it should also be noted that of the 20 less developed economies for which visitor expenditure accounts for between 5% and 10% of GDP only two economies are not either coastal destinations or islands, while the majority are also long-haul destinations.

The susceptibility of the less developed economies identified in Table 2.3 is also reinforced by the assessments of several other studies of climate change, which have consistently identified developing nations in Africa, the Caribbean, Indian Ocean, Oceania, and South and South-east Asia as the most at-risk tourism destinations from 2025 to the mid-21st century. Table 2.4 provides an overview of these assessments.

Using the same criteria, a number of 'winners and losers' from climate change were recognized in the developed world. Gössling and Hall (2006d), for example, identified the south-west USA and the Mediterranean as the most at-risk destinations with respect to climate change because of the cumulative effects of a number of elements of global environmental change while with respect to specific factors, the Gold Coast (Australia) and Florida were also identified at risk from sea-level rise, coastal California and Florida from urbanization, and Australia

Table 2.3. Tourism and developing economies: vulnerability to climate change.

Developing economies	Region	UNCTAD economic groupings	Nominal GDP 2006 ($m)	Total expenditure of visitors 2006 ($m)	Visitor expenditure as % of GDP 2006	Ecotourism/ Nature-based tourism	Coastal	Islands	Long-haul destination
>50% tourism GDP									
China, Macao SAR	Eastern Asia	A	14,293	9,337	65.3			x	
Palau	Oceania	A, F	156	90	57.6			x	x
Anguilla	Caribbean	A	201	107[a]	53.2			x	x
Cook Islands	Oceania	B	177	90	50.8			x	x
25–<50% tourism GDP									
Maldives	Southern Asia	B, F, G	907	434[a]	47.9			x	x
Seychelles	Eastern Africa	A, F	707	323	45.7			x	x
Aruba	Caribbean	A	2,380	1,076	45.2			x	x
Turks and Caicos Islands	Caribbean	A	648	292[b]	45.1			x	x
Saint Lucia	Caribbean	A, F	933	347[a]	37.2			x	x
Vanuatu	Oceania	B, F, G	361	109	35.6			x	x
Antigua and Barbuda	Caribbean	A, F	(e)1,002	347[a]	34.6			x	x
Bahamas	Caribbean	A, F	(e)6,175	2,079	33.7			x	x
Barbados	Caribbean	A, F	3,446	978[a]	28.4			x	x
Cape Verde	Western Africa	B, F	1,116	286	25.6			x	x

(*Continued*)

Table 2.3. (Continued)

Developing economies	Region	UNCTAD economic groupings	Nominal GDP 2006 ($m)	Total expenditure of visitors 2006 ($m)	Visitor expenditure as % of GDP 2006	Type of vulnerability			
						Ecotourism/ Nature-based tourism	Coastal	Islands	Long-haul destination
10–<25% tourism GDP									
Lebanon	Western Asia	A	22,064	5,491	24.9		x		x
Saint Kitts and Nevis	Caribbean	A, F	487	116[a]	23.8			x	x
Saint Vincent and the Grenadines	Caribbean	B, F	(e)480	113[a]	23.5			x	x
Grenada	Caribbean	A, F	(e)413	93[b]	22.5			x	x
Dominica	Caribbean	B, F	316	68[b]	21.5			x	x
Samoa	Oceania	B, F, G	(e)429	91	21.2			x	x
Belize	Central America	B	1,217	253[a]	20.8	x	x		x
Cayman Islands	Caribbean	A	2,447	509	20.8			x	x
Fiji	Oceania	B, F	3,103	636	20.5			x	x
Jamaica	Caribbean	B, F	10,316	2,094	20.3			x	x
Mauritius	Eastern Africa	B, E	6,413	1,302	20.3			x	x
Zimbabwe	Eastern Africa	C, E	1,765	338	19.2	x			
São Tomé and Príncipe	Middle Africa	C, D, F, G	74	14[a,b]	18.9			x	
Montserrat	Caribbean	A	46	8[a]	17.4			x	

	Region	UNCTAD groups			%			
Cambodia	South-eastern Asia	C, G	(e)6,648	1,080	16.2		X	X
Jordan	Western Asia	B	14,336	2,008	14.0			X
French Polynesia	Oceania	A	5,643	785	13.9		X	X
Gambia	Western Africa	C, D, G	511	69	13.5	X		X
Dominican Republic	Caribbean	B	31,593	3,792[b]	12.0		X	X
Bahrain	Western Asia	A, H	(e)15,884	1,786	11.2		X	X
Morocco	Northern Africa	B	65,365	6,899	10.5	X		X

(e) Estimate.
[a] Visitor expenditure excluding transport.
[b] Most recent available figure.

UNCTAD economic groupings:
A – 2000 per capita current GDP above US$4,500: High-income (42)
B – 2000 per capita current GDP between US$1,000 and US$4,500: Middle-income (50)
C – 2000 per capita current GDP below US$1,000: Low-income (65)
D – Heavily indebted poor countries – HIPCs (41);
E – Landlocked developing countries – LLDCs (31)
F – Small island developing States – SIDS (29)
G – Least developed countries – LDCs (49)
H – Major petroleum exporters (22)
I – Major exporters of manufactured goods (12)
J – Emerging economies (10)
K – Newly industrialized economies (8)
(From: Derived from UNCTAD (2008) data).

Table 2.4. Estimated climate change vulnerability of tourism in developing regions.

Study	Timeframe assessed	Vulnerability categories	Regions
Deutsche Bank Research, 2008	2030	Negatively affected (slightly or strongly)[a]	South America, Caribbean/ Mexico, South-east Asia (including China and India), Middle East, Africa[b]
Gössling and Hall, 2006d; Hall, 2008a	Mid-21st century	Moderately to strongly negatively impacted[c]	Africa, Asia, especially coastal China, Latin America, Small Island Nations
Halifax Travel Insurance, 2006	2030	Identifies at-risk destinations[d]	Caribbean, North Africa (Morocco and Tunisia), India and the Indian Ocean, Maldives and Seychelles
Hamilton *et al.*, 2005	2025, +4°C warming scenario	Negative impact on tourist arrivals[e]	Caribbean/Mexico, South America (except Chile), Africa (except Zambia and Zimbabwe), Middle East, South-east Asia (except China)
Scott *et al.*, 2008a	Mid-21st century	Vulnerability hotspots[f]	Caribbean, Indian and Pacific Ocean Small Island Nations[g]

[a]Impact criteria considered: climatic changes, regulatory burdens, substitution effects, adaptation capacities. Data sources and indicators for these criteria were not identified.
[b]Many nations in the Middle East and Africa were 'not examined', however no rationale was provided regarding availability of information for selected nations.
[c]Impact criteria considered: land and marine biodiversity loss, urbanization, water security, sea level rise, regime change, fuel costs, temperature changes, disease potential.
[d]Impact criteria not stated, although items notes included climate changes, sea level rise, changing weather patterns, no rationale was provided regarding availability of information for selected nations.
[e]Impact criteria considered: change in annual average temperature.
[f]Impact criteria considered: summer and winter climatic change, increases in extreme events, sea level rise, land and marine biodiversity loss, water scarcity, political destabilization, health impacts/disease potential, transportation costs, and relative importance of tourism to the economy (also utilizing Gössling and Hall (2006d) results).
[g]South America, Africa, Middle East, South-east Asia were identified as potentially vulnerable, but not listed as 'hotspots' due to insufficient information on magnitude of potential impacts.
From: After Gössling *et al.* (2009a).

from water security. In the European context it has also been argued that countries bordering the Mediterranean will suffer substantially from climate change (Hamilton *et al.*, 2005; Gössling and Hall, 2006a, d; Deutsche Bank Research, 2008). In contrast, those that may gain include the Benelux countries, Denmark, Germany, and the Nordic and Baltic countries. However, the greater capacity of developed countries such as France, Italy and Spain to adapt to climate change means that forecasts as to the demise of tourism in those countries at least in the medium term may be quite problematic as adaptation mechanisms such as changes in seasonality may mean that while there may be a decline in visitor numbers in summer as a result of extremely high temperatures, visitor numbers may increase in winter thereby balancing the overall contribution of tourism to the economy. Indeed, it may even be possible to develop destination management scenarios in the European Mediterranean coastal destinations that will provide more balanced seasonal tourism demand than what exists at present (Hall and Lew, 2009).

Conclusions

There is now a substantial policy gap between the perspectives of climate change researchers of what is required to limit the negative effects of climate change and the actions of governments around the world – and the gap appears to be widening. For example, in February 2009 Professor Chris Field, one of the lead authors of the North America chapter in the 2007 IPCC report on climate change (Parry *et al.*, 2007), speaking at the American Science conference in Chicago, said future temperatures 'will be beyond anything' predicted, 'fresh data showed greenhouse gas emissions between 2000 and 2007 increased far more rapidly than expected … We are basically looking now at a future climate that is beyond anything that we've considered seriously in climate policy' (BBC News, 2009). Similarly, James Hansen, another leading climate change scientist, wrote in an opinion piece in *The Observer* that 'Coal-fired power stations are death factories. Close them' (Hansen, 2009).

The reasons for the highly charged policy environment primarily relate to the implications of the costs of any mitigation and adaptation strategies (Monbiot, 2006). For example, application of the 'polluter pays' principle to an area such as aviation would have significant impacts on costs of airline passenger and freight costs and therefore levels of demand (Hall, 2008a). In addition, climate change is now part of wider political debates and appears to be emerging as a factor in electoral campaigns (Hall and Lew, 2009). Nevertheless, economic interests and especially fears of an economic and employment crisis still dominate the political agenda over a climatic and environmental crisis. Many organizations in the tourism industry, such as the World Tourism Organization (WTO) and the World Travel and Tourism Council (WTTC), also advocate the economic significance of tourism while at the same time seeking to position it as an environmentally friendly industry. Yet as this chapter has indicated it may be extremely difficult to reconcile the extent to which long-haul travel contributes to emissions to being a 'green industry' (Gössling *et al.*, 2009b).

There are clearly enormous practical political difficulties in reducing the ecological footprint of tourism yet still achieving the economic benefits that tourism may bring, As discussed above, tourism is proportionately economically more important to LDCs, and it is germane to the present volume that those economies for which visitor expenditure represents a proportion of GDP above 5% are nearly all coastal destinations and island states. However, it is also clear that there are enormous knowledge gaps in understanding tourism and climate change relationships. With respect to emissions for example, there is a lack of detail of the contribution of cruise ships and other marine passenger services. Nevertheless, the greatest knowledge gaps exist with the specific effects of climate change on tourism in particular locations and for specific types of tourism activity. Although the IPCC has produced excellent macro-accounts of climate change impacts, some regions, such as Asia, Africa and South America, have had very little research conducted specifically on climate change effects and tourism (see also Scott *et al.*, 2008a; Simpson *et al.*, 2008). Such gaps also make it extremely difficult to understand the extent to which adaptation and mitigation processes can be effectively engaged in by the tourism sector or by government at various levels. Perhaps most importantly though, it needs to be realized that tourism is only a relatively small, albeit significant part, of a much bigger picture of environmental, economic and political debate.

References

Access Economics (2005) *Measuring the Economic and Financial Value of the Great Barrier Reef Marine Park*. Report by Access Economics for Great Barrier Reef Marine Park Authority. Great Barrier Reef Marine Park Authority, Townsville.

Access Economics (2008) *Economic Contribution of the GBRMP, 2006–07*. Great Barrier Reef Marine Park Authority, Access Economics, Canberra.

Alcamo, J., Moreno, J.M., Nováky, B., Bindi, M., Corobov, R., Devoy, R.J.N., Giannakopoulos, C., Martin, E., Olesen, J.E. and Shvidenko, A. (2007) Europe. In: Parry, M.L., Canziani, O.F., Palutikof, J.P., van der Linden, P.J. and Hanson, C.E. (eds) *Climate Change 2007: Impacts, Adaptation and Vulnerability*. Cambridge University Press, Cambridge, pp. 541–580.

Amelung, B. and Viner, D. (2006) Mediterranean tourism: exploring the future with the tourism climatic index. *Journal of Sustainable Tourism* 14, 349–366.

BBC News (2009) Global warming 'underestimated'. BBC News, Sunday, 15 February 2009, http://news.bbc.co.uk/1/hi/sci/tech/7890988.stm (Accessed: 15 February 2009).

Berkelmans, R., De'ath, G., Kininmonth, S. and Skirving, W.J. (2004) A comparison of the 1998 and 2002 coral bleaching events of the Great Barrier Reef: spatial correlation, patterns and predictions. *Coral Reefs* 23, 74–83.

Boko, M., Niang, I., Nyong, A., Vogel, C., Githekol, A., Medany, M., Osman-Elasha, B., Tabo, R. and Yanda, P. (2007) Africa. In: Parry, M.L., Canziani, O.F., Palutikof, J.P., van der Linden, P.J. and Hanson, C.E. (eds) *Climate Change 2007: Impacts, Adaptation and Vulnerability*. Cambridge University Press, Cambridge, pp. 433–467.

Bruno, J. (Lead Author) and McGinley, M. (Topic Editor) (2008) Coral reefs and climate change. In: Cleveland, C.J. (ed.) *Encyclopedia of Earth*. Environmental Information Coalition, National Council for Science and the Environment, Washington DC (first published in the *Encyclopedia of Earth*, 19 December 2007; last revised 26 August 2008), www.eoearth.org/article/Coral_reefs_and_climate_change (Accessed: 12 February 2009).

Cruz, R.V., Harasawa, H., Lal, M., Wu, S., Anokhin, Y., Punsalmaa, B., Honda, Y., Jafari, M., Li, C. and Huu Ninh, N. (2007) Asia. In: Parry, M.L., Canziani, O.F., Palutikof, J.P., van der Linden, P.J. and Hanson, C.E. (eds) *Climate Change 2007: Impacts, Adaptation and Vulnerability*. Cambridge University Press, Cambridge, pp. 469–506.

Deutsche Bank Research (2008) Climate Change and Tourism: Where Will the Journey Take Us? Deutsche Bank Research, Berlin.

Field, C.B., Mortsch, L.D., Brklacich, M., Forbes, D.L., Kovacs, P., Patz, J.A., Running, S.W. and Scott, M.J. (2007) North America. In: Parry, M.L., Canziani, O.F., Palutikof, J.P., van der Linden, P.J. and Hanson, C.E. (eds) *Climate Change 2007: Impacts, Adaptation and Vulnerability*. Cambridge University Press, Cambridge, pp. 617–652.

Gössling, S. and Hall, C.M. (eds) (2006a) *Tourism and Global Economic Change*. Routledge, London.

Gössling, S. and Hall, C.M. (2006b) Uncertainties in predicting tourist flows under scenarios of climate change. *Climatic Change* 79(3–4), 163–173.

Gössling, S. and Hall, C.M. (2006c) An introduction to tourism and global environmental change. In: Gössling, S. and Hall, C.M. (eds) *Tourism and Global Environmental Change. Ecological, Social, Economic and Political Interrelationships*. Routledge, London, pp.1–34.

Gössling, S. and Hall, C.M. (2006d) Conclusion: Wake up... This is serious. In: Gössling, S. and Hall, C.M. (eds) *Tourism and Global Environmental Change. Ecological, Social, Economic and Political Interrelationships*. Routledge, London, pp. 305–320.

Gössling, S., Bredberg, M., Radnow, A., Svensson, P. and Swedlin, E. (2006) Tourist perceptions of climate change: a study of international tourists in Zanzibar. *Current Issues in Tourism* 9(4–5), 419–435.

Gössling, S., Lindén, O., Helmersson, J., Liljenberg, J. and Quarm, S. (2007) Diving and global environmental change: a Mauritius case study. In: Garrod, B. and Gössling, S. (eds) *New Frontiers in Marine Tourism: Diving Experiences, Management and Sustainability*. Elsevier, Oxford.

Gössling, S., Peeters, P. and Scott, D. (2008) Consequences of climate policy for international tourist arrivals in developing countries. *Third World Quarterly* 29(5), 873–901.

Gössling, S., Hall, C.M. and Scott, D. (2009a) The challenges of tourism as a development strategy in an era of global climate change. In: *Development and Climate Change*. Ministry of Foreign Affairs, Helsinki.

Gössling, S., Hall, C.M. and Weaver, D. (eds) (2009b) *Sustainable Tourism Futures: Perspectives on Systems, Restructuring and Innovations*. Routledge, New York.

Government of the Maldives (2001) First National Communication of the Republic of Maldives to the United Nations Framework Convention on Climate Change. Government of Maldives, Malé.

Halifax Travel Insurance (2006) Holiday 2030: Climate change to drive radical changes in global tourism. Halifax Press Release, 1 September 2006, www.hbosplc.com/media/pressreleases/articles/halifax/2006-09-01-05.asp (Accessed: 1 April 2007).

Hall, C.M. (2005) *Tourism: Rethinking the Social Science of Mobility*. Prentice Hall, Harlow.

Hall, C.M. (2006a) Tourism urbanization and global environmental change. In: Gössling, S. and Hall, C.M. (eds) *Tourism and Global Environmental Change: Ecological, Economic, Social and Political Interrelationships*. Routledge, London, pp. 142–156.

Hall, C.M. (2006b) Tourism, biodiversity and global environmental change. In: Gössling, S. and Hall, C.M. (eds) *Tourism and Global Environmental Change: Ecological, Economic, Social and Political Interrelationships*. Routledge, London, pp. 211–225.

Hall, C.M. (2008a) Tourism and climate change: Knowledge gaps and issues. *Tourism Recreation Research* 33, 339–350.

Hall, C.M. (2008b) Santa Claus, place branding and competition. *Fennia* 186(1), 59–67.

Hall, C.M. and Higham, J. (eds) (2005) *Tourism, Recreation and Climate Change*. Channel View Publications, Clevedon, UK.

Hall, C.M. and Lew, A. (2009) *Understanding and Managing Tourism Impacts: an Integrated Approach*. Routledge, London.

Hamilton, J.M., Maddison, D.J. and Tol, R.S.J. (2005) Climate change and international tourism: a simulation study. *Global Environmental Change* 15, 253–266.

Hansen, J. (2009) Coal-fired power stations are death factories. Close them. *The Observer*, Sunday 15 February 2009, www.guardian.co.uk/commentisfree/2009/feb/15/james-hansen-power-plants-coal (Accessed: 15 February 2009).

Hoegh-Guldberg, O. (2004) Coral reefs in a century of rapid environmental change. *Symbiosis* 37, 1–31.

Lamers, M. and Amelung, B. (2007) The environmental impacts of tourism, to Antarctica. A global perspective. In: Peeters, P.M. (ed.) *Tourism and Climate Change Mitigation. Methods, Greenhouse Gas Reductions and Policies*. NHTV, Breda.

Mimura, N., Nurse, L., McLean, R.F., Agard, J., Briguglio, L., Lefale, P., Payet, R. and Sem, G. (2007) Small islands. In: Parry, M.L., Canziani, O.F., Palutikof, J.P., van der Linden, P.J. and Hanson, C.E. (eds) *Climate Change 2007: Impacts, Adaptation and Vulnerability*. Cambridge University Press, Cambridge, pp. 687–716.

Monbiot, G. (2006) *Heat: How to Stop the Planet Burning*. Allen Lane, London.

Nicholls, R.J., Wong, P.P., Burkett, V.R., Codignotto, J.O., Hay, J.E., McLean, R.F., Ragoonaden, S. and Woodroffe, C.D. (2007) Coastal systems and low-lying areas. In: Parry, M.L., Canziani, O.F., Palutikof, J.P., van der Linden, P.J. and Hanson, C.E. (eds) *Climate Change 2007: Impacts, Adaptation and Vulnerability*. Cambridge University Press, Cambridge, pp. 315–356.

Nurse, L. and Moore, R. (2005) Adaptation to global climate change: an urgent requirement for Small Island Developing States. *Review of European Community and International Environmental Law* 14, 100–107.

Parry, M.L., Canziani, O.F., Palutikof, J.P., van der Linden, P.J. and Hanson, C.E. (eds) (2007) *Climate Change 2007: Impacts, Adaptation and Vulnerability*. Contribution of Working Group II to the Fourth Assessment Report of the Intergovernmental Panel on Climate Change. Cambridge University Press, Cambridge.

Payet, R. and Obura, D. (2004) The negative impacts of human activities in the Eastern African region: an international waters perspective. *Ambio* 33, 24–33.

Rosenzweig, C., Casassa, G., Karoly, D.J., Imeson, A., Liu, C., Menzel, A., Rawlins, S., Root, T.L., Seguin, B. and Tryjanowski, P. (2007) Assessment of observed changes and responses in natural and managed systems. In: Parry, M.L., Canziani, O.F., Palutikof, J.P., van der Linden, P.J. and Hanson, C.E. (eds) *Climate Change 2007: Impacts, Adaptation and Vulnerability*. Cambridge University Press, Cambridge, pp. 79–131.

Scott, D., Wall, G. and McBoyle, G. (2005) The evolution of the climate change issue in the tourism sector. In: Hall, C.M. and Higham, J. (eds) *Tourism, Recreation and Climate Change*. Channel View Publications, Clevedon, UK, pp. 44–60.

Scott, D., Amelung, B., Becken, S., Ceron, J.-P., Dubois, G., Gössling, S., Peeters, P. and Simpson, M. (2008a) Technical Report. In: *Climate Change and Tourism: Responding to Global Challenges*. United Nations World Tourism Organization, United Nations Environment Programme and World Meteorological Organization, Madrid, pp. 23–250.

Scott, D., Gössling, S. and de Freitas, C.R. (2008b) Preferred climates for tourism: case studies from Canada, New Zealand and Sweden. *Climate Research* 38, 61–73.

Simpson, M.C., Gössling, S., Scott, D., Hall, C.M. and Gladin, E. (2008) *Climate Change Adaptation and Mitigation in the Tourism Sector: Frameworks, Tools and Practices*. UNEP, University of Oxford, UNWTO, WMO, Paris.

Stern, N. (2006) *The Economics of Climate Change: The Stern Review*. Cambridge University Press, Cambridge.

UNCTAD (2008) UNCTAD *Handbook of Statistics 2008*. UN, New York and Geneva.

UNFCCC (2008) Physical and Socio-economic Trends in Climate-related Risks and Extreme Events, and Their Implications for Sustainable Development. Technical Paper FCCC/TP/2008/3, 20 November 2008. UNFCCC, Geneva.

UNWTO, UNEP and WMO (2008) *Climate Change and Tourism: Responding to Global Challenges*. United Nations World Tourism Organization, United Nations Environment Programme, World Meteorological Organization, Madrid.

Uyarra, M.C., Cote, I., Gill, J., Tinch, R., Viner, D. and Watkinson, A. (2005) Island-specific preferences of tourists for environmental features: implications of climate change for tourism-dependent states. *Environmental Conservation* 32, 11–19.

Wall, G. (1998) Climate change, tourism and the IPCC. *Tourism Recreation Research* 23(2), 65–68.

Wilbanks, T.J., Romero Lankao, P., Bao, M., Berkhout, F., Cairncross, S., Ceron, J.-P., Kapshe, M., Muir-Wood, R. and Zapata-Marti, R. (2007) Industry, settlement and society. In Parry, M.L., Canziani, O.F., Palutikof, J.P., van der Linden, P.J. and Hanson, C.E. (eds) *Climate Change 2007: Impacts, Adaptation and Vulnerability*. Cambridge University Press, Cambridge, pp. 357–390.

3 Managing the Coastal Zone: Learning from Experience?

MICHAEL PHILLIPS

Introduction

The coastal zone has evolved in response to many natural and anthropogenic factors and processes. Therefore, it is logical these should be integrated within management strategies. Climate change and sea level rise now pose significant threats to coastal regions and, consequently, many tourism destinations. Accepted strategies to manage coastal areas under threat are:

- hold the line;
- advance the line;
- retreat from the line; and
- do nothing.

However, each of these options comes with its own problems and consequences. Ketchum (1972) identified six major spheres of human activity in the coastal zone, which still hold true: residency, recreation and tourism; industrial and commercial; waste disposal; agricultural, aquaculture and fishing; conservation; military and strategic. However, these activities are increasingly in conflict with one another as well as with natural processes. Consequently, the point at issue is how to protect and manage our coastal resources while accommodating growing development pressures. An evaluation of the present-day status of a coastline is fundamental in deciding whether to actively manage or refrain from intervention (Simm, 1996). In many vulnerable coastal areas beaches lie in front of built defences and it is important to differentiate between the general health of a beach and its function in coastal defence. A beach may be at a very low level and its volume may be reducing, but this does not necessarily mean that the beach needs managing to improve its defensive capability (Simm, 1996). Micallef and Williams (2002) argued that very little research work adequately addressed beach management needs and addressed this in their recent book (Williams and Micallef, 2009). Managing the coastal zone involves policies at various geographical scales and the implementation of techniques to achieve these policy objectives. Consequently, this chapter will examine coastal management in response to climate change and sea level rise. It will consider problems caused by human interaction with physical processes, assess options for protecting coastal assets, examine policy options based on available capacity and conclude with strategic management recommendations.

Coastal Problems

The following case studies give examples of development and consequences of human attempts to provide a stabilized shoreline. Figure 3.1 shows a recently constructed cliff-top road in Praia, Cape Verde. It represents a significant infrastructure investment to support tourism development in the island.

There is already evidence of settlement and repairs have been undertaken. Unfortunately, undercutting and erosion will be an ongoing process, causing further future problems. The decision to site the road at this location highlights a common coastal problem, in that coastal processes are not considered in development planning. Another example of an inappropriate development location is shown in Fig. 3.2. Here a property along the same coastal frontage in Praia is threatened by cliff retreat and the problem has been managed using rock armour at the cliff toe. However, ground movement has reduced armour effectiveness and further remedial actions will be necessary to prevent this property falling into the sea. Protection will be an ongoing and expensive process.

Fig. 3.1.   Praia, Cape Verde.

Fig. 3.2. Property under threat, Praia, Cape Verde.

Cliff-top development in Albufeira, Portugal is clearly threatened by erosion (Fig. 3.3). This is a common problem along the Algarve coastline and some properties are now uninhabited. They are left vacant, in some cases by local authority enforcement, as a safety precaution due to the risk of collapsing into the sea.

Figure 3.4 shows cliff protection measures near Cadiz, Spain. A hotel at the cliff top is the only property under threat should there be extensive cliff-falls. The local authority placed rock armour at the cliff toe along the coastal frontage and secured the cliff face with netting to contain rock falls and prevent potential injury to beach users.

These cliff protection measures represent a significant investment by the municipality while the beach itself evidences erosion and narrowing at many locations along its length. This increases the incidence of storm waves attacking the cliffs, resulting in further management costs. The paradox is that cliff material should naturally replenish the beach and adopted management strategies have reduced local sediment input. Consequently, this has increased beach erosion and has resulted in greater wave energy/storm impacts along the whole coast-line. It could therefore be argued that the local authority has invested in long term shoreline degradation. However, military land at Barry Buddon, near Dundee, Scotland has evolved naturally with little disturbance and, consequently, the coastal dune system shows no evidence of degradation (Fig. 3.5).

Adjacent land to the west has for centuries been used for various industries and activities. It has also been used as a landfill site and latterly for recre-ational activities. Human use over time has necessitated stabilization and

Fig. 3.3. Coastal development in Albufeira.

Fig. 3.4. Cliff protection measures.

Fig. 3.5. Military coastal land.

these measures have themselves caused erosion. Figure 3.6 shows rock armour protecting the dunes, but in reality, it is preventing natural reworking of the shoreline. In front of the armour, embryo dunes form as part of the natural process of coastline evolution.

South Wales, UK has many examples of development subsequently being in conflict with coastal processes. In Porthcawl, the Esplanade seawall of 1887 was replaced in 1906 and again in 1934, as erosion continually undermined previous constructions (Carter, 1988). Beach levels continued to fall and in 1984, the coastal protection authority paved the beach with bitumen macadam (Fig. 3.7). While not aesthetically pleasing, only minor repair works have subsequently been needed and high value human infrastructure has been protected.

A tidal harbour at Port Talbot, constructed for importing iron ore and coal, subsequently caused significant erosion of the adjacent coastline. The promenade and tourism infrastructure were themselves all constructed in a former sand-dune area. Here seawalls constructed to protect the promenade were undermined and coastal defence measures to protect seawalls fronting the promenade and industrial hinterland include rock armour revetments (Fig. 3.8; Phillips, 2009).

The construction of the Millennium Park, Millennium Coastal Path and Earth Structure at Llanelli, South Wales, UK stimulated a tourism and domestic property redevelopment strategy. However, this took place without due consideration of coastal processes and location. Furthermore, because of previous dereliction and lack of valuable infrastructure, temporal coastal data had not been collected

Fig. 3.6. Rock armour protecting dunes.

Fig. 3.7. Bitumen revetment.

Fig. 3.8. Aberavon promenade.

Fig. 3.9. Catastrophic failure of coastal path.

as part of strategic monitoring. Consequently, following storm events the coastal path suffered catastrophic failure (Fig. 3.9), the Earth Structure suffered erosion and significant damage became apparent on many newly constructed homes. Existing seawalls were undermined and required rock armour protection and their ability to protect recent developments is now in question. Causes and effects included inappropriate siting of infrastructure, advancing the line without due consideration of coastal processes and relocation of nearshore river channels. Lessons had not been learned following similar construction patterns elsewhere (Phillips *et al.*, 2009).

Protecting Coastal Assets

Without sufficient data to enable accurate assessment of coastal processes and dynamics, it is unlikely that effective long-term protection of coastal assets will be achieved. However, the collection of quantitative data is often expensive and time consuming (Galofre and Montoya, 1995). Phillips (2008a) identified unique short-term changes in coastal processes which had caused significant infrastructure failure and similar work at another location showed marine aggregate dredging was not the significant cause of local beach erosion (Phillips, 2008b). Without analysis of long-term datasets neither of these outcomes would have been achieved. Qualitative data should enable identification of socio-economic and environmental values associated with coastal use. Ideally, collection of data on coastal processes and sediment-related characteristics should include both physical and environmental components and be complemented by subsequent long-term monitoring programmes. Identification of local characteristics and/or problems and the socio-economic value of resources are vital for effective decision-making. Protection measures should be considered as a function of socio-economic pressures and physical environmental constraints. Micallef and Williams (2002) considered analysis in this context was often linked to understanding an environmental system, examining active management if present and identifying problems. Spatial assessment should evaluate external events, such as resort development which can influence natural beach dynamics, while temporal analysis should address timeline variation and causal change, such as sea level trends. Therefore, as argued by Bowman and Pranzini (2008), it is necessary to decipher the effects of time and space at different scales, on shoreline behaviour when designing an optimal coastal monitoring strategy. Remote sensing technologies utilizing satellite imagery, LiDAR and video systems are increasingly used to assess coastal change, and these are supported by numerical models that generate wave climates, sediment transport mechanisms, etc. Importantly, as stressed by Barale (2008), both in situ and remote sensing techniques should be integrated. In the UK, Shoreline Management Plans based on sediment cells provide large-scale risk assessments associated with coastal processes such as tidal patterns, wave height, wave direction and movement of beach and seabed materials. Their aim is to help reduce risks to people and the developed, historical and natural environments.

Historically, human development in coastal areas has been protected from the sea by hard engineering structures, such as seawalls, breakwaters and groynes. A worldwide tendency to coastal erosion (Cipriani *et al.*, 2004) has been locally aggravated by some of the very strategies implemented to reverse the pattern (Gillie, 1997; Weerakkody, 1997). While reducing coastal erosion locally, these structures tend to interfere with the natural transport of sand and cause coastal erosion further down the coast. Following port developments at Marina di Massa, Tuscany, Cipriani *et al.* (1999) reported that in order to protect the seaside resort, each kilometre of coastline was protected by 1.4 km of hard structures. Later work identified 2.2 km of hard structures protecting every kilometre at Marina di Pisa, Tuscany (Cipriani *et al.*, 2004). Of the 875 km of European coastlines that started to erode within the past 20 years, 63% are located less than 30 km from coastal areas altered by recent engineering works (Europa, 2007a). Europe's coast is under increasing threat from erosion. A fifth of the enlarged EU's coastline is already severely affected, with coastlines retreating by between 0.5 and 2 m/year and by 15 m in a few dramatic cases (Europa, 2007b). However, Basco (1999) believed there are many misconceptions that seawalls increase erosion and believed policy decisions to locate infrastructure in the coastal zone are the cause. Seawalls are needed to protect inappropriately sited construction from storm damage but then are blamed for subsequent beach erosion. Kosyan *et al.* (2005) highlighted a similar situation when seawalls were built to protect the Black Sea coastal railway. Wiegel (2002) considered that seawalls cause erosion in special circumstances where they prevent erosion of an upland source of sand for a beach downdrift, whilst van der Weide *et al.* (2001) recognized that engineering works along the coast often cause erosion and accretion.

Because of the problems associated with hard engineering in the nearshore zone, not least cost and maintenance, alternative soft engineering techniques that work in conjunction with natural coastal processes are increasingly being used. These include the construction of submerged breakwaters that reduce the effective depth offshore and consequently reduce wave power and beach erosion (Aminti *et al.*, 2002). Beach nourishment is another soft engineering method used on eroded beaches worldwide. Although some argue it is unsustainable in the long term, it improves beach conditions, supports tourism and enhances beach appearance. A good example is Miami Beach, which by the mid-1970s had virtually no beach. Following beach nourishment and infrastructure improvements, visitor numbers grew and this has resulted in an annual return of almost US$500 in foreign exchange alone, for every US$1 invested (Houston, 2002). Beach nourishment was undertaken at Marina di Massa, Italy, where offshore sand was dredged and dumped on the beach (Cipriani *et al.*, 1999). The project was funded by bathing establishment owners and the local authority. The mean grain size of the borrow material was finer than the native beach sediment, which resulted in approximately 66% of borrow material disappearing within 1 year. Beach quality also worsened due to the fine sediments making the beach dusty. Although financially successful in terms of tourist revenue, it led to a loss of faith in a soft engineering solution by private owners, tourism operators and local authorities alike. Subsequent work by Micallef *et al.* (2001) on a proposed beach nourishment project at St George's Bay, Malta showed a high probability (0.95) of a mild impact during the post-construction phase with fine-grained sediment as against a high probability (0.86) of a negligible impact with coarse-grained sediment. Had these findings been applied at Marina di Massa, nourishment would have been more successful. Nourishment is commonly practised along the North Adriatic coast and 10 million m^3 has been used in 10 years along a 45 km coastal stretch. Studies of beach nourishment's potential to reconstruct beach/dune systems are currently being evaluated and early results showed beach management practices and shoreline orientation to be critical (Bezzi *et al.*, 2009). However, Bochev-van der Burgh *et al.*'s (2009) studies on the central Netherlands coast found that noticeable changes in foredune morphology were not evident until several years after commencement of nourishment activities.

The lesson is beach nourishment can be a sustainable way to manage coastal erosion provided that coastal processes are appropriately considered. Following nourishment, the new wider beach protects the shore from storm impacts while increasing recreational benefits and tourism-related opportunities (Benassai *et al.*, 2001). Issues include estimation of required sand volumes, locating sediments on the continental shelf, environmental compatibility, extraction techniques and projected costs (Lupino and Riccardi, 2001). Beach nourishment is now the preferred US coastal erosion response (Leatherman, 1997; Harris *et al.*, 2009) and, as argued by Symes and Byrd (2003), there is a natural symmetry to combating coastal erosion with sand won from the sea. However, as specified by Williams and Micallef (2009), when carrying out beach nourishment it is important to adhere to established guidelines and procedures, otherwise repercussions include large scale changes to geomorphological and ecological characteristics.

Another soft engineering solution, which has been used internationally to good effect on eroding coastlines, is beach drainage (Turner and Leatherman, 1997). The link between groundwater flow and beach erosion/accretion has been documented by many authors, including Turner and Nielsen (1997). Lower groundwater levels allow a relatively large volume of water in the run-up phase to percolate through the beach face, which in turn reduces the erosive back-wash effects. Piccini *et al.* (2006) assessed its application in Ravenna, Italy and found that although successful, the presence of an impermeable clay layer significantly reduced the beach drainage system's efficiency. Bowman *et al.* (2007) showed beach accretion and shoreline advance at Alassio Beach, northern Italy, but also found inefficiencies in the beach drainage system. Conversely, at Enoe and Hornbæk in Denmark, beach drainage has been completely successful and at the former location, erosion has stopped and annual beach nourishment cancelled. As part of a long term strategy to protect Venice against the effects of climate change and sea level rise, dune systems seaward of the Venice Lagoon are being restored. In Avalon, New Jersey, municipal economic resources have been used to enhance landforms as protection structures. Dunes have been restored and heightened, sand fences installed and sediment budgets controlled. Consequently, one of the wealthiest communities ranks in the lowest 1% of state property taxes and has the lowest property insurance costs (Nordstrom *et al.*, 2009). The value of using natural processes to protect coastal assets is becoming increasingly clear.

Coastal Management

The seminal work on Integrated Coastal Zone Management (ICZM) by Cicin-Sain and Knecht was first published in 1998 and it is still the major reference on this topic. It is an academic and practitioners' guide for developing and implementing effective coastal management, giving guidance on resolving difficult policy issues. Sauer (1963) identified the general management problems of integrating physical and cultural environments, exemplified by Granja's (2001) assertion that lack of coastal management had irreversibly contributed to the gradual degradation of Portugal's natural heritage, including the landscape that is one of its key elements. She further argued that management implies an understanding of geoforms, their generation, longevity and relationship with the ecosystems dependent on them. Therefore, to promote conservation and management of the coastal zone, it is important to understand not only present-day factors and processes, but also those that have been active in the recent geological past.

> Strategic planning for the management of our coasts relies implicitly upon an understanding of the physical processes responsible for shaping coastal morphology.
>
> (Reeve and Spivack, 2001:55)

The coastal zone has evolved from many natural and anthropocentric factors and processes and it is logical that management concepts inherent to these factors should be integrated. This has not always been the case, demonstrated by the coastal examples earlier in this chapter. The approach suggested by van der Meulen *et al.* (2001) is that ICZM is a cyclic process of problem recognition, planning, implementation and monitoring. This includes recognition of the country's institutional setting in terms of stakeholders and the respective mandate, capacity, commitment and financial potential. Calado *et al.* (2009) assessed geographical, environmental, cultural, political and institutional aspects of the Azores archipelago when devising a new management strategy for the Azores Marine Park, while Coutinho *et al.* (2009) recognized the importance of geological classification and hazard assessment in constructing management and constraints maps. It is important to accept differences amongst stakeholders and understand potential conflict when deciding who has most rights. Policy and implementation will be influenced by strategic and socio-economic potential in conjunction with available techniques for defending the coastline. Society's socio-cultural matrix (Ferreira *et al.*, 2009), inefficient institutional frameworks (Mercado *et al.*, 2009) and science–management barriers (O'Connor *et al.*, 2009) are seen as preventing effective ICZM. However, these limitations could be overcome utilizing multi-criteria decision-making techniques (Mosadeghi *et al.*, 2009).

> increasing populations and development are placing significant stresses on coastal resources; rising sea level is causing land loss, creating a collision course of social and sea level trends.
>
> (Leatherman, 2001:181)

The cost and sustainability of technological solutions will be a critical factor as the use of seawalls to protect the coastline is now being questioned on the basis of expense and effectiveness (Cipriani *et al.*, 1999; van der Weide *et al.*, 2001; Wiegel, 2002). However, as advocated by van der Weide *et al.* (2001), to design appropriate mitigating measures, causes should be properly analysed and the technical and economic feasibility of such mitigating measures should be evaluated. Groyne-field techniques to facilitate sedimentation (Kunz, 1999), submerged groynes to reduce nearshore wave energy (Jackson *et al.*, 2002; Robertson *et al.*, 2002), beach drainage (Turner and Nielsen, 1997) and beach nourishment (Cipriani *et al.*, 1999; Benassai *et al.*, 2001; Lupino and Riccardi,

2001; Micallef *et al.*, 2001) work in conjunction with natural coastal processes. Decision makers will need to consider these aspects when deciding future coastal management policies.

Granja and Carvalho (2000) recognized that it was unrealistic to believe that all coastlines can be protected from impending sea level rise and subsequent coastal erosion. They suggested managed retreat and selective conservation of parts of the coast that are important to society and to use technological developments, where possible, to halt inland beach migration. It may be argued on socio-economic grounds, however, that hard engineering with its associated problems will still be necessary. If human activities and global change result in coastal zone losses, risk assessments will have to be undertaken to consider overall consequences. These will include costs for defending buildings and infrastructure, environmental issues, and associated socio-economic benefits. Stakeholders will be unwilling to allow areas of high value real estate to be abandoned to the will of the sea unless cost–benefit analysis and, more importantly, political will prove otherwise. Interestingly, Martins *et al.*'s (2009) study of coastal community shoreline retreat perceptions found the majority of respondents would accept having their homes relocated, provided there was evidence to support them being in danger.

Beach management and sea defences can be justified on socio-economic grounds for a particular region and community that depends on the beach, even though these may cause the acceleration of coastal erosion further along the coastline. Consequently, the use of risk assessment tools in conjunction with benefit–cost analyses (Granja and Carvalho, 2000) could be used to justify policies of managed retreat where irreversible loss is evident. Strategies for management of the coastal zone generally agree with those suggested for coping with the negative effects of climate change. According to the *Environmental Scientist* (1999), they include prevention of loss, tolerance of loss and changing activities and location, while the mechanisms to achieve these strategies include institutional, legal, financial and technological aspects. Difficult decisions will need to be taken irrespective of stakeholder interests and there will be economic consequences (Leatherman, 2001). Policies will therefore need to integrate the complex inter-relationships of Ketchum's (1972) spheres of human coastal activity. Geographical Information Systems (GIS) analysis can aid this process by producing spatial datasets that have direct value for coastal stakeholders, planners and decision makers. Furthermore, these systems can be tailored on a regional basis or for individual shorelines (Kalliola and Laurila, 2009).

Summary and Future Strategies

According to Johnson and Scholes (1988), strategic management involves the following:

1. Analysis, where one seeks to understand the content of a system, the status of existing management, if any, and whether one should take any action.

2. Choice of the different courses of action available.

3. Implementation, where the chosen option is put into effect.

Strategic management for coastal tourism destinations with respect to climate change and sea level rise must address the following:

- Increased storminess: this will significantly impact on coastal infrastructure;
- Sea level rise: this will vary, even along the same coastline, leading to increased erosion/beach loss. Coupled with increased storms, impacts and coastal damage will worsen;
- Resilience: how quickly will tourism economies of affected coastal communities recover? This will be a critical issue for Small Island Developing States (SIDs); and
- Risk: vulnerability analysis and adaptive capacity.

Results of research and monitoring must be evaluated in the context of strategic management, and management options justified for coastal environmental protection. For climate change and sea level rise, understanding of the coastal region will rely on temporal and spatial data collection. Existing and proposed developments should be assessed alongside predicted change and decisions should be taken on socio-economic grounds. Shoreline trends can be determined from aerial photographs, remote sensing data and physical monitoring techniques. Trend impacts on infrastructure should be analysed in the context of existing management, e.g. seawalls, breakwaters, etc., and economic value. GIS is an excellent planning tool whereby spatial and temporal change can be represented alongside cultural use. From a policy perspective, decision makers can evaluate options such as 'hold the line' and subsequently assess available methods by which this can be achieved, using hard or soft engineering. Once implemented, monitoring should continue and strategies be re-evaluated on a cyclical basis. Unfortunately, some countries will be restricted on available adaptation choices. For SIDs, climate change and sea level rise impacts will be disproportionally compounded. Inundation and low elevations will affect available options. Therefore, vulnerability analyses will underpin adaptive strategies, which unfortunately must be based on response capacity. Many SIDs rely on their tourism economies and resilience will be the major driver. If strategic options are not evaluated with appropriate forward planning, coastal destinations will be under even more threat. There is now an opportunity to learn from past mistakes, otherwise we may have to pave all our beaches (Fig. 3.7).

References

Aminti, P., Cipriani, L.E., Iannotta, P. and Pranzini, E. (2002) Beach erosion control along the Golfo di Fallonica (Southern Tuscany): actual hard protection vs. potential soft solutions. In: Veloso-Gomes, F., Taveira-Pinto, F. and das Neves, L. (eds) *Littoral 2002, The Changing Coast.* Vol. 2. Eurocoast Portugal and EUCC, Porto, pp. 355–363.

Barale, V. (2008) The European marginal and enclosed seas: an overview. In: Barale, V. and Gade, M. (eds) *Remote Sensing of the European Seas.* Springer Science and Business Media B.V., Berlin, pp. 3–22.

Basco, D.R. (1999) Misconceptions about seawall and beach interactions. In: Ozhan, E. (ed) *Land–Ocean Interactions: Managing Coastal Ecosystems. Proceedings of the Medcoast-EMECS Joint Conference.* Vol. 3. Medcoast, Ankara. pp. 1565–1578.

Benassai, E., Calabrese, M. and Uberti, G.S.D. (2001) A probabilistic prediction of beach nourishment evolution. In: Ozhan, E. (ed.) *Medcoast 01: Proceedings of the Fifth International Conference on the Mediterranean Coastal Environment.* Vol. 1. Medcoast, Ankara, pp. 1323–1332.

Bezzi, A., Fontolan, G., Nordstrom, K.F., Carrer, D. and Jackson, N.L. (2009) Beach nourishment and foredune restoration: practices and constraints along the Venetian shoreline, Italy. *Journal of Coastal Research* (Special Issue) 56, 287–291.

Bochev-van der Burgh, L.M., Wijnberg, K.M. and Hulscher, S.J.M.H. (2009) Dune morphology along a nourished coast. *Journal of Coastal Research* 56 (Special Issue), 292–296.

Bowman, D. and Pranzini, E. (2008) Shoreline monitoring: review and recommendations. In: Pranzini, E. and Wetzel, L. (eds) *Beach Erosion Monitoring.* BEACHMED-e/ OpTIMAL Project, Nuova Grafica Fiorentina, Italy, pp. 15–24.

Bowman, D., Ferri, S. and Pranzini, E. (2007) Efficacy of beach dewatering – Alassio, Italy. *Coastal Engineering* 54, 791–800.

Calado, H.M., Lopes, C., Porteiro, J., Paramio, L. and Monteiro, P. (2009) Legal and technical framework of Azorean protected areas. *Journal of Coastal Research* (Special Issue) 56, 1179–1183.

Carter, R.W.G. (1988) *Coastal Environments: an Introduction to the Physical, Ecological and Cultural Systems of Coastlines.* Academic Press, London, 617pp.

Cicin-Sain, B. and Knecht, R.W. (1998) *Integrated Coastal and Ocean Management: Concepts and Practices.* Island Press, Washington, DC, 543pp.

Cipriani, L.E., Pelliccia, F. and Pranzini, E. (1999) Beach nourishment with nearshore sediments in a highly protected coast. In: Ozhan, E. (ed.) *Land–Ocean Interactions: Managing Coastal Ecosystems.* Proceedings of the Medcoast–EMECS Joint Conference. Vol. 3. Medcoast, Ankara, pp. 1579–1590.

Cipriani, L.E., Wetzel, L., Aminti, D.L. and Pranzini, E. (2004) Converting seawalls into gravel beaches. In: Micallef, A. and Vassallo, A. (eds) *Management of Coastal Recreational Resources – Beaches, Yacht Marinas and Coastal Ecotourism.* ICoD, Malta, pp. 3–12.

Coutinho, R., Pacheco, J., Wallenstein, N., Pimentel, A., Marques, R. and Silva, R. (2009) Integrating geological knowledge in planning methods for small islands coastal plans. *Journal of Coastal Research* (Special Issue) 56, 1199–1203.

Environmental Scientist (1999) Living in the greenhouse. *Environmental Scientist* 8(1), 1–3.

Europa (2007a) *European Commission puts spotlight on coastal erosion.* http://ec.europa.eu/ fisheries/press_corner/press_releases/archives/com04/com04_21_en.htm (Accessed: 4 January 2008).

Europa (2007b) *Coastal Zone Policy.* http://ec.europa.eu/environment/iczm/home.htm (Accessed: 4 January 2008).

Ferreira, J.C., Silva, L. and Polette, M. (2009) The coastal artificialisation process. Impacts and challenges for the sustainable management of the coastal cities of Santa Catarina (Brazil). *Journal of Coastal Research* (Special Issue) 56, 1209–1213.

Galofre, J. and Montoya, F.J. (1995) A case study of the behaviour of urban beach: El Miracle, Tarragona. In: Ozhan, E. (ed.) *Proceedings of the Second International Conference on the Mediterranean Coastal Environment, MEDCOAST 95.* Medcoast, Ankara, Turkey, pp. 1119–1130.

Gillie, R.D. (1997) Causes of coastal erosion in Pacific Island nations. *Journal of Coastal Research* (Special Issue) 24, 173–204.

Granja, H.M. (2001) Paleoenvironmental indicators from the recent past: a contribution to CZM purposes. In: Ozhan, E. (ed.) *Medcoast 01: Proceedings of the Fifth International Conference on the Mediterranean Coastal Environment.* Vol. 1. Medcoast, Ankara, pp. 59–70.

Granja, H.M. and Carvalho, G.S. (2000) Inland Beach Migration (Beach Erosion) and the Coastal Zone Management (The Experience of the Northwest Coastal Zone of Portugal). *Responsible Coastal Zone Management, Periodicum Biologorum* 102(1), 413–424.

Harris, M.S., Wright, E.E., Fuqua, L. and Tinker, T.P. (2009) Comparison of shoreline erosion rates derived from multiple data types: data compilation for legislated setback lines in South Carolina, USA. *Journal of Coastal Research* (Special Issue) 56, 1222–1228.

Houston, J.R. (2002) The economic value of beaches – a 2002 update. *Shore and Beach* 70(1), 9–12.

Jackson, L.A., Tomlinson, R.B. and D'Agata, M. (2002) The challenge of combining coastal processes and improved surfing amenity. In: Veloso-Gomes, F., Taveira-Pinto, F. and das Neves, L. (eds) *Littoral 2002, The Changing Coast.* Vol 1. Eurocoast Portugal and EUCC, Porto, pp. 257–263.

Johnson, G. and Scholes, K. (1988) *Exploring Corporate Strategy.* Prentice-Hall, Hemel Hempstead, UK, 218pp.

Kalliola, R. and Laurila, L. (2009) Contributing Coastal Zone Management by GIS analyses – the case of Finnish marine coast. *Journal of Coastal Research* (Special Issue) 56, 1233–1236.

Ketchum, B.H. (ed.) (1972) *The Waters Edge.* MIT Press, Massachusetts, 393pp.

Kosyan, R., Krylenko, M., Petrov, V. and Yaroslavtsev, N. (2005) Study of beach state and coastal protection in the neighbourhood of Sochi City. In: Ozhan, E. (ed.) *Medcoast 05: Proceedings of the Seventh International Conference on the Mediterranean Coastal Environment.* Vol. 2. Medcoast, Ankara, pp. 1007–1016.

Kunz, H. (1999) Groyne field technique against the erosion of salt marshes, renaissance of a soft engineering approach. In: Ozhan, E. (ed.) *Land–Ocean Interactions: Managing Coastal Ecosystems. Proceedings of the Medcoast–EMECS Joint Conference.* Vol. 3. Medcoast, Ankara, pp. 1477–1490.

Leatherman, S.P. (1997) Sea-level rise and small island states: an overview. *Journal of Coastal Research* (Special Issue) 24, 1–16.

Leatherman, S.P. (2001) Social and economic costs of sea level rise. In: Douglas, B.C., Kearney, M.S. and Leatherman, S.P. (eds) *Sea Level Rise – History and Consequences.* Academic Press, San Diego, USA, pp. 181–223.

Lupino, P. and Riccardi, C. (2001) Utilisation of marine sand for beach nourishment in the western Mediterranean. In: Ozhan, E. (ed.) *Medcoast 01: Proceedings of the Fifth International Conference on the Mediterranean Coastal Environment.* Vol. 3. Medcoast, Ankara, pp. 1347–1358.

Martins, F., Betamio de Almeida, A. and Pinho, L. (2009) Have you ever listened to coastal inhabitants? Know what they think. *Journal of Coastal Research* (Special Issue) 56, 1242–1246.

Mercado, V., Malvarez, G., Alburqurque, F. and Navas, F. (2009) Impact of the changing economic models in the development of societal and environmental structures of coastal natural parks. *Journal of Coastal Research* (Special Issue) 56, 1247–1251.

Micallef, A. and Williams, A.T. (2002) Theoretical strategy considerations for beach management. *Ocean and Coastal Management* 45, 261–275.

Micallef, A., Williams, A.T. and Cassar, M. (2001) Environmental risk assessment: application to a proposed beach nourishment, Malta. *Shore and Beach* 69(3), 13–17.

Mosadeghi, R., Tomlinson, R., Mirfenderesk, H. and Warnken, J. (2009) Coastal management issues in Queensland and application of the Multi-Criteria decision making techniques. *Journal of Coastal Research* (Special Issue) 56, 1199–1203.

Nordstrom, K.F., Jackson, N.L. and de Butts, H.A. (2009) A proactive programme for managing beaches and dunes on a developed coast: a case study of Avalon, New Jersey, USA. In: Williams, A.T. and Micallef, A. (eds) *Beach Management: Principles and Practice*. Earthscan, London, Case Study 7, pp. 307–316.

O'Connor, M.C., Cooper, J.A.G. and McKenna, J. (2009) Integrating science into shoreline management practice and policy: an Irish perspective. *Journal of Coastal Research* (Special Issue) 56, 1267–1270.

Phillips, M.R. (2008a) Consequences of short term changes in coastal processes: a case study. *Earth Surface Processes and Landforms* 33(13), 2094–2107.

Phillips, M.R. (2008b) Beach erosion and marine aggregate dredging: a question of evidence? *The Geographical Journal* 174(4), 332–343.

Phillips, M.R. (2009) Beach consequences of an industrial heritage. In: Williams, A.T. and Micallef, A. (eds) *Beach Management: Principles and Practice*. Earthscan, London, Case Study 12, pp. 353–362.

Phillips, M.R., Powell, V.A. and Duck, R.W. (2009) Coastal regeneration at Llanelli, South Wales, UK: lessons not learned. *Journal of Coastal Research* (Special Issue) 56, 1276–1280.

Piccini, M.F., Gonella, M., Teatini, P. and Gabbianelli, G. (2006) Modelling groundwater response to beach dewatering at Ravenna shoreline. In: Micallef, A., Vassallo, A. and Cassar, M. (eds) *Management of Coastal Recreational Resources – Beaches, Yacht Marinas and Coastal Ecotourism*. ICoD, Valetta, Malta, pp. 169–178.

Reeve, D.E. and Spivack, M. (2001) Stochastic prediction of long-term coastal evolution. In: Brebbia, C.A. (ed.) *Coastal Engineering V.* WIT Press, Southampton, UK, pp. 55–64.

Robertson, A., McGrath, J. and Tomlinson, R. (2002) Formulation of a master plan for the Palm Beach protection strategy. In: Veloso-Gomes, F., Taveira-Pinto, F. and das Neves, L. (eds) *Littoral 2002, The Changing Coast* 1, 255–272.

Sauer, C.O. (1963) Morphology of landscape. In: Leighly, J. (ed.) *Land and Life*. University of California Press, Berkeley, pp. 315–350.

Simm, J.D. (ed.) (1996) *Beach Management Manual*. CIRIA Report 153. CIRIA, London, 448pp.

Symes, C. and Byrd, T. (2003) Ship to shore. *Surveyor,* 13 November, London, pp. 19–20.

Turner, I.L. and Leatherman, S.P. (1997) Beach dewatering as a 'soft' engineering solution to coastal erosion – a history and critical review. *Journal of Coastal Research* 13(40), 1050–1063.

Turner, I.L. and Nielsen, P. (1997) Rapid water table fluctuations within the beach face: implications for swash zone sediment mobility. *Coastal Engineering* 32, 45–59.

Van der Meulen, F., Misdorp, R. and Baarse, G. (2001) ICZM, from planning to implementation: success or failure? In: Ozhan, E. (ed.) *Medcoast 01: Proceedings of the Fifth International Conference on the Mediterranean Coastal Environment*. Vol. 1. Medcoast, Ankara, pp. 1–16.

Van der Weide, J., de Vroeg, H. and Sanyang, F. (2001) Guidelines for coastal erosion management. In: Ozhan, E. (ed.) *Medcoast 01: Proceedings of the Fifth Interna-*

tional Conference on the Mediterranean Coastal Environment. Vol. 3. Medcoast, Ankara, pp. 1399–1414.

Weerakkody, U. (1997) Potential impact of accelerated sea-level rise on beaches of Sri Lanka. *Journal of Coastal Research* (Special Issue) 24, 225–242.

Wiegel, R.L. (2002) Seawalls, seacliffs, beachrock: what beach effects? Part 1. *Shore and Beach* 70(1), 17–27.

Williams, A.T. and Micallef, A. (2009) *Beach Management: Principles and Practice.* Earthscan, London, 445pp.

4 Definitions and Typologies of Coastal Tourism Beach Destinations

ALLAN WILLIAMS

Introduction

Some 50% of the world's coastline is currently under threat from development and it is estimated by Finkl and Kruempfel (2005) that by 2025, *circa* 75% of the world's population will live within 60 km of the sea; Povh (2000) stated the same percentage by the year 2020. This will result in a major thrust for coastal tourism, one of the world's largest industries (Klein *et al.*, 2004). Currently, in several coastal areas of France, Italy and Spain, the built-up area exceeds 45% (EEA, 2006), and in these plus Greece and Turkey, tourism receipts account for some 5% of the gross domestic product (WTO, 2006). These countries account for 'the most significant flow of tourists. ... a sun, sea and sand (3S) market' (Dodds and Kelman, 2008:58). In 2006, global tourism was worth US$733 billion, employed 8% of the global workforce and estimates were for 1.6 billion international tourists by 2020 (www.Tourism.concern). 'Travel & Tourism' worldwide, is expected to grow at a level of 4.0% per year over the next 10 years and is one of the largest growth industries in the world (www.wttc.org).

This means that beaches will be in even greater demand – they are big business and good beaches are worth billions of tourist dollars (Clark, 1996). As beaches worldwide take huge numbers of tourists in order to accommodate this development, a sound infrastructure should be in place in order to realize the real economic and social values of the 'beach industry', otherwise unregulated tourism development will continue to devastate environments, degrade cultures and destroy traditional livelihoods. From a number of coastal-marine ecosystems peer-reviewed non-market valuation studies (1970–2006) carried out by Wilson and Liu (2008:130), beach recreation 'got inordinate attention in the economic literature.' This emphasizes that environmental scientists should be very involved in tourism issues (Hall, 1997).

In the Mediterranean region, tourism is the most important activity with 298 million international tourist arrivals in 2008, followed by approximately

400 million domestic tourism arrivals. However, it is highly seasonal, being just 3 months and mainly concentrated upon the coastal strip, which has a permanent population of circa 460 million, a figure which is postulated to grow to 520 million by 2025 (Eurostat, 2009). Visitors to the coastal zone were estimated as some 250 million (international and domestic) in 2008 and this number will increase substantially, in line with a forecasted 368 million tourists by 2020 (UNEP and UNWTO, 2008). In the UK, tourism surveys show that >40% of all tourism is motivated by visits to the coast; is worth £110 billion and employs more than 1.3 million people – some 5% of all employed people (www.visitbritain.co.uk).

In California, beaches have >567 million visits compared to 286 million to all US National Park Service lands, and the Government between 1995 and 1999 received US$14 billion in tax revenues annually from tourists (King, 1999). Houston (2002) stated that travel and tourism is the USA's largest industry, employer, and earner of foreign exchange and beaches were the major factor in this tourism market. At Miami Beach, Florida, expenditure of circa US$65 million for a beach nourishment scheme has produced some US$2.4 billion annually in foreign exchange from tourists and, each year, some 85 million tourists to Florida contribute US$65 billion to the state's economy (Houston, 2002). In Barbados, local beaches are deemed to be worth >US$13 million to the local economy (Dharmaratne and Braithwaite, 1998).

Beach Types

There are a variety of beach classifications. To a geomorphologist, they can be linear (long, straight), e.g. beaches found on the barrier islands of South Carolina and Virginia, USA (Fig. 4.1), pocket as found at the head of a bay, e.g. St Georges Bay, Malta and Durdle Door, UK (Fig. 4.2), or zeta (curved at one end), e.g. Half Moon Bay, California, USA and Rhosilli, Wales, UK (Fig. 4.3). They can also cover a spectrum ranging from dissipative (many waves in the surf zone, low beach gradient) to reflective (small number of waves, a steeper beach face), essentially based on wave climatology (high–low energy) and beach material composition. To both geomorphologist and tourist they can be viewed as being composed of mud, sand, pebbles, cobbles, boulders, with an emphasis on sand for the tourist, although the same beach can exhibit sand in summer under constructive waves and pebbles in winter when destructive waves tend to be far more common – hurricane/typhoon areas excepted (Fig. 4.4). In Barbados, they classify beaches according to usage: heavy, medium and dense (CEES, 2006).

Beaches can also be either natural or artificial (sediment brought in from elsewhere, e.g. Miami). In Italy, >20 million m^3 of marine sand have been used for nourishment (Pranzini, 2004). Therefore pioneering gravel beach nourishment schemes have been introduced aimed primarily for coastal defence and these beaches (Carrarra marble in some instances) have become intensively used for recreation during summer months and are a valuable adjunct to the tourist industry (Cipriani et al., 1999, 2004; Cammelli et al., 2004). The beaches have low cost/maintenance factors and gravel is one of nature's best methods of

Fig. 4.1. A linear beach, Virginia, USA.

Fig. 4.2. A pocket beach, Durdle Dor, UK.

protecting a coastline, as it results in wave force diffusion. The current artificial fad, is for beaches to be temporarily placed in the main squares of cities during summer months, e.g. Paris, France (Fig. 4.5) and Birmingham and Nottingham in the UK.

Fig. 4.3. A zeta curve beach, Rhosilli, Wales, UK.

(a)   (b)

Fig. 4.4. The same beach (a) summer and (b) winter.

Fig. 4.5. 'Paris plage' – a nourished city beach.

However, the following classification (resort to rural) covers all beaches that a tourist might find anywhere in the world (Williams and Micallef, 2009).

Resort

Walton (2000:21) asked a question regarding UK resorts: 'How important does the holiday industry have to be in a town before it can be classed as a resort? This is increasingly important in the early C21st as old resorts transmute into commuter or retirement centres and begin to lose their generic cultural distinctiveness.' The following are not universals but are recurrent, in that resorts are recognizable as distinctive town types, but have as many variations as colour in a chameleon. As seaside resorts approached their UK popularity peak in 1951, >100 resorts had 5.7% of the population, which indicated their importance (Theroux, 1983:21). UK resorts are very distinctive, and may be best summed up in the words of Theroux (1983:349–351):

> The character (of seaside resorts) was fixed, and although few coastal places matched their reputation, every one was unique…. And there was such a thing as a typical resort on the coast … There was always an Esplanade, and always a Bandstand on it; always a war Memorial and a Rose Garden…. A Lifeboat station and a Lighthouse, and a Pier. A Putting Green, a Bowling Green, a Cricket Pitch, and a church the guidebook said was Perpendicular. The pier has been condemned. It was threatened with demolition…. The railway had been closed down … and the fishing industry folded five years ago. The art-deco cinema was

now a bingo hall…. The new bus shelter has been vandalised. It was famous for its whelks. It was raining.

As a genus, especially in tourist 'hot spots' e.g. the Caribbean and the Mediterranean, coastal resorts should be located on a beach adjacent to an accommodation complex (hotel/apartment/camp site), where a substantial proportion of beach users are resident and management is the responsibility of the complex. A host of facilities is usually prevalent, e.g. windsurfing, speedboat towing activities (e.g. 'rings', 'bouncy castles', 'bananas'), as recreation is the main aim; Club Med epitomizes this type of resort.

Urban

These serve large populations that have well-established public services, e.g. primary school(s), bank(s), religious centre(s), internet cafés, with a clearly demarcated central business district and commercial activities, e.g. harbours and marinas. Urban beaches are located within/adjacent to the urban area and are in the main freely open to the public.

Village

These are found outside the main urban environment (Fig. 4.7). They have a small, permanent population reflecting access to organized but small-scale community services such as a primary school(s), religious centre(s) and shop(s).

Fig. 4.6.   A resort beach, Weston-super-Mare, UK.

Fig. 4.7. A village beach, Newton, Wales, UK.

This also includes 'tourist villages', mainly utilized in the summer months, as well as 'ribbon development' between urban and rural environments. It is arguably the most difficult definition of the five bathing area types. The beach area can be reached by public/private transport.

Rural

These would be found outside the urban/village environment. They are not readily accessible by public transport and have virtually no facilities – perhaps a small summer shop, car park and/or toilet. In the Mediterranean context, permanent land-based recreational amenities (such as golf courses) and summer-time beach-related recreational facilities (e.g. banana boats, jet skiing etc., which are typical of resorts) may be found. Housing is limited in number (generally 0–10 but may be more depending on the size of the coastal stretch) and is usually of a temporary (summer) nature, although a permanent (year long) residency can occur, but there is no permanent community focal centre (religious centre, primary school, shops, cafés, bars). The beaches have little or no beach front development and are greatly valued by beach users for their quietness and natural (unspoilt) qualities.

Remote

These may be defined by difficulty of access, largely by boat or on foot – a walk of up to or over 300 m. They can be adjacent to either village or rural areas but

Fig. 4.8. A remote beach, Falkland Isles.

rarely with urban areas (Fig 4.8). They are not supported by public transport and have very limited (<5 if any) temporary summer housing. In the Mediterranean, restaurants/secondary summer homes may be found in the summer season but permanent dwellers are few and far between.

Tourist Preferences

Beach type

From a study carried out in Wales, UK (n = 854), only 3% preferred a large resort, e.g. Llandudno and Rhyl, 6% preferred an urban beach, e.g. Swansea, 30% a village, e.g. Saundersfoot, while 416 (48%) preferred a rural beach with basic facilities only, i.e. toilet, refreshments and car park, e.g. Southerndown, and 13% a beach with no facilities (remote). Even users at large resorts expressed these sentiments (Fig. 4.9). This may be attributed to the fact that companions and children have other needs that can be satisfied in such large resort beaches, but also location and access availability comes into the decision-making process. This could have far-reaching implications for tourism promotion.

This was investigated further in Malta, an island with an area of some 316 km² and a population of *circa* 400,000. Tourism, the third largest industry after construction and finance, constitutes some 24% of the gross domestic product and 27% of the country's employment (MTA, 2004). Out of 154 beach users who were interviewed, 42% expressed a preference for a beach with basic

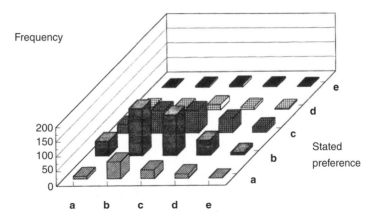

Fig. 4.9. Preferred beach type versus beach preference where interviewed: a, no facilities; b, basic; c, village; d, urban; e, resort (adapted from Morgan, 1996).

facilities when visiting alone or with a partner, contrasting with 18% when children were involved. Only 2% expressed preference for a resort beach when with a partner, but this rose to 14% when children were involved; for a beach with no facilities the figures were 18% and 2%, respectively; similarly, figures of 7% and 17% were recorded for urban beaches.

Beach requirements

Having established five types of beach areas, what does a 'typical tourist' require? Surveys were carried out on beach user preferences in Wales, UK (n = 2345, 98% locals), Hollywood beach, Florida, USA (n = 83, 76% locals), the Costa Dorado, Spain (n = 157, 95% locals), Malta (n = 154, 65% local and 34% northern European) and Turkey's Aegean coast (n = 245, 12% local and 88% northern European). Fifty beach aspects were given in a questionnaire and results showed that five parameters were of the greatest importance: safety, facilities, water quality, litter and scenery (Table 4.1). These should be weighted in that tourists at a remote beach would not expect to find lifeguards, sun-loungers, showers etc. at the beach area, whereas these would be mandatory at any resort beach area. Water quality and safety dominated the results (Table 4.1) with the other parameters jostling for position.

Table 4.1. Ranking of the five main preference parameters (1 = highest).

Parameters	Malta	UK	Turkey	Spain	USA
Facilities	3	5	3	4	3
Water Quality	1	3	1	2	5
Litter	4	4	2	3	1
Scenery	5	1	5	5	2
Safety	2	2	4	1	4

Water quality
User preferences showed that this was of prime importance. However, it should be noted that problems associated with microbiological sampling of sea water are well documented and fraught with difficulty (Fleisher, 1985, 1990; Jones *et al.*, 1990; Rees, 1997). Several factors apply to beach quality sampling, e.g. variation between analysts, methods, culture mediums, choice of sampling location, number of transects from which samples are taken, number of sampling points on any stretch of beach, time of sampling (spring to neap tides), sampling frequency, wind, tide, currents and sunlight can all contribute to result inconsistency. Therefore is it possible to take a representative sample? Rees (1997:1) has commented that, 'Current bathing water quality monitoring regimes are so fundamentally flawed that we can have little or no confidence in the accuracy of respective, arbitrary and almost limitless variable set of statistics. It is impossible to guarantee the quality of a bathing water, as a beach award implies to the unknowing'. In many ways we pay lip service to this parameter, as a sample taken for example on a weekly/fortnightly basis from a beach can in no way be statistically justified as representative of that beach area, albeit analysis for the many parameters is carried out quite diligently. It is noteworthy that the EC has introduced a new directive (CEC, 2006), which now profiles water quality at beaches and is a much better system than the old one (CEC, 1976).

Safety
Safety on urban and resort beaches is paramount (Fig. 4.10a, b). This would involve zoning a beach for swimming, water sports etc., lifeguard presence (including equipment, telephones and first aid), adequate signage of potential problem areas together with a site risk assessment analysis. The high priority given to lifeguards in Spain is perhaps reflected in beach sea slope steepening, as a result of coarse-grained sediment beach nourishment schemes (Table 4.2). These materials result in steeper beach gradients that may prove socially unacceptable. Breton and Esteban (1995) and Breton *et al.* (1996) have commented on the negative public perception of coarse sediment beaches off Barcelona, Spain, that had to undergo profile re-grading by the municipality due to what was considered to be unsafe bathing waters for children. Results indicated that beach users also liked flatter beaches and smaller waves, again reinforcing safety aspects. In the design of recreation beaches rather than conservation, special attention should be given to consideration of social preferences and priorities and local environmental characteristics.

Facilities
These include a host of parameters, e.g. boating, surfing, swimming, sunbathing, showers, toilets, etc. (Fig. 4.11), and Table 4.2 shows sound conformity for many of the parameters. In all countries, the presence of adequate clean toilets was a major aspect. A low value given to absence of catering odours in Malta may be explained by the fact that in an intensely urbanized island, food kiosks are found on the backshore of the beach, which is usually bounded by a road. Similarly, the presence of traffic fumes scored highly in the case of Malta. For all five countries investigated, light tan colour for beach sediment was the preferred option.

(a)

(b)

Fig. 4.10. (a) Safety: a standard lifeguard station, Turkey and (b) a de luxe lifeguard station, Barbados.

Table 4.2. Percentage of beach rating for some selected parameters.

Beach aspect	Turkey	Spain	Malta
Clean toilets	4.1	3.6	3.7
No visible sewage debris	3.5	3.4	4.1
No litter	3.5	4.0	3.1
Water clarity	3.1	3.7	2.7
Water quality	3.6	4.1	3.4
Lifeguards	2.7	3.7	3.0
No traffic fumes	3.5	3.5	3.9
Absence of dangerous rocks	3.3	3.7	2.6
Catering odours	2.1	2.8	1.1
Sun-loungers	2.3	1.5	1.9
Showers	2.2	3.1	2.4
Noise	3.4	3.4	4.1

The colour of any new beach nourishment needs re-assessing, as people prefer the original beach colour, but very little work seems to have been carried out on this aspect of nourishment (Grove, 2007).

A Maltese case study regarding beach priorities between native Maltese and overseas visitors, indicated that local Maltese gave a lower priority to 'facilities' ($p < 0.01$) and 'sand (litter) and water quality' ($p < 0.01$). In contrast, overseas visitors gave lower priority to beach 'access and car parking' ($p < 0.01$), probably due to the population density of the island, which has > 1 million visitors in summer – nearly three times the indigenous population – and parking is very difficult. (Fig. 4.12) indicates the importance given to water quality and litter, followed by safety. Compared to beach users from other European non-Mediterranean countries, British visitors gave higher priority to absence of sewage pollution ($p < 0.01$), but a lower priority to scenic quality of the beach environment ($p < 0.01$).

Litter
Depending upon location, litter either has a marine origin, i.e. from shipping, oil rigs, etc., or is derived from a land source, i.e. riverine inputs or from beach users, with the land source being predominant on a world basis. It is patently obvious that tourists do not want to see beach litter and Fig. 4.13 shows some marine litter that was gathered on a Fijian beach. The key question relates to attributing litter to a source and whether it is cleaned from the beach or not. For any resort or urban beach, i.e. ones that are used primarily for recreation, it is usually imperative to clean the beach daily during the bathing season. This is normally done via mechanical means rather than hand picking. The former involves motorized equipment utilizing a sieve mesh that scoops up sand, which then filters back to the beach via the sieve which retains the litter – retention is a function of sieve size. However, most machines are coarse grained allowing items such as cigarette stubs and cotton bud sticks (Q tips) to pass through. In areas where hazardous waste (medical or sewage related debris) occurs, it cuts down

(a)

(b)

Fig. 4.11. Facilities: (a) Rows of sun-loungers, Italy. (b) Poorly designed shower facilities, Caribbean. (c) Well designed shower facilities, a foot shower, drinking fountain and access for the less able, Spain. (d) Simple, well designed beach changing facilities, Croatia. (*Continued*)

(c)

(d)

Fig. 4.11.   (*Continued*)

the need for picking up material, so reducing potential health risks to individuals. The machine interferes with beach ecology and it is a costly method (Acland, 1994), and obviously cannot be utilized on pebble/gravel beaches. It is fast and can provide an apparently pristine beach for visitors.

Manual beach cleaners can pick up small items missed by a machine, raise community awareness of the litter problem and help source litter (Earll *et al.*, 1996). Indirect action, such as education, award schemes and legislation, is also

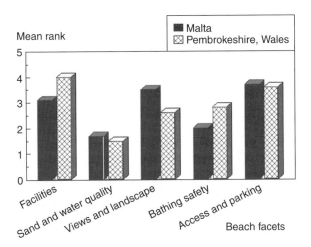

Fig. 4.12. Ranking of beach facets: Wales versus Malta.

Fig. 4.13. Marine-based litter, Fiji.

part of litter picks. The direct/indirect costs of dealing with Kent (UK) coast litter has been given at over £11 million (Gilbert, personal communication); it costs £937,000 to clean the Bohuslan coast of Sweden (Olin *et al.*, 1994) and over US$1 million was spent in 1988–1999 cleaning litter from the coasts of Santa Monica and Long Beach in California (Kauffman and Brown, 1991). At Studland, Dorset, UK, one million visitors per year along a 6 km stretch of beach resulted in 12–13 t of litter, collected weekly in the summer months at a cost of £36,000 per annum. Additional costs are incurred when hazardous containers are found and have to be recovered from beaches (Dixon, 1992).

Fig. 4.14.   Scenery, class I: Ursa, Portugal.

Scenery
Objective assessment of scenery is a difficult task as people perceive the same
scene differently. The technique proposed by Ergin *et al.* (2004), is one of the
first to semi-quantify scenic assessment via objective mathematical means (utilizing fuzzy logic), and grouped scenery into one of five categories, one being the
highest (Fig. 4.14). The three Mediterranean areas rated this as the least important of the 'Big Five' parameters (Table 4.1). This is most likely due to the fact
that most tourists came for swimming and/or sun, as virtually every beach user
enters the sea. In the UK, the percentage of bathers to non-bathers varies greatly,
as a function of the weather, but a figure of around 1.40 has been found in our
surveys. Therefore if bathing is 'out', scenery comes 'in' and this is probably why
it was ranked first in the UK (Table 4.1). In the USA study, the beach area was
located in a 'retirement area', so that people interviewed tended to be 'older than
usual'. Swimming did not appear high on their agenda, hence a low score for
water quality and safety, but a high score for scenery and beach litter.

Conclusions

Many types of beaches exist and this chapter considered them as bathing areas
based on an anthropogenic scale, i.e. resort, urban, village, rural and remote
beaches. In UK beaches, 48% of beach users interviewed were of the opinion
that beaches with just basic facilities (toilet, car park, café) were the preferred
choice if alone or with a partner. This prompted a similar study in Malta and 42%

expressed a similar finding, with the proviso that if children were involved this number dropped to 18%. From surveys in the UK, Malta, USA, Turkey and Spain, the main items in considerations of a 'good beach' were safety, facilities, litter, scenery and water quality. Weightings associated with these are a function of beach type, for example, safety and facilities are not expected at remote beaches whereas at resort areas they would be mandatory.

References

Acland, B. (1994) Resort management. In: Earll, R.C. (ed.) *Coastal and Riverine Litter: Problems and Effective Solutions.* Marine Environmental Management and Training, Kempley, UK, pp. 18–20.

Breton, F. and Esteban, P. (1995) The management and recuperation of beaches in Catalonia. In: Healy, M.G. and Doody, P. (eds) *Directions in European Coastal Management.* Samara Publishing, Cardigan, UK, pp. 511–517.

Breton, F., Clapés, J., Marquès, A. and Priestley, G.K. (1996) The recreational use of beaches and consequences for the development of new trends in management: the case of the beaches of metropolitan Region of Barcelona (Catalonia), Spain. *Ocean and Coastal Management* 32, 153–180.

Cammelli, C., Jackson, N.I., Nordstrom, K.F. and Pranzini, E. (2004) Assessment of a gravel nourishment project fronting a seawall at Marina di Pisa, Italy. *Journal of Coastal Research* (Special Issue) 39, 770–775.

Cipriani, L.E., Pelliccia, F. and Pranzini, E. (1999) Beach nourishment with nearshore sediments in a highly protected coast. In: Ozhan, E. (ed.) *Proceedings of Medcoast 99.* Medcoast Secretariat, Middle East Technical University, Ankara, Turkey, pp.1579–1590.

Cipriani, L., Wetzel, L., Aminti, P.L. and Pranzini, E. (2004) Converting sea walls into gravel beaches. In: Micallef, A. and Vassallo, A. (eds) *Proceedings of the 1st International Conference on the Management of Coastal Recreational Resources – Beaches, Yacht Marinas and Ecotourism, Malta.* Euro-Mediterranean Centre on Insular Coastal Dynamics (ICoD), Valletta, Malta, pp. 3–12.

CEC (1976) EC Directive, 76/160, 1976. Directive on bathing water quality, 8 December 1975, (76/160/EEC). *Official Journal of the European Communities* L31/1, 5/2/76.

CEC (2006) European Parliament and the European Council 2006. Directive 2006/7/EC of the European Parliament and of the Council of 15 February 2008 concerning the management of bathing water quality and repealing Directive 76/160/EEC. *Official Journal of the European Communities* L64 of 4.3.2006.

CEES (Coastal & Environmental Engineering Solutions Inc.) (2006) Beach Management Project: Best Practices Guidelines for 50 Beaches along the Coastline of Barbados. Draft report submitted to the Government of Barbados, 62pp.

Clark, J.R. (1996) *Coastal Zone Management Handbook.* CRC Press, Boca Raton, Florida, USA.

Dharmaratne, G.S. and Braithwaite, A.E. (1998) Economic valuation of the coastline for tourism in Barbados. *Journal of Travel Research* 37(2), 138–144.

Dixon, T. (1992) *Coastal Survey of Packaged Chemicals and Other Hazardous Items.* PECD, Reference Number 7/8/188. ACOPS, London, 111pp.

Dodds, R. and Kelman, I. (2008) How climate change is considered in sustainable tourism policies: a case of the Mediterranean islands of Malta and Mallorca. *Tourism Review International* 12, 57–70.

Earll, R.C., Everard, M., Lowe, N., Pattinson, C. and Williams, A.T. (1996) *Measuring and Managing Litter in Rivers, Estuaries and Coastal Waters. A guide to methods.* Working document. Marine Environmental Management and Training, Kempley, UK, 78pp.

EEA (2006) *The Changing Face of Europe's Coastal Areas.* Breton, F. and Meiner, A. (eds) EEA Report No. 6. Office for Official Publications of the European Communities, Luxembourg, http://reports.eea.europa.eu/eea_report_2006_6/en/eea/report_2006.pdf (Accessed: 6 March 2010).

Ergin, A., Karaesmen, E., Micallef, A. and Williams, A.T. (2004) A new methodology for evaluating coastal scenery: Fuzzy logic systems. *Area* 36(4), 367–386.

Eurostat (2009) Population Reference Bureau. The Publications Office of the European Union Official Journal and Access to Law Directorate Legal and Documentary Issues, Consolidation and Copyright Unit Copyright, Luxembourg (http://epp.eurostat.ec.europa.eu/portal/page/portal/publications/eurostat_yearbook).

Finkl, C.W. and Kruempfel, C. (2005) Threats, obstacles and barriers to coastal environmental conservation: societal perceptions and managerial positionalities that defeat sustainable development. In: Veloso-Gomez, F., Taveira Pinto, F., da Neves, L., Sena, A. and Fereira, O. (eds) *Proceedings of the 1st International Conference on Coastal Conservation and Management in the Atlantic and Mediterranean Seas.* University of Porto, Portugal, pp. 3–28.

Fleisher, J.M. (1985) Implications of coliform variability in the assessment of the sanitary quality of recreational water. *Journal of Hygiene* 94, 193–200.

Fleisher, J.M. (1990) Conducting recreational water quality surveys: some problems and suggested remedies. *Marine Pollution Bulletin* 21(12), 562–567.

Grove, S.H. (2007) Physical aspects of south Californian beaches and how people perceive them: considerations for beach nourishment planning. *Shore and Beach* 75, 11–21.

Hall, D. (1997) The tourism debate and environmental scientists. *Environmental Scientist* 6(5), 1–2.

Houston, J.R. (2002) The economic value of beaches – a 2002 update. *Shore and Beach* 70(1), 9–12.

Jones, F., Kay, D., Stanwell-Smith, R. and Wyer, M. (1990) An appraisal of the potential health impacts of sewage disposal to UK coastal waters. *Journal of the Institution of Water and Environmental Management* 4, 295–303.

Kauffman, J. and Brown, M. (1991) California marine debris action plan. In: Magoon, O.T., Converse, H., Tippie, V., Tobin, L.T. and Clark, D. (eds) *Coastal Zone '91. Proceedings of the Seventh Symposium on Coastal and Ocean Management.* Long Beach, California, pp. 3390–3406.

King, P. (1999) *The Fiscal Impact of Beaches in California.* Public Research Institute, University of California, USA.

Klein, Y.L., Osleeb, J.P. and Viola, M.R. (2004) Tourism generated earnings in the coastal zone: a regional analysis. *Journal of Coastal Research* 20(4), 1080–1088.

MTA (Malta Tourism Authority) (2004) *Frequently Asked Questions on Tourism.* www.mta.com.mt/index.p1/faq_on_tourism (Accessed: 10 March 2010).

Morgan, R. (1996) Beach user opinions and the development of a beach rating quality scale. PhD thesis. University of Glamorgan, UK, 38pp.

Olin, R., Carlsson, B. and Stahre, B. (1994) The west coast of Sweden – the rubbish tip of the North Sea. In: Earll, R. (ed.) *Coastal and Riverine Litter: Problems and Effective Solutions.* Marine Environmental Management and Training, Kempley, UK, pp. 12–14.

Povh, D. (2000) Economic instruments for sustainable development in the Mediterranean Region. Responsible Coastal Zone Management. *Periodicum Biologorum* 102(1), 407–412.

Pranzini, E. (2004) *La forma della Costa*. Zanichelli, Bologna, Italy, 246pp.

Rees, G. (1997) Lies, damned lies and beach awards. *Current Quality* 1, 1 (May).

Theroux, P. (1983) *The Kingdom by the Sea*. Penguin, London, 246pp.

UNEP and UNWTO (2008) *Making Tourism More Sustainable: A Guide for Policy Makers*. United Nations Environment Programme, World Tourism Organization, Paris, 209pp.

Walton, J.K. (2000) *The British Seaside*. Manchester University Press, 216pp.

Williams, A.T. and Micallef, A. (2009) *Beach Management: Principles and Practice*. Earthscan, London, 445pp.

Wilson, M. and Liu, S. (2008) Non market values of ecosystem services provided by coastal and nearshore and marine systems. In: Patterson, M. and Glavovicic, B. (eds) *Ecological Economics of the Oceans and Coasts*. Edward Elgar, Cheltenham, UK, pp. 119–139.

WTO (World Tourism Organization) (2006) International tourism up 4.5% in the first four months of 2006. www.world-tourism.org/newsroom/Releases/2006/June/baro,eter. html (Accessed: 4 March 2010).

Websites

www.tourismconcern.org.uk
www.visitbritain.co.uk
www.wttc.org

5 Climate Change: Risk Management Issues and Challenges

Ian Jenkins

Australians will be affected in a major way, and to an increasing extent, by climate change and its impacts on the coastal zone. In Australia the highest concentration of people, housing, infrastructure and industry is within the coastal zone. Due to the sea change phenomenon, this exposure is increasing.

(Australian Government, 2008:1)

Evidence suggests that *Homo sapiens* have survived upon planet earth for between 100,000 and 160,000 years (Amos, 2003), but possibly more skilfully over the last 10,000 years. It is asserted that our ancestors have in the past suffered a much wider diversity of risks than those currently faced by the developed world. Evidence suggests that a significant area of risk which our ancestors survived is that of climate change. Only some 10,000 years ago the last Ice Age gripped much of Europe and it is conspicuous that the human race endured, unlike other creatures such as the woolly rhinoceros and woolly mammoth (Johnson, 2008). Hence the current predictions of accelerated climate change should, to some degree, be somewhat expected, as the earth has *always* had climatic change (Montaigne, 2004) and, as of yet, the human race seems to have adapted and continued to exist. That said, humans could be viewed as 'inexperienced' at surviving climate shocks (considering other animals who have greater lineages) and this is possibly the prophetic idiom (Montaigne, 2004) that is being heralded at the moment by world institutions. The IPCC suggests that speed of climate change is exponential and not akin to past climate variations, which have previously taken millennia, thereby allowing adaptation (IPCC, 2008).

It is asserted that risk is a human concept and one that all humans are familiar with (Denney, 2005). Just to survive, humans have to manage risk; consequently climate change can be viewed as another form of 'risk management' and scientists seem to indicate, if acted upon now, not beyond the capacity of human beings to manage (Davos Declaration, 2007; IPCC, 2008). Commentaries and narratives concerning risk seem to believe that it is a definable unit and therefore manageable, as demonstrated by statisticians who produce tables of the risks populations face and the likelihood of survival. In many circumstance the importance of risk, to us as individuals, is simply the perception of risk, rather than the actuality. In addition, perceptions of risk are easily manipulated by a number of different institutions, none more so powerful than the media.

Societal risks are nearly always about possible loss (asymmetric) (Denney, 2005) and it is essential to be very clear regarding what loss is being defined, especially when we look at climate change and its relationship with tourism markets. Ultimately, all risk is personal; accordingly risks of climate change will to some extent become individual, depending upon how tourism reacts and develops with the changes that are forecast to occur. Risks are also unmistakably associated with economics and this factor in particular seems to be the driving force behind the current climate change debate.

Risk: What Risk?

In order to assess the risks that may occur, it is necessary to identify how climate change will affect the natural resources on which tourism is based. The latest reports identify landscape typology and environs as the variables that will be affected by climate change (IPCC, 2001; Australian Government, 2005; Scholze *et al.*, 2006; Davos Declaration, 2007). The last few years may give an indication of what the future holds for tourism. Since 2000 there have been a number of climate events that have affected the tourism market, such as hurricanes, floods, droughts, ice storms, heat waves (Löw, 2008), which give the impression of changes in climate and the devastation that this will cause on societal and tourism resources.

Risk and Hazard

When evaluating climate change it is necessary to consider the two variables that are components of adverse change: namely, risk and hazard. Both are different concepts and should be treated and managed in different ways, even though they are the components of risk management. Risk management through Safety Management Systems (SMS) can be seen as the holistic approach to controlling adverse events and trying to ensure a minimum risk environment (Glendon and McKenna, 1995).

Risk is usually recognized as having two aspects, namely magnitude and frequency. It is frequently understood in terms of a formula that produces a statistic comparing other phenomena, resulting in the creation of measures for management control. Risk management constructs have different levels of risk, for example high, medium, low or no risk outcomes (Glendon and McKenna, 1995). The importance to tourism may be seen in these outcome risk levels; namely, how frequently will unpleasant/adverse events transpire and at what magnitude will they happen. This is a simple but important concept if one is to try and manage the effects of climate change by adapting tourism destinations and markets. This principle can be seen already in tourism locations where natural hazards pose a risk to tourists such as mountain tourism and in particular avalanche management (BBC TV, 1999). Recent events relating to avalanche management show that risk management systems are certainly not infallible. During the winter of 1998/99 (BBC TV, 1999) the Alps saw an extreme amount of snowfall, resulting in avalanches that were outside the safe prediction zone of risk management models (BBC TV, 1999). So predictions of risk are not infallible, including climate change predictions.

It is asserted that climate change risks are mainly human (Inter-American Development Bank, 2003; Davos Declaration, 2007) and could be seen in a number of forms: the risk to human life, property and capital. These risk areas form the central focus of the debate on climate change and are in essence economic. Again, it is argued that economics is at the heart of climate change and management, although this is not always clearly alluded to and certainly, without humans, there is no tourism (Durkin, 2005). Indeed, one of the major purposes of tourism is economic exchange and development. Much of the literature on climate change relates to the effects that this will have on economic systems (Australian Government, 2005, 2008) and essentially all risks, as well as being individual, are economic (leaving aside the moral aspect of the loss of human life through disasters).

There is also another consideration relating to the climate risk debate, which is the level of climate change that is and is not acceptable. Climate risk management must decide on what is an acceptable change (if any) to the climate and how the tourism industry can exist or adapt to such a change. This can be seen within the context of acceptable and tolerable risk (Glendon and McKenna, 1995; Hillson and Murray-Webster, 2007). Unfortunately, however, the decision on what is or is not acceptable in terms of climate change is influenced, and thus complicated, by the person who is assessing the risk within the industry. Is it the consumer, company, or government institution? Each will have different perspectives and expectations on what constitutes an 'acceptable' change.

Quintessentially, it is mooted that climate change will need tourist destinations to react to the hazards that are already known (flood, heat wave, drought, severe storms etc.) and it is possible that previous disasters could be used as risk management plans for climate change. Some governments already have 'disaster agencies' and perhaps these should now be adapted to look at climate change risks and hazards. What is perhaps difficult to manage are the perceived risks to the tourist and how these will be managed. It becomes evident that sagacious prediction of climate change is the foundation of a risk management strategy and the Davos Agreement (Davos Declaration, 2007) indicates the need for this. For example, Australia already identifies the locations likely to be at high risk (Australian Government, 2005).

Climate Risk Models

Another aspect that needs to be considered is how predictions are ameliorated in order to make sense of the climate change that will affect tourism businesses and markets. The literature (Strachan, 2007) suggests that the current models, used for predictions, are designed for different purposes. Presently, there appear to be two approaches to risk modelling. Strachan (2007:1) notes that: '[c]atastrophe modeling [political and financial] is traditionally based on statistical (stochastic) models, which use synthetic event-sets to project the incidence of destructive weather events, such as tropical cyclones, windstorms and floods. Climate science, on the other hand, uses dynamical models of the earth's climate system to simulate past, present and future climate conditions, using observational data to validate simulations.' This to an extent illustrates that measuring the risk to humans and hence to tourism business activity is a complex task and that climate prediction models are not necessarily linked to catastrophe models. It should also be remembered that models are themselves abstractions of reality, simplifying the world systems that exist. In addition, some natural systems such as the weather have been attributed to the theory of 'chaos systems' (*The Tech*, 2008), which, by its very nature suggests an inability to predict outcomes.

The weather is a classic example where 5-day forecasts are reasonably reliable, but prediction of yearly weather seems beyond the application and scope of these models. This might also raise doubts on the accuracy of the climate model (Pearce and Le Page, 2008). In addition, some of the stochastic risk models also result in singular outcomes with a 'risk factor' attached; this is frequently true for models that predict political risk.

There are also political risk models (Alon and Martin, 1998) that might be adapted to measure the notion of climate change to particular countries, but many of these give single factor outputs. The World Resources Institute (2007) is another organization that produces a model of each country for different aspects, including social and environmental issues. Perhaps an amelioration of these models could, as suggested by Stacy (2006), be the way ahead to actually produce a climate tourism model that would be able to predict change with some certainty.

There are critics of single outcome risk models (Piekarz, 2009); even though a risk factor is an indication of risk, this is sometimes too general and not representative of the whole case. For example, a predictive climate change model might isolate Thailand as being high risk in the future, but risk of climate change hazards, such as high wind, flooding and increased sea levels, might only affect certain parts of the country. Other areas of Thailand might not be affected and so tourism could be developed in new areas that have a lower exposure to climate change hazards. Applying then a contextual application to climate risk models would emulate new developments of political instability models (Piekarz, 2009). There are some models that attempt to link climate inputs with specific effects on tourism activities. For example, Shih *et al.* (2009) have attempted just this at ski resorts in Michigan, USA, and have predicted what variable temperatures might do to economic outputs based upon ski usage, if the snow was to vary at these resorts.

It seems that future climate prediction models need to relate their outcomes to business risk including tourism and will need to reflect the notion of 'contextualization', rather than single risk scores for countries. Perhaps amelioration of mixed method risk models is needed to include dynamic models.

This raises a further question relating to the predictive strength and accuracy of these climate change models and the effect they will have on tourism (Pearce and Le Page, 2008). If one considers tourism in its simplest form, climate is a major tourism motivator and one could also advocate it is a source of tourism change (World Tourism Organization, 2003). Tourism in its basic form is composed of two attraction elements, namely climate and culture. One could even advocate that culture is a consequence of climate, as the position of a tourism location on the earth's surface defines its culture. Consequently, climate change may well be a precursor to adaptation of different types of tourism and concomitantly change in cultural response at each location.

Currently it is asserted that climate change predictions are no indication of tourism business risk. This is based upon the premise that the climate predictive systems measure different outcomes (change of temperature, vegetation, precipitation etc.) (Davos Declaration, 2007). They do not indicate how these will affect the more stochastic models of anthropological variables (business investment, tourism choice etc.) and anthropological variables are far more difficult to forecast, even though there have been predictions of what will happen to tourist regions and destinations (WTO, 2003). This then is possibly the way forward, developing climate:tourism models where climate variables are predictive for key tourism change variables such as tourism investment, customer expectations and behaviour.

Hazard Identification

Hazards are the elements that will give rise to risk if left unmanaged. A hazard is an item or condition that gives rise to loss or damage (Waring, 1996; Denney, 2005) and it is important to realize that this would also include human actions (moral and morale) and conditions (Adams, 1995). Currently, hazard identification, from the wealth of climate change documents, focuses upon the physical environment. Human attitude and action are often factors left out of any risk management framework, as it is easier to deal with the natural visible hazards, rather than those that are unseen. In many circumstances it is human action, or lack of it, that engenders or exacerbates the risk and this is a principle that needs to be addressed in climate change (Davos Declaration, 2007).

In terms of physical hazards that will arise from climate change, there is now more or less agreement on climate change outcomes, for example:

- greater intensity of storm surges;
- more frequent flooding;
- heavier intensity of rainfall;
- increased frequency of very hot days;
- greater intensity and frequency of droughts;
- increased storm incidence and greater intensity; and
- increased velocity of wind speeds (WTO, 2003; Australian Government, 2005; IPCC, 2008; Simpson *et al.*, 2008).

For human hazards these are:

- lack of human preparation;
- inappropriate knowledge and prediction;
- increase of non-insurable losses;
- moral inaction to potential threats;
- immoral business/political actions; and
- economic deprivation (Davos Declaration, 2007).

Evaluation of Risk Management Tools

One of the key elements of the Davos Declaration (Davos Declaration, 2007) is to encourage the development of techniques that can assess risk and develop cost–benefit analyses. In order to reduce the climate risk to acceptable levels there is a need for risk management models to be used and consolidated. Risk literature is suffused with a wide array of risk management models and it is suggested that some of these models could be adapted by the tourism industry and certainly destination management, to help with predicting climate change. Risk management is used here as a blanket term. None the less, for climate change this will have to be viewed on a number of levels, namely the strategic, the supply chain, destination and the market, together with a micro approach which, for most tourists, is the most important (what happens at their destination and the method of transport they use). The components of risk management will have to include government, private companies, transport and destination. This is also noted by the Davos Declaration (2007).

Risk management would include a number of aspects and possibly one of the most important is risk assessment. Risk assessment is not a new concept and there are a number of models used in evaluating risk and implementing management controls. There are numerous models that have been applied to reduce risk in various industries and circumstances. For example, FMAEA (Failure Mode and Effect Analysis) and FTA (Fault Tree Analysis) (Warring, 1996) are models that have been commonly used for a long time and were developed to look at complex systems. FMAEA is an evaluation made of the system failure of a product and a risk rating is constructed based upon the likelihood of failure of a component and the resulting damage this might cause to a system.

FTA (Warring, 1996) tries to identify possible hazards and then produces a series of logical evaluations, which are used to systematically identify how a system might fail resulting in loss or high risk to a product or person. However, both these systems are designed for contained controlled environments, unlike the chaos of a climate system. That said, the actual hazards that climate change are forecast to produce are known hazards (see above). Hence knowledge of these hazards can enable risk management at a tourism destination to develop systems to combat such outcomes. These models could be adapted to be used on climate risks at tourism destinations. But there are many others types of frameworks and models that are being currently used, for example as shown in Fig. 5.1.

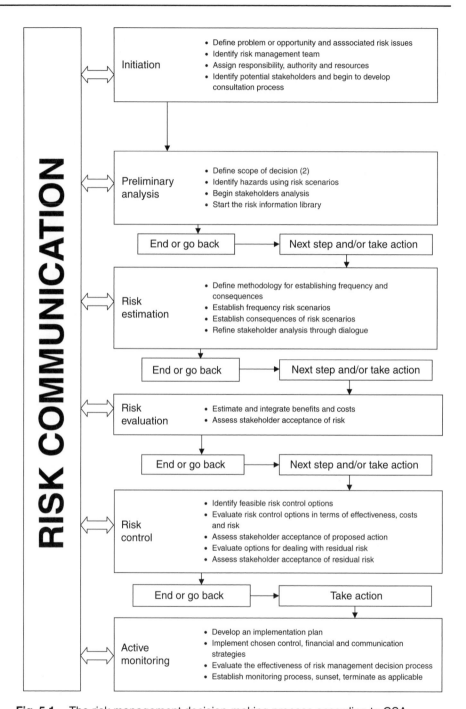

Fig. 5.1. The risk management decision-making process according to CSA (From: adapted from CSA, 1997, p.7 cited in Saner, 2005). Note: the combination of 'preliminary analysis' and 'risk estimation' is called 'risk assessment'.

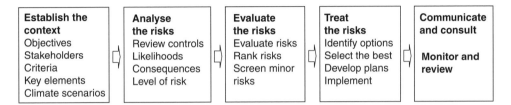

Establish the context	Analyse the risks	Evaluate the risks	Treat the risks	Communicate and consult
Objectives Stakeholders Criteria Key elements Climate scenarios	Review controls Likelihoods Consequences Level of risk	Evaluate risks Rank risks Screen minor risks	Identify options Select the best Develop plans Implement	Monitor and review

Fig. 5.2. Adapted model of risk management: steps in the risk management process Communicate and Consult Monitor and Review Model (cited in Saner, 2005). At each of the stages there should be consultation and monitoring with the concerned 'actors'.

Another example can be found in Fig. 5.2, which is the risk management framework provided by the Australian and New Zealand Standard AS/NZS 4360 to use in the assessment of climate change hazards.

This framework allows an examination of the output effects on the environment, and the Australian Government have come up with the following areas that are likely to be affected; they note that the following environmental locations will 'reflect … considerations of climate vulnerability, the significance of the systems at risk and the likely need for government intervention to encourage a timely and efficient adaptation response'.

Australian vulnerability of ecosystems and biodiversity

- alpine regions;
- reef systems (such as Ningaloo and the Great Barrier Reef);
- tropical rainforest areas;
- heathland systems in south-west Western Australia;
- coastal mangrove and wetland systems (such as Kakadu); and
- rangelands.

Within this group, particular priority should be given to World Heritage listed systems.

(Australian Government, 2005)

Another simpler approach to assessing climate risks could be the system illustrated in Fig. 5.3. Here, the notion is to identify and prioritize areas that are threatened by the hazards of climate change using just three variable inputs: exposure, sensitivity of the landscape and the adaptive capacity of the location/ecosphere.

Climate Time Bomb: Business

A number of sources (WTO, 2003; Davos Declaration, 2007; Simpson *et al.*, 2008) have emphasized that the current proposition of climate change is likely to affect business in a serious way. For example: 'The 2007 IPCC report showed that the three hottest years ever recorded were 1998, 2003 and 2005. In Europe, the 2003 heatwave led to around 30,000 premature deaths, and projections show that 1:500 year events like this will become normal summers by around the middle of the century' (CCRM, 2005).

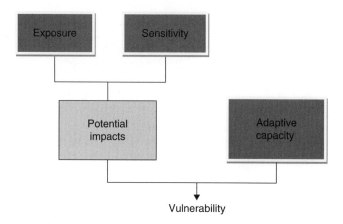

Fig. 5.3. Vulnerability and its components. Adapted from D. Schroter and the ATEAM consortium 2004, *Global Change Vulnerability – Assessing the European Human–environment System*, Potsdam Institute for Climate Impact Research. (From: Australian Government, 2005.)

Evidence also predicts that global warming is accelerating and could reach as much as 4°C by the end of this century (Simpson *et al.*, 2008). The prediction is that this will disrupt the environment, inevitably affecting business. Rising sea levels will cause flooding and disruption to transport routes, droughts will compound the supply of food, thereby increasing the death rate in certain parts of the globe. Both events, if frequent enough and sustained, are likely to have social and political consequences, giving rise to negative effects and destabilizing countries; this in turn is bound to affect business investment and solidity. Climate change then could act in the same way as political and economic instability acts now; hence the earlier section suggesting that the present political instability models be adapted to involve predictions of climate change. This appears necessary to determine climate change effects on business.

Business could be affected in a number of ways. Firstly, the uncertainty of investment will be compounded as the environment deteriorates and the number of politically unstable states starts to increase. This will then start to affect competition and share holders may start to lose money on their investments in locations of high climate risk. In addition, the concept of responsible tourism will start to increase in an effort to try and counter the effects of climate change. This means that companies will have to invest in new approaches to their products and investments. Some companies have already begun this process, for example BP has clearly embraced the idea of climate change and tried to reposition itself as an ethical energy provider.

Insurance costs

The Association of British Insurers (ABI) suggest that, if present weather trends continue, subsidence claims are set to double in bad years to £1.2bn by 2050.

Claims for storm damage are expected to treble to £7.5bn. In a worst-case scenario, inland flood damage from bursting rivers is likely to treble to £4.5bn over the same period (CCRM, 2005). This is further reiterated by Stacy (2006), who notes that after the present global credit shock, risk assessments of possible effects are now even more important.

The current debate on climate change illustrates the impact of climate on insurance claims. Recent tourism disasters have highlighted the cost and devastation that climate can bring to tourist destinations. The tsunami in South-east Asia (although not climate induced) resulted in horrific loss of life and billions of pounds of damage (BBC, 2005). If these events continue, then it is predicted that many tourists will not be covered by insurance in high risk destinations, affecting the demand for tourism and redirecting it to less risky areas of the globe. It is argued that this is likely to occur on two platforms. First, investment at high risk tourist destinations will be unavailable and second, this will be compounded by tourist demand switching to more stable and safer tourist destinations.

However, another scenario could also be envisaged: the development of 'risk savvy' tourists who are prepared to travel to higher risk regions. Already we have tourists who venture to war zones and dark tourism sites (Cambodia) and perhaps climate change will induce a more risk conscious and savvy tourist, who is able to adapt and deal with these changing circumstances. In one aspect this could be seen as a new product similar to current 'allocentric' tourists. It could also be more beneficial to the location as the provision of accommodation and supply of services would inevitably be local, thus minimizing any likely leakages that current mass tourism markets exhibit. It could be asserted that tourists are becoming more competent in risk management, and the increase of climate risk could mean that tourists readapt to high risk destinations where they manage their own risk factors (Piekarz, 2009). The use of modern technology coupled with the internet is one possible management tool that would provide customers with up to the minute risk information on possible destinations (Buhalis, 2006).

Change of business culture

There does now appear to be evidence that the business community is taking the threat of climate change seriously (Goldenberg, 2009). In fact, the sea change of the USA is a good example of the opportunities that climate change will bring, as well as the threats (Goldenberg, 2009). There are some schools of thought that see climate change as another control principle used by the rich western countries on the poorer developing regions of the world (Durkin, 2005). Ironically, it is also these poorer regions that are more likely to be seriously affected by climate change. Evidence suggests that the rich technological countries of the developed world will be able to adapt and survive climate change better than the developing countries (Blakie *et al.*, 1994).

Some developing countries also see the World Summits as control factors on their economic developments; India and China have both voiced these concerns (Lingle, 2009). Developing countries are not prepared to be penalized, especially as it is clear that the developed countries have already caused environmental and climate change through their industries.

As suggested in the earlier section, the threat of disaster could bring new products and changes to the tourism industry and this seems to have been acted upon by certain companies who will be affected by climate change. Interestingly, a number of companies have seen the need to change their persona and brand image. They appear to have seen the advantage of becoming a 'green' company, even though their past may not have been so environmentally responsive.

A good example of this is BP (British Petroleum) who has rebranded, within the notion of an environmentally welcoming company. Yet this is the industry that has possibly contributed most to climate change, selling fossil fuels, which are stated as the most important of the variables to affect the climate. BP state now that they are 'being green and yellow' and further add 'BP has a decade-long track record of advocating and taking precautionary action to address climate change' (BP, 2009).

A review of their website and reports identifies a global shift towards the idea of sustainability and that BP is now 'doing its part' to help with global warming. It also seems that BP was aware of the need to be more environmentally friendly and advocating that it has been changing towards a greener future for the last 10 years (BP, 2009). If a global corporation, which is in fact a possible initiator of global climate change, is now changing should not all business emulate this stance? BP will not have undertaken this image change without careful consideration of its product and its profitability.

Therefore, it may be argued that climate change will provide business with a new view of profitability, not necessarily economic loss or costs. In fact a recent survey carried out on Tourism and Hospitality Alumni which acquired information on future business development, identified green products and sustainability as management priorities (GIHE, 2008). The results emphasize the importance that 'green products' and 'green image' seems to be having on business and the tourism industry in a global market.

None the less, what seems to be apparent is that to a certain extent the market is consumer led, which introduces the notion of risk elasticity of demand for climate-sensitive products. If green products cost more, will consumers actually purchase these if non-green items cost less? To what extent are consumers price sensitive and are they really becoming more ethical? Perhaps there is a need for the tourism market to form its own 'green' cartel, which only offers 'sustainable' goods, and limiting the competition of unethical climate products. This may not seem such a draconian idea, as the present markets are in fact not free. They require controls, checks and balances to ensure freedom of competition, so why not then do this for ethical climate products?

If the world is facing climate-induced disaster then surely there is a need to ensure that the products on offer are limited to positive climate outputs, whilst at the same time limiting or even outlawing the use of climate-damaging goods? This opens up a whole new 'Pandora's box' in terms of considered ethical products. Technology certainly influences variables that affect climate change as does the availability of resources. The 1970s, for example, foresaw a very grave future for the world and the document *Blue Print for Survival* (Goldsmith, 1972) predicted that by the year 2000 the world would have nearly run out of most of its resources, and in particular, fossil-based energy by 2040 (Goldsmith, 1972). This prediction seemed to be based upon the consumption and growth of the world without considering advances in technology. Since 1970 a number of industries in the UK have all but disappeared, the coal industry being one, not because stocks have been exhausted, but as a result of global competition and the efficiency of extraction (Buckley, 2007). Access to new oil fields has also been made possible due to changes in technology and the greater efficiency of consumer appliances (*The Economist*, 2001). So should not advances in technology be included as an important factor in present models of climate change?

As with BP, more and more travel companies are realizing the need to create a positive environmental image. Virgin is, as one might expect, responding to this need. As a brand appealing to and reflecting the views and concerns of young people, it is only to be expected that it would foster an ethical image and endeavour to become environmentally friendly. Indeed, Virgin Holidays state: '[w]e're committed to taking care of everyone and everything that matters to our business in the long run. ... But we're also determined to look after the world we all share and the people who live in it. From investing our profits in renewable energy to developing sustainable tourism projects worldwide, we are active in caring for the future of our planet' (Virgin Holidays, 2009).

This corresponds with the hypothesis that businesses need to look towards the future and the possibility of climate change. Virgin Holidays is more than a transport company; it provides the complete package for a holiday maker and has quickly recognized the need to appear green and sustainable (Virgin Holidays, 2009). Richard Branson clearly supports this environmental stance and states: 'Our generation has inherited an incredibly beautiful world from our parents and they from their parents. It is in our hands whether our children and their children inherit the same world. We must not be the generation responsible for irreversibly damaging the environment – Sir Richard Branson (Sept 2006)' (Virgin Holidays, 2009). Plainly, Virgin Holidays seem committed to this venture, even though, paradoxically, global air transport is a definite contributor to GHGs, all be it only 2% (Kaletsky, 2007).

Additionally, Virgin offers responsible tourism awards, which enhance the Company's status but also encourages other operators to engage in responsible tourism (Virgin Holidays, 2009). 'Explore' is an adventure tourism company that seems to fit into the new category of combining business ethics and sustainable tourism, responding positively to the threat of climate change. 'Explore' have won the Virgin 'Responsible Tourism Prize' and it is a company that has been operating for some 30 years (Explore, 2009a). Interestingly, they have now adopted the responsible tourism aspect, even though the sector of the market that they operate in is to some extent a niche and diminutive.

To reiterate their intention to offer an environmentally friendly product, Ashley Toft, Explore's Managing Director, says (Explore, 2009b): '[w]e have thought long and hard about the current environmental concerns and are convinced that carbon offsetting all customers' flights is a step in the right direction. We take our responsibilities towards the environment very seriously and that is why we have included carbon offsetting in tour costs from 2008 onwards.'

However, carbon offsetting could be viewed as simply a 'get out' clause where carbon emissions are not really reduced but simply passed on to other members of the global community; a luxury that only the developed nations are able to utilize. One has to question whether travelling to these global communities is either climate friendly or conducive to the climate change debate. On the other hand, it should be applauded that environmental considerations are being chosen by these companies in their search to find an ethical business solution to climate change.

TYF is an adventure tourism company, located in Wales, UK, within the Pembrokeshire National Park. They appear committed to fostering a green tourism product. On their website you will find the following statement: 'From running the first carbon neutral outdoor adventure company in the world to buying fair trade tea and coffee, The TYF Group is doing everything it can to make "spaceship earth" a better place' (TYF, 2009). They claim to be the first to run an eco-friendly hotel, which is supplied with green electricity. They further state: 'We aim to run our business as a leading example of sustainable business practice and in doing so, demonstrate that good business is good sense. To minimize our impact on the environment, influence others and protect the environment for future generations of life on earth' (TYF, 2006).

They have a clear environmental policy which incorporates:

- tackling climate change;
- green our supply chains;
- reduce, reuse and recycle waste; and
- work in partnership with others to protect the environment.

The TYF Group will also continue to:

- Operate an environmental management system that complies with the requirements of the Green Dragon Environmental Standard.
- Monitor and improve environmental performance on an ongoing basis, keep up to date, and comply with all environmental legislation and avoid pollution.
- Enforce the TYF Group's ban on the use of synthetic horticultural pesticides on company property.

The TYF Group's environmental policy is constantly maintained, developed and updated, and undergoes a significant annual review. This policy is regularly communicated to all customers, suppliers and staff, and made available to all interested parties (TYF, 2006).

Clearly, this organization appears to be effectively reacting to predicted climate change, whilst maintaining the company's success through environmental tourism products. Furthermore, its environmental policy may effectively enhance the product it offers, especially as the basis of the company is centrally focused upon the use of the environment, which might eventually be transformed as a result of climate change.

The Future?

The future is uncertain and change is inevitable. Yet change is not new and is what the world has experienced for eons. The task ahead is adaptation, to ensure that risk and hazard predictions are as accurate as humanly possible. Past prediction and forecast have not been very accurate and there is now an even greater need to ensure that new risk models of prediction are developed. The difficulty is trying to use these on a system (weather) that is clearly extremely complex and chaotic. Weather predictions are notoriously inaccurate for the long term (a year). How safe are they for a hundred years?

The development of new climate prediction models relating to tourism impacts is necessary and it is suggested that they require greater rigour than the current stochastic models. This would ensure that a more qualitative understanding is gained rather than a single factor outcome relating to a country's risk factor. Countries vary greatly in terms of their geography and climate and a more detailed construction is needed to explore the effects of climate change on the different regions of each country.

There is also a need to understand management planning related to risk predictions, so that the hazards that will result from climate change can be minimized. Again there is a need to attempt to forecast the likely effects and then instigate MR (minimum risk) management systems to assist and adapt tourist destinations and products to meet these changes. From previous examples, developing countries are more likely to be the worst affected in terms of the extremes of climate change. That said, climate change has engendered positive reactions from some countries and companies, global and national, illustrating that, yet again, adaptation and new product development will be the way ahead. King Canute couldn't stop the sea advancing, but he could have sailed on it.

References

Adams, J. (1995) *Risk*. UCL Press, London.

Alon, I. and Martin, M.A. (1998) A normative model of macro political risk assessment. *Multinational Business Review*, http://findarticles.com/ (Accessed: 23 March 2009).

Amos, J. (2003) Oldest human skulls found by staff. *BBC News Online* science, 11 June, http://news.bbc.co.uk/2/hi/science (Accessed: 8 May 2009).

Australian Government (2005) *Climate Change: Risk and Vulnerability*, Report to Department of Climate Change, Promoting an Efficient Adaptation Response in Australia – Final Report, March 2005, Report to the Australian Government, Australian Greenhouse Office, Department of the Environment and Heritage, www.climatechange.gov.au/impacts (Accessed: 23 March 2009).

Australian Government (2008) Department of Climate Change, Submission to the House of Representatives Standing Committee on Climate Change, Water, Environment and the Arts, Inquiry into Climate Change and Environmental Impacts on Coastal Communities, 12 June 2008.

BBC (2005) At-a-glance: Countries hit. http://news.bbc.co.uk (Accessed: 6 May 2009).

BBC TV (1999) Anatomy of an Avalanche. BBC Two, *Horizon*, November, BBC, London.

Blakie, P., Cannon, T., Davis, I. and Wisner, B. (1994) *At Risk: Natural Hazards, People's Vulnerability, and Disasters*. Routledge, London.

BP (British Petroleum) (2009) BP brand and logo. www.bp.com (Accessed: 23 March 2009), BP, London.

Buckley, C. (2007) UK Coal pleads for state commitment. *The Times Online*, 2 March, http://business.timesonline.co.uk (Accessed: 8 May 2009), Times Newspapers Ltd, London.

Buhalis, D. (2006) *Tourism Management Dynamics: Trends, Management, Tools*. Elsevier, London.

CCRM (Climate Change and Risk Management) (2005) Why your business should take climate change seriously. www.ccrm.co.uk (Accessed: November 2008), CCRM, Oxford.

Davos Declaration (2007) *Declaration Climate Change And Tourism Responding To Global Challenges*, Davos, Switzerland, 3 October 2007.

Denney, D. (2005) *Risk and Society*. Sage, London.

Durkin, M. (2005) The Great Global Warming Swindle. *C4*, March 2007, documentary film, UK.

Explore (2009a) Responsible travel and tourism. www.explore.co.uk/responsible-travel/ (Accessed: 23 March 2009).

Explore (2009b) Carbon Offsetting. www.explore.co.uk/responsible-travel/carbon-offsetting.htm (Accessed: 23 March 2009).

GIHE (Glion Institute of Higher Education) (2008) *Alumni Survey of Priority Areas for Business*. LRG, Bulle, Switzerland.

Glendon, A.I. and McKenna, E.F. (1995) *Human Safety and Risk Management*. Chapman & Hall, London.

Goldenberg, S. (2009) Barack Obama's $1.8bn vision of greener bio fuel. www.guardian.co.uk (Accessed: 6 May 2009), *The Guardian*, London.

Goldsmith, E. (1972) *A Blueprint for Survival*. Penguin Books, London.

Hillson, D. and Murray-Webster, R. (2007) *Understanding and Managing Risk Management Attitude*. Gower, Aldershot, UK.

Inter-American Development Bank (2003) *Adaptation to Climate Change and Managing Disaster Risk in the Caribbean and South-East Asia*. Report of a Seminar, Barbados, 24–25 July.

IPCC (Intergovernmental Panel on Climate Change) (2001) *Climate Change 2001: Synthesis Report*. WMO UNEP.

IPCC (2008) *Climate Change and Water*. WMO UNEP.

Johnson, K. (2008) Climate change, then humans, drove mammoths extinct. *National Geographic News*, 1 April, http://news.nationalgeographic.com/news (Accessed: 8 May 2009).

Kaletsky, A. (2007) Rise above the hot air and carry on flying – cracking down on air travel won't stop climate change. *The Times Online*, 11 January, www.timesonline.co.uk (Accessed: 8 May 2009), Times Newspapers Ltd, London.

Lingle, C. (2009) Climate change superstitions put human well being at risk. *Jakarta Post*, www.thejakartapost.com/news (Accessed: 23 March 2009), Jakarta.

Löw, P. (2008) Weather-related Disasters Dominate. Worldwatch Institute, 2 October, www.worldwatch.org/node/1005 (Accessed: 8 May 2009), Washington, DC.

Montaigne, F. (2004) Signs From Earth: No Room to Run. Republished from the pages of *National Geographic* magazine, September, http://environment.nationalgeographic.com/environment/global-warming (Accessed: 8 May 2009).

Pearce, F. and Le Page, M. (2008) Climate change: The Next Ten Years. *New Scientist* 199, 2669.

Piekarz, M. (2009) Political risk. PhD thesis, Cranfield University, Shrivenham, UK.

Saner, M. (2005) Information Brief on International Risk Management Standards, to Support the Discussion on the Government Directive on Regulating, 30 November 2005. Institute on Governance, Ontario.

Scholze, M., Knorr, W., Arnell, N.W. and Prentice, I.C. (2006) A climate-change risk analysis for world ecosystems. *Proceedings of the National Academy of Science of the United States of America (PNAS)*, www.pnas.org/content (Accessed: November 2008).

Shih, C., Nicholls, S. and Holeck, D.F. (2009) Impact of weather on downhill ski lift ticket sales. *Journal of Travel Research* 47(3), 359–372.

Simpson, M.C., Gössling, S., Scott, D., Hall, C.M. and Gladin, E. (2008) *Climate Change Adaptation and Mitigation in the Tourism Sector: Frameworks, Tools and Practices.* UNEP, University of Oxford, UNWTO, WMO/Paris, France.

Stacy, M. (2006) Insurers must report exposure to climate change risk. Solve Climate, http://solveclimate.com (Accessed: 23 March 2009), Science First Inc.

Strachan, J. (2007) Harnessing The Power of Super-Computers for Climate Risk Assessment – The Use of High-Resolution Global Climate Models for Climate Risk Assessment. www.willisresearchnetwork.com (Accessed: 23 March 2009), Walker Institute for Climate System Research, Reading, UK.

The Economist (2001) REPORTS Into deeper water. Technology Quarterly, 6 December, www.economist.com/science (Accessed: 8 May 2009), *The Economist* print edition, Economist.com.

The Tech (2008) Obituary: Edward N. Lorenz ScD '48. *The Tech*, 18 April 2008, Vol. 128, http://tech.mit.edu/V128/N20/lorenzobit.html (Accessed: 8 May 2009), MIT, Cambridge, USA.

TYF (2006) Environmental Policy. www.tyf.com (Accessed: 23 March 2009).

TYF (2009) People, Planet and Places. www.tyf.com (Accessed: 23 March 2009).

Virgin Holidays (2009) www.virginholidays.co.uk/info/about/who_are_we (Accessed: 23 March 2009).

Waring, A. (1996) *Safety Management Systems.* Chapman & Hall, London.

World Resources Institute (2007) Earth Trends. The Environmental Information Portal, www.wri.org.

WTO (2003) *Climate Change and Tourism, Proceedings of the 1st International Conference on Climate Change and Tourism*, Djerba, Tunisia, 9–11 April 2003, WTO.

6 Climate Change – Law, Environment and Tourism

PAUL OSBORNE

The subject of climate change is now a permanent fixture in today's society. Certainly, despite the implications of a global conference at Copenhagen in December 2009, a day rarely passes without expressions of concern somewhere in the media. This chapter addresses the policy steps that respective governments in the UK have taken to address the issues presented by climate change as it impacts on both the UK and internationally. The chapter will address the impact of international law in relation to climate change and then focus on UK government strategy, finally focusing on the Welsh dimension, in terms of the Welsh Assembly Government (WAG) approach to this issue.

International Law and Climate Change

> The political, scientific and economic complexity of tackling climate change has presented the international community with a considerable challenge.
>
> (Birnie et al., 2009:357)

Indeed, as early as 1988 and 1989 the United Nations General Assembly had declared 'Climate Change is a common concern of mankind' (Sands, 2003:358). A detailed analysis of the preamble to the Framework Convention on Climate Change 1992 ('the Convention') is contained in both of these publications and is beyond the scope of this chapter, although the Convention's ultimate objective is articulated within Article 2: 'to stabilise greenhouse gas concentrations in the atmosphere at a level that would prevent dangerous anthropocentric interference with the climate system'. Despite the reference to effects and adverse effects of climate change (Sands, 2003:362), the Convention itself contains no intention in relation to any form of commitments. It has been suggested the language within the Convention is 'convoluted' (Sands, 2003:364) with even the commitments that are evident, based on common but differentiated responsibility, representing a 'compromise between various OECD members and different interests in and between developed and developing states'. Certainly, the Convention acknowledges the necessity to strengthen commitments in the light of new scientific information and it is suggested that it may thus be viewed as a bold attempt to address climate change subject to overarching national interests, hence the convoluted language. The crucial work of the Intergovernmental Panel on Climate Change (IPCC) must be related at this stage. Formed in 1988, this intergovernmental body set up under the auspices of the World Meteorological Association (WMO) and United Nations Environmental Programme (UNEP) has published (to date) four Assessment Reports on climate change, which are seen as authoritative. The evidence-based regime provided (inter-alia) by the IPCC Assessment Reports has brought a clearer coherence to the climate change debate at international level and is fundamental in the assessment of the potential impacts of climate change.

The first Conference of the Parties to the Framework Convention met in Berlin in 1995, resulting in the Berlin Mandate, which acknowledged that new obligations were required as the existing commitments in Article 4(2)a and b of the Framework Convention were 'not adequate' (Sands, 2003:369). Subsequently, at the second Conference of the Parties (COP) in Geneva in July 1996 a Ministerial Declaration was adopted 'by which Ministers urged their representatives to accelerate negotiations on a legally binding protocol or another legal instrument'. Obligations were formulated and adopted within the Kyoto Protocol, which was opened for signature in March 1998. The impact of the Protocol has been manifest in that it has highlighted the divisions that exist between the conference parties, indeed 'the key feature of the Kyoto Protocol is its establishment for the first time of quantitative restrictions on emissions from industrialised economies' (Birnie *et al.*, 2008:360–361). Despite a consensus being reached on the 'flexibility mechanisms' in Articles 6, 12 and 17 the process of further negotiation has proven difficult. This has been most significant in the announcement by President George Bush in March 2001 that the USA would not ratify the Protocol. Despite the obstruction of the USA, the Kyoto Protocol entered into force on 16 February 2005 with ratification by Russia. Ironically, between 1 and 3 February 2005 the Hadley Centre for Climate Prediction and Research hosted the 'Avoiding Dangerous Climate Change' conference. The Final Report of the Steering Committee reported what the impacts of proposed rises in temperature could be; providing stark warnings of, inter alia: species extinction, migration, land loss and ecosystem instability. Indeed, Sir David King, the UK government's chief scientist, acknowledged there was now a consensus among climate scientists that the problem was a 'globally serious and urgent issue on which we need to take action' (www.guardian.co.uk/climatechange/story/0,12374,1404453,00.html).

In its Fourth Assessment Report (AR4) (IPCC, 2007), published in February 2007, the IPCC reported on a series of 'robust findings and key uncertainties'. In relation to the former, with regard to observed changes in climate and their effects and their causes: 'warming of the climate system is unequivocal'; 'many natural systems on all continents and in some oceans, are being affected by regional climate change'; 'Global total anthropogenic GHG emissions, weighted by their 100-year GWPs, have grown by 70% between 1970 and

2004'; 'Most of the global average warming over the past 50 years is very likely due to anthropogenic GHG increases and it is very likely that there is a discernible human-induced warming averaged over each continent (except Antarctica); 'Anthropogenic warming over the last three decades has likely had a discernible influence at a global scale on observed changes in many physical and biological systems'. The IPCC acknowledge the existence of key uncertainties, including, inter alia: limited climate data coverage in some regions; the difficulty of monitoring and analysing changes in extreme events; how effects of climate change on human and some natural systems are difficult to detect due to adaptation and non-climatic drivers. The magnitude of CO_2 emissions from land use change and CH_4 emissions from individual sources remain as key uncertainties.

Reflecting on the conclusions of AR4, which of the issues will be most significant for a legal agreement in the Copenhagen Summit in December 2009? The United Nations Framework Convention on Climate Change (UNFCCC) negotiations within the COP resulted in elements of the 'Bali roadmap', an umbrella term for the 2-year negotiation process, which will lead to the Copenhagen Climate Summit, related the following issues: mitigation, adaptation, technology and investment and finance. In relation to mitigation the decision as adopted by the COP keeps the distinction between developed and developing countries, calling for 'measurable, reportable and verifiable appropriate mitigation'. The briefing note of the Pew Center on Global Climate Change relates that 'For developed countries, this is further defined as "commitments or actions, including quantifiable emission limitation and reduction objectives" ... For developing countries, the decision calls for "actions ... supported by technology and enabled by financing and capacity building" which are to be "measurable, reportable and verifiable".'

Additionally, the decision calls for new efforts to support adaptation to climate impacts; to remove obstacles to, and provide financial support for 'the development and transfer of technology' to developing countries; and other positive incentives for mitigation and adaptation by developing countries (www.pewclimate.org/road_to_bali/cop13).

Despite the stark reality expressed by AR4 and the significance of a newly elected President in the USA, the roadmap has started to resemble a 'potholed pavement' with difficult, protracted negotiation on the run into the Copenhagen Summit in December 2009.

Despite the significance of the statements made in AR4 at the time of writing (November 2009), negotiations between developed and developing countries appear at an impasse prior to the Copenhagen Summit in December 2009. It has been clearly related by Yvo de Boer (Executive Director of the UN Convention on Climate Change) that 'it is physically impossible under any scenario to complete every detail of a treaty in Copenhagen' (http://unfccc.int/meetings/intersessional/barcelona_09/items/5024.php).

The suggestion has instead been the adoption of a COP decision, which 'would be politically but not legally binding and would form the basis for a treaty to be negotiated post-Copenhagen' (Bodansky blog: http://opiniojuris.org/2009/11/06/bodansky-update-from-barcelona-climate-change-negotiations/).

However, Bodansky suggests that even a political outcome will be difficult and require significant compromises by all sides. He suggests a possible 'wish list' but these elements 'given the current state of negotiations ... remains a very ambitious objective for Copenhagen'. Given the present antipathy towards politicians in the UK (and a recent by-election in Glasgow North-East which heralded a 33% turn out – which some commentators have blamed ironically on the weather!), do the public trust politicians with so sensitive and significant a matter?

The UK Climate Change Strategy

The UK has a rich and diverse tradition of legislation and policy in relation to air pollution, which has, until the Environmental Protection Act 1990, been pre-dominantly reactive in nature. The issue of climate change was first addressed via the Climate Change Programme, launched in 2000 ('CCP 2000'). The pro-gramme contained an ambitious programme of measures, which has subse-quently been accused of 'optimism bias in relation to its predictions about the impact, on emissions, of its measures' (Bell and McGillivray, 2008:527). Never-theless, the UK saw greenhouse gas emissions fall in the 1990s (15.3% between 1990 and 2002) although it is acknowledged that these cuts were 'one off gains' due to the switch from coal to gas, de-industrialization/modernization and greater reliance on nuclear energy (the House of Commons Select Committee on Envi-ronment, Transport and Regional Affairs in its Fifth Report referred to this as a 'fortuitous coincidence rather than the result of any strategy' (www.publications. parliament.uk/pa/cm199900/cmselect/cmenvtra/194/19402.htmat at 89). The Select Committee noted two aspects (at 91.) towards the framing of a long-term climate change policy: 'enabling industry to invest with confidence and starting to educate and persuade individuals to change their behaviour.' The question at UK level therefore is has this happened?

The Royal Commission on Environmental Pollution (RCEP) in its 22nd Report, *Energy: The Changing Climate* (www.rcep.org.uk/reports/22-energy/22-energyreport.pdf) had, inter alia, already addressed these two issues with the Commission favouring the 'contraction and convergence' approach, which would allow an equal per-capita emission allowance to every citizen of the world, thus 'the result of this new allocation would, of course, be an enormous reduction for the current high emitters and some scope for emissions growth by developing countries' (http://jel.oxfordjournals.org/cgi/pdf_extract/13/2/287).

What is interesting is the broad conclusion of the 22nd Report; a reduction by industrialized countries of 60% or more by the year 2050, was formally adopted by the UK Government in the Energy White Paper of 2003 (DTI, 2003), only to be taken to a legally binding target of at least an 80% cut in greenhouse gas emissions by 2050 with a reduction in emissions of at least 34% by 2020 by the Climate Change Act 2008.

The first UK Climate Change Programme (CCP 2000) was based upon the following: reducing industrial emissions through integrated pollution prevention and control (IPPC) permits; energy efficiency measures; the promotion of renewable sources of energy; investment in transport measures to reduce pollution caused by traffic congestion; and the use of economic instruments (namely a Climate Change Levy and a national emissions trading scheme) (Bell and McGillivary, 2008:527). CCP 2000 was subject to a review initiated by the Government in November 2004, which resulted in a revised programme published in March 2006 (Climate Change: The UK Programme Cm 6764) (CCP 2006). This programme, whilst carrying on with issues from the original programme, also included: a commitment to produce annual reports to Parliament on emissions, future plans, and progress on domestic climate change; a commitment to plan for adaptation to climate change; and a renewable transport fuel obligation (Bell and McGillivary, 2008:528).

The National Atmospheric Emissions Inventory 2007 (www.theccc.org.uk/images/nat_as_map_jpg) illustrates how energy producers (power) have traditionally been the most significant atmospheric emitters in the UK. This was evidenced in the traditional UK approach, which 'tended to focus on the supply side – that is, that it has traditionally tried to limit emissions by energy producers' (Bell and McGillivray, 2008:528). This approach is now questionable and thus brings into sharp focus a move from tackling suppliers to an actual reduction in energy demand. This movement to reducing energy demand is evident in CCP 2006 with significant increases in the Voluntary Agreements with car manufacturers to reduce CO_2 emissions from cars (0.1 to 2 MtC from 2010 to 2020) and Product Policy (0.2 to 0.6 MtC from 2010 to 2020) (Defra, 2007:11).

The Climate Change and Sustainable Energy Act 2006 also stated as its principal purpose to enhance the UK's contribution to combating climate change. This was carried out by s.2, which made it a legal requirement of the Secretary of State to report annually on the level of greenhouse gas emissions in the UK and the steps taken by government departments during the previous year to reduce those emissions. In July 2007 the first annual report on the UK Climate Change Programme (www.decc.gov.uk/en/content/cms/what_we_do/change_energy/tackling_clima/programme/programme.aspx) (as stated in s.2 above) was laid before Parliament. The report acknowledges that 'The reduction in greenhouse gases has, since 1990, mainly been driven by restructuring, especially in the energy supply industry; energy efficiency; pollution control measures in the industrial sector' (p.12). Soon after publication of this report the Climate Change Bill was introduced to Parliament (November 2007) becoming law in November 2008. Its primary aims were to improve carbon management, helping the transition to a low carbon economy in the UK and to demonstrate UK leadership internationally (www.decc.gov.uk/en/content/cms/legislation/cc_act_08/cc_act_08.aspx).

The 2008 Annual Report to Parliament (www.decc.gov.uk/en/content/cms/what_we_do/change_energy/tackling_clima/programme/programme.aspx) again highlighted the move towards demand factors and away from the energy suppliers. The report summarizes the main areas for action: energy efficiency, buildings, transport, environmental markets, technology and innovation, energy production and fuel poverty. The table (Table 6, p.25) of the report highlights the significant contribution to greenhouse gas emissions made by transport, which has risen (despite some incremental declines between 1997–2002 from 124.4 MtCO$_{2e}$ in 1990 to 139.3 MtCO$_{2e}$ in 2006). These figures are against a decline in all other measured categories within the table (with the exception of Residential, which recorded a marginal rise of 2.6 $MtCO_{2e}$ between the base year and 2006).

The Annual Reports on the UK Climate Change Programme have now been augmented by the reports of the Committee on Climate Change (a statutory committee since the Climate Change Bill become law on 1 December 2008). The first report – Building a low-carbon economy – The UK's contribution to tackling climate change (published in December 2008) (www.decc.gov.uk/en/content/cms/legislation/cc_act_08/cc_act_08.aspx) suggests, inter alia, a reduction by the UK in Kyoto greenhouse gas emissions of 80% by 2050 against 1990 base levels. This target, along with the recent supplementary supporting evidence of Defra (Adapting to Climate Change UK Climate Predictions June 2009) (www.defra.gov.uk/environment/climate/documents/uk-climate-projections.pdf) provides a clear indication to those countries who attend the Copenhagen Summit in December 2009, showing that the UK and its devolved regions are taking a clear leadership role in tacking climate change.

The Welsh Assembly Government

The Welsh Assembly Government strategy on Climate Change (Climate Change Strategy – High level policy statement consultation) (http://wales.gov.uk/docs/desh/consultation/090116climateconsultationen.pdf) is currently under consultation, having originally been open to a first consultation in January 2009 (for 6 weeks) with a detailed analysis of the consultation exercise published in March 2009. The second consultation, which closed in October 2009, sets out proposals for new policies and programmes to tackle climate change in: transport, business, public sector, agriculture and land use, waste and at home. Additionally, it also details proposals for an adaptation framework in Wales (see http://wales.gov.uk/consultations/environment and countryside/climate change action/;js). This dual consultation will contribute to a final Climate Change Strategy bringing together the High Level Policy Statement and the Programme of Action at the end of 2009.

Prior to the consultation exercise related above, the Welsh Assembly had established a Climate Change Commission with four subgroups (adaptation; baseline methodology and economics; communication; emission reduction), which commenced work in 2008. This Commission is both cross-party and cross-sector, although the work of the four groups, whilst important and relevant, appears embryonic in nature at this stage. Nevertheless, as is stated within the Climate Change Strategy – High level policy statement consultation, climate change is acknowledged as a 'social justice issue', something which can be addressed in conjunction with policies to tackle climate change. Clearly (as related in responses to the February consultation), The Welsh Assembly Government must take on a leadership role in climate change (already clear in the One Wales: One Planet consultation – with a strong target of an annual 3% reduction in greenhouse gas emissions in areas of devolved competence from 2011) as well as effective communication and engagement with people and communities across Wales. However, it is suggested that the parts are only a percentage of the whole and, as such, the Welsh nation must see the impact of its climate change strategy in both a UK but more importantly a global picture.

Conclusion

It was only on April 2, 2009, that the US Supreme Court in Massachusetts *v.* EPA (549 US 497) 2007, stated that greenhouse gases are air pollutants covered by the Clean Air Act. This has led to a subsequent Proposed Endangerment Finding (www.epa.gov/climatechange/endangerment.html) by the EPA Administrator, Lisa Jackson, where she 'proposes to find that atmospheric concentrations of greenhouse gases endanger public health and welfare within the meaning of section 202(a) Clean Air Act'(ibid). This finding was made 'specifically with respect to six greenhouse gases that together constitute the root of the climate change problem: carbon dioxide, methane, nitrous oxide, hydroflourocarbons, perfluorocarbons, and sulphur hexafluoride' (see Federal Register Vol. 74 No. 78 April 24th 2009/Proposed Rules). Subsequently, the US House of Representatives passed the American Clean Energy and Security Act of 2009 (ACES Act), H.R. 2454, on 26 June by a vote of 219 to 212. The Pew Center on Global Climate Change reported that 'this comprehensive national climate and energy legislation would establish an economy-wide, greenhouse gas (GHG) cap-and-trade system and critical complementary measures to help address climate change and build a clean energy economy' (www.pewclimate. org/docUploads/Waxman-Markey-short-summary-revised-June26.pdf).

President Barack Obama has, at the time of writing, decided to attend the Copenhagen Summit, or at least some of it. As the only developed nation not to ratify the Kyoto Protocol the USA seems to hold the key to the success of Copenhagen. Clearly, with the publication of the next IPPC report imminent and mounting scientific evidence of the dangers of climate change, Obama must follow the example of Europe and play a central part in negotiations before it is too late to talk.

References and Bibliography

Books and journals

Bell, S. and McGillivray, D. (2008) *Environmental Law* (7th edn). Oxford University Press, Oxford.

Birnie, P., Boyle, A. and Redgewell, C. (2009) *International Law and the Environment* (3rd edn). Oxford University Press, Oxford.

Defra (2007) 'Synthesis of Climate Change Policy Appraisals'. January 2007, p.11.

DTI (2003) *Our Energy Future: Creating a Low Carbon Economy*. White Paper. DTI, The Stationery Ofiice, London.

IPCC (2007) Summary for Policymakers. In: Solomon, S., Qin, D., Manning, M., Chen, Z., Marquis, M., Avery, K.B., Tignor, M. and Miller, L. (eds) *Climate Change 2007:*

The Physical Science Basis. Contribution of Working Group I to the Fourth Assessment Report of the Intergovernmental Panel on Climate Change. Cambridge University Press, Cambridge, UK and New York, USA.

Sands, P. (2003) *Principles of International Environmental Law* (2nd edn). Cambridge University Press, Cambridge, UK.

Internet sources

International

http://opiniojuris.org/2009/11/06/bodansky-update-from-barcelona-climate-change-negotiations/ (Accessed: 3 November 2009).

http://unfccc.int/meetings/intersessional/barcelona_09/items/5024.php   (Accessed: 3 November 2009).

www.epa.gov/climatechange/endangerment.html (Accessed: 7 June 2009).

www.guardian.co.uk/climatechange/story/0,12374,1404453,00.html   (Accessed: 1 November 2009)

www.pewclimate.org/docUploads/Waxman-Markey-short-summary-revised-June26.pdf (Accessed: 7 June 2009).

www.pewclimate.org/road_to_bali/cop13 (Accessed: 3 November 2009).

UK

http://jel.oxfordjournals.org/cgi/pdf_extract/13/2/287 (Accessed: 4 November 2009).

www.decc.gov.uk/en/content/cms/legislation/cc_act_08/cc_act_08.aspx (Accessed: 4 June 2009).

www.decc.gov.uk/en/content/cms/what_we_do/change_energy/tackling_clima/programme/programme.aspx (Accessed: 5 November 2009).

www.defra.gov.uk/environment/climate/documents/uk-climate-projections.pdf (Accessed: 6 June 2009).

www.publications.parliament.uk/pa/cm199900/cmselect/cmenvtra/194/19402.htmat (Accessed: 4 November 2009).

www.rcep.org.uk/reports/22-energy/22-energyreport.pdf (Accessed: 4 November 2009).

www.theccc.org.uk/images/nat_as_map_jpg (Accessed: 4 November 2009).

Welsh Assembly Government

http://wales.gov.uk/consultations/environment and countryside/climate change action/;js (Accessed: 7 June 2009).

http://wales.gov.uk/docs/desh/consultation/090116climateconsultationen.pdf   (Accessed: 7 June 2009).

7 Climate Change, Tourism and the Media: Developing a Research Agenda

PETER BURNS AND LYN BIBBINGS

Introduction

As stated elsewhere in this book, climate change represents one of the greatest environmental, social and economic threats facing the planet; a fact now firmly recognized by world governments (including President Obama's US government) and scientists as an issue of extreme concern for the global population (Oreskes, 2004; Nicholls, 2006). Hall and Higham (2005) state that in recent years, interest in the weather has grown as heavy storms, floods, droughts, snowstorms and extremely high temperatures have become more likely and are associated with changes in the global climate. Moreover, they mention, for instance, that at the time of writing 11 of the 12 past years were among the 12 warmest ones since recording temperatures began in 1850. The year 2003 is probably the one that will most stay in mind with 14,802 heat related deaths in France alone (Higham and Hall, 2005). Extreme weather events include, for example, hurricanes Katrina in 2005 and Kyrill in January 2007.

The UNWTO (2007:2) underpinned the importance of tourism in the global challenges of poverty reduction and climate change with the Davos Declaration, made at the 2nd International Conference on Climate Change and Tourism, and agreed on the 'urgent need to adopt a range of policies encouraging sustainable tourism regarding environmental, social, economic and climate responsiveness'. In practice, this includes mitigation (i.e. prevention of causes) of greenhouse gas (GHG) emissions (particularly those derived from transport and accommodation activities), adaptation by tourism businesses and destinations to changing climate conditions, and the application of new and existing technologies to improve energy efficiency. However, the development of appropriate policies has been very limited overall, primarily due to a lack of research in sectors such as tourism and energy regarding the relationship between climate change and impacts at a global scale (OECD, 2003, cited in Becken and Hay, 2007).

Climate change also presents a global security threat, as argued by David King, Chief Advisor to the UK Government, who refers to climate change as the 'most severe problem we are facing today, more serious even than the threat of terrorism' (King, 2004:176). Higham and Hall (2005) note that King's comments originated in a leaked US security assessment of climate change. Hall *et al.* (2004, cited in Higham and Hall, 2005:18) consider the issue of climate change as a security threat as well, and identify 'environmental security, including climate change, as a major issue facing tourism policy and development'. Higham and Hall (2005:18) identify four sets of relationships 'between more traditional notions of security and the concept of environmental security:

- The relationship between environmental security and the potential for resource wars fought over increasingly scarce resources such as water;
- Direct threats to environmental health because of environmental change and bio-security threats;
- Mass migration of ecological refugees who are abandoning resource-poor or damaged areas; and
- Environmentally destructive capability of the military itself.'

These changes will lead to major impacts on biodiversity and ecosystem services (which have already been recorded on every continent (UNWTO, 2007b)), on economic activities, and on human health and welfare, including the loss of life and forced migration, with associated implications for international stability and equality. Watkiss *et al.* (2005) mention effects on energy use because of unusual changes in temperature, including heating and cooling as well as effects on agriculture. In addition, effects to human health from changes in cold- and heat-related effects, as well as from disease will occur. Water supply and quality are threatened, too, and therefore also have to be considered in the context of tourism consumption as tourists consume far more water than local residents in tourism destinations (UNWTO, 2003). Furthermore, resulting water stress is likely to arise within areas that already suffer from inherent water shortages. Moreover, Watkiss *et al.* (2005) state that global warming effects are likely to be greatest in high latitudes and most evident in the autumn and winter seasons, though the equatorial regions will also experience noticeable warming. In general, wetter weather is to be expected in the mid-latitudes, with drier weather in the subtropics.

Most of the effects mentioned above are inter-related. Negative impacts on unique or threatened systems and risks from extreme climate events occur with a temperature change of 1°C, and these impacts and risks are projected to become significant for changes of 2 to 3°C. Above a 2°C temperature increase, the majority of market impacts are predicted to be negative and most regions will suffer adverse effects from climate change. Risks from large-scale discontinuities become significant above a temperature change of 3°C (Watkiss *et al.*, 2005). Finally, changes to tourism potential and destinations can occur, as tourism is very climate sensitive (Viner, 2005).

Tourism activity itself is a contributor to the problem of climate change due to its dependency on fossil fuel consumption (Nicholls, 2006; Becken and

Hay, 2007), the UNWTO (2007a) estimates that tourism's contribution of CO_2 emissions accounts for about 5% (though the methodology for the calculation is unclear and the basis for calculation seems different from the calculation that proposes tourism as the 'world's largest industry'). Consequently, tourism and climate change represent a two-way relationship termed 'tourism as vector and victim' (UNWTO, 2003): on the one hand, tourism must minimize its negative impacts on the environment (i.e. reduce the emission of GHGs which causes climate change); on the other hand, as mentioned above, climatic change will have a significant impact on tourism destinations, resulting in changes for the tourism industry, e.g. in terms of market changes, as well as for other economic sectors that profit indirectly from tourism. Interestingly, the majority of international tourism generation occurs in the countries that are themselves the major contributors to greenhouse gases (Higham and Hall, 2005).

In summary, the UNWTO (2007b) suggests four broad categories for the above-mentioned impacts:

1. Direct climatic impacts, referring primarily to changes of global seasonality in tourism demand, which in turns influences operating costs such as heating, cooling, snowmaking or food and water supply, as well as impacts upon competitive relationships between destinations, which includes the shift towards higher latitudes/altitudes as well as the vulnerabilities among winter sport destinations due to declining natural snowfall.

2. Indirect environmental change impacts, including biodiversity loss, reduced landscape aesthetic, increased natural hazards, etc. The UNWTO argues that these impacts are likely to be largely negative, and there are still major knowledge gaps of how climate change will actually affect natural but also cultural resources (e.g. Venice, Italy) that are critical for tourism.

3. Impacts of mitigation policies on tourist mobility, whereby increased transportation costs (especially air travel) may alter leisure mobility patterns, initially impacting long-haul destinations that can only be reached by air travel, such as Australia or the Caribbean, but eventually affecting European short-haul travel. However, on the other hand, there might be opportunities for low carbon emission transport modes such as rail and coach travel, which would help destinations that are closer to main markets to revitalize.

4. Indirect societal change impacts might occur, which includes risks regarding future economic growth and political stability of some countries. The Stern Review (2006) reinforces that view by stating that whereas a global warming of 1°C might even benefit the global GDP, any warming above 1°C is likely to damage economic growth at a global scale. Furthermore, such impacts will lead to the climate security issues mentioned above.

This chapter reiterates the idea widely promulgated throughout this book that the impacts of climate change on tourism are potentially important and very diverse. Impacts do and will vary significantly by geographic regions and market segments, not least depending upon the competitors' impacts, and importantly, climate change will generate both positive and negative impacts in the tourism sector as a whole.

Social Responses to Climate Change and Tourism

The year 2007 saw something of a cultural turn or tipping point for the general debate on climate change: public opinion seemed to shift under the sheer weight of scientific evidence following the publication of IPCC 4 and in the UK and Europe as public response to the Stern Report on the Economics of Climate Change. However, citizens remain cynical about government attempts to seize the green initiative, especially in the case of ecotaxes that are not directly hypothecated to ameliorating carbon emissions.

There also emerged a clearer public understanding of the implications behind the two key phrases 'global warming' and 'climate variability', with the former referring to anthropogenic causes (notably burning fossil fuels) and the latter to non-human factors such as the general propensity for temperature change in the earth over time and solar variation. This understanding was helped by massive news coverage in the popular media underpinned by a dramatic rise in scientific research into climate change and its causes.

With the growing realization that virtually all powered human mobility causes carbon emissions, the role of tourism (and in particular flying) as a contributing factor to global warming came into the spotlight. The comfortable democracy of cheap flights brought about by air deregulation and heated competition was cast into doubt by negative publicity epitomized by the phrase 'binge flying', coined rather ironically by Mark Ellingham, founder of the Rough Guide travel book organization (Hill, 2007). His basic premise is that the middle classes of the developed world are somehow addicted to leisure mobility, which is making a considerable contribution to climate change:

> The tobacco industry fouled up the world while denying [it] as much as possible for as long as they could,' said Ellingham. 'If the travel industry rosily goes ahead as it is doing, ignoring the effect that carbon emissions from flying are having on climate change, we are putting ourselves in a very similar position to the tobacco industry.
>
> (Hill, 2007)

The desire for instant gratification, a consumer mentality and hypermobility bought about by ennui and fuelled by the postmodern 'forest of media' (Hughes, 1980) provides an ever changing backdrop of compelling media communications for travel products that creates confusion in the mind of the tourist as consumer. The EU predicts that by 2020, aviation emissions are likely to be more than double that of 2006 (Barbot, 2006; Europa, 2006). If air travel continues to grow at this rate then it may be impossible to achieve carbon reduction targets. In 2006, the Tyndall Centre on Climate Research reported that aviation could account for 100% of the UK's carbon allocation by 2050. At the same time, the Chief Executive of the British Airports Authority insisted that capacity should not be reduced at a time when people want to fly more. This contradiction is the basis of aviation being a central issue in debate on how climate change can be stabilized, and one where both government action and individual changes in attitude and behaviour will be necessary. Ironically (and unsurprisingly), the global financial crisis is slowing down international travel 'drastically' (UNWTO, 2008:1) and far more effectively than green lobbying or government eco-actions.

The Media

A fundamental question for modern societies in the age of mass media and instant communication is about how mass communications shape public discourses surrounding climate change and tourism (especially air travel, which has received particular attention). Mass communication is crucial in determining which issues the public prioritizes for resolution by policy makers and businesses. Most importantly, the publication of the Stern Report on the Economics of Climate Change (2007) marked a period of more intensive mass communication about climate change, its effects, and actions to take by a range of actors (the 'tipping point' mentioned above). Since then, discussions about climate change by the press, new social movements, the government and from individuals have increased significantly, especially via the internet. Air travel in particular has been a source of contentious debate. The diverse contradictions inherent in air travel (e.g. the introduction of a green aviation tax while embarking on airport expansion, greenhouse gas emissions vs. notions of personal freedom associated with air travel) make it particularly important to understand how public discourses are framed and communicated.

In August 2006, before the publication of the Stern review, the Institute for Public Policy Research (IPPR) published its report 'Warm Words: how are we telling the climate change story and can we tell it better?' The research found that the climate change discourses in the UK were confusing, contradictory and chaotic. It concluded that the overarching message for the public is that 'nobody really knows', but that this was beginning to change with some identifiable streams of discourse emerging: a pessimistic 'alarmist' repertoire, and two more optimistic streams: 'it'll be alright'; and 'it'll be alright as long as we do something'. The report went on to recommend engaging the public in discourses to an extent that would result in changing attitudes and, ultimately, behaviour. In the USA the FrameWorks Institute, as part of the Climate Message Project (2006) on discourses on climate change, media, and environmental groups' communications, revealed that the way in which climate change was being reported was counterproductive and immobilizing people.

The ESRC Expert Workshop on Social Science Research for Environment, Energy and Climate Change (11 December 2006, Cardiff University) recognized the role of the media in relation to a number of post-Stern research topics including 'Discourses and Media'. The ESRC experts acknowledged 'the importance and power of discourses [that] can mobilise reflection and action about climate change.' Significantly for this proposal, the experts suggested that 'It will be important to understand the role of the media in *framing the debate* relating to … climate change by constructing notions of citizenship, consumption and well-being' (ESRC, 2006, emphasis added).

However, conflicting information also abounds about climate change (Weingart *et al.*, 2000; Boykoff and Boykoff, 2004) and its relationship to the tourism–leisure mobility continuum (Gössling and Akerman, 2007; Heyer, 2007) from a variety of media, government and independent organizations. In particular, there seems to be no agreement about the level or effect of aviation emissions on the atmosphere. There are also conflicting debates on what actions may be taken in terms of individual flying habits, whether we contribute to carbon offsetting schemes or whether individuals or governments take responsibility for action for seeking solutions. The presentation of material is contradictory. For example, in February 2007, *The Independent on Sunday* produced a double-page report on the latest findings of the International Panel on Climate Change and the urgent need to take action. About a quarter of the total space was taken up by an advertisement from American Airlines proclaiming its 'lowest ever fares' (at £199) to New York, presenting to the reader closely juxtaposed competing messages.

In addition, there is increasing activity in mass communication from new social movements concerned with the climate change and our patterns of consumption. For example, Plane Stupid, Campaign on Climate Change, Greenskies all have a very high profile, and contribute significantly to media debates. It is essential to examine this mass communication and the role it plays in the framing of thinking about climate change and air travel.

The availability of the internet makes it much more possible for individuals to participate in public debate through e-mails to newspaper letter pages, media weblogs set up on specific issues or articles, and personal weblogs/travelblogs on their own travel experiences. Examining these as part of the public debate that influences individuals and policy makers is an important part of the whole picture.

Investigating the complex web of issues is underpinned by five assumptions that are a constant throughout the present book:

1. Tourism transport emissions are growing at 4–5% a year (Peeters, 2007);
2. Technological fixes are unlikely to divert this trend (Adams, 2001);
3. Significant behavioural and institutional changes are required (Giddens, 2006);
4. There is a key contradiction in the EU's Lisbon agenda that promotes economic growth while limiting environmental deterioration (Amelung and Scott, 2007);
5. The present era is characterized by a fundamental transformation in mobility patterns whereby the symbolic power of the 'freedom to travel' locates the problem firmly in the post-industrial milieu of consumer attitudes, belief systems and behaviours (Urry, 2003, 2006).

Given the ubiquitous 'forest of media' that accompanies almost every step we make in modern society, the news media have a particularly significant role in both reporting and analysing behaviour and responses to climate change. The capacity to set the political agenda is also an aspect of media (especially the print media) and it has been suggested that for politicians, the media is a proxy for public opinion (Gilliam and Bales, 2001). Understanding the framing and ensuing narratives is thus critical to finding solutions to public problems.

Thus the cognitive processes where actors interpret events through existing 'frames of reference' can be located into bigger systems of values and meanings.

This is a method ideal for investigating socio-political events, accompanying discourses, and identifying alternative frames within which to locate messages that will influence target audiences.

Setting a Research Agenda for Climate Change, Tourism and Media

Given the complex and under-nuanced relationship between climate change, tourism and media and the simplistic ways in which lobbying groups on both sides marshal their arguments, it is self-evident that more research is needed. In the light of this, the purpose of the present chapter is to propose an agenda that could be usefully addressed to help bridge the knowledge gap. By identifying, analysing and deconstructing the conceptual frames people are using to think about climate change and tourism (but most specifically air travel) in the period immediately following publication of the Stern review and prior to the 2009 financial crisis, at least four key objectives could be achieved:

1. Sources (Government and pressure groups) of competing and coherent discourses on hyper-consumption, lower carbon footprint lifestyles, the role of air travel in freedom could be clearly identified, thus leading to greater understanding of the well-being and the norms, values and arguments that underpin these contradictory behaviours and contradictions.
2. By examining individual personal narratives in response to public discourses on climate change and air travel the influencing factors that may lead to change in attitude and/or behaviour will be identified.
3. A toolkit could be developed for analysing the relationship between discourse and motivating reflection and behavioural change in this arena.
4. A benchmark set of attitudinal frames could be established and used for measuring the impact of the 2009 financial crisis on travel and tourism.

The research agenda could be addressed in part by a series of research questions:

1. How do the print media frame public discussions of the relationship between tourism, air travel and climate change, including the competing discourses of hyper-consumption and the pressure for more restrained lifestyles with a lower carbon footprint?
2. How do 'New Social Movements' (the new puritans, ethical consumers, environmental activists, anti-flying pressure groups) frame tourism and air travel in relation to climate change?
3. How does the government frame its communications and policies in relation to air travel?
4. How do online travel commentaries written by members of the public as weblogs/travelblogs, frame the relationship between tourism and climate change?

Answering these questions would help identify the dominant frames of public understanding and the dynamic role that the media plays in creating and activating particular frames. This approach would not only identify and deconstruct the current frames that drive thinking about climate change and air travel, but also cast light on to the interaction and inter-relationships between the frames of various actor groups.

At the very least, research in this area would deliver new knowledge in terms of identifying contradictions and challenges likely to confront policy makers and individuals as they seek change, and linked to this, clearer identification of attitudinal barriers to change and the provision of strategies for overcoming these. Such research would also provide much needed evidence for travel companies wishing to take a more socially responsible attitude towards the provision of travel products. The primary impact of such research could be on the academic community as insights into changing attitudes and behaviour towards climate change and air travel emerge, and on policy makers and lobbyists as they, too, gain greater understanding of the cultural dynamics that accompany social policies and anticipate attitudinal/behavioural barriers to mitigation, and improved ways of framing communication to achieve better reception of key messages aimed at mitigation.

References

Adams, J. (2001) Hypermobility: too much of a good thing? RSA Lecture Programme. RSA, London.

Amelung, B. and Scott, D. (2007) *Tourist Climate Requirements*. Paper submitted to the E-CLAT Technical Seminar Policy Dialogue on Tourism Transport and Climate Change: Stakeholders meet Researchers. 15 March 2007. UNESCO, Paris.

Barbot, C. (2006) Low-cost airlines, secondary airports, and state aid: an economic assessment of the Ryanair-Charleroi Airport agreement. *Journal of Air Transport Management* 12(4), 197–203.

Becken, S. (2004) How tourists and tourism experts perceive climate change and carbon-offsetting schemes. *Journal of Sustainable Tourism* 12(4), 332–345.

Becken, S. and Hay, J. (2007) *Tourism and Climate Change: Risks and Opportunities*. Channel View Publications, Clevedon, UK.

Boykoff, M. and Boykoff, J. (2004) Balance as bias: global warming and the US prestige press. *Global Environmental Change* 14, 125–136.

ESRC (2006) www.brass.cf.ac.uk/events/Previous_BRASS_Events--ESRC_Expert_Workshop.html (Accessed: 15 January 2008).

Europa (2006) Climate change: Commission proposes bringing air transport into EU Emissions Trading Scheme. IP/06/1862. Brussels, 20 December 2006.

Giddens, A. (2006) Climate Change EAC debate, House of Lords, 14th July 2006. Hansard, London.

Gilliam, F. and Bales, S. (2001) Strategic Frame Analysis. *Social Policy Report* 4, 1–23.

Gössling, S. and Akerman, J. (2007) *Hypermobile Travellers*. E-CLAT Technical Seminar: Policy Dialogue on Tourism Transport and Climate Change: Stakeholders meet Researchers, 15 Mar 2007, UNESCO, Paris, France.

Hall, C.M. and Higham, J. (eds) (2005) *Tourism, Recreation and Climate Change*. Channel View Publications, Clevedon, UK.

Heyer, H. (2007) Global Warming and Tourism: where do you stand? *Travel Industry Review*. www.travelindustryreview.com/news/5777 (Accessed: 12 March 2007).

Hill, A. (2007) Travel: the new tobacco. *The Observer*, 6 May 2007 www.guardian.co.uk/travel/2007/may/06/travelnews.climatechange (Accessed: 8 May 2007).

Independent on Sunday (2007) The temperature is rising and humans are to blame. *Independent on Sunday*, 3 February 2007.

Nicholls, S. (2006) Climate change, tourism and outdoor recreation in Europe. *Managing Leisure* 11, 151–163.

Peeters, P. (2007) *The Impact of Tourism on Climate Change*. E-CLAT, Paris.

UNWTO (2003) Djerba Declaration on Tourism and Climate Change. Available at: www.unwto.org/sustainable/climate/decdjerba-eng.pdf (Accessed 29 March 2008).

UNWTO (2007a) Another record year for world tourism. www.unwto.org/newsroom/Releases/2007/january/recordyear.htm (Accessed: 25 June 2008).

UNWTO (2007b) Application of the General Program of Work, Addendum 1: progress report on the ST-EP (note by the Secretary General). UNWTO Commission for the Americas, El Salvador.

Urry, J. (2003) *Globalizing the Tourist Gaze*. Department of Sociology, Lancaster University, Lancaster, UK, www.comp.lancs.ac.uk/sociology/papers/Urry-Globalising-the-Tourist-Gaze.pdf (Accessed: 15 May 2008).

Urry, J. (2006) *Cars, Climates and Complex Futures*. Department of Sociology, Lancaster University, Lancaster, UK.

Viner, D. (2005) éCLAT – das wissenschaftliche Netzwerk rund um Klimawandel, Umwelt und Tourismus. *Integra* 2/05, 9–10.

Viner, D. (2006) Editorial: Tourism and its Interactions with Climate Change. *Journal of Sustainable Tourism* (Special Issue) 14(4), 317–321.

Watkiss, P., Downing, T., Handley, C. and Butterfield, R. (2005) The impacts and costs of climate change. Oxford. Available at: http://ec.europa.eu/environment/climat/pdf/final_report2.pdf (Accessed: 10 December 2007).

Weingart, P., Engels, A. and Pansegrau, P. (2000) Risks of communication: discourses on climate change in science, politics, and the mass media. *Public Understanding of Science* 9(3), 261–283.

8   Climate Change and the Mediterranean Southern Coasts

Giorgio Anfuso and Driss Nachite

Introduction

Global climate change is a scientific hypothesis proposing that anthropogenic impacts on the environment, such as greenhouse gas emissions and land use, may be responsible for local and global climate changes at present and into the future. Furthermore, although anthropogenic emissions of greenhouse gases associated with the use of fossil fuels are mainly from the rich industrialized countries, the impacts of climate change will be more severe in poor developing countries. Any environmental impacts in the world's coastal zones may be significant because coastal development is continually expanding from current levels: projections are that approximately 75% of the global population of 7.1 billion in the year 2020 will live within 60 km of the coastline. Because of this, the effect of predicted global sea level rise (SLR) due to climate change has become one of the major concerns for coastal managers in recent years.

The local change in sea level at a particular coastal location and the interconnected coastal risks depend on the global mean SLR and regional deviation from this mean (Church and White, 2006). While the global SLR results from the expansion of the ocean due to the increase in ocean temperature and melting of ice caps, regional factors are caused by non-uniform patterns of temperature and salinity changes in the ocean. In detail, sea warming raises sea level whereas a salinity increase causes sea level to drop because of increased seawater density. Moreover, salinity contributions to SLR constitute at most 20% of the temperature contributions (Maes, 2000).

Locally, vertical land movements also occur due to various geological and human induced processes such as tectonics and isostatic adjustments, sediment loading, and underground water pumping and gas extraction.

In addition, commonly documented outcomes of climate change on coastal environments include changes on storm sequencing and storm arrival patterns, storm surge increase and tropical storm variability. However, a less documented

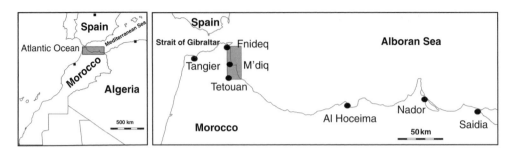

Fig. 8.1. Location map of the most important coastal cities along the Mediterranean littoral of Morocco.

aspect is greater wave climate variability, even if some studies have found that changes are already evident and many will continue into the future (Keim *et al.*, 2004). In general, sea level variations are surveyed through high-precision satellite altimetry and tidal gauges; the latter are referenced by a point on land, thus including land movements that can significantly contaminate the sea level signal (Emery and Aubrey, 1991).

The present study deals with climate change effects in the Mediterranean littoral of Morocco, which is one of the most vulnerable countries within the Mediterranean region (GIEC, 2007), especially the low-lying areas located in the eastern, i.e. Nador and Saidia areas, and western parts, i.e. Tangier and Tetouan areas (Fig. 8.1).

According to the methodology proposed by GIEC (2001), the future scenario of climatic change in Morocco includes a clear increasing trend of the mean annual temperature, with values ranging from 0.6 to 1.1°C by 2020; a reduction in rainfall precipitation of 4% in 2020, with respect to the figures for 2000; an increase of the frequency and intensity of dry periods in the southern and eastern parts of the country; changes in the rainfall precipitation with winter rainfall concentrated in a short period and a reduction in the duration of snowing period and in the extension of ice cover.

The aforementioned changes will greatly impact most vulnerable activities, i.e. tourism and agricultural activities, which are especially developed in coastal areas. Different aspects of climatic change characteristics and impacts will be analysed in following sections.

Sea Level Rise Trend in the Mediterranean Littoral of Morocco

Tsimplis and Baker (2000) used tide gauges to study SLR for the coastal Mediterranean Sea. A negative trend, because of an increase in average atmospheric pressure, was observed during the 1960–1990 period while an average increase of 1.1–1.3 mm/year was recorded for the 20th century. Cazenave *et al.* (2001) investigated sea level changes in the Mediterranean Sea in the 1993–1999 period through data obtained by the Topex/Poseidon space mission, which provided absolute measurements of sea level variations. Authors observed that the Mediterranean sea level has been rising almost everywhere since early 1993. In detail, according to Cazenave *et al.* (2001), within the western Mediterranean, sea level is increasing 5–10 mm/year in the Alboran Sea, i.e. south-east Spain and north-east Morocco Mediterranean littoral areas, which was confirmed by tidal gauge data at Malaga and Alicante.

There are several possible causes for the recent sea level trend observed in the Mediterranean Sea. In detail, the observed trend essentially depends on seawater volume change due to density changes in response to temperature and salinity variations, and mass change due to water exchange with the atmosphere and land through precipitation, evaporation and river runoff, and exchange of water through the Gibraltar Strait (Ross *et al.*, 2000). Quantitative estimations of each contribution for the 1993–1999 period were not feasible due to the lack of suitable observations. Cazenave *et al.* (2001) were able to correlate sea surface temperature trend with observed SLR, obtaining a correlation coefficient of 0.72 for the whole Mediterranean Sea, the detailed spatial pattern showing that surface warming has been about twice as large in the eastern than in the western basin. Cyclic variations are superimposed on the trend, with periods around 2–3 and 4–5 years.

Noticeable increase of the temperature and salinity of deep waters of the western Mediterranean Sea has been observed by several hydrographical studies conducted since the 1960s (Bethoux *et al.*, 1990, 1998). Salinity increase has been attributed to freshwater deficit due to reduced rainfall in the 1990s and damming of major rivers for agricultural purposes (Bethoux *et al.*, 1998; Bethoux and Gentili, 1999). Overall, for the western Mediterranean Sea, Ross *et al.* (2000) affirmed that hydraulic changes of surface and deep water flow through the Strait of Gibraltar may participate in raising sea levels. Fenoglio-Marc *et al.* (2004) used differences in sea surface heights measured by tide gauges and Topex/Poseidon altimeter to estimate vertical land movement in the Mediterranean region, obtaining smaller rates in the north-western area.

More recent studies, i.e. Marcos and Tsimplis (2008), used available tide gauge records for the period 1960–1990 to investigate sea level trends in the Mediterranean Sea and Atlantic Iberian coasts. They separated the direct atmospheric forcing and steric contributions from the other forcing factors and presented the residual trends. By this means, Marcos and Tsimplis used the HIPOCAS (Hindcast of Dynamic Processes of the Ocean and Coastal Areas of Europe) data to correct atmospheric pressure and wind-induced sea level variations and MEDAR database for the Mediterranean Sea to correct temperature and salinity related sea level variations. The postglacial rebound was considered for the Mediterranean in the order of ±0.3 mm/year. The authors utilized Cádiz, Tarifa, Málaga and Ceuta tide gauge records, with data spanning from 40 to 60 years, to try to reconstruct sea level trend in the Gibraltar Strait area. They observed important variations between the tide gauge records, which prevented a common value being calculated for the area. In detail, tide gauges recorded sea level rise at Málaga (2.4 ± 0.4 mm/year) and Ceuta (0.6 ± 0.1 mm/year) and steric contributions in Ceuta were evaluated as −2.1 ± 0.6 mm/year.

Naizi (2007) affirmed that no data are available on land movement and local SLR causes in the Tetouan region, and proposed a SLR value of

2.5 mm/year, which is the value obtained for the western Mediterranean Sea by the Topex/Poseidon and Jason-1 satellite mission during the 1993–2006 period. The author, in order to estimate maximum and minimum hypothetical storm surge elevations for the western Mediterranean littoral of Morocco, took into account two hypotheses: (i) no increase of present SLR trend, i.e. sea level would record an increase of 15 and 27.5 cm by 2050 and 2100, respectively; and (ii) rapid increase of SLR trend, with different scenarios and associated SLR values ranging between 21 and 47 cm by 2050 and between 36.5 and 115.5 cm by 2100.

Lastly, for both the eastern and western Mediterranean areas (Fig. 8.1), Warrick *et al.* (1996) proposed SLR values ranging from 20 to 86 cm for 2100, with a best estimate value of 49 cm.

Coastal Erosion and Flooding Hazards

The impact of climate change will acquire a great importance on littoral areas because of coastal erosion and flooding processes, which will be emphasized by SLR, especially considering that almost all the Morocco Mediterranean beaches are recording important erosion processes (Nachite, 2009a) and are heavily urbanized (Fig. 8.2). In the 1958–2003 period, the littoral of Tetouan recorded coastal retreat rates of 2 m/year (Anfuso *et al.*, 2007; Nachite, 2009b), and lost about 3,900,000 m^2 of beach surface (Niazi, 2007); it presents a great vulnerability to coastal flooding (Benavente *et al.*, 2007).

Fig. 8.2. Human structures on the backshore and dune ridges. Buildings under construction south of Marina Smir (a and b, photo May 2006), summer houses (c, photo October 2003) and a promenade (d, photo May 2006) at M'diq.

According to the previous observations, erosion and flooding processes will affect economic activities and human settlements in different areas, generating a great impact on tourist activities, which represent the most important income for the country. The effects of erosion and flooding processes on different sectors, i.e. Tangier and Tetouan, in the western littoral, and Saidia-Ras El Ma–Al Hoceiema in the eastern Mediterranean littoral (Fig. 8.1) will be described here. The littoral between the last two areas is essentially composed by cliffed sectors that do not record erosion or flooding processes and have very limited tourist and economic activities.

Snoussi *et al.* (2009), following SLR values proposed by Warrick *et al.* (1996), estimated that 10% and 24% of the area of Tangier will be at risk of flooding for minimum and maximum hypothetical storm surge elevations of 4 and 11 m, respectively. Beaches (97% and 99.9%, respectively, for the minimum and maximum storm surge elevations), tourist (69.1% and 84.5%) and harbour (97.5% and 99.9%) infrastructures will be heavily impacted and shoreline erosion would affect nearly 20% and 45% of the total beaches, in 2050 and 2100, respectively.

For the Tetouan area, Niazi (2007) forecasted the flooding of 20% and 27% of the coastal area and important damage for 57% and 63% of urbanized areas of Fnideq, M'diq, Cabo Negro, Martil and Tetouan because of hypothetical storm surge elevations of 5 and 10 m, respectively. The littoral between Cabo Negro and Martil essentially comprises a low lying coastal plain that is very exposed to flooding processes (Fig. 8.3), which would produce the loss of about 25% of its original extension.

According to Snoussi *et al.* (2008), in the eastern Mediterranean littoral, 24% and 59% of the littoral located between Cape Ras El Ma and Saidia village will be flooded for minimum and maximum hypothetical storm surge elevations of 2 and 7 m, respectively. The most severely impacted sectors are expected to be the residential, recreational and agricultural areas, and natural areas with their important ecosystems. Shoreline erosion will affect 50% and 70% of the area in 2050 and 2100, respectively.

Lastly, river-flooding processes will affect economic activities and human settlements in low lying areas close to rivers, especially because of the inappropriate and heavy (94%) urbanization of these areas. In the Mediterranean region, river-flooding processes acquire a great importance because of the characteristics of river basins (high slopes, low vegetal cover, high rates of soil erosion: 3000 t/km^2/year as observed by Oubalkace (2007) along most of the Mediterranean river basins) and location of human settlements (more than 80 villages present a great risk of inundation). Examples of this during last decades have been the flooding in the Tetouan–Martil (1996, 1998, 2000) and Al Hoceima (2003, 2004, 2008) areas, which produced huge damage and loss of human lives (Fig. 8.4).

Water Management Problems

The regional increase of temperatures and lower levels of precipitation over the last decades, and the inter-annual seasonal variability and changes in precipitation

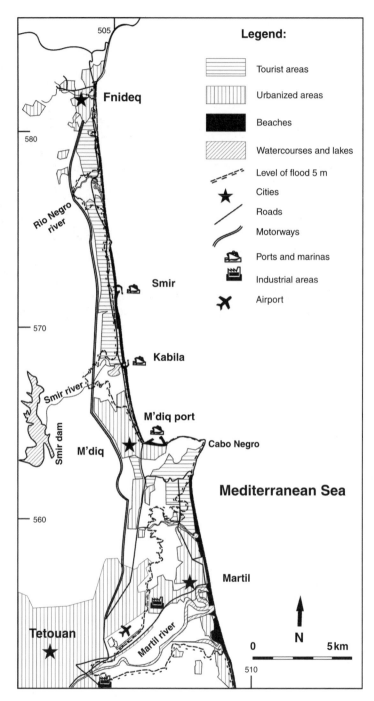

Fig. 8.3. Land uses and vulnerability to flooding, for the 5 m maximum storm surge case, for the area between Fnideq and M'diq. Modified from Nachite (2008, 2009b) and Niazi (2007).

Fig. 8.4. Flooding at Tetouan on 27 December 2000.

distribution, make water resource management an important and imperative issue in Morocco, especially in the Mediterranean littoral, which is a semi-arid region (Tekken *et al.*, 2009). It must also be taken in mind that agricultural and tourism-related activities, which are well developed in the Mediterranean littoral, are highly water consuming.

Today, water resource difficulties cover the basic human necessities, water availability ranging from 180 to 1850 m³/person/year for the southern and northern parts of Morocco, respectively. MATEE (2001) predicted a scenario by the year 2020 of a decrease for water resources of 10–15%, with an average national value of 720 m³/person/year. By the 2020 scenario, according to the previous predictions, about 14 million inhabitants (i.e. 35% of the total population) will have less than 500 m³/person/year (Oubalkace, 2007).

Alibou (2002) predicted, by 2020, a decrease of 3.3% and 2.3% of rainfall, respectively, for the north-western and eastern sectors of the Mediterranean littoral of Morocco. It is estimated that this situation will produce a deficit of 109 million m³/year in the Tangier, Loukkos and other Mediterranean coastal basins, and of 60 million m³/year in the Moulouya basin (Oubalkace, 2007). For the latter area (i.e. Moulouya basin), Tekken *et al.* (2009) observed that average annual precipitation dropped about 10% in the last century, with most important decreases recorded in spring, winter and autumn and small increases in summer, the latter being too marginal to contribute to the regional water balance because of high summer evapotranspiration values.

Groundwater resources are threatened by changing temperature and precipitation and damming, intensive withdrawal of water and SLR. As a result, coastal aquifers along the Mediterranean littoral are presently experiencing sea water intrusion especially in the lower coastal plains. Example of this are observed at Smir, Martil-Alila, Oued Laou, Ghis-Nekor, Bouareg and at the coastal plain of Saidia (ABHL, 2006; Meneoui, 2008; Nachite 2009b). Niazi (2007) predicted vulnerability to sea water intrusion for 45% and 52% of Smir and 30% and 46% of Martil-Alila aquifers, by the 2050 and 2100 scenarios, respectively.

All these previous problems will be greatly emphasized by temperature increase, which will produce a migration of vegetation and a consequent expansion of arid zones towards the north, i.e. an increase of desertification processes. Not only human activities are threatened by temperature and precipitation changes but also several coastal lagoons of great ecological interest, i.e. Kabila, Smir and Nador (Castro et al., 2006).

Agricultural and Tourist Activities

In Morocco, agriculture and farming are basic activities of the local economy that contribute to smallholder subsistence. Agriculture employs approximately 60% of the working population and utilizes more than the 80% of the total amount of water resources; as a result, it will be greatly affected by the reduction of water availability. From present predictions to a 2020 scenario, the Cropwat Model (FAO, 2001) predicted a decrease in the winter cultivation of cereals by 10% and 50% in normal and dry years, respectively, with a reduction at national level of about 30%. Thibault (2008) predicted an increase in the necessity of water for irrigation purposes, a reduction in the duration of the vegetative cycles of cultures, an increase of soil erosion, and a reduction of agricultural activities in littoral areas because of sea water intrusion in soils and aquifers, especially in the Mediterranean region, where most of the agricultural lands are located on the coastal plain.

Human occupation of littoral areas has also been growing during the last decade, with 2,532,714 inhabitants, 8% of the total population of Morocco, living in the Mediterranean littoral. Most of the cities of the northern area of Morocco are coastal cities (15 out of 20). The seasonal character of tourism in the area produces a doubling of the population during summer (July and August), which is essentially constituted by national tourists. Most important tourist beaches are Saidia, Nador, Al Hoceima and littoral areas of Tangier and Tetouan (Fig. 8.1).

At Saidia, the growth in coastal area occupation was about 9% per annum for the period 2004–2010 (taking into account constructed and projected buildings) and urbanized areas are projected to be about 75% of the whole coastal area by 2010. The same processes achieve critical dimensions in the western part of the littoral; in fact in the Tetouan littoral area, about 40 km long, coastal occupation was about 95% in 2007, with an average growth of occupation for the 1969–2007 period of 2% per annum, with maximum values of 5% per annum for the 2004–2007 period (Nachite, 2008).

Dealing with such tourist activities, the conference on tourism held in Marrakech in 2001 marked a turning point in the tourism policy of Morocco, which opted for the promotion of the tourist sector, putting in place an ambitious strategy named 'Vision 2010': as such, tourism is supposed to play a principal role in socio-economic development of the country.

The 'Vision 2010' objectives are very ambitious (both in terms of quantity and quality): (i) the arrival of 10 million tourists by 2010; (ii) the increase of hotel capacity of 160,000 beds (130,000 in coastal tourist resorts and 30,000 in cultural destinations of the country), putting the national capacity up to 230,000 beds; (iii) the increase of investments, the volume being expected to reach 8 to 9 billion Euros, because of the planning of new sea tourist resorts, infrastructure, hotels, leisure and entertainment; (iv) revenues expansion expected to reach 48 billion Euros; (v) the creation of 600,000 new jobs; and (vi) the increase of tourism contribution to the GDP, which is forecast to rise annually from today's 8.5% average, to be about 20% by 2010.

The plan is essentially based on the increase of coastal and beach-related tourism through the 'Plan Azure' and 'Azure extension' focused on littoral tourism. The main aim is to increase, by 2015, beach tourism to 70% of the total offer at national scale and to 90% at the Mediterranean littoral.

Several problems potentially arise from the present tourist development trends and the 'Vision 2010' plan, i.e. a chronic deficit of water resources and a large increase in the population living on the littoral. Substantial increases in water demand are also linked to the 3 million tourists that visit Morocco each year and which require 30% more water than a local person. Furthermore, they produce about 180 l of waste water per person (EEA, 2000). In addition, Morocco is going to receive about 172,000 tourists for playing golf (ONMT, 2006) by 2010, and the Mediterranean littoral especially will record a great increase in the construction of golf camps, this way highlighting the necessity of new, important water resources.

Conclusions

Although many European countries have qualitative data on SLR and climatic change processes and related effects and impacts, further studies must be carried out in Morocco to properly understand the potential physical and social consequences of such processes. In particular, the following areas will require special attention.

- Coastal erosion and flooding processes will generate, in the near future, important losses of beach and coastal area surfaces, this way producing severe economic damage to coastal tourism, the main economic activity for the Mediterranean littoral of Morocco.
- Rainfall diminution, sea water intrusion and excessive groundwater exploitation are generating an increase in the water demand–supply gap. This issue will seriously penalize both tourism developments and agricultural activities, the latter representing the unique income for a large part of the rural population of Morocco.

Lastly, in Morocco, appropriate vulnerability assessment and adaptation strategies to SLR and climate change are required at regional and national scale to improve the tools for correct coastal zone management. During recent decades, these have been greatly neglected because of more urgent requirements and problems or essentially the wish to create rapid economic growth linked to coastal urbanization and tourism.

References

ABHL – Agence du Bassin Hydraulique du Loukkos (2006) Les ressources en eau au niveau de la zone d'action de l'Agence du Bassin Hydraulique du Loukkos: Etat des lieux et perspectives de leur développement et leur sauvegarde. Débat national sur l'eau, November 2006, 29pp.

Alibou, J. (2002) Impact des changements climatiques sur les ressources en eau et les zones humides du Maroc. Table Ronde Régionale en Méditerranée, Athens, Greece, 10–11 December 2002, 41pp.

Anfuso, A., Martinez del Pozo, J.A., Nachite, D., Benavente, J. and Macias, A. (2007) Morphological characteristics and medium-term evolution of the beaches between Ceuta and Cabo Negro (Morocco). *Environmental Geology* 52, 933–946.

Benavente, J., Bello, E., Anfuso, G., Nachite, D. and Macias, A. (2007) Sobreelevación debida a temporales y cambios producidos en las playas del litoral NE marroquí. *Cuaternario & Geomorfología* 21(1), 13–15.

Bethoux, J.P. and Gentili, B. (1999) Functioning of the Mediterranean Sea: past and present changes related to freshwater input and climate changes. *Journal of Marine Systems* 20, 33–47.

Bethoux, J.P., Gentili, B., Raunet, J. and Tailliez, D. (1990) Warming trend in the western Mediterranean deep water. *Nature* 347, 660–662.

Bethoux, J.P., Gentili, B. and Tailliez, D. (1998) Warming and freshwater budget change in the Mediterranean since the 1940s, their possible relation to the greenhouse effect. *Geophysical Research Letters* 25, 1023–1026.

Castro, M., Arroyo, G., Bekkali, R., Nachite, D. and Anfuso, G. (2006) Características ambientales del entorno de la laguna de Smir. In: Anfuso, G. and Nachite, D. (Coords). Dep. Legal: CA/206/06. 40pp.

Cazenave, A., Cabanes, C., Dominh, K. and Mangiarotti, S. (2001) Recent sea level change in the Mediterranean Sea revealed by Topex/Poseidon satellite altimetry. *Geophysical Research Letters* 28(8), 1607–1610.

Church, J.A. and White, N.J. (2006) A 20th century acceleration in global sea level rise. *Geophysical Research Letters* 33(1), L01602, doi: 10.1029/2005GL024826.

EEA (2000) *State and Pressure of the Marine and Coastal Mediterranean Environment.* Office for Official Publications of the European Communities (Environmental assessment report, no 5), Luxembourg.

Emery, K.O. and Aubrey, D.G. (1991) *Sea Levels, Land Levels and Tide Gauges.* Springer, Berlin, 237pp.

FAO (2001) CropWat Model, version 7.0. www.fao.org/ag/AGL/aglw/cropwat.stm (Accessed: 10 January 2009).

Fenoglio-Marc, L., Dietz, C. and Groten, E. (2004) Vertical land motion in the Mediterranean Sea from altimetry and tide gauge stations. *Marine Geodynamics* 27(3), 683–701.

GIEC (2001) *Climate Change 2001: The Scientific Basis*. Contribution of Working Group I to the Third Assessment Report of the Intergovernmental Panel on Climate Change, Cambridge. Cambridge University Press.

GIEC (2007) Groupe de travail I du GIEC. Quatrième Rapport d'évaluation, Bilan 2007 des changements climatiques les bases scientifiques physiques, Résumé à l'intention des décideurs, 25pp.

Keim, B., Muller, R. and Stone, G. (2004) Spatial and temporal variability of coastal storms in the North Atlantic Basin. *Marine Geology* 210, 7–15.

Maes, C. (2000) Salinity variability in the equatorial Pacific ocean during the 1993–1998 period. *Geophysical Research Letters* 27, 1659–1662.

Marcos, M. and Tsimplis, M. (2008) Coastal sea level trends in Southern Europe. *Geophysical Journal International* 175, 70–82.

MATEE (2001) Communication Nationale Initiale à la Convention Cadre des Nations Unies sur les changements climatiques, October 2001, 101pp.

Meneoui, M. (2008) Vulnérabilité des écosystèmes du Littoral Méditerranéen Oriental à l'élévation du niveau de la mer. Projet ACCMA, 44pp.

Nachite, D. (2008) *L'aménagement touristique de la côte méditerranéenne du Maroc et ses impacts environnementaux*. Journées internationales de sensibilisation aux enjeux de la Gestion Intégrée des Zones côtières (GIZC) dans le bassin méditerranéen et en Amérique latine. 9–11 January 2008 (Projet LITMED 21), Université de Nice Sophia-Antipolis – France. http://podcast.unice.fr/groups/conferences/weblog/68c1d/ (Accessed: 10 January 2009).

Nachite, D. (2009a) Diagnostic environnemental – PAC Rif central du Maroc, activité GIZC, PAP/CAR, January 2009, 74pp.

Nachite, D. (2009b) Le développement touristique du littoral de la région Tanger-Tétouan: une évolution vers des scénarios non désirables? In: S. Dominguez Bella and A. Maate (eds) *Geología y geoturismo en la orilla sur del estrecho de Gibraltar*. MCN-UCA Cadiz, 59–78.

Niazi, S. (2007) Evaluation des impacts des changements climatiques et de l'élévation du niveau de la mer sur le littoral de Tétouan (Méditerranée occidentale du Maroc): Vulnérabilité et Adaptation. Doctorat es-sciences Univ. Mohammed V – Agdal (Maroc), 296pp.

ONMT (2006) Le Maroc se fixe pour objectif d'accueillir plus de 172.000 touristes golfeurs en 2010. Office National Marocain du Tourisme. MAP, 30 June 2006. www.fmdt.ma/details.php?id=2757 (Accessed: 10 January 2009).

Oubalkace, M. (2007) Suivi des progrès et promotion de politiques de gestion de la demande en eau: *Rapport national du Maroc*. Gestion de la demande en eau en Méditerranée, progrès et politiques. ZARAGOZA, 19–21 March 2007, 121pp.

Ross, T., Garett, C. and Le Traon, P.Y. (2000) Western Mediterranean sea level rise: changing exchange flow through the Strait of Gibraltar. *Geophysical Research Letters* 27(18), 2949–2952.

Snoussi, M., Ouchani, T. and Niazi, S. (2008) Vulnerability assessment of the impact of sea-level rise and flooding on the Moroccan coast: The case of the Mediterranean eastern zone. *Estuarine, Coastal and Shelf Science* 77, 206–213.

Snoussi, M., Ouchani, T. and Niang-Diop, I. (2009) Impacts of sea-level rise on the Moroccan coastal zone: quantifying coastal erosion and flooding in the Tangier Bay. *Geomorphology* 107(1–2), 32–40.

Tekken, V., Costa, L. and Kropp, J.P. (2009) Assessing the regional impacts of climate change on economic sectors in the low-lying coastal zone of Mediterranean east Morocco. *Journal of Coastal Research* (Special Issue) 56, 272–276.

Thibault, H.L. (2008) Changement climatique et énergie en méditerranée. Plan Bleu, Centre d'Activités Régionales, Sophia Antipolis, July 2008, 49pp.

Tsimplis, M.N. and Baker, T.F. (2000) Sea level drop in the Mediterranean Sea: an indicator of deep water salinity and temperature changes? *Geophysical Research Letters* 27(12), 1731–1734.

Warrick, R.A., Le Provost, C., Meier, M.F., Oerlemans, J. and Woodworth, P.L. (1996) Changes in sea level. In: Houghton, J.T., Meira Filho, L.G., Callander, B.A., Harris, N., Kattenberg, A. and Maskell, K. (eds) *Climate Change 1995. The Science of Climate Change*. Cambridge University Press, Cambridge, UK, 365–405.

9 Climate Change and Coastal Tourism in the Azores Archipelago

HELENA CALADO, KIAT NG, PAULO BORGES, FÁTIMA ALVES AND LISA SOUSA

Introduction

The Azores, a Portuguese Autonomous Region located in the North Atlantic, is a beautiful archipelago consisting of nine volcanic islands with stunning coast and ocean, and year-round mild weather. It is considered as one of the seven Outermost Regions (OR) in the EU and has been recognized by the EU to possess specific problems pertaining to small islands such as remoteness, insularity, small size, difficult topography and climate, and economic dependence on a few products (CEC, 2007). Thus, Article 299(2) of the EC Treaty and the two Communications adopted by the Commission in 2004 stress the need to address the special nature of ORs and to implement a genuine European strategy to support them (CEC, 2007). The three key elements to this strategy are to reduce the accessibility deficit and the effects of the other constraints on the ORs, to make them more competitive, and to strengthen their regional integration (CEC, 2007). This strategy is founded on an active partnership between the European institutions, the Member States and the OR. Thus in particular, extra attention should be paid to mitigate or eliminate any accessibility or competitiveness problems arising for the OR.

Accessibility is vital to the current and future Azorean regional development, both due to the distance that separates the archipelago from the Portuguese mainland (around 1500 km) and other countries, and the inter-island discontinuity of nine small islands spreading over 600 km of ocean. This issue became even more prominent when regional government started developing its tourism sector.

Tourism in the Azores only started growing in the mid-1990s despite its obvious growth potential. Since then, tourism has grown rapidly over the last decade and has gained considerable interest by the regional government especially when it comes to strategizing its economic and social development (Azores Regional Government, 2008). To illustrate its tourism quality, the Azores was ranked second among 111 world island destinations for sustainable tourism by National Geographic Traveler in 2008. In addition to the economic benefits of tourism to the region, it is also socially beneficial in terms of demographics as it may contribute to the settlement of young and innovative people in the smaller and less developed islands through new opportunities of services for tourists.

Concurrently, climate change concerns in the Azores are gaining interest due to increasing global warming awareness, as well as EU and global climate change policies. Researches on climate change and its associated impacts, and impact of climate change policies on the Azores are at their infancy stage. With tourism becoming an important economic sector for the Azores and the coast being the main tourist attraction, there is a growing need to understand the impacts of climate change and especially on how current EU policies could impact on its coastal tourism. The latter is crucial because the EU policies could have disastrous effects on the Azores and may further limit the potentialities of these regions in comparison with other mainland territories. This chapter thus addresses the impact of climate change on coastal tourism in the Azores and, in particular, discusses whether the EU-wide climate change policies are economically reasonable and feasible at a local scale for the Azores. The chapter will present a background study of the Azores, an overview of coastal tourism in the Azores, climate change and its associated effects in the Azores, the impacts of climate change on coastal tourism quality in the Azores, climate change policies, impacts and current effort of the Azores in combating climate change, and finally conclusions and recommendations.

Background on the Study Area

The Azores archipelago, a Portuguese Autonomous Region, is located in the North Atlantic about 1500 km from Lisbon and about 3900 km from the east coast of North America (Fig. 9.1). The Azores archipelago consists of nine islands of volcanic origin located between 37 to 40°N and 25 to 31°W. The islands of the Azores archipelago are geologically young and are located in a tectonically and volcanically active region. The islands are scattered along a 600 km WNW–ESE-trending strip. The Azores is located near the triple junction of the American (west), Eurasian (northeast) and African (south) plates (Fig. 9.1).

The Azores occupies an area of 2333 km² and has a population of roughly 240,000 inhabitants. Despite its small land area, the Azores archipelago encompasses an Exclusive Economic Zone (EEZ) of approximately 940,000 km². The Azores coastline has diverse coastal forms, ranging from low rocky coasts to bluffs, plunging cliffs, pocket beaches, coastal dunes and lagoons.

The Azores climate is influenced by its geographic location in an open oceanic basin, open to the North Pole and the tropics (Ferreira, 1980). Marine air masses interact with cold or temperate air masses from the pole. In addition, local factors such as distance from the coast, altitude and the exposed island slopes are major influences (Agostinho, 1941). The Azores climate can be considered as marine temperate, which is reflected by the low thermal amplitude, high precipitation, high air humidity, and persistent wind. The altitude and the

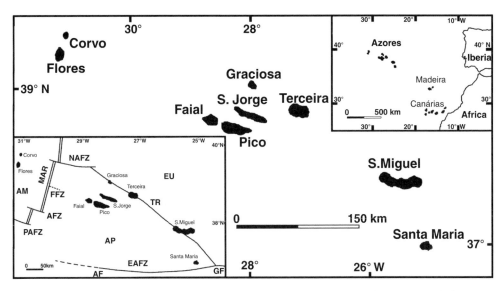

Fig. 9.1. Location map of the Azores islands in the North Atlantic and main tectonic features for the Azores region. AF – African Plate; AFZ – Azores Fracture Zone; AM – American Plate; AP – Azores Plateau; EAFZ – East Azores Fracture Zone; EU – Eurasian Plate; FFZ – Faial Fracture Zone; GF – Gloria Fault; MAR – Mid Atlantic Ridge; NAFZ – North Azores Fracture Zone; PAFZ – Princess Alice Fracture Zone; TR – Terceira Ridge (modified from Krause and Watkins, 1970; Laughton and Whitmarsh, 1974; Needham and Francheteau, 1974; Abdel-Monem *et al.*, 1975; Searle, 1980; Forjaz, 1983; Luis *et al.*, 1994; França *et al.*, 2001; Borges *et al.*, 2007; Fontiela, 2009; on the background of the insert is shown the bathymetry from Smith and Sandwell, 1997).

exposure of the terrain to the dominant winds are important variables that regulate the spatial distribution of precipitation in the archipelago (Agostinho, 1941; Bettencourt, 1979). Naturally, the large-scale atmospheric circulation also plays an important role in the precipitation distribution among the different groups of islands in the Azores (Andrade *et al.*, 2008; Marques *et al.*, 2008).

As discussed by Calado *et al.* (2010), seven coastal environmental hazards have been identified as posing significant threats to the Azores coasts. They are mainly: (i) sea-level rise; (ii) coastal storm; (iii) stream flooding; (iv) coastal erosion; (v) tsunami; (vi) landslide; and (vii) seismicity and volcanism. Although not listed specifically as a coastal environmental hazard, Calado *et al.* (2010) stated that human activity contributes significantly to human vulnerability along the coast.

Coastal Tourism in the Azores

Coastal tourism emerged as a new sector in the mid-1990s. Until then, there were very few hotels and direct air connections. The adoption of tourism growth-enhancing policies by the regional government led to the provision of air connections and promotion of brand awareness spawning a boom in hotel construction with the total number of hotel beds growing from 3000 in 1995 to 10,000 in 2005 (SREA, 2009). Tourist nights spent in touristic accommodations increased from 407,000 in 1995 to over 1,200,000 in 2006 (SREA, 2009). The recently approved Tourism Development Plan in the Autonomous Region of the Azores (POTRAA) projects a maximum tourist load of 15,500 beds by 2015 (ATA, 2008). With regards to air connections, currently there are several charter carriers offering direct connections and tour packages to, among others, the Nordic countries, Germany, the UK, Spain and the Netherlands. As a means to alleviate regional economic asymmetries, the Azores Regional Government (2008) promotes inter-island hopping to spread the economic benefits from tourism across the islands.

De Menezes *et al.* (2008) stated that nature, landscape, remoteness and weather are parameters that will promote longer expected stays in the Azores. Coastal recreational activities are certainly major tourist attractions. Some of the main activities include sailing, yachting, boat tour, cruise tourism, scuba diving, whale and dolphin watching, swimming with dolphins, and sport fishing.

The Azores Tourism Association (ATA) presented its new 2008–2010 Strategic Marketing Plan for the Azores, which focuses on market niches, that is projected to double current tourism revenue (ATA, 2008). ATA (2008) stated that the Azores has been one of Portugal's most successful destinations and that it is now approaching maturity. The new plan proposes investment in certain niches such as nature lovers within the source markets that have already been targeted to date. The plan projects the creation of more than one thousand jobs and a significant increase in the number of overnights in terms of both quantity and value, in addition to doubling of its current tourism revenue (ATA, 2008).

Climate Change in the Azores and its Associated Effects on the Coasts

Santos *et al.* (2004) indicated that there would be a slight temperature increase in the Azores due to a projected increase in greenhouse emissions by the end of 21st century. The moderating effect of the ocean on temperature field shields the islands from drastic increases in temperature. The possible main associated concerns due to climate change in the Azores are as follows: (i) changes in precipitation pattern; (ii) sea-level change; (iii) increase in coastal storms; (iv) increase in coastal erosion; (v) increase in stream flooding; (vi) increase in landslide events; and (vii) changes in water resources.

Precipitation pattern

One of the main characteristics of the Azores climate is the well-established difference between the dry season and the colder, wet season (Ferreira, 1980). About 75% of the annual precipitation occurs between October and March (winter season). The distribution of rain is highly influenced by topography, with very wet high ground and drier coastal areas (Santos *et al.*, 2004). The average annual precipitation in the Azores is 1930 mm exceeding by far the average annual actual evapotranspiration, which is 581 mm (DROTRH-INAG, 2001).

The postulated biggest impact of global warming on the Azores may be the change in annual precipitation distribution, with an increase in winter precipitation and decreases in other seasons (Santos *et al.*, 2004; Miranda *et al.*, 2006). Increased winter precipitation could also escalate stream flooding and especially devastating landslide events that are already major concerns in the Azores.

Sea-level change

Using 10 years of historical data from the tidal gauge station of Angra do Heroísmo (Terceira Island) provided by PSMSL (2002) and converted to a universal datum (Revised Local Reference), Borges (2003) obtained a sea-level rise trend of 16.8 mm/year. According to Borges (2003) and using the 'Bruun model' (Bruun, 1962, 1983), this rate of sea-level rise implies a coastal erosion of 1.68 m/year. However, the trend observed by Borges (2003) is inconclusive of whether there is a long-term increasing trend. This is because for sea-level data, a 10-year time period could just be part of an inter-decadal variation. More monitoring data are needed to determine if there is indeed a rising trend. Nevertheless, with sea-level rise being a major result of climate change in general, the potential significant impact of sea-level rise needs to be taken into consideration, which includes the alteration of ecosystems and habitability in coastal regions (Douglas, 2001). According to IPCC (2001), the main physical effects of sea-level rise are erosion of beaches and bluffs, increased flooding and storm damage, inundation of low-lying areas, saltwater intrusion into aquifers and surface waters, and higher water tables.

Increase in coastal storms

According to Borges *et al.* (2002), the long fetch that characterizes the Azores results in a high-energy wave climate where both sea and swell are relevant sources of energy to the coast, with the northern-facing shore of each island being more exposed in general. Additionally, the wave climate of the North Atlantic Ocean appears to be increasing according to Bacon and Carter (1991) and Bouws *et al.* (1996). In line with this observed phenomenon, the storminess of the Azores increased slightly over the last 150 years (Borges, 2003). The storminess in the Azores is characterized by its elevated inter-annual and inter-decadal variation. The recent paper of Andrade *et al.* (2008) indicates that the average storm lasts for 2.3 days and the average storm frequency is 3.1 storms/year. The paper also states that low intensity storms occur four times every 5 years, while an extreme storm occurs on average once every 7 years. The storms are usually short, frequent and intense (Borges, 2003). The extreme storm usually occurs with south-westerly waves of maximum significant wave height of

11.7 m and highest wave height of 22.2 m (Borges, 2003). These events usually also result in coastal flooding.

The tide, which characterizes the littoral as microtidal to low mesotidal, does not pose a threat to the coastal zones in the Azores. However, the tide becomes a major concern in the concurrent events of coastal storm and storm surge, especially during the period of high tide in spring tides. The compounded effect results in an amplified mean sea-level, which could result in coastal flooding (Calado et al., 2010).

Increase in coastal erosion

The sea and swell are relevant sources of energy to the Azorean coasts (Borges et al., 2002), illustrating the high-energy wave climate characterized by the long fetch of the Azores relative to the North Atlantic. Considering the possibility of increasing trends in the wave climate of the North Atlantic Ocean (e.g. Bacon and Carter, 1991; Bouws et al., 1996), as well as in the storminess of the Azores archipelago (Borges, 2003), it is expected that these factors will, in the near future, contribute to amplify the coastal erosion rates on the Azorean shores.

Upon comparison of the Azorean recession rates with other places in the world (e.g. Sunamura, 1992) and the materials eroded from the scarps and cliffs, the result suggests that the mesoscale values of the Azores recession rates are in general less significant (Borges, 2003). However, it is important to note that in relation to the relatively small size of the Azores, the mesoscale coastal erosion rates might represent a significant reduction on the already limited land availability there.

Increase in stream flooding

In the Azores, many of the streams are ephemeral and torrential with occasional flash floods. Some of the coastal fringes that are attractive for settling correspond to flood plains of streams with perennial nature. Areas like Povoação, Faial da Terra and Ribeira Quente villages in São Miguel Island are some examples of such coastal areas that are exposed to stream flooding risk. Based on historical data, villages have experienced stream flooding as a result of heavy rain episodes that were mostly associated with storms (Raposo, 1998). These events resulted in extensive destruction such as buildings and bridges. Impacts from landslides were responsible for some of the damage (Raposo, 1998). In some of these reported flood events, coastal flooding occurred in addition to stream flooding (Borges, 2003).

One of the impacts of climate change for the Azores region is the increase in intense precipitation events in winter (Santos et al., 2004; Miranda et al., 2006). Heavy rains imply an increasing trend in both the frequency and intensity of storms in the Azores (Borges, 2003). Consequentially, the incidence of flooding in villages located in flood plains and landslide occurrences is expected to increase.

Increase in landslide events

Landslide is one of the most common natural hazards in the Azores, resulting in considerable deaths and economic losses. For example, the 31 October 1997 event at São Miguel Island resulted in 29 deaths and approximately €21 million losses (Raposo, 1998; Cunha, 2003). Since the settlement of the archipelago in the 15th century, there have been records of landslide events of different magnitudes that were triggered by namely earthquakes, volcanic eruptions or heavy rain episodes. The loose and unconsolidated nature of the rocks and soils characteristic of these volcanic islands also contributes significantly to the coastal vulnerability to landslides (Malheiro, 2006).

Heavy rainstorms typically trigger a large amount of landslides (e.g. nearly 1000 on 31 October 1997; Valadão *et al.*, 2002). These are usually shallow slope movements with the vast majority of them originating near the crest of very steep slopes that spread over the complete length of the slope (Marques *et al.*, 2008). Vulnerability of the volcanic soils due to over-saturation with long periods of continuous precipitation is a major contributing factor to landslide events (Gaspar and Guest, 1998). With a postulated increase in precipitation in winter due to climate change, there will be a higher probability of landslide occurrences.

Changes in water resources

The Azores archipelago relies mostly on groundwater for freshwater supply (Cruz, 2003). The basal aquifer system in the coastal area has a very low hydraulic gradient in general and groundwater is mainly extracted using drilled wells (Cruz, 2003). Cruz and Silva (2000) stated that saltwater intrusion in the groundwater of the Azores is a concern as observed in many of the wells that were drilled to the basal aquifer. In fact, several wells have been abandoned due to saltwater intrusion in a few of the islands, resulting in severe economic losses (Cruz, 2003). The decreased precipitation in summer implies an increase in groundwater pumping during that period of time unless other alternatives are available. With the combined effect of sea-level rise and likely increased groundwater pumping, saltwater intrusion into the groundwater freshwater aquifer is a likely scenario. This could result in a long-term reduction in freshwater supply for the Azores.

Impact of Climate Change on Coastal Tourism Quality in the Azores

The five major tourism concerns that could be affected by climate change are namely: (i) weather; (ii) freshwater supply; (iii) lodging; (iv) recreational activities; and (v) safety.

Weather

There will be a slight temperature increase in the Azores with probably warmer and wetter winters due to climate change in the Azores (Santos *et al.*, 2004;

Miranda *et al.*, 2006). In general, the number of tourists visiting the Azores is very low during winter because of the coldness and wetness. Hence, the temperature increase in winter might not be a negative factor for the Azores with regards to tourism. More tourists would visit if winter becomes milder as they will be able to enjoy some outdoor recreational activities in pleasant weather. Interestingly, climate change might actually help the Azores in improving tourist visits in off-season winter times.

Freshwater supply

Water resources of the Azores could be reduced as mentioned above. There are currently very few rainwater catchment reservoirs and apparently no alternative plans to obtain more freshwater supply through means other than groundwater and springs. With a reduction in precipitation in summer, risk of saltwater intrusion in groundwater and an increased demand by growing tourism in the summer in the Azores, there is a likelihood of freshwater shortage in the future. Unless certain measures are taken, this will probably be one of the most limiting issue for tourism growth in the Azores.

Accommodation

With increasing threat of sea-level rise, coastal erosion and landslides, there will be a restriction on the number of hotels and commercial buildings that can be constructed along the coasts. The reduction in ocean-view hotels could have a minor impact on tourism.

Recreational activities

Sandy beaches are not very common coastal forms in the Azores archipelago. They could be reduced due to coastal erosion and sea-level rise as a result of climate change. However, also as a consequence of climate change, the probable increase of cliff and bluff erosion, coastal landslides and stream flooding will certainly provide an increment of sediment amount for nursing the beaches. According to Borges (2003), these are the main sources of sediment for the Azorean sandy beaches. The scenario concerning the sandy beaches is thus uncertain. Nevertheless, with limited beaches in the Azores, mitigation measures are essential in curbing further beach erosion.

   With beaches not being the main tourist attraction in the Azores, it is important to evaluate the impact on other coastal recreational activities, which, in this case, might not be negatively impacted. According to an on-going survey of whale-watching companies in the Azores, marine species of tourist interest are more commonly spotted in the Azores waters over the last few years. The most exciting of all is the increase in frequency of whale sharks that were being spotted in the Azores during 2008 and 2009 (Fig. 9.2). Though this could be due to more

Fig. 9.2. Whale shark in the Azores. (From: Photograph taken by Nuno Sá.)

interest and observers of marine species now than before, it could also be due to change in migratory pattern as a result of a possible change in water conditions (Calado, 2009, unpublished research report on survey of whale-watching companies in the Azores).

Safety

The climate change could increase coastal storms, coastal erosion and land-slides. However, with appropriate mitigation measures in place such as coastal protection and setback rules on construction, tourist vulnerability along the coasts does not appear to be significantly increased.

Climate Change Policies

In 2008, Directive 2008/101/EC was adopted amending Directive 2003/87/EC to include aviation activities within the EU in the Emission Trading Scheme (ETS; EU, 2008). This law aims to promote the reduction of emissions in a cost-effective and economically-efficient manner. Each business operator receives an initial amount of allowance and may increase through market purchases (EU, 2008). This system will enter into force in 2012 for all flights to or from an aerodrome located in the territory of a Member State of the EU, with exceptions to flights that are with low take-off weight or for public service purposes (EU, 2008). In order to assess whether these policies are applicable or reasonable for the

Azores, the following areas need to be considered: (i) impact of climate change policies on tourism in the Azores; and (ii) current effort in combating climate change in the Azores.

Impact of climate change policies on tourism in the Azores

The ETS imposed on aviation activities will result in an increase in airfare with a more significant impact on the Azores than mainland Member States. It will aggravate the accessibility of tourists and diminish the economic potentialities of the Azores (Azores Regional Government, 2008). It should be noted that the sacrifice imposed upon the development of the Azores is proportionally much bigger, when compared to mainland regions and even island regions. This is very straining for the Azores and its growing tourism, and will place the Azores in a very disadvantageous position in comparison to other mainland territories. Thus, this policy is not in line with the EU's aim of achieving a cost-effective economically-efficient manner for the region.

Current effort in combating climate change in the Azores

It is very important to recognize that the Azores is an insignificant emitter of greenhouse effect (GHE) gases in a global context (Azores Regional Government, 2008). Additionally, it is essential to note that the Azores has invested a greater effort in developing and employing renewable energy than most developed territories in the EU and is in fact well ahead of the global objectives set by the EU for this area (Azores Regional Government, 2008). In 2001, the energy produced by its geothermal power plants contributed to approximately 19% of the total energy consumption in the Azores, while 5% was contributed by hydraulic power plants and 2% by eolic parks (ARENA, 2009). All Azorean islands have potential for eolic parks, and there are plans of installing more eolic parks to increase the current capacity. Other efforts include a private biomass power plant using pig manure to supply energy to pig farms, a pilot power plant using wave energy that is also a great potential for all islands, and the use of solar panels by individuals (ARENA, 2009). Also in preparation is the Green Islands Project (MIT-Portugal) with a specific goal of finding sustainable conditions that are required to change the energy trend to a 'green' path.

Conclusions and Recommendations

Climate change research in the Azores is at its initial stage. To date, there has not been enough research carried out on the impact of climate change on the Azores, let alone on tourism. Based on preliminary findings as discussed above, the most significant effects of climate change for coastal tourism in the Azores are freshwater shortage as a result of saltwater intrusion into its freshwater aquifer and reduction in coastal developments of resorts due to coastal erosion and landslide hazards.

However, the former issue could be mitigated by building reservoirs to collect rainwater as another source of water supply, or a more costly option of desalination. The latter, on the other hand, does not appear to have a very significant impact on tourism based on current evaluation.

Without doubt, the policies of climate change of the EU could be beneficial to combat global warming. However, being a remote, isolated and small island with great dependence on air transportation for its tourism, the resulting higher cost of airfares will have a significant impact on the Azores. The tourism growth strategy for this emerging sector greatly depends upon frequent air transportation with competitive prices. Accessibility is thus an indispensable element to maintain the attraction and competitiveness of the destination. As stated by CEC (2007), one of the recommended steps to improve cohesion for the ORs is to foster the competitiveness and sustainability of the tourism industry, in particular through support of sustainable management of destinations. Thus, a review of the function of Directive 2003/87/EC in relation to aviation activities is necessary and should take into account the structural dependence on aviation of territories that have no alternative means of transport, and therefore are highly dependent on air transports. This is especially important because this law imposes great economic impact specifically on the Azores where tourism has the potential to become a big contribution to its gross domestic product. The region cannot, therefore, be gravely impaired and discriminated in a vital sector for their development, when they have demonstrated greater effort than other more developed regions within EU in combating climate change, particularly in the emission of GHE gases and renewable energy (Azores Regional Government, 2008).

The Azores is not a disappearing destination based on current preliminary climate change impact assessment on coastal tourism. However, it is important to note that the main convenient mode of transportation to this remote archipelago is via air travel. The recent EU climate change policies will result in higher air travel cost. These policies would largely impede the growing tourism in the Azores unless they are adapted for the Azores by taking into consideration the following five main factors: current and projected climate change impact on the Azores; the contribution of the Azores to the global warming-based GHE emission; the greater effort than other developed Member States that the Azores has made in combating climate change with respect to being self-sufficient in energy; the accessibility issue, which explains the dependence on air travel; and the lacking competitiveness and economic repercussions for the Azores, which the EU is trying to improve.

More research needs to be carried out to understand better the predicted impact and corresponding mitigation strategies and implementations to combat climate change in the Azores. However, the EU climate change policies also need to be tailored to a local scale level in order for the Azores to remain competitive. Considering the difficult mobility and accessibility conditions of the Azores, which have no alternative to air transportation, there needs to be a special local-specific applicable system for the region. With no exclusion or compensation mechanism, the increase in transportation prices will greatly aggravate the accessibility conditions and tourist mobility in relation to the mainland and international countries, as well as inter-island. This will diminish the Azorean potential as a tourism destination, with negative repercussions on its economy (Azores Regional Government, 2008). Furthermore, the climate change policies can be foreseen to extend to maritime transportation, implying higher direct and indirect travel costs (Azores Regional Government, 2008). Hence, if these policies are not adapted, taking into account the above considerations, the Azores, though not a disappearing destination in terms of its touristic qualities based on preliminary climate change impact assessment, could however become a disappearing tourist destination due to undesirable travel cost as a result of climate change policies.

References

Abdel-Monem, A., Fernandez, L.A. and Boone, G.M. (1975) K/Ar ages from the eastern Azores group (Santa Maria, São Miguel and the Formigas Islands). *Lithos* 4, 247–254.

Agostinho, J. (1941) Clima dos Açores. *Açoreana* 2(4), 224–267 (in Portuguese).

Andrade, C., Trigo, R.M., Freitas, M.C., Gallego, M.C., Borges, P. and Ramos, A.M. (2008) Comparing historic records of storm frequency and the North Atlantic Oscillation (NAO) chronology for the Azores region. *The Holocene* 18(5), 745–754.

ARENA (2009) A utilização de recursos renováveis nos Açores e a produção de electercidade. http://arena.com.pt/er.html (Accessed: 12 September 2009).

ATA (2008) New marketing plan for the Azores – revenue and overnights in the second quarter of 2008. Associação de Turismo dos Açores, 20pp.

Azores Regional Government (2008) An assessment of 'Strategy for the Outermost Regions: Achievements and Future Prospects'. Regional Government, The Autonomous Region of the Azores.

Bacon, S. and Carter, D. (1991) Wave climate changes in the North Atlantic and the North Sea. *International Journal of Climatology* 11, 545–558.

Bettencourt, M.L. (1979) *O Clima de Portugal*. Instituto Nacional de Meteorologia e Geofísica, Portugal, XVIII, 103pp (in Portuguese).

Borges, J.F., Bezzeghoud, M., Buforn, E., Pro, C. and Fitas, A. (2007) The 1980, 1997 and 1998 Azores earthquakes and some seismo-tectonic implications. *Tectonophysics* 435, 37–54.

Borges, P. (2003) Ambientes litorais nos grupos Central e Oriental do arquipélago dos Açores, conteúdos e dinamîca de microescala. PhD thesis, University of Azores, 413pp (in Portuguese).

Borges, P., Andrade, C. and Freitas, C. (2002) Dune, bluff and beach erosion due to exhaustive sand mining – the case of Santa Bárbara, S. Miguel (Azores, Portugal). *Journal of Coastal Research* (Special Issue) 36, 89–95.

Bouws, E., Jannink, D. and Komen, G. (1996) The increasing wave height in the North Atlantic. *Bulletin of the American Meteorological Society* 77(10), 2275–2277.

Bruun, P. (1962) Sea-level rise as a cause of shore erosion. *Journal of Waterways Harbors Division* 88, 117–130.

Bruun, P. (1983) Review for conditions for uses of the Bruun Rule of erosion. *Coastal Engineering* 7, 77–89.

Calado, H., Borges, P., Phillips, M., Ng, K. and Alves, F. (2010) The Azores Archipelago, Portugal: Improved Understanding of Small Island Coastal Hazards and Mitigation Measures. *Natural Hazards* (in press).

CEC (2007) *Strategy for the Outermost Regions: Achievements and Future Prospects*. Communication from the Commission to the European Parliament, the Council, the European Economic and Social Committee and the Committee of the Regions. Communication from the European Communities, COM(2007) 507 Final, Brussels, 13pp.

Cruz, J. (2003) Groundwater and volcanoes: examples from the Azores archipelago. *Environmental Geology* 44, 343–355.

Cruz, J. and Silva, M. (2000) Groundwater salinization in Pico island (Azores, Portugal): origin and mechanisms. *Environmental Geology* 39(10), 1181–1189.

Cunha, A. (2003) The October 1997 landslides in San Miguel Island, Azores, Portugal. In: Javier, H. (ed.) Lessons learn from landslide disasters in Europe. *European Commission Joint Research Centre* 92, 27–32.

De Menezes, A., Moniz, A. and Vieira, J. (2008) The determinants of length of stay of tourists in the Azores. *Tourism Economics* 14(1), 205–222.

Douglas, B.C. (2001) An introduction to sea level. In: Douglas, B.C., Kearney, M.S. and Leatherman, S.P. (eds) *Sea Level Rise: History and Consequences*. Academic Press, San Diego, CA, 1–11.

DROTRH-INAG (2001) Plano regional da água. Relatório técnico. Versão para consulta pública. DROTRH-INAG, Ponta Delgada (in Portuguese).

EU (2008) Directive 2008/101/EC of the European parliament and of the council of 19 November 2008 amending Directive 2003/87/EC so as to include aviation activities in the scheme for greenhouse gas emission allowance trading within the Community. *Official Journal of European Union*.

Ferreira, D.B. (1980) *Contribution a l'étude des ventes et de l'humidité dans les Îles centrales de l'archipel des Açores*. Centro Estudos Geográficos, Lisbon (in French).

Fontiela, J. (2009) Human losses and damaged expected in future earthquakes in Faial Island – Azores; a contribution to risk mitigation. MSc thesis, University of the Azores, 106pp (in Portuguese).

Forjaz, V.H. (1983) Azores tectonic sketch, Ponta Delgada, Açores Centro de Vulcanologia INIC, 1 pp. Unpublished Technical Report (in Portuguese).

França, Z., Forjaz, V.H., Nunes, J.C., Cruz, J.V. and Borges, P. (2001) Pico (Azores) composite volcano – a model for explaining the migration of the summit vent. *Extended Abstract Book of the Workshop on the Geodynamics of the Western Part of Eurasia-Africa Plate Boundary (Azores–Tunisia)*. San Fernando, Spain, 2pp.

Gaspar, J.L. and Guest, J. (1998) The 31st October 1997 landslides at S. Miguel Island, Azores: a dramatic lesson for the future, Volcanic Hazard Assessment, Monitoring and Risk Mitigation. Advanced Study Course, European Commission, 43.

IPCC (2001) *Climate Change 2001: Impacts, Adaptations and Vulnerability*. Contribution of Working Group II to the Third Assessment Report. Intergovernmental Panel on Climate Change. Cambridge University Press, Cambridge UK and New York, USA.

Krause, D.C. and Watkins, N.D. (1970) North Atlantic crustal genesis in the vicinity of the Azores. *Geophysical Journal of the Royal Astronomical Society* 19, 261–283.

Laughton, A.S. and Whitmarsh, R.B. (1974) The Azores–Gibraltar plate boundary. In: Kristjansson, L. (ed.) *Geodynamics of Iceland and the North Atlantic Area*. Reidel Publishing Company, Dordrecht, 63–81.

Luis, J.F., Miranda, J.M., Galdeno, A., Patriat, P., Rossignol, J.C. and Victor, L.A.M. (1994) The Azores triple junction evolution since 10 Ma from an aeromagnetic survey of the mid-Atlantic ridge. *Earth and Planetary Science Letters* 125, 439–459.

Malheiro, A. (2006) Geological hazards in the Azores archipelago: volcanic terrain instability and human vulnerability. *Journal of Volcanology and Geothermal Research* 156, 158–171.

Marques, R., Zêzere, J., Trigo, R., Gaspar, J. and Trigo, I. (2008) Rainfall patterns and critical values associated with landslides in Povoacão County (São Miguel Island, Azores): relationships with the North Atlantic Oscillation. *Hydrological Processes* 22, 478–494.

Miranda, P.M.A., Valente, M.A., Tomé, A.R., Trigo, R., Coelho, M.F., Aguiar, A. and Azevedo, E.B. (2006) O clima de Portugal nos séculos XX e XXI. In: Santos, F.D. and Miranda, P.M.A. (eds) *Alterações climáticas em Portugal: cenários, impactos e medidas de adaptação (Projecto SIAM II)*. Gradiva, Lisbon, pp.47–113 (in Portuguese).

Needham, H.D. and Francheteau, J. (1974) Some characteristics of the rift valley in the Atlantic ocean near 3648' north. *Earth and Planetary Science Letters* 22, 29–43.

PSMSL (2002) Sea Level Data. Proudman Oceanographic Laboratory, Birkenhead, UK. www.pol.ac.uk/psmsl/psmsl_individual_stations.html (Accessed: 25 November 2002).

Raposo, A.G.B. (1998) Os desabamentos na bacia hidrográfica da Ribeira Quente e sua freguesia, na madrugada de 31 de Outubro de 1997. *Açoreana* 8(4), 571–590 (in Portuguese).

Santos, F.D., Valente, M.A., Miranda, P.M.A., Aguiar, A., Azevedo, E.B., Tomé, A.R. and Coelho, F. (2004) Climate change scenarios in the Azores and Madeira Islands. *World Resource Review* 16(4), 473–491.

Searle, R. (1980) Tectonic pattern of the Azores spreading center and triple junction. *Earth and Planetary Science Letters* 51, 415–434.

Smith, W.H.F. and Sandwell, D.T. (1997) Global seafloor topography from satellite altimetry and ship depth soundings. *Science* 277, 195–196.

SREA (2009) Serviço Regional de Estatísticas dos Açores. www.srea.ine.pt (Accessed: 8 September 2009).

Sunamura, T. (1992) *Geomorphology of Rocky Coasts*. Wiley, Chichester, UK, 302pp.

Valadão, P., Gaspar, J.L., Queiroz, G. and Ferreira, T. (2002) Landslides density map of S. Miguel Island, Azores archipelago. *Natural Hazards and Earth System Sciences* 2, 51–56.

10 Climate Change and Coastal Tourism in Ireland

J.A.G. COOPER AND S.W. BOYD

Introduction

This chapter assesses coastal tourism for the whole island of Ireland (Republic of Ireland and Northern Ireland), addressing first the context in which tourism occurs, the nature of visitor flows and change, the mix of visitor attraction and the position coastal tourism attractions and beaches play in overall visitor choice, and the economic benefits of tourism. Coastal regions as tourist space are discussed. Present climate and future changes are discussed and the effect of such changes on coastal regions and tourism products is assessed.

Tourism in the Republic of Ireland and Northern Ireland

The history against which tourism has developed in the Republic of Ireland and Northern Ireland is one of contrast. The former has always enjoyed the required antecedents for tourism to develop (an attractive, safe environment and accessible environment), whereas the latter has suffered from a negative image of a dangerous environment where 30 years of civil unrest has made it difficult to perceive the destination as having potential for out-of-state visitors; only in the past decade have tourist numbers grown substantially to the extent that at present numbers visiting Northern Ireland are double those recorded in the mid-1960s. In 2008, 7.4 million visitors came to the Republic of Ireland, compared to 2.1 million to Northern Ireland, where the industry is worth €6.3 billion and £573 million, respectively (Fáilte Ireland, 2009a; Northern Ireland Tourist Board (NITB), 2009). When direct and indirect spending is accounted for, tourism directly accounts for 30,000 jobs in Northern Ireland and 90,000 in the Republic of Ireland. In terms of Gross National Product, tourism in the Republic of Ireland is worth 2.3% of total expenditure in the economy and 5.2% of the overall labour force, whereas in Northern Ireland it accounts for 3.7% of Gross Value Added

(CogentSI, 2007; Fáilte Ireland, 2009a). 'Marine tourism and leisure' in the Republic of Ireland was valued at €709 million per annum between 1999 and 2003 (Douglas-Westwood, 2005).

Visitor Flows and Principal Attractions

Tourism statistics in 2008 for both regions of the island reveal a distinctive pattern of purpose of visit. The majority of visitors to the Republic of Ireland come for a holiday (48%), followed by visiting friends and relatives (VFR) (30%), with business accounting for 15% of all visits (Fáilte Ireland, 2009a). In contrast, the majority of visits to Northern Ireland are to visit friends and relatives (45%), followed by holiday (24%) and then business (23%) (NITB, 2009). The latter region has always had a higher proportion of VFR visitors where 'holiday' was not the main purpose, though this position is starting to be reversed as it is now the second main reason, albeit only slightly more important than 'business' visits. Only the Republic of Ireland statistics record the main activities that visitors engage in. These are hiking and walking (53%), followed by golf (14.5%), angling (14.5%), cycling (12.4%) and equestrian (5%). Northern Ireland Tourist Board has identified key markets that they term 'winning themes'. The activity tourism market, which is what the above statistics reflect, is one of these themes, along with city breaks, culture and heritage, business, and excellent events.

A cursory glance of what attractions receive the most visitors (Table 10.1) reveals that the top attractions are mostly found in coastal regions, particularly in Dublin, counties Clare and Cork in the case of the Republic of Ireland, and Belfast and the North Coast, for Northern Ireland (Fig. 10.1). It is not surprising that Dublin and Belfast receive the most visitors to Ireland overall, recording 5.7 million (of which 4.4 million are overseas visitors) and 2.2 million (of which 1.6 million are overnight visits), respectively (Fáilte Ireland, 2008a; www.belfastcity. gov.uk

Table 10.1 also reveals that while many of the top visitor attractions are found in coastal cities (Belfast and Dublin), few are natural heritage attractions located in coastal regions. Instead, the focus is with heritage and cultural visitor centres and recreation/entertainment spaces. Those attractions that are directly located on the coastline are the Giant's Causeway, County Antrim, a World Heritage Site inscribed in 1986, Carrick-a-Rede Rope Bridge, County Antrim and the Cliffs of Moher, County Clare. Statistics are not collected on visitor numbers to beaches in the Republic of Ireland and visitor numbers exist only for those beaches in Northern Ireland that are under National Trust ownership. Of these, Portstewart Strand beach was last ranked in the top ten visitor attractions in 2000 (rank no. 8) with over 140,000 recorded visitors. Much higher numbers are claimed for many urban beaches; Crawfordsburn County Park near Belfast has 600,000 visitors annually to its beaches, most of whom are local residents walking dogs and exercising.

Unfortunately, the statistics fail to link activities that visitors engage in with where these engagements occur. It is reasonable to assume that a considerable proportion of hiking and walking and golf takes place along the coastlines of

Table 10.1.   Top ten visitor attractions in Northern Ireland and the Republic of Ireland, 2007.

NI attraction	Visitor numbers (2007)	RoI attraction	Visitor numbers (2007)
Giant's Causeway Visitor Centre (North Coast)	712,714	Guinness Storehouse (Dublin)	946,577
Belfast Zoo (Belfast)	294,935	Cliffs of Moher Visitor Experience (Clare)	940,455
W5 Science Museum (Belfast)	247,506	Dublin Zoo	900,005
Carrick-a-Rede Rope Bridge (North Coast)	222,613	National Gallery of Ireland (Dublin)	740,407
Oxford Island Nature Reserve	216,713	Book of Kells (Dublin)	567,632
Historic Walls of Derry	213,415	National Aquatic Centre (Dublin)	565,085
Belfast Lough RSPB Reserve	210,000	Irish Museum of Modern Art (Dublin)	485,000
Belleek Pottery	171,569	National Museum of Ireland – Archaeology (Dublin)	407,202
Ulster Folk and Transport Museum (Belfast)	168,866	Blarney Castle (Cork)	401,567
Ulster American Folk Park	157,325	St Patrick's Cathedral (Dublin)	388,559

From: NITB, 2008a; Fáilte Ireland, 2008b.

both the Republic of Ireland and Northern Ireland. The main activities listed by Nairn (2005) on the Irish coast are surfing, sailing, windsurfing, scuba diving, sea kayaking, sea and shore angling, birdwatching, whale and dolphin watching, seal watching, coastal walks and rock climbing.

The product portfolio for the Republic of Ireland focuses on scenery, culture, heritage and friendly and hospitable people, and sells the Irish experience by encouraging visitors to explore an 'Island of unique character and characters'. This is supported by the 2008 visitor attitudes survey, which reiterates Ireland's strong performance as a destination that stands out for the beauty of its scenery and friendliness and hospitality of its people. These two factors remain the most prominent positive discriminators for Ireland compared with other holiday destinations (Fáilte Ireland, 2009b). In Northern Ireland, visitors are invited to 'experience our awakening' and 'uncover our stories', where the product portfolio comprises four segments, namely cities (attractions, shopping, nightlife, Titanic, Walled City, festivals, events and public realm), culture and heritage (living culture, heritage, the arts, St Patrick/Christian Heritage), sports tourism activities and waterways (golf, soft adventure, walking, cycling and water-based activities), and business tourism (association, corporate/incentive) (NITB, 2008b).

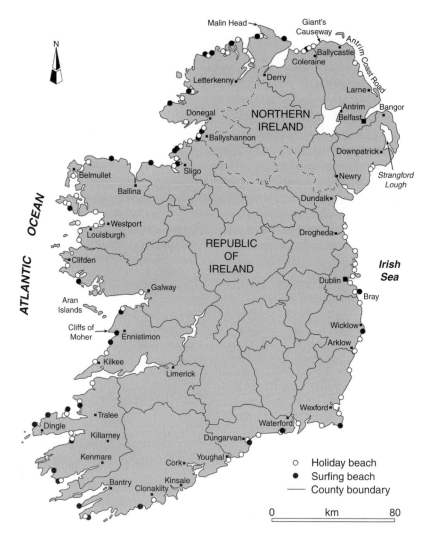

Fig. 10.1. Map of Ireland, showing main surfing and holiday beaches and localities referred to in the text (after Nairn, 2005).

Coastal Regions as Tourist Spaces

Given the product portfolio, the coastal regions around the island play an integral role in meeting visitor expectations of beautiful scenery and the opportunity to engage in sports tourism and water-based activities. For instance, the Causeway Coastal Route in Northern Ireland takes the visitor around the North Coast, linking the three Signature Projects (projects that offer international standout) of The Walled City of Londonderry/Derry, the Giant's Causeway World Heritage

Site and the Titanic/Maritime quarter of Belfast. The route was described by Jacob's Creek in 2008 as one of the top touring routes in the world.

Ireland has some stunningly beautiful beaches, both urban and rural, along its 7500 km coast (Fig. 10.1). It is, however, important to make the distinction between urban and rural beaches. The former (Fig. 10.2) are linked to seaside resorts that have a long history of resort development stemming back to the late 1800s/early 1900s (e.g. Bundoran, County Donegal, Portrush, County Antrim, Newcastle, County Down and Bray, County Wicklow), where the beach surroundings have been modified with urban seawalls, promenades running parallel to the coastline, and visitor accommodation has been built in close proximity to the beach or overlooking it. In contrast, the vast majority of beaches around Ireland are rural in character, with little modification, and the virtual absence of a built environment designed to accommodate visitors (Fig. 10.3). In recent years, authorities have sought to achieve certain award status for beaches (e.g. Blue Flag) and stretches of coastline (e.g. Green Coast). Blue Flag status is awarded to beaches for their cleanliness, water quality, safety and level of environmental protection (www.blueflag.org). In contrast, the more recent Green Coast award is made to more rural beaches that are recognized for their natural unspoilt beauty, water quality and cleanliness (www.tidynorthernireland.org). In 2009, 75 Blue Flags and 40 national Green Coast awards were made in the Republic of Ireland (Table 10.2). In Northern Ireland there were six Blue Flag beaches, four Green Coast awards and ten Seaside Award beaches (Table 10.3).

Fig. 10.2. Facilities at Portrush are typical of urban seaside resorts.

Fig. 10.3.   Kinnego Bay, County Donegal, is typical of the scenic attraction of Ireland's many undeveloped rural beaches.

Table 10.2.   Blue Flag beaches by county in the Republic of Ireland in 2009 (From: www.antaisce.ie).

Region	Number
Louth	3
Dublin	1
Wicklow	3
Waterford	2
Wexford	4
Cork	8
Kerry	12
Clare	8
Galway	8
Mayo	13
Sligo	1
Donegal	12

   While there are no formal statistics recorded on the levels of domestic visitor numbers to Ireland's coastline, domestic visitors are as important as out-of-state visitors to the economic life of Ireland's resort communities. Over the past decade, there has been considerable change to the mix of accommodation available with

Table 10.3. Blue Flag, Green Coast and Seaside Awards for Northern Ireland in 2009 (From: www.tidynorthernireland.org).

Name of beach	County
(a) Blue Flag beaches	
Magilligan, Benone Strand	Londonderry
Cranfield Bay	Down
Portstewart	Londonderry
Murlough	Down
Portrush, Whiterocks	Antrim
Tyrella	Down
(b) Green Coasts	
Cranfield Bay	Down
Murlough	Down
Tyrella	Down
Helen's Bay	Down
(c) Seaside Award beaches	
Downhill (R)	Londonderry
Portrush West (R)	Antrim
Portrush East (R)	Antrim
Portstewart Strand (R)	Antrim
Carnlough (r)	Antrim
Ballygally (r)	Antrim
Millisle (r)	Down
Cranfield Bay (R)	Down
Murlough (R)	Down
Tyrella (R)	Down

R, resort; r, rural.

the decline of guest houses and Bed and Breakfast establishments and the rise of second homes along the coastline (Fig. 10.4) and within the resort communities of the North Coast to the extent that in some resorts second-home ownership comprises between 33 and 65% of all housing stock (Boyd, 2006). This has had many unforeseen social implications (Cooper and McKenna, 2009a). Many resorts throughout Ireland have recently undergone redevelopment in an attempt to move away from stagnation and avoid the decline stage of the Butler resort model (Butler, 1980). At the West Strand region of Portrush the local Borough Council has embarked on a strategy to rejuvenate the once recognized jewel of the North Coast region by redevelopment of tourism infrastructure that is juxtaposed to the beach and the resort's harbour. New accommodation is being considered along with a range of water-based, recreation and entertainment facilities back from the beach itself (GVA Grimley Associates, 2007).

Fig. 10.4.   Second-home development at Culdaff typified the development boom of the early 2000s on the Irish coast. During this phase many traditional homes, hotels and businesses were converted to apartments and additional new builds proliferated at the coast.

The Climate of Ireland in Relation to Tourism

A number of studies have shown a strong link between tourism and climate (e.g. Mieczkowski, 1985; Lise and Tol, 2002). Tourism is, however, influenced by many other aspects of the destination such as cultural, landscape and historical attributes, recreational opportunities and family ties. Factors such as cost, proximity, ease of access and language also influence choice of destination.

Ireland's climate is influenced mainly by its position as an island on the margin of the Atlantic Ocean (Rohan, 1986). It is warmed by the north-flowing North Atlantic Drift and its maritime climate is characterized by high levels of rainfall, strong winds and low hours of sunlight. The west coast has high wave energy that diminishes rapidly into the Irish Sea around both north and south coasts. Off the west coast the average wave height is 2.5–3 m, whereas on the east coast it is 0.5 m or less.

The following characteristics of Ireland's climate derive from the Irish Meteorological Service (www.met.ie/climate/climate-of-ireland.asp). Average annual temperature is about 9°C. In the east, summer mean daily maximum is about 19°C and winter mean daily minimum is about 2.5°C. The mean daily maximum temperature at coastal stations of Valentia (west coast) and Dublin (east coast), in the warmest month (July), is between 12 and 19°C. Air temperature falls below zero on only about 10 days per year at the coast, compared to about 40 days per year inland. Ireland normally experiences only between 1400 and 1700 h of sunshine annually and on about 50% of days there is 100% cloud cover.

The west and north-west coasts of Ireland are renowned as the windiest places in Europe. At Malin Head, gales are recorded on more than 50 days each year on average. Only between 0.8 and 3.3% of the time are calm conditions recorded at the coast compared to up to 9% inland. Mean annual wind speed ranges from 7 m/s in the north-west to 4 m/s in the east midlands.

Rainfall is normally associated with Atlantic low pressure systems and there is consequently a strong rainfall gradient (around 1000–1250 mm/year in the west to 750–1000 mm/year in the east). The south-east coast has only around 150 days per year of rain (>1 mm), compared to 225 in the west. Although rain is common, it is not particularly intense; average hourly rainfall amounts in Ireland usually range from 1 to 2 mm. High rainfall intensity (15 to 20 mm/h) has a recurrence interval of about 5 years. Rainfall is highest in winter and lowest in early summer; April is the driest month in most of Ireland, except in the south, where June holds that distinction.

Ireland's seawater is 7° to 8°C warmer than the average global sea temperature at such latitudes. Surface water temperatures at Malin Head in 2008 ranged from a low of 7.9°C in February to a high of 15.1°C in August. Average February sea temperatures vary from 10°C in the south-west to <7°C in the north-east, while August temperatures range from 16°C in the south to 13°C in the north-east.

In terms of its role in tourism, climate contributes largely to the landscape character of Ireland and also its resulting culture. It is also an important factor in limiting some outdoor recreational activities (e.g. sea bathing) and promoting others (e.g. surfing). The weather on any given day plays an important role in tourist behaviour and selection of visitor sites (Fahy *et al.*, 2005). It is, however, probably true to say that Irish tourism exists in spite of its climate and weather conditions.

Climate Change and the Irish Coast

Several historical records and other indicators provide historical evidence of climate change in Ireland. These records are of variable length and are unevenly scattered geographically, however, collectively they provide an impression of the main changes that have been occurring in Ireland historically. Since the 1980s there has been a general warming trend of 0.3–0.7°C per decade in Irish waters (Dunne *et al.*, 2009). On land, Sweeney *et al.* (2003) noted a mean annual temperature increase of 0.5°C during the 20th century, with a more rapid rise in the 1990s. Significant decreases in frost frequency and increases in 'hot day' frequencies also occurred during this time and substantial increases in winter precipitation occurred in the north-west with a decrease in summer rainfall in the south-east (Sweeney *et al.*, 2003).

Climate change in Ireland has been the subject of several recent reports (e.g. Sweeney *et al.*, 2002, 2003; Dunne *et al.*, 2009) and its implications for the marine environment specifically were considered by Boelens *et al.* (2005) who noted that:

- Land temperatures will increase by up to 1.5°C in winter and 2.0°C in summer by 2055;
- Average winter rainfall will increase by 10% by 2055 while summer rainfall will fall by 10% to 40% in summer;
- An increase in sea levels similar to the global mean prediction of 0.49±0.08 m by the end of the century; and
- An increase in the number of extreme events (e.g. more intense storms, hotter summers).

Dunne *et al.* (2009) presented the following scenarios on the basis of a suite of models of global atmospheric circulation, ocean surge and wave climate:

- Temperature increases of 3–4°C towards the end of the century;
- Increase in autumn and winter rainfall by 15–25% towards the end of the century;
- Summers to become drier by 10–18%;
- No change in mean wind speeds over the coming decades, but an overall reduction by 4–5% towards the end of the century;
- Increased frequency of very intense cyclones;
- Sea water warming of 0.3–0.4°C per decade in the Atlantic and 0.6–0.7°C per decade in the Irish Sea;
- Increased frequency of storm surge events;
- Extreme wave heights to increase in most regions.

The effect of global sea level rise at the coast is expressed as relative sea level change (the relationship between land and sea) and this is markedly variable around Ireland because of the underlying effect of land uplift. In the north, relative sea levels have changed little in the past 50 years (Orford *et al.*, 2006) because land uplift has approximately equalled sea level rise, whereas in the south they have increased at rates similar to the global average (Devoy, 2008). Recent projections (Orford *et al.*, 2007) suggest sea levels will rise around the entire island during the next few decades as global sea level rise begins to exceed rates of land uplift.

Climate Change and Irish Coastal Tourism

Climate change not only affects human activity directly through temperature, rainfall and wind, but also indirectly through changes in the natural landscape, its morphology, habitats and species, driven mainly by changes in sea level and wave conditions. These indirect impacts arise through coastal erosion and accretion and flooding. The response by humans to perceived impacts can also have profound implications for the environment and human activities (Cooper, 2009).

Increased air and water temperatures, reduced rainfall and wind are likely to improve the conditions for outdoor activities in Ireland. Using the Tourism

Climatic Index (TCI; Mieczkowski, 1985), Amelung and Viner (2006) suggest that north-west Europe may develop a more favourable climate than Mediterranean destinations leading to increases in home holidays. Ireland could attain 2–4 'very good months' by the end of the century (it currently has none) (Nicholls and Amelung, 2008). Since visitor numbers are strongly correlated with daily temperature (Viner and Agnew, 1999), this will probably increase visitor numbers to the coast. While this might be regarded as good for the tourism economy, it creates some issues. Since most visitors use a car to travel to the coast, the current carrying capacity as determined by car parking availability and road traffic volumes might be exceeded. Traffic is currently an issue at some rural Irish beaches and resorts in summer. Rossnowlagh, County Donegal, for example, has an emergency traffic management scheme for such occasions (Cooper and McKenna, 2009b). Large numbers of pedestrians can also cause serious erosion problems on dunes as documented at Brittas Bay, County Wicklow by Quinn (1977) and this can require control measures to be put in place. Increases in numbers can also increase pressure for good quality environments and enhanced facilities (Phillips and Jones, 2006).

Coasts respond to increased wave height and sea level rise by changes in shape and position. The most common manifestations of this change are coastal erosion and flooding in low-lying areas. In Ireland, this will simply exacerbate trends that are already evident in the south, but lead to a complete change in the north where sea levels have been stable historically and coastal erosion has not been a major issue. Structures on or near the shore will be at risk from such coastal changes but the geological record shows that in general terms, coastal depositional systems (beaches, tidal flats, marshes) continue to exist but tend to move upwards and landwards as sea level rises.

With accelerated sea level rise cliffs may erode at faster rates and shore platforms will become more active than during the recent past. Increasing contrasts between dry and wet periods and increased storm intensity are likely to contribute to enhanced cliff instability. At the Giant's Causeway, the rise in sea level may mean that access to parts of the site becomes more difficult as extreme water levels occur more frequently. Cliff paths may become more difficult to maintain in the face of more instability (Orford *et al.*, 2007).

Many of the most iconic cultural sites on the Irish coast are historical defensive sites such as Dun Aengus, County Galway or Dunluce Castle, County Antrim. Built on cliff-top locations, these sites are prone to periodic erosion. The increased frequency of cliff erosion will probably make this more of a management issue in the future. An indication of the importance of such sites is that in County Londonderry the Mussenden Temple, an iconic 18th-century building on the cliff top, was protected by strengthening of the surrounding cliff edge.

When cliff recession threatens infrastructure, management problems can arise. The main access road to the Dingle peninsula is heavily utilized by tourist traffic during the peak season from June to September. Erosion of sea cliffs caused part of the road to collapse in April 2007. This threatened the entire Dingle tourism industry and a rapid intervention by Kerry County Council (at a cost of €4 million) was necessary to stabilize the cliff and rebuild the road (O'Connor *et al.*, 2009). At a smaller scale, access to several (mainly holiday) homes was cut by coastal erosion of an access road built on a soft dune cliff at Kilmichael, County Wexford in December 2007 (Cooper and McKenna, 2008). Popular tourist drives, such as the Antrim Coast Road, are likely to require more frequent maintenance and even capital upgrades in the face of increased erosion threats from sea level rise. The same issues pertain to many access roads and railway lines in Ireland that follow the coastline. The east coast railway line has had to be defended against erosion because of its coastal location. Occasional blockage of roads and railway lines by rockfalls and landslides may increase in frequency with the projected changes in precipitation and greater contrasts between wet and dry periods.

Beaches respond much more rapidly to changed environmental conditions than rock coasts. Ireland's beaches are overwhelmingly rural in nature and, left to themselves, they can adjust readily to changes in sea level by changing their morphology. There is, however, an aversion in Ireland to such entirely natural behaviour and many beaches and dunes have been damaged by rock armour and seawalls. Indicative of the public perception is a statement by a government Minister that 'Ireland must continue to protect our coastline, sections of which are constantly under threat from erosion. Being an island community, our coastline is one of our most important natural resources and is of particular importance to our tourism industry. The coastal protection programme aims to construct works that slow or even halt erosion in places where the coastline is at its most vulnerable' (www.agriculture.gov.ie/press/pressreleases/2008/april/title,13657,en.html). Similarly, an MEP stated 'The ongoing erosion at Lisfannon threatens the future of Inishowen's most popular beaches, as the Council's recent efforts have failed to stop erosion at the beach it is time to look at the possibility of creating a permanent erosion prevention structure' (www.jimhiggins.ie/html/press_current. html). These sentiments illustrate one of the major misconceptions highlighted by Cooper and McKenna (2008) regarding the meaning of coastal protection. In these statements, 'protection' means only protection of land and infrastructure. In many cases this unfortunately also means degradation or destruction of the natural coastal system, particularly beaches. Clearly, degradation is not beneficial to many aspects of tourism, which data show to be reliant on a high quality environment and scenic beauty.

Links-type golf courses are major offenders here (Fig. 10.5), but caravan parks (Fig. 10.6) and, worse still, houses built in ill-advised locations (Fig. 10.7) have all been defended even when the erosion is purely a seasonal or episodic response to storms and when the infrastructure is poorly sited. Under a rising sea level coastal defences cut off the sediment supply to the beach causing it to narrow and even disappear altogether. Similar effects can be produced by efforts to halt erosion of the cliffs, which cuts off the supply of sediment to some beaches and leads to their demise.

It is a particular challenge in Ireland to maintain the coastal scenery and maintain the coastal resilience by not armouring and finding alternative approaches, such as the proactive one of not permitting building in high risk zones and the responsive one of relocating threatened infrastructure. The human response to coastal erosion is therefore critical in influencing its effect on future tourism.

Fig. 10.5. Rock armouring of a dune to protect a golf course at Portrush.

Fig. 10.6. Informal armouring of the coast at a caravan site creates an unsightly landscape.

Fig. 10.7. Walls built to defend private homes degrade the beach environment. Millisle, County Down.

On Ireland's resort beaches the choices are more difficult, because many beaches have been backed by seawalls and promenades for more than a century (Fig. 10.8) and this infrastructure, plus the buildings and infrastructure behind it, have become an integral part of the tourism landscape. The 'bucket and spade, ice cream and arcade entertainment spaces' experience still holds resonance with a large sector of the population; any physical changes that climate change may bring to these environments will not lessen the demand for this type of product. The narrowing and loss of beaches in front of such seawalls (Taylor *et al.*, 2004), however, leads to loss of recreational space accompanied by loss of environmental quality. There has been significant historical loss of beach area at Bray, County Wicklow and Portrush, County Antrim, both of which have seawalls and promenades at the rear of the beach. To maintain the resource in such instances will precipitate several choices, all involving expenditure. With increased sea level and storminess, seawalls themselves will come under increasing wave attack requiring maintenance and even enlargement. To maintain the beach requires either that the seawall be shifted landward or removed (a difficult choice given the infrastructure that is typically located behind such structures), or that the beach be artificially nourished with sand brought in from an external source. This is common practice in other parts of the world, but in Ireland has been limited to only a few undertakings at Rosslare, Courtown and Cahore (all in County Wexford). Beach nourishment is an expensive activity that replaces sand or gravel being removed by wave action. Nourishment requires an open-ended

Fig. 10.8.   A seawall and promenade at Portrush prevents adjustment of the
beach and has degraded the natural beach resource. It provides amenities for the
traditional Irish seaside resort experience.

commitment if the beach is to be maintained and is usually confined to resorts
whose economic situation depends on maintenance of the beach. In many cases
it is a response to human-induced erosion. Worryingly, nourishment was also proposed proactively as a remedial action to counter the effects of erosion that would
be caused by the construction of a marina at Greystones, County Wicklow.

Sea level rise in estuaries in particular has implications for the habitats that
occur there. Some of the most important birdwatching sites in Ireland are associated with tidal flats and saltmarshes in estuaries (e.g. the RSPB bird reserve in
Belfast, North Bull Island, Dublin, Shannon Estuary, Strangford Lough). Left to
themselves, these environments tend to evolve under rising sea levels by extending landward. Unfortunately, the shorelines of many estuaries are now armoured.
Most of central Dublin and central Belfast is built on formerly intertidal land that
was progressively reclaimed (Fig. 10.9). This land thus needs to be defended
against flooding. With rising sea level, the defences themselves face increased
risk of overtopping, which means that they are likely to require capital upgrading
or enhanced maintenance in the future. Many of Ireland's coastal cities (Cork,
Dublin, Belfast) experience episodic problems with flooding. A storm surge in the
Irish Sea in February 2002 led to the highest water levels recorded in Dublin
since 1923. The water level was about 50 cm above the highest water level experienced each year in the Port. That storm caused damage throughout the Irish
Sea with flooding from Dublin to Belfast and the collapse of the seawall in front

Fig. 10.9. Central Dublin and its port is built largely on reclaimed intertidal land that is at increased risk of flooding under rising sea levels.

of the Slieve Donard Hotel in Newcastle, County Down. Insurance losses in Ireland amounted to €37 million. A rise in sea level of 50 cm would mean that the 2002 extreme water levels would be reached almost every year (Cooper, 2009). The scale of losses sustained in 2002 could clearly not be withstood at this frequency and the most probable response in urban areas is likely to be improved defences. In some cases, such as Belfast, tidal barrages built to reduce flood risk have become tourism attractions in themselves. The Belfast system is interpreted in the Lagan Lookout Centre. In less developed areas, other options may prove both economically and environmentally more appropriate.

In highly developed urban settings the only short-term option for coping with sea level rise is likely to be to continue defending the shorelines. This means that tidal flats and saltmarshes will reduce in area or even be squeezed out altogether. At sites with less development, other options exist that might permit intertidal habitats to evolve. A number of sites have already experienced collapse of sea defences as it has become uneconomic to maintain them. Near Rathmullan, County Donegal, for example, a formerly reclaimed agricultural area has been flooded by the sea since the earth embankments were breached and not repaired. The fields are now reverting to saltmarsh.

In Strangford Lough, a mainly rural area in County Down, a 1 m sea level rise could cause the loss of 50% of the intertidal area (Orford *et al.*, 2007). At this site up to 60,000 wildfowl and wading birds (including 75% of the world population of Light-bellied Brent Geese) congregate in winter where they feed on the resources provided by the tidal flats. Management options include accepting the loss, creating compensatory habitat elsewhere, removing the sea defences and permitting the habitats to migrate. All such options have important consequences for the natural habitats and associated tourism activity. There are potential additional linked impacts of habitat loss for tourism activities. Loss of habitat affects the entire ecosystem and has implications for angling species as well as bait organisms (much bait digging is done on intertidal flats).

The retreat or coastal realignment option has the potential to enable coastal systems to operate naturally and maintain high quality coastal landscapes. The landward removal of tourism infrastructure and historic buildings has also been considered elsewhere. Such options, however, are not currently supported by current practice or public opinion in Ireland. The fact that Ireland has had one of the highest rates of coastal development of any EU country between 1990 and 2000 (EEA, 2006) is inevitably going to lead to increased future calls for 'protection' of property and consequent environmental degradation under existing practices. The long term implications of this approach for tourism in Ireland (outside major cities and a few resorts) are likely to be highly damaging.

References

Amelung, B. and Viner, D. (2006) The sustainability of tourism in the Mediterranean: Exploring the future with the Tourism Climatic Index. *Journal of Sustainable Tourism* 14, 349–366.

Boelens, R., Minchin, D. and O'Sullivan, G. (2005) Climate Change: Implications for Ireland's Marine Environment and Resources. Marine Foresight, Series 2. www.marine.ie/NR/rdonlyres/113A2AB9-1A83-4E91-B256-A3BDE5DE19D1/0/ClimateChangeImplications.pdf (Accessed: 12 July 2009).

Boyd, S.W. (2006) Second Homes and Tourism Development on Northern Ireland's North Coast: Social Benefit, Social Cost. Paper presented at the IGU regional conference, Queensland University of Technology, Brisbane, 3–7 July.

Butler, R.W. (1980) The concept of a tourist area cycle of evolution: implications for management of resources. *Canadian Geographer* 24(1), 5–12.

Carter, R.W.G. (1988) *Coastal Environments*. Academic Press, London.

CogentSI (2007) Tourism in the Northern Ireland Economy. Report commissioned by Department of Trade Investment and Enterprise (DETI) and NITB.

Cooper, J.A.G. (2009) Coastal economies and people. In: Baxter, J.M., Buckley, P.J. and Frost, M.T. (eds) Marine Climate Change Ecosystem Linkages Report Card 2009. Online science reviews, 18pp. www.mccip.org.uk/elr/coasts (Accessed: 12 July 2009).

Cooper, J.A.G. and McKenna, J. (2008) Working with natural processes: the challenge for Coastal Protection Strategies. *Geographical Journal* 174, 315–331.

Cooper, J.A.G. and McKenna, J. (2009a) Boom and bust: the influence of macroscale economics on the world's coast. *Journal of Coastal Research* 25, 533–538.

Cooper, J.A.G. and McKenna, J. (2009b) Managing cars on beaches: a case study from Ireland. In: Williams, A.T. and Micallef, A. (eds) *Beach Management*. Earthscan, London, pp. 136–146.

Devoy, R. (2008) Coastal vulnerability and the implications of sea-level rise for Ireland. *Journal of Coastal Research* 2, 325–341.

Douglas-Westwood Limited (2005) Marine industries global market analysis. *Marine Foresight Series, 1*. Marine Institute, Ireland.

Dunne, S., Hanafin, J., Lynch, P., McGrath, R., Nishimura, E., Nolan, P., Ratnam, J.V., Semmler, T., Sweeney, C., Varghese, S. and Wang, S. (2009) Ireland in a Warmer World – Scientific Predictions of the Irish Climate in the Twenty-First Century (2001-CD-C4-M2) STRIVE Report, Environmental Protection Agency, Dublin, www.epa.ie/downloads/pubs/research/climate/STRIVE_27_Dunne_C4I_web.pdf (Accessed: 12 July 2009).

EEA (European Environment Agency) (2006) The changing faces of Europe's coastal areas. *EEA Report 6/2006*. EEA, Copenhagen.

Fahy, G., Griffin, J., Henry, D., Jones, M., Kelly, D., Kennedy, A., Lane, L., Smith, R. and Wolchover, S. (2005) *Climate Change and the Visitor Economy of the Sefton Coast*. School of Planning and Landscape, University of Manchester, UK.

Fáilte Ireland (2008a) *Dublin Visitor Statistics 2003–2007*. Fáilte Ireland.

Fáilte Ireland (2008b) *Visitor Attractions Statistics 2003–2007*. Fáilte Ireland.

Fáilte Ireland (2009a) *Tourism Facts 2008*. Fáilte Ireland.

Fáilte Ireland (2009b) *2008 Visitor Attitude Survey*. Fáilte Ireland.

GVA Grimley Associates (2007) Portrush Regeneration Strategy West Strand Region. Report produced for Portrush Regeneration Group, Coleraine Borough Council.

Lise, W. and Tol, R.S.G. (2002) Impact of climate on tourist demand. *Climatic Change* 55, 429–449.

Mieczkowski, Z. (1985) The Tourism Climatic Index: a method of evaluating world climates for tourism. *Canadian Geographer* 29, 220–233.

Nairn, R. (2005) *Ireland's Coastline*. The Collins Press, Dublin.

Nicholls, S. and Amelung, B. (2008) Climate change and tourism in north-western Europe. *Tourism Analysis* 13, 21–31.

NITB (2008a) *Tourism Facts 2007*. Northern Ireland Tourist Board.

NITB (2008b) *Planning Our Route to Success: NITB Corporate Plan 2008–2011*. Northern Ireland Tourist Board.

NITB (2009) *Northern Ireland Visitor Tourism Figures (Jan–Dec 2008)*. Northern Ireland Tourist Board.

O'Connor, M.C., Lymbery, G., Cooper, J.A.G., Gault, J. and McKenna, J. (2009) Practice versus policy-led coastal defence management. *Marine Policy* 33(6), 923–929.

Orford, J.D., Murdy, J. and Freel, R. (2006) Developing constraints on the relative sea-level curve for the northeast of Ireland from the mid-Holocene to the present day. *Philosophical Transactions of the Royal Society* A 364, 857–866.

Orford, J.D., Betts, N., Cooper, J.A.G. and Smith, B. (2007) *Future Coastal Scenarios for Northern Ireland*. Report to National Trust, Northern Ireland.

Phillips, M.R. and Jones, A.L. (2006) Erosion and tourism infrastructure in the coastal zone: problems, consequences and management. *Tourism Management* 27, 517–524.

Quinn, A.C.M. (1977) *Sand Dunes: Formation, Erosion and Management*. An Foras Forbartha, Dublin.

Rohan, P.K. (1986) *The Climate of Ireland*. The Stationery office, Dublin.

Sweeney, J., Donnelly, A., McElwain, L. and Jones, M. (2002) *Climate Change: Indicators for Ireland* (2000-LS-5.2.2-M1). Environmental Protection Agency, Dublin, 54pp.

Sweeney, J., Brereton, T., Byrne, C., Charlton, R., Emblow, C., Fealy, R., Holden, N., Jones, M., Donnelly, A., Moore, S., Purser, P., Byrne, K., Farrell, E., Mayes, E.,

Minchin, D., Wilson, J. and Wilson, J. (2003) *Climate Change: scenarios and impacts for Ireland* (2000-LS-5.2.1-M1). Environmental Protection Agency, Dublin, 229 pp.

Taylor, J.A., Murdock, A.P. and Pontee, N.I. (2004) A macroscale analysis of coastal steepening around the coast of England and Wales. *The Geographical Journal* 170, 179–188.

Viner, D. and Agnew, M. (1999) *Climate Change and its Impacts on Tourism, Climatic Research Unit*. Report prepared for the WWF-UK, University of East Anglia, Norwich, UK.

www.antaisce.ie An Taisce announce 115 beach awards for Ireland (Accessed: 20 June 2009).

www.belfastcity.gov.uk Press Release 9 June 2009. Visitor Numbers Continue to Increase (Accessed: 19 June 2009).

www.blueflag.org Blue Flag History (accessed: 20 June 2009).

www.tidynorthernireland.org Local beaches among the best in the world (Accessed: 20 June 2009).

11 Climate Change – Coral Reefs and Dive Tourism in South-east Asia

PHILIP DEARDEN AND PETCH MANOPAWITR

Introduction

Tourism is a major economic force in the world today and South-east Asia is a region that has shown large gains in tourism. Thailand in particular has shown strong gains in the past, averaging a 7.4% annual growth in visitor numbers between 1998 and 2007 (Tourism Authority of Thailand, 2009). Other countries in the region such as Laos and Cambodia now show some of the strongest growth rates in the world, although all countries have been affected by the economic downturn of 2008. For example, in Cambodia, after a 12.6% increase in the first half of 2008, growth in international tourist arrivals declined –1.2% in the second half of 2008. The final result was 2.125 million international tourist arrivals to Cambodia, representing a growth of 5.5% compared to 2007 (Ministry of Tourism, 2009). None the less, this rate is still one of the strongest in the world and compares with an overall global increase of 2% in 2008 (World Tourism Organization, 2009a). The WTO predicts that global tourism will reach 1.6 billion arrivals by 2020 and that East Asia and the Pacific will experience the greatest increase in market share over this period (World Tourism Organization, 2009b).

Coastal tourism is a strong component of the tourism industry both at the global level and also in South-east Asia. Thailand has been particularly strong in this regard (Hitchcock *et al.*, 2009; Yasue and Dearden, 2008). Clearly, there are significant economic benefits related to the growth of coastal tourism, but there are also challenges related to negative environmental and social impacts (e.g. Harriott, 2004; Yasue and Dearden, 2006). At its best, coastal tourism can provide not only employment and economic benefits but also act as an incentive to local communities to develop effective stewardship of coastal and marine resources. Tourists are not attracted to visit degraded ecosystems. This is particularly true of dive tourists and the purpose of this chapter is to discuss the implications of global climate change on dive tourism in South-east Asia.

Dive Tourism in South-east Asia

Dive tourism has become a major component of the tropical marine tourism industry. Improvements in dive equipment, the ease and low cost of obtaining SCUBA certification, increased mobility and the global reach of the international tourism industry has brought sites all over the world in easy reach of mass tourism markets. The range of engagement varies, with some divers taking dedicated 2-week offshore cruises that concentrate solely on diving and others taking in a recreational dive as an adventitious part of a vacation. The number of certified divers has grown rapidly over the last two decades. PADI, the world's largest dive certification organization, records over 900,000 certifications per year with a cumulative certification base of over 17 million divers in 2008 (PADI, 2009).

South-east Asia is a major centre for dive tourism. With one of the world's fastest growing tourism industries, warm waters, high biodiversity, extensive reefs, cheap prices and good infrastructure, South-east Asia has become a prime dive destination. Most diving is concentrated in the Coral Triangle sites of Indonesia, Malaysia and the Philippines and in Thailand, although there are also growing industries in Cambodia and Vietnam. Diving takes place throughout this region but in Indonesia it is concentrated in Flores, Manado and Pulau Seribo, in the Philippines in Batangas and the Visayas and in Malaysia on the east coast of Sabah. Diving in Thailand occurs both in the Gulf of Thailand and also on the Andaman coast. Although there is some of the world's best wall diving, such as at Komodo, Kupang, Manado and Irian Jaya in Indonesia, Sipadan and Layang Layang in Malaysia, and Verde, Anilao, Nsugbu, Apo in the Philippines and also wreck dives, most diving is concentrated on shallow coral reefs and this will be the focus of this chapter. Although most diving is by day boats close to population centres, there are numerous live-aboard dive boats including some of the world's largest, that access even the most remote reefs in the region.

South-east Asia is home to the world's most diverse and largest coral reefs, with 34% of the world's total (Tun et al., 2008). The area has over 600 species of hard coral and 1300 reef-associated fish species and is recognized as the global centre of marine tropical biodiversity. At the same time more than 60% of the region's burgeoning 557 million people live within 60 km of the coast and pressures on reefs are high. This region has the highest proportion of Vulnerable and Near Threatened coral species as a chronic result of anthropogenic disturbance and the effects of climate change (Carpenter et al., 2008). Recent analyses (e.g. Bruno and Selig, 2007) show that the condition of the reefs is declining rapidly and has been underestimated in previous assessments. Even the area of reef cover is not well established and Tun et al. (2008) suggest that in Thailand, for example, reef areas may be ten times lower than previously estimated.

Thailand is South-east Asia's most popular dive destination and touted as 'one of the most comfortable and safe diving environments to be found anywhere in the world' (Espinosa et al., 2002:147). Diving is focused on four main areas in two seas, the Andaman Sea, in the eastern Indian Ocean and the Gulf of Thailand, part of the South China Sea. Diving occurs all along the Andaman coast but is mainly focused in Phuket, offering access to diving at the spectacular offshore sites of Koh Similan and Koh Surin as well as up into Burma's Mergui

Archipelago. These sites have grown enormously in popularity over the last few years, leading to concerns about the sustainability of the dive industry (Bennett et al., 2003). Other dive centres are all in the Gulf of Thailand including Koh Tao and Koh Samui on the west side of the Gulf and Pattaya and the recently emerging centre of Koh Chang on the eastern side of the Gulf.

The empirical data on the economic value of diving tourism in South-east Asia are largely lacking, with a few exceptions. For instance, Koh Similan, one of most popular and relatively well-protected diving areas, was estimated to receive US$158.38 million per annum in term of the economic value from Scuba diving activity (Tapsuwan and Asafu-Adjaye, 2008). Total benefit of tourism at Phi Phi islands, a similar and equally popular diving site near Phuket, Thailand, was estimated at US$102.7 million per year (Seenprachawong, 2003). Even from these isolated statistics it can be assumed that coral reefs create an annual income in South-east Asia of several billion dollars and play an important role in sustaining local livelihoods and improving societal welfare.

A recent assessment of coral reefs showed over 80% of reefs along Thailand's Andaman Coast and over 50% of reefs along the Gulf as either in 'fair', 'bad', or 'very bad' condition (a quality measured by the ratio of live to dead coral) and concluded that these reefs are at risk of continued degradation (ONEP, 2004). The World Bank (2006) estimate that with about 57 km^2 (or 37% of the total of Thailand's coral reef area) of rich coral reef categorized as degraded or very degraded, coral reef deterioration represents a loss in potential value of about US$8.5 million each year.

Climate Change

The impacts of global climate change on the ocean are becoming better understood, but many uncertainties remain. Changes include global sea level rise, increased oceanic temperatures, acidification, changes in oceanic currents, rises in UV concentrations and increased frequency of extreme weather events such as cyclones (IPCC, 2007). These changes are already having negative impacts on reefs and will have increasingly serious impacts on coral reef ecosystems in the future. Already about 20% of the world's coral reefs are lost and another 26% are under imminent threats of irrecoverable damage (Wilkinson, 2006). Coral reefs may be the first marine ecosystem to sustain extreme damage and possible collapse from climate change (Wilkinson, 2008). Increased temperatures result in coral bleaching, the breakdown in the symbiosis between their symbiotic zooxanthellae and the corals. Bleached corals are still living but will not survive if stressful conditions do not subside soon enough. The extent and severity of mass coral bleaching events have increased dramatically worldwide since the early 1980s (Hughes et al., 2003; Baker et al., 2008). Ocean acidification as a result of the buildup of atmospheric CO_2 also has deleterious impacts for coral reefs by decreasing growth rate and skeletal density, increasing erosion and reducing recruitment, resulting in death as corals can no longer form skeletons (Hoegh-Guldberg et al., 2007). Increased frequency and severity of extreme weather events may lead to increased breakage on shallow reefs and sediment redistribution and there are also suggestions that some reefs may be drowned by increasing sea levels (Grigg *et al.*, 2002), although increased turbidity as a result of coastal erosion is now thought to be a more significant impact (Buddemeier *et al.*, 2004).

These changes will lead to a vastly different distribution and biodiversity of reefs in the future. The impacts will vary markedly from place to place as a result of the differing characteristics of the reefs and the stresses they will encounter. Scientists distinguish between the resistance of a site, that is its ability to withstand disturbance without losing function and structure and resilience, which is the ability of the site to absorb or recover from disturbance. Overall, as temperatures increase, those corals most resistant to thermal stress such as *Porites* will be favoured, perhaps along with rapidly colonizing genera such as *Acropora*, although the latter are thermally sensitive. Ultimately even the thermally tolerant and rapid colonizing genera may be stressed beyond their tolerance levels and macroalgae will start to dominate large areas leading to a major loss of biodiversity, including coral-associated fish and vertebrates. Once the change to an algae-dominated phase occurs then the chances of recovery to a coral-dominated phase, especially given the changing environmental conditions, is very remote.

Climate Change and Dive Tourism

In light of the drastic changes in reef ecology resulting from global climate change a major question is the likely impacts that this will have on the coral-reef based dive industry. This will differ according to the nature of the reefs in the area under consideration, the type of diving on the reefs and the adaptive capacity of the communities and countries in which the diving takes place. These factors will be examined in this section.

Reef vulnerability

Reefs that are more resistant and resilient to change should be able to continue to support a dive industry much longer than those where stress is already resulting in significant change. Several factors have been identified that may contribute to certain reefs being more resistant and resilient to the effects of global change.

Coral bleaching, as described above, is a major concern and Mather *et al.* (2005) suggest that by 2020 bleaching on corals in South-east Asia may be an annual event. Shallow reefs will be more vulnerable to bleaching, as will those that are already close to the thermal maximum for coral growth. As pointed out above, some corals are more thermally sensitive than others and so coral genus and growth form will also be contributing factors. Overall location is also important as offshore reefs may be more removed from polluting influences of the land. So inshore, shallow reefs close to their thermal maximum and dominated by thermally sensitive corals will be most vulnerable from a biophysical point of view. Important additional factors will be the health of the reef and the management capacity available to maintain that health.

Already stressed reefs will be more vulnerable to the effects of climate change, especially if the management regime is incapable of addressing the stress factors.

In East Africa, well-managed coral reefs showed more resilience to climate change and faster recovery after major bleaching events (McClanahan *et al.*, 2009).

Diver response

A key question in ascertaining diver response is to examine why divers dive, what are their motivations, and see how these may be impacted by the projected changes resulting from global climate change. Several authors have examined diver motivations and there is a strong consensus that motivations centre around the natural characteristics of the dive experience, such as diversity and size of marine organisms, clear waters and unpolluted sites (Musa, 2002; Todd *et al.*, 2002; Bennett *et al.*, 2003; Fitzsimmons, 2009). With the projected declines in the health of reefs it would seem a straightforward projection to suggest that diver attendance on these reefs will decline as the effects of climate change become more obvious.

However, there are some complicating factors in considering how divers might respond to the changes. One factor is the so-called Shifting Baselines syndrome (SBS). Coined in the mid-1990s (Pauly, 1995), the term refers to knowledge extinction over time because younger generations are not aware of past biological conditions, and personal amnesia, where knowledge extinction occurs as individuals forget their own experience (Papworth *et al.*, 2009). How divers might adjust their frame of reference over time in relationship to climate change is unknown. New divers will have no previous frame of reference to compare new conditions against and may be satisfied with what previously might have been considered very mediocre marine viewing opportunities. There is some evidence on this response from the Indian Ocean tsunami of 2004. Following the tsunami, assessments of reef damage were made on the reefs in the Phuket region by members of the Dive Operators Club of Thailand, mainly dive masters. When asked to subsequently rate tsunami damage on these sites, over 85% of the 342 recreational divers failed to perceive any damage on DOCT-assessed damaged sites (Main and Dearden, 2007). The dive masters conducting the original survey had a very current frame of reference and could easily detect damage. Coming new into the situation, most recreational divers were unable to detect any damage.

Differences in motivations, satisfactions, spending and other factors between less-experienced, generalist divers and more specialized divers have been discussed by several authors (e.g. Todd *et al.*, 2002). Dearden *et al.* (2006) compared the motivations of generalist and specialist divers in Phuket on Thailand's Andaman coast. They found that expected flora and fauna at the dive site became significantly more important as the level of specialization increased. Less specialized divers, by way of contrast, placed much more emphasis on improving their dive skills, the dive trip experience (e.g. good views) and the social aspects of the activity. Furthermore, in the Phuket study satisfaction with features

such as variety and amount of marine wildlife, clear unpolluted sites and undam-
aged dive sites declined as specialization increased.

These findings suggest that specialized divers are more likely to be affected
by declining conditions on the reefs than generalist divers. They are also less
likely to be affected by the SBS discussed above. This differential impact is also
supported by evidence from social carrying capacity studies that show that more
specialized divers have lower levels of tolerance for crowded conditions on dive
sites (Dearden *et al.*, 2006; Leujak and Ormond, 2007). One possible effect of
global climate change is that there will be a reduced number of sites on which to
dive. Dive sites that have relatively deep conditions with cooling ocean currents
may be little affected for some time. However, shallow reefs with little cold water
circulation may be some of the first casualties. If overall diver numbers are maintained, this will mean the same number of divers diving on fewer sites, resulting
in more crowding at those sites. The crowding will have a larger impact on more
specialized divers and suggests that, over time, there will be an increasing number
of generalist divers.

The Phuket study showed that specialized divers already have lower satisfaction levels than generalist divers with their dive experience and are less likely
to return to Phuket than generalist divers. With additional reductions, their satisfactions may well fall below the level at which they will continue to participate in
the activity. Hence in the future there may well be a reduction in the overall
experience level of the dive fraternity, to one that becomes dominated by generalist, in comparison to experienced, divers. Leujak and Ormond (2007) found a
shift in clientele over time at South Sinai's coral reefs as the reefs became more
degraded and generalists replaced specialists. These changes in clientele over
time will be discussed in more detail below in relation to the industry response.

From both resource conservation and economic perspectives such a change
is undesirable for several reasons. First, the Phuket study showed that specialist
divers are higher yielding tourists than generalist divers who tend to dive less and
at cheaper prices. Second, there is a wide range of evidence that suggests that
generalist divers have higher impacts on the reef when they dive (Hawkins
et al., 2005). Finally, as will be discussed later, a powerful and informed dive
community will be a tremendous asset in building monitoring and enhancement
capabilities in response to global change.

Dive industry characteristics

The dive industry has grown along with the number of divers. The growth over
time in the industry can be represented by the model shown in Fig. 11.1. The
model has three essential characteristics:

1. The growth over time is represented by a logistic curve with a slow start to the
industry in a given area, followed by a rapid growth as the industry becomes established and growth slowing as 'carrying capacity' levels are reached. Ultimately
the curve may decline (point D in Fig. 11.1) as conditions become unsuitable for
diving either as a result of impacts from the industry itself or by exogenous forces.

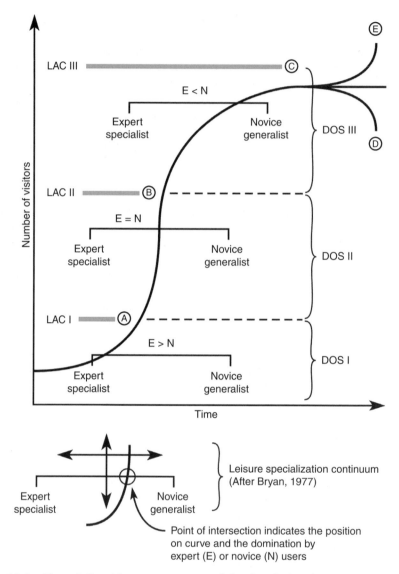

Fig. 11.1. The relationship among user specialization, limits of acceptable change (LAC I-III) and stages in evolution of a dive tourism site (A to E) over time. DOS (I-III) is the Diver Opportunity Spectrum used as a basis for matching dive site characteristics with specialization levels (from Dearden *et al.*, 2006).

2. The 'carrying capacity levels' are represented by the more comprehensive concept of Limits of Acceptable Change (Roman *et al.*, 2007). As the number of companies (and divers) grows so do the associated impacts on both the ecological and social conditions. In the absence of monitoring of these conditions and management interventions to forestall them it is possible that LACs are so violated that overcrowding and decline in reef health lead to the downturn shown in Fig. 11.1.

3. As growth progresses there is an associated change in the nature of the clientele. In the early stages of evolution, the clientele is often dominated by more experienced, explorer-type divers. As the site becomes more widely known an increasing number of inexperienced and generalist divers hear about the site, until ultimately their presence dominates the site. They are able to displace the more specialized divers since the latter have less tolerance for crowded conditions and the higher impacted sites created by the more damaging generalists. This process has been described in more detail in the previous section on diver characteristics.

The model suggests the need to understand the evolution of sites and identify desirable conditions regarding the quality of the environment, crowding and type of clientele and instigate management interventions that will produce those results. For example, in relationship to diving out of Phuket, Dearden *et al.* (2006) use the model to suggest a zoning scheme that would help maintain a full range of diver opportunities in the area. At the moment considerable numbers of inexperienced, low-paying divers are diving on the more pristine dive sites where they create more damage. This will not result in a sustainable dive industry as the entire area slides to the top of the curve. Dearden *et al.* suggest a zoning scheme, whereby access to the most pristine reefs is reserved for more specialized higher-paying divers and numbers of divers are limited (Dive Opportunity Spectrum 1 in Fig. 11.1). Such a restriction will encourage the continuation of the full range of opportunities for divers of varying abilities and interests, as well as yield higher economic returns and a more sustainable industry over the long term.

In general, the industry model might change in a number of ways under the stress of climate change. In terms of the shape and extent of the growth, several changes might be expected from the original curve (curve A, Fig. 11.2). Southeast Asia is remote from the main clientele that make up the diving fraternity, primarily from northern Europe, North America and North-east Asia. In the future it is likely that air travel will rise considerably in cost as governments seek ways to reduce carbon footprints. Taxes on air fares will probably increase and increased scarcity of fossil fuels will lead to further increases. The overall result is likely to be less international travel, especially the long-haul international travel that dominates the dive industry in South-east Asia. For example, Gössling *et al.* (2002) found that for travellers to the Seychelles, 97% of the energy footprint was a result of air travel. Not only energy and financial costs might reduce the ease of long haul travel but increased security precautions, threats of disease transmission and other factors will also contribute (Gössling, 2005). In addition, some destinations, particularly tropical ones, may become so hot in the future that they exceed the tolerance levels of potential tourists (Mather *et al.*, 2005).

In general, these changes will probably lead to a lower number of divers on reefs in South-east Asia (curve B, Fig. 11.2) in the future. This will, in all likelihood, be accompanied by a reduction in the number of dive companies. This effect was documented by Main and Dearden (2007) in response to the tsunami.

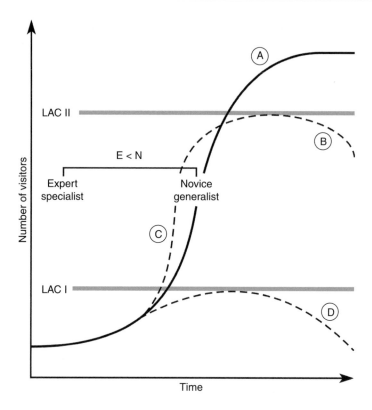

Fig. 11.2. Potential adaptation of the dive site evolution model under the stress of climate change.

In Phuket, dive company numbers fell by about one-third. However, this may not be a bad thing. As Dearden *et al.* (2006) pointed out, excessive competition for customers amongst the proliferating dive companies in Phuket was leading to very low margins of profitability and a great temptation for dive companies to cut their costs by employing unsustainable practices on ill-equipped vessels. Following the tsunami, many of the more marginal dive companies went bankrupt, leading to a sense of greater cooperation amongst the remaining dive companies.

The shape of the curve will vary widely according to local conditions. Resistant and resilient dive sites may see steeper growth curves (curve C, Fig. 11.2); sites with lower resistance may see very attenuated growth curves and then collapse (curve D, Fig. 11.2) as the effects of global change become more obvious on reef conditions. Much will depend on where the particular dive site is on the curve as to the resulting trajectory. Virtually all sites will face more restricted Limits of Acceptable Change, which will result in earlier flattening of the growth curve and potential collapse. The environmental LACs will be reached sooner as the reefs are under greater stress than previously (LAC I, Fig. 11.2); social LACs will likely be approached earlier on 'successful' reefs as divers crowd the few remaining healthy reefs (LAC II, Fig. 11.2). The reefs will become dominated by generalist divers earlier in the progression than in the original model. As with the original model, the main requirement is to have effective monitoring systems that detect unacceptable limits of change in reef conditions, both biophysical and social, and have management interventions designed for ready implementation. Some of these will be discussed in the final section.

Another factor to be considered in the industry response is the mobility of the industry. Shore-based dive facilities based on shallow reefs are likely to be more vulnerable than live-aboards that can access a large number of deeper offshore reefs. For example, in Thailand sites such as Koh Tao in the Gulf of Thailand are likely to be more vulnerable than the Andaman coast sites where there are a greater number of live-aboards with access to offshore sites, such as Koh Similan and Koh Surin.

Social adaptive capacity

McClanahan *et al.* (2008) point out the importance of social adaptive capacity in determining the response to climate change of reef-dependent communities in five countries in the western Indian Ocean. They undertook their analysis at the community and household levels to assess different capacities and this level of analysis will also be important for assessing adaptability for diving. For example, communities with higher social capital should have a stronger base on which to build to implement adaptive strategies. The same is true for national social adaptive capacity. In more developed countries with higher indices of wealth and education and other associated factors (such as are reflected in the UN's Human Development Index, HDI) there are greater resources to deploy in adapting to climate threats to reefs. There should be greater scientific capacity and understanding, greater depth of experience, and more effective protection agencies. Communities should have a wider range of alternative livelihoods to draw upon. Thailand, for example, has several well-developed marine research centres, graduate programmes in marine biology and conservation and a large and experienced National Parks Department. Thailand is ranked 81st in the world in terms of its HDI (UNDP, 2009) Cambodia, on the other hand, has no dedicated marine research centres, few highly qualified personnel in this area and a nascent National Parks Department just cutting its teeth on the terrestrial scene and with little marine experience. It is ranked 136th in the world for HDI (UNDP, 2009). This comparison suggests that Thailand will have a higher national social adaptive capacity for addressing the impacts of global change on coral reefs than might be found in Cambodia.

The new Coral Triangle Initiative on Coral Reefs centred around high-level political commitments and proactive implementation by six governments of the Coral Triangle area, and supported by private sector, international agency and civil society (NGO) partners, could provide a model and a major contribution toward safeguarding the region's marine and coastal biological resources for sustainable development. The new initiative is very well funded and could serve as a platform to build local capacity region-wide.

Differing Vulnerabilities

The foregoing suggests that we can start to identify situations where some dive industries will be more vulnerable to the impacts of climate change than others. These are summarized in Table 11.1. The next step in this analysis would be to test empirically some of these relationships. The upshot of the analysis would be a relative assessment of the potential abilities of dive industries in different locations to persist in the face of climate change. At one end of the scale, there might be highly vulnerable shallow inshore reefs attracting long-haul, specialist divers in a highly competitive industry with little effective management in a country with a low HDI. At the other end of the scale might be deep, offshore reefs attracting a more general and local market served by a cooperative dive industry using live-aboards and with a high HDI and effective protection for the reefs. The more vulnerable end of the scale would suggest a policy of limited investment, a triage approach. The top end of the scale would have much more time and capacity to adapt. The main challenges will come in the middle of the scale, and the question becomes what can be done?

Building Resilience

Many of the adaptations currently thought of in relation to global warming involve building physical infrastructure such as seawalls and locks. In many

Table 11.1. Summary of some of the main factors potentially influencing the impacts of global climate change on the dive industry in South-east Asia.

Characteristics	More vulnerable	Less vulnerable
Reefs	Shallow	Deep
	Close to thermal maximum	Far from thermal maximum
	Thermally intolerant coral	Thermally tolerant coral
	Nearshore	Offshore
	Degraded	Healthy
Divers	Specialists	Generalists
Industry	Long haul	Short haul
	Reefs sole attraction	Diversified attractions
	Reefs shallow	Reefs deep
	Industry not well managed	Industry well managed
	Shore based	Live-aboard based
	Highly competitive industry	Less competitive industry
Adaptive Capacity	Low HDI	High HDI
	Few alternative livelihoods	Many alternative livelihoods
	Reefs not well managed	Reefs well managed
	Low scientific capacity	High scientific capacity
	Low social capital	High social capital

HDI, Human Development Index (UN)

cases, however, as pointed out by the World Ocean Congress in Manado, it will be more effective and economical to use nature's infrastructure first. Coral reefs are one of the most effective means of breaking powerful storm waves from flooding coastal lands and eroding shorelines. In Thailand, for example, coastal erosion is already reported to be between 15–25 m/year in many locations (Asian Development Bank, 2009). Reefs have survived for millennia and healthy reefs will re-grow following breakage if favourable conditions can be maintained. It is therefore of considerable importance that reef maintenance and enhancement not be seen merely as a financial cost but considered within the framework of the opportunity costs of not maintaining the reefs and having to construct man-made infrastructure. As Hughes *et al.* (2003) pointed out, although climate change is a global issue that needs international collaboration, local conservation efforts can help greatly in maintaining and enhancing resilience and in limiting the longer-term damage from bleaching and human impacts. Managing coral reef resilience through networks of marine reserves integrated with management of adjacent areas will be crucial to any practical solution to the challenges of global climate change.

One of the best ways to protect the reefs is to provide incentives for local people to do so. Developing a sustainable dive industry where local people derive the benefits is an important component of this task and helps build local stewardship. Although the analysis in the preceding section suggests that overall diving numbers will decline, there are also possibilities of increases in some areas. This will occur as healthy dive sites become more scarce, but may also occur on sites where damage is being sustained. Dearden *et al.* (2007), for example, found that witnessing damage to a dive site during a dive was one of the most powerful motivators for divers to become engaged in future reef conservation activities and conclude that 'exposure to field conditions can act as a major catalyst for future conservation activities.' (p. 314). Disaster tourism has emerged as an interest over the last few years and some suggest that climate change tourism (Aall and Hoyer, 2005) might also emerge as a focus of interest. For divers this might well involve engagement in activities to address the damage that is occurring.

There will be much scope for active management of reefs in the future as impacts grow. Eakin *et al.* (2008), for example, suggest the need for possible shading and cooling of reefs during major bleaching events in the future. There may also be a need to restore reefs, to assist in the propagation of more resilient corals and other such tasks. Already scientific resources are stretched to the limit and there is great potential to harness the power of the recreational diving sector to aid in these tasks. Thousands of divers are already involved in citizen science through monitoring programmes such as ReefCheck and Reefbase, and many more will be required as the range of tasks increases in the future.

The potential of the dive industry to contribute significantly in this way was clearly illustrated in the response in Thailand to the Indian Ocean tsunami of 2004. Main and Dearden (2007) describe the highly competitive nature of the industry and the impacts this was having on dive sites before the tsunami. However, the tsunami resulted in unprecedented cooperation amongst dive companies, and between the dive companies and the government. When faced with an external threat of staggering proportions the result was a coordinated and effective response that otherwise could not have been conceived of. If the changes wrought by climate change become as drastic and rapid as predicted by scientists then this may again create an environment of cooperation and mobilization to act in the common good. In fact, the dive industry may become key players in actually implementing climate change adaptation strategies on coral reefs. Self interest is a powerful and not unworthy motivating force.

The dive industry also has detailed local knowledge gained after daily dives over long time periods that exceeds that of many research institutions and can prove very valuable in assessment of conditions and design of restoration projects. For example, following the tsunami, in April 2005, two diving companies donated boats and staff to facilitate a gorgonian seafan restoration project at the Similan Islands. This was a joint government and university initiative with the purpose of restoring seafans that had been dislodged and damaged during the tsunami. Restoration team members included university professors from Thailand and Japan, scientists from Phuket Marine Biological Centre, volunteer biologists from abroad and dive professionals from Phuket. The trip was preceded by a series of meetings with all groups to determine optimal strategies for attempting to reattach tsunami-dislodged massive gorgonian seafans to the seafloor. The knowledge of local dive professionals regarding site-specific characteristics and diving conditions was essential in planning and undertaking the initiative.

There are also dangers involved with a potential increase in divers to assist in restoration projects. Although diving is generally less damaging than other extractive uses of the reef, it is not a benign activity, and a significant body of literature indicates that diving is a source of stress on reefs and on reef-associated fish communities (Prior *et al.*, 1995; Schleyer and Tomalin, 2000; Zakai and Chadwick-Furman, 2002; Barker and Roberts, 2004; Dearden *et al.*, 2010). Hawkins and Roberts (1992) pointed out that heavily used dive sites may be less able to recover from other stressors such as hurricanes, storms and disease and climate-induced stressors can certainly be added to this list and indicate the need for greatly improved dive management in the future, which may well involve more restrictions on divers and the dive industry.

One of the main needs in the future is to gain better understanding of reef ecosystems and how they work (Bouchet, 2006). Knowledge of functional relationships is still very elementary. However, scientists have difficulties in unravelling these relationships because of the vast range of human impacts already extant on most reefs. There are few pristine sites to act as natural laboratories, and even where they do exist, such as on remote, uninhabited and protected atolls in the central Pacific Ocean and north-western Hawaiian islands, it is difficult to know how broadly results on these reefs can be applied to reefs that may be thousands of kilometres away. MPAs, in theory, should provide sites where human impacts are less severe and relationships more intact. Many MPAs have zones where no extractive uses are allowed, but few have zones where no access at all, including diving, is allowed, and this might be exactly what is needed in future if we are to allow for the need for scientific study of reefs in a wide variety of locations.

However, ultimately the greatest challenge in climate change adaptation strategies is changing human behaviour. The educative impact of diving has been shown to be amongst the activity's strongest impacts. Many authors have called for improved educational programmes and dive-master training and this need will only increase in the future.

Conclusions

Scientists are only recently starting to understand more about reef dynamics, and knowledge of potential impacts of global change on reefs is building slowly. However, there has been relatively little analysis of the knock-on effects of these changes on industries such as diving. Broad patterns can be suggested, as above, but much empirical work remains to be done. Knowlton and Jackson (2008) conclude after their review of the impacts of global change on coral reefs that finding ways for effective management at the local level in the face of global change is the central challenge in reef conservation today. Given the tremendous economic and educational values of diving it would be a mistake not to harness these forces to aid in achieving improved reef management at the local level through financial incentives.

References

Aall, C. and Hoyer, K.G. (2005) Tourism and climate change adaptation: the Norwegian case. In: Hall, C.M. and Higham, J. (eds) *Tourism, Recreation and Climate Change*. Channel View Publications, New York, pp. 209–222.

Asian Development Bank (2009) *The Economics of Climate Change in Southeast Asia*. ADB, Manila.

Baker, A.C., Glynn, P.W. and Riegl, B. (2008) Climate change and coral reef bleaching: an ecological assessment of long-term impacts, recovery trends and future outlook. *Estuarine, Coastal and Shelf Science* 80, 435–471.

Barker, N.H. and Roberts, C.M. (2004) Scuba diver behaviour and the management of diving impacts on coral reefs. *Biological Conservation* 120, 481–489.

Bennett, M., Dearden, P. and Rollins, R. (2003) The sustainability of dive tourism in Phuket, Thailand. In: Landsdown, H., Dearden, P. and Neilson, W. (eds) *Communities in SE Asia: Challenges and Responses*. Centre for Asia Pacific Initiatives, University of Victoria, pp. 97–106.

Bouchet, P. (2006) The magnitude of marine biodiversity. In: Duarte, C.M. (ed.) *The Exploration of Marine Biodiversity: Scientific and Technical Challenges*. Fundacion BBVA, Madrid, pp. 31–64.

Bruno, J.F. and Selig, E.R. (2007) Regional decline of coral cover in the Indo-Pacific: timing, extent, and subregional comparisons. *PLoS ONE* 2(8), e711.doi:10.1371/journal.pone.0000711.

Bryan, H. (1977) Leisure value systems and recreational specialization: the case of trout fishermen. *Journal of Leisure Research* 9, 174–187.

Buddemeier, R.W., Kleypas, J.A. and Aronson, R.B. (2004) *Coral Reefs and Global Climate Change: potential contributions of climate change to stresses on coral reef ecosystems*. Pew Center for Global Climate Change, Arlington, USA, 33pp.

Carpenter *et al.* (2008) One-third of reef-building corals face elevated extinction risk from climate change and local impacts. *Science* 321, 560–563.

Dearden, P., Bennett, M. and Rollins, R. (2006) Dive specialization in Phuket: implications for reef conservation. *Environmental Conservation* 33(4), 353–363.

Dearden, P., Bennett, M. and Rollins, R. (2007) Perceptions of diving impacts and implications for reef conservation. *Coastal Management* 35, 305–317.

Dearden, P., Theberge, M. and Yasué, M. (2010) Using underwater cameras to assess the effects of snorkeler or SCUBA diver presence on coral reef fish abundance, family richness and species composition. *Environmental Monitoring and Assessment* (in press).

Eakin C.M., Kleypas, J. and Hoegh-Guldberg, O. (2008) Global climate change and coral reefs: rising temperatures, acidification and the need for resilient reefs. In: *Status of Coral Reefs of the World*. Global Coral Reef Monitoring Network and Reef and Rainforest Research Centre, Townsville, Australia, pp. 29–34.

Espinosa, D., Mitchell, H., Muller, K., Nichols, F. and Williams, J. (2002) *Diving Southeast Asia*. Periplus Pub., Singapore.

Fitzsimmons, C. (2009) Why dive? And why here? A study of recreational diver enjoyment at a Fijian eco-tourist resort. *Tourism in Marine Environments* 5, 159–174.

Gössling S. (2005) Tourism's contribution to global environmental change: space, energy, disease, water. In: Hall, C.M. and Higham, J. (eds) *Tourism, Recreation and Climate Change*. Channel View Publications, New York, pp. 286–300.

Gössling, S., Borgstrom-Hansson, C., Horstmeier, O. and Saggel, S. (2002) Ecological footprint analysis as a tool to assess tourism sustainability. *Ecological Economics* 43, 199–211.

Grigg, R.W. *et al.* (2002) Drowned reefs and antecedent karst topography, Au'au Channel, S.E. Hawaiian Islands. *Coral Reefs* 21, 73–82.

Harriott, V.J. (2004) Marine tourism impacts on the Great Barrier Reef. *Tourism in Marine Environments* 1, 29–40.

Hawkins, J.P. and Roberts, C.M. (1992) Effects of recreational SCUBA diving on fore-reef slope 414 communities of coral reefs. *Biological Conservation* 62, 171–178.

Hawkins, J.P., Roberts, C.M., Kooistra, D., Buchan, K. and White, S. (2005) Sustainability of scuba diving tourism on coral reefs of Saba. *Coastal Management* 33, 373–387.

Hitchcock, M., King., V.T. and Parnwell, M. (eds) (2009) *Tourism in Southeast Asia: Challenges and New Directions*. NIAS Press, Copenhagen.

Hoegh-Guldberg, O., Mumby, P.J., Hooten, A.J., Steneck, R.S., Greenfield, P. *et al.* (2007) Coral reefs under rapid climate change and ocean acidification. *Science* 318, 1737–1742.

Hughes, T. *et al.* (2003) Climate change, human impacts, and resilience. *Science* 301, 929.

IPCC (2007) *Climate Change 2007: The Physical Science Basis. Contribution of Working Group I to the Fourth Assessment Report of the Intergovernmental Panel on Climate Change*, Solomon, S. *et al.* (eds). Cambridge University Press, Cambridge, UK, and New York.

Knowlton, N. and Jackson, J.B.C. (2008) Shifting baselines, local impacts, and global change on coral reefs. *PLoS Biol* 6(2), e54. doi:10.1371/journal.pbio.0060054.

Leujak, W. and Ormond, R.F.G. (2007) Visitor perceptions and the shifting social carrying capacity of South Sinai's coral reefs. *Environmental Management* 39, 472–489.

Main, M. and Dearden, P. (2007) Tsunami impacts on Phuket's diving industry: geographical implications for marine conservation. *Coastal Management* 35(4), 1–15.

Mather, S., Viner, D. and Todd, G. (2005) Climate and policy changes: the implications for international tourism flows. In: Hall, C.M. and Higham, J. (eds) *Tourism, Recreation and Climate Change*. Channel View Publications, New York, pp. 63–85.

McClanahan, T.R., Cinner, J.E., Maina, J., Graham, N.A.J., Daw, T.M., Stead, S.M., Wamukota, A., Brown, K., Ateweberhan, M., Venus, V. and Polunin, N.V.C. (2008) Conservation action in a changing climate. *Conservation Letters* 1, 53–59.

McClanahan, T.R., Muthiga, N.A., Maina, J., Kamukuru, A.T. and Yahya, S.A.S. (2009) Changes in northern Tanzania coral reefs during a period of increased fisheries management and climatic disturbance. *Aquatic Conservation: Marine and Freshwater Ecosystems* 19(7), 758–771.

Ministry of Tourism (2009) *Tourism Statistical Report 2008*. Phnom Penh.

Musa, G. (2002) Sipidan: an over-exploited scuba-diving paradise? An analysis of tourism impact, diver satisfaction and management priorities. *Tourism Geography* 4(2), 195–209.

ONEP (2004) *Thailand's Coastal Resources and Environment Profile*. Developed in collaboration with Chula Unisearch and Southeast Asia Global Changes System for Analysis, Research and Training Regional Center.

PADI (2009) Statistics, graphs and history about PADI Scuba diving certification. www.padi.com/scuba/about-padi/PADI-statistics (Accessed: 28 May 2009).

Papworth, S.K., Rist, J., Coad, L. and Milner-Gulland, E.J. (2009) Evidence for shifting baseline syndrome in conservation. *Conservation Letters* 2(2), 92–100.

Pauly, D. (1995) Anecdotes and the shifting baseline syndrome of fisheries. *Trends in Ecology and Evolution* 10, 430.

Prior, M., Ormand, R., Hitchen, R. and Wormald, C. (1995) The impacts on natural resources of activity tourism: a case study of diving in Egypt. *International Journal of Environmental Studies* 48, 201–209.

Roman, G., Dearden, P. and Rollins, R. (2007) Application of zoning and 'Limits of Acceptable Change' to manage snorkeling tourism. *Environmental Management* 39, 819–830.

Schleyer, M.H. and Tomalin, B.J. (2000) Damage on South African coral reefs and an assessment of their sustainable diving capacity using a fisheries approach. *Bulletin of Marine Science* 67, 1025–1042.

Seenprachawong, U. (2003) Economic valuation of coral reefs at Phi Phi Islands, Thailand. *International Journal of Global Environmental Issues* 3, 104–114.

Tapsuwan, S. and Asafu-Adjaye, J. (2008) Estimating the economic benefit of SCUBA diving in the Similan Islands, Thailand. *Coastal Management* 36, 431–442.

Todd, S.L., Graefe, A.R. and Mann, W. (2002) Differences in diver motivation based on level of development. In: Todd, S.L. (ed.) *Proceedings of the 2001 Northeastern Recreation Research Symposium*. Gen Tech rep NE 289. USDA Forest Service, Northeastern Research Station, Newtown Square, Pennsylvania, pp. 107–114.

Tourism Authority of Thailand (2009) *Tourism Statistics*. Bangkok, www2.tat.or.th/stat/web/static_index.php (Accessed: 10 June 2009).

Tun, K., Ming, C.L., Yeemin, T., Phongsuwan, N., Amri, A.Y., Ho, N., Sour, K., Long, N.V., Nanola, C., Lane, D. and Tuti, Y. (2008) Status of reefs in Southeast Asia. In: Wilkinson, C. (ed.) *Status of Coral Reefs of the World*. Global Coral Reef Monitoring Network and Reef and Rainforest Research Centre, Townsville, Australia, pp. 131–144.

UNDP (2009) *Human Development Indices: a statistical update 2008*. UNDP, Nairobi.

Wilkinson, C. (2006) Status of coral reefs of the world: summary of threats and remedial action. In: Cote, I.M. and Reynolds, J.D. (eds) *Coral Reef Conservation*. Zoological Society of London, Cambridge University Press.

Wilkinson, C. (ed.) (2008) Executive Summary in *Status of Coral Reefs of the World*. Global Coral Reef Monitoring Network and Reef and Rainforest Research Centre, Townsville, Australia, pp. 5–28.

World Bank (2006) *Thailand Environment Monitor 2006*: *Marine and Coastal Resources*. World Bank Office, Bangkok.

World Tourism Organization (2009a) World Tourism Barometer. January 2009.

World Tourism Organization (2009b) Tourism 2020 Vision. WTO, Madrid.

Yasué, M. and Dearden, P. (2006) The potential impact of tourism development on habitat availability and productivity of Malaysian plovers, *Charadrius peronii*. *Journal of Applied Ecology* 43, 978–989.

Yasué, M. and Dearden, P. (2008 was in press) Methods to measure and mitigate the impacts of tourism development on tropical beach-breeding shorebirds: the Malaysian plover in Thailand. *Tourism in Marine Environments* 5, 287–299.

Zakai, D. and Chadwick-Furman, N.E. (2002) Impacts of intensive recreational diving on reef corals at Eilat, northern Red Sea. *Biological Conservation* 105, 179–187.

12 Tourism and Climate Impact on the North American Eastern Seaboard

ZOE HUGHES

Introduction

With attractions such as New York City, Virginia Beach, the Florida Keys and the autumn colours of New England, the East Coast of the United States is a popular destination. Global warming has the potential to have both dramatic and adverse consequences for human society, resulting from changes in temperature, precipitation, sea level, storms, air quality and ecosystems. The potential impact of climate change on the international tourist industry and recreational use by US nationals is complex, yet of great concern. Travel and tourism in the USA generate an estimated US$746 billion per annum, supplying 10% of the Gross Domestic Product and making it the second largest contributing industry (Houston, 1995). During 2007, the USA drew over 56 million international visitors (UNTWO, 2008). Four of the top ten ports of entry for international visitors lie on the Eastern Seaboard, with Miami and New York City ranking first and second (US Dept of Commerce, 2009). The US coast also receives over 180 million recreational visitors annually, coastal states producing 85% of the national revenue related to tourism (Cicin-Sain and Knecht, 1998). Activities such as saltwater fishing, recreational boating, outdoor (non-pool) swimming and birdwatching attract millions of participants and each generates tens of billions of dollars annually (Cicin-Sain and Knecht, 1998).

The shore of the East Coast graduates from a rocky glaciated coastline in the north (e.g. Maine and New Hampshire) to coral reefs and mangroves in the south (Florida). In contrast to the tectonically active West Coast, the East Coast is situated far from active plate boundaries with a broad coastal plain and continental shelf. Much of the shoreline is characterized by protective barrier islands, which sit just offshore of the mainland and have extensive wetlands and lagoons behind them. These barriers dominate the coasts of Virginia, North Carolina, South Carolina and Georgia, but smaller systems also occur in Massachusetts and New Hampshire. The sandy barrier islands are often topped by dune systems and are popular destinations for tourists. As a result it is common for barrier islands to be highly developed, the property being partly residential and partly vacation homes. The marshes and lagoons of the back-barrier provide sheltered waterways and wetlands perfect for hunting, fishing and pleasure boating. However, the low elevation of these barrier systems makes them susceptible to changes in sea level and increased storminess.

The impact of climate change on any region is a function of the physical setting but also the ability of the population to adapt to the alterations. The vulnerability of the US shoreline and the potential for managing the coastal zone in the face of global warming has been the focus of studies spanning the past 20 years (Titus *et al.*, 1991; Thieler and Hammer-Klose, 1999; Titus and Richman, 2001; Gornitz *et al.*, 2002; Nicholls, 2003; Nicholls *et al.*, 2007; Rowley *et al.*, 2007; FitzGerald *et al.*, 2008; Titus and Wang, 2008; CCSP, 2009), each new study improving the accuracy of the assessment, as models, and the underlying science, progress. This chapter examines the shorelines and the coastal plain of the US Eastern Seaboard, their potential response to global climate change and the consequent impact on the expansive tourist industry, which thrives upon them.

Vulnerability to the Impacts of Global Warming

Climate change will manifest in a number of ways including: increases in average temperatures; changes in precipitation patterns; and increased storminess (IPCC, 2007). The north-east is expected to experience a warming of between 2 and 5°C, with a predicted increase in precipitation ranging from 0–25% (IPCC, 2007). The south-east is forecast to receive about 20–30% more rain on the whole, but to be more prone to heat waves and droughts and similar temperature rises to the north-east (IPCC, 2007; Karetinkov *et al.*, 2008).

Global temperature increases will result in the melting of glaciers and ice packs, releasing terrestrial water stores and increasing global sea level (presently increasing at ~2 mm/year; IPCC, 2007). Additionally, local temperature changes will increase sea level through steric effects (expansion) and, as a consequence, the warmer Mid-Atlantic and southern zones of the East Coast may experience higher rates of sea level rise. High precipitation can enhance weathering and erosion of rocks and soils, which may produce increased shoreline retreat, as cliffs and bluffs erode, but will also introduce new sediment into the littoral system. A warming climate may also be associated with increases in frequency or intensity of storminess, which in turn, may amplify coastal flooding by storm surge.

Of the potential impacts of global warming, sea level rise (SLR) is perhaps the most relevant to the shoreline and the coastal plain (Pilkey and Cooper, 2004; FitzGerald *et al.*, 2008), particularly on the East Coast where coastal populations continue to expand (Crossett *et al.*, 2004; Poulter *et al.*, 2009). Model estimates of sea level at the end of this century indicate increases of ~0.18–0.59 m (IPCC, 2007), however, it is likely this figure may be nearer to 1 m as the projected rates do not consider variation in the rates of melting on the

Greenland and Antarctic ice sheets (Rahmstorf, 2006). Between them, these two reservoirs contain sufficient water to induce a SLR of 63.9 m (Bamber *et al.*, 2001; Lythe and Vaughan, 2001).

The raising of mean sea level can induce one or more of the following processes within the coastal plain (FitzGerald *et al.*, 2008; CCSP, 2009):

- land loss by inundation of low-lying lands;
- land loss due to erosion (removal of material from beaches, dunes, and cliffs);
- barrier island migration, breaching and segmentation;
- wetland accretion and migration;
- wetland drowning (deterioration and conversion to open water);
- expansion of estuaries;
- saltwater intrusion (into freshwater aquifers and surface waters); and
- increased frequency of storm flooding (especially of uplands and developed coastal lands).

These physical changes will have dramatic impacts on coastal populations and ecosystems. For example, in New Jersey, approximately 142 km^2 of the coastal plain lies within 0.61 m of present mean sea level (Cooper *et al.*, 2005) and over 5900 km^2 of coastal North Carolina lies ~1 m below present mean sea level (Poulter *et al.*, 2009). What is of equal concern however, is the rate at which the sea level changes. Slow changes allow time for physical, environmental and socio-economical adaptation, however, sea level rise is predicted to accelerate, enhancing the stress on the coastal zone (Field *et al.*, 2007). Several studies indicate this increase in SLR has already begun, initiating in the mid-19th to 20th centuries (Donnelly, 2006; Jevrejeva *et al.*, 2008).

Vulnerability to natural phenomena can be defined as the degree to which a natural or social system is at risk to damages or losses (Cooper *et al.*, 2005). The physical setting of a coastal region is a major control on its vulnerability to the impacts of climate change. Coastline response to sea level rise is likely to be modulated by the antecedent geology (Belnap and Kraft, 1985). This will include the exploitation of existing estuaries and bays by the encroaching waters, and the influence of the initial elevation of a coastal zone, as well as the rate at which elevation increases with distance from the coastline (i.e. the slope of the land). In addition to global or steric SLR, local land movements occur as a result of such processes as local subsidence (relating to overburden and compaction of sediment) or glacial isostatic adjustment (GIA; Fig. 12.1; FitzGerald *et al.*, 1994). This produces site-specific 'relative sea level rise' rates which deviate from global trends (Douglas, 2001).

Relative SLR along the East Coast is varied (Fig. 12.2). Glaciation has had a significant impact on the north-east, scouring sediment from the mainland to be deposited offshore during the retreat of the ice sheets. Cape Cod and the Islands (Nantucket and Martha's Vineyard) are composed of the sandy moraines left by ice lobes at the seaward extent of the Laurentide ice sheet about 11,000 years ago. However, the surrounding coastline is considered sediment starved; riverine inputs to the littoral system are relatively low compared to rivers in the south-east (Meade, 1972). Far northern regions may

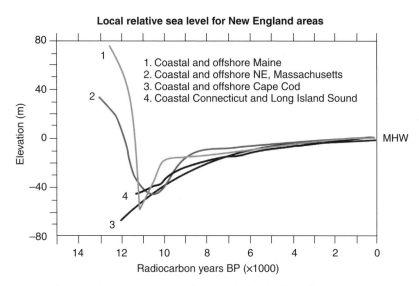

Fig. 12.1. Sea level curves since the last glaciation in New England (after FitzGerald *et al.*, 1994).

still be experiencing a positive GIA, masking global SLR (Figs 12.1, 12.2). In contrast, the south-east is richer in sediment supply as a result of agricultural deforestation and a wider coastal plain, and as a result many coastal areas are experiencing subsidence and compaction of deltaic sediments (FitzGerald *et al.*, 2008). In some cases this response is further exacerbated by a sudden reduction in sediment deposition related to dams upriver (e.g. the Santee Delta, South Carolina; Hughes *et al.*, 2009).

In an assessment of the vulnerability of the Eastern Seaboard, Thieler and Hammer-Klose (1999) consider six variables: geomorphology, coastal slope, relative sea-level rise, shoreline erosion/accretion rate, mean tide range and mean wave height. These physical parameters are integrated into a coastal vulnerability index. The entire East Coast will experience changes relating to sea level rise, however it is clear that the mid-Atlantic region (New York, New Jersey, Delaware, Maryland, Virginia, North and South Carolina) are most severely at risk, and consequently have been the specific focus of recent vulnerability assessments (e.g. CCSP, 2009).

Changes in climate and sea level are not new phenomena, and both have varied throughout geological history. Sea level has risen approximately 120 m since the last glacial maximum (Fairbanks, 1989). This rise slowed to a near standstill (0.1 mm/year) about 3000 years ago, allowing the development of coastal societies and increasing coastal populations (Day *et al.*, 2007). This trend continues today with coastal counties in the USA being home to 153 million people in 2000, increasing to 160 million in 2008, accounting for 53% of the population (Culliton, 1998; Crossett *et al.*, 2004). In 2003, coastal counties in the USA accounted for 23 of the 25 most densely populated counties, a pattern reflected globally. The resulting coastal infrastructure and real estate on the East Coast is estimated at over US$3 trillion (Evans, 2004). While the beauty of

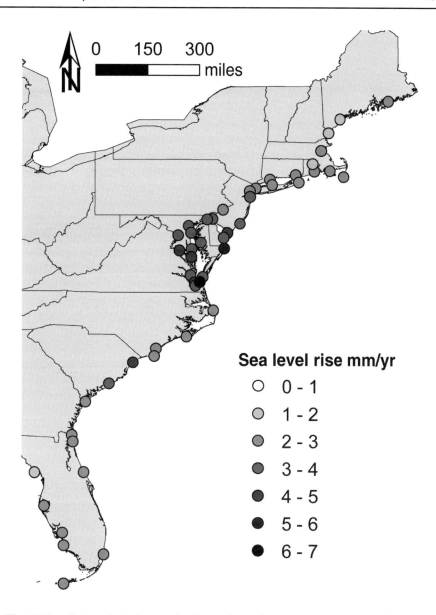

Fig. 12.2. Rates of relative sea level rise, in mm/year, along the Eastern Seaboard (data from NOAA http://tidesandcurrents.noaa.gov/sltrends/index.shtml).

natural coastlines is undoubtedly a draw, these populations centres are culturally and historically of interest to tourists and a magnet for visitors. Both cultural wealth and population density must be a further consideration in terms of potential value and vulnerability. Coastal population density is about three times that of inland areas in the USA (Crossett *et al.*, 2004). Crowell *et al.* (2010) estimate that 7.9% of the total US population lives within zones exposed to erosion on an open coast or in a region that has been determined by FEMA

(Federal Emergency Management Agency) as having a 1% annual chance coastal flood hazard. A sea level rise of 0.91 m increases the US land area at risk of flooding to 67,330 km^2, increasing insured property values by 100–200% (FEMA, 1991). Households in the USA at risk of flood would increase from ~2.7 million to 5.7 million and 6.8 million by the year 2100 assuming a 0.3 m and 0.91 m rise in sea level, respectively (FEMA, 1991).

New York is subsiding due to GIA and relative sea level rise is around 2.8 mm/year (Douglas, 1991). The vulnerability of the city was highlighted in December 1992, when an extra-tropical storm (or 'Nor'easter') produced high winds and some of the worst flooding on record due to a 2.6 m storm surge. Many critical transportation systems sit only 2–6 m above current sea level. As a result of the storm, the Metropolitan transportation system (the Metro) had to be shut down and many waterfront communities evacuated. Had the water been just 30 cm higher, the rail system would have been inundated, flooding the subway tunnels and potentially resulting in the loss of life (NAST, 2000). Given the predicted SLR by 2100, a storm of the same or lower magnitude would have produced a lot more damage.

Nor'easter storms produce significant storm surges in high to mid-latitudes, though recent studies indicate that global warming is pushing these systems further north (Gutowski et al., 2008). Karl et al. (2008) conclude that, in the future, these storms will become more intense with stronger winds and more extreme wave heights. The frequency of these storms is likely to increase in the north and decrease to the south, because of the northerly shift in the weather patterns, raising the threat to areas such as Cape Cod, where sandy systems can be heavily altered and eroded during Nor'easters (Adams and Giese, 2008).

Atlantic hurricanes regularly threaten the East Coast with storm surges of up to 5 m (Karl et al., 2008). Recent investigations indicate that the intensity of these storms has increased over the past 30 years (Emanuel et al., 2004, 2008; Emanuel, 2005, 2008; Elsner et al., 2008; Komar and Allan, 2008). As sea surface temperatures increase, this trend is likely to continue (IPCC, 2007; Karl et al., 2008). Whether climate change will impact the frequency of these storms is still uncertain (Elsner et al., 2008; Emanuel et al., 2008), however, the increase in intensity alone is enough to cause concern, as it will lead to higher winds, waves and storm surges and, thus, an increasing flood and erosion risk to the shoreline and coastal properties.

Coastal Response to Climate Change

While the threat of individual processes, such as inundation or increased wave energy, to a coastline is profound, the non-linear interaction among responses may enhance the rate and extent of shoreline alterations, further heightening the coastal hazard (Stive, 2004; Nicholls et al., 2007). Certain systems may have tipping points, experiencing a gradual or negligible response to climate forcing, until eventually a threshold is met, after which catastrophic and irreversible damage may occur. This is thought to be true of both coastal wetlands and coral reefs (Morris et al., 2002; FitzGerald et al., 2006; Reed et al., 2008; CCSP, 2009).

Furthermore, our predictions rely on observations of systems where change may lag the forcing, and the assumptions made within our models may not always be applicable or realistic (Cooper and Pilkey, 2004; Kirwan and Murray, 2007). Feedbacks between processes can become very complex, muddying our understanding and thus reducing the accuracy of our forecasts. The impacts of relative SLR, however, are already evident in many areas and are likely to increase over the coming century (FitzGerald *et al.*, 2006, 2008; Nicholls *et al.*, 2007; Hughes *et al.*, 2009). Despite the difficulty in estimating the compound response of coastlines to climate change, some general conclusions can be drawn (CCSP, 2009) and in order to do this, it is necessary to consider different coastal morphologies and their distribution along the Eastern Seaboard.

Rocky headlands, bays and pocket beaches dominate much of the northeast coast. Further south the higher sediment supplies and wide continental shelf lend themselves to sandy barrier shorelines, characterized by shore-parallel islands separated by tidal inlets, and protecting extensive lagoons, wetlands or estuaries (Meade, 1972; Psuty and Ofiara, 2002). The few barrier islands in the north-east are smaller, isolated systems and the back-barrier marshes sit at a higher elevation than those further south. Tidal range varies along the coast, a function of the shape of the local coastline. The tides are mostly micro-tidal (<2 m), ranging from less than 0.3 m in parts of Florida and Maryland, to over 2 m at a few sites in parts of Maine, Massachusetts, New York and Georgia (NOAA, http://tidesandcurrents.noaa.gov). There are very few macro-tidal areas and these are limited to the far north, within the Bay of Fundy. The funnelling shape of Chesapeake Bay and the Bay of Fundy produce large tidal ranges; however, a great deal of the open shoreline is dominated by waves (e.g. North Carolina) or mixed-energy (e.g. Georgia).

It is virtually certain that headlands will experience increased erosion over the next century (CCSP, 2009) and SLR will dramatically alter sandy beaches and barrier island coasts. These impacts go beyond simple inundation and involve the permanent or long-term loss of sand from beaches. Barriers support a thriving tourist industry and residential communities, for example, Figure Eight Island, North Carolina, a single 7-km-long barrier, has a tax base of more than US$2 billion (FitzGerald *et al.*, 2008). Tourism plays a major part in the economies of coastal regions, and the success of this industry depends on the vitality of the beaches. On the Eastern Seaboard, almost 90% of beaches that are not anthropogenically stabilized or engineered in some way are experiencing long-term erosion (Galgano *et al.*, 1998). US East Coast beaches have retreated an estimated 23.8 m on average for each 0.3 m of sea level rise over the last century (Zhang *et al.*, 2004). Widespread beach erosion is a result of a combination of inundation, which allows waves to act higher up the beach profile, changes in storm intensity, and human interference (Thieler and Hammer-Klose, 1999; Zhang *et al.*, 2004). Beach erosion actively transfers sediment from the beach to the offshore, reducing the available sediment supply; however, because of the interaction of this process with inundation, it is difficult to quantify the relationship between SLR and shoreline change (Stive, 2004; Zhang *et al.*, 2004).

Spits and barrier islands are expected to experience increased erosion and overwash (a mechanism by which some barriers migrate landward). This change will probably be dynamic; erosion at one site may lead to deposition further along the beach due to longshore transports. It is probable, however, that at some point a threshold will be met, and these features will be significantly reduced in size or removed (CCSP, 2009). Existing studies indicate that barriers have thinned in some areas over the last century and evidence of barrier migration is not widespread on the mid-Atlantic coast (CCSP, 2009). Barrier island chains in Louisiana (e.g. Chandeleur Islands and Isle Dernieres) have undergone a significant land loss in recent years in response to a limited sediment supply, accelerated rates of SLR and permanent erosion of sand by hurricanes (see reviews in FitzGerald et al., 2008 and CCSP, 2009). Recent studies of the North Carolina Outer Banks indicate that Abermarle and Pamlico Sounds have experienced fully open-ocean conditions at lease twice in the last 2000 years, suggesting the removal or segmenting of the barrier islands in the past (Culver et al., 2007, 2008). These conditions may well occur again. The same may be true of the extensive barrier systems in Virginia, much of which comprises a wildlife reserve, but these have been undergoing increased shoreline erosion since the 1970s (Fenster and Dolan, 1994). The barrier islands sit close to sea level and their transgression is evident as marsh and trees, once part of the back-barrier, are incorporated into the beach front as overwash pushes the islands back towards land (personal communication, M. Fenster).

Coastal wetlands are especially vulnerable to changes in SLR given their flat morphology and elevations close to mean sea level. Marsh plants respond to increased inundation by increasing productivity, thus enhancing both organic and inorganic accretion, allowing them to keep pace with SLR (Redfield, 1972). A recent study by Langley et al. (2009) demonstrates that increases in atmospheric CO_2 may actually stimulate the productivity in coastal wetlands, perhaps assisting this accretion. Differences in the hydrodynamics, sediment supply and dominant species of vegetation within different marshes leads to a high potential for variation in coastal wetland response to climate change. However, a threshold inundation exists at which the marsh plants cease to enhance in productivity and ultimately perish (Morris et al., 2002), consequently, the marsh platform is submerged as vertical accretion ceases. It is virtually certain that tidal wetlands are already experiencing submergence due to SLR and associated high rates of loss (CCSP, 2009).

Reed et al. (2008) make an opinion-based assessment of the vulnerability of coastal wetlands along the New York–New Jersey coast. They project with a moderate level of confidence that wetlands presently keeping pace with sea-level rise would only survive a 2 mm/year acceleration in SLR under optimal hydrology and sediment supply conditions, and would not survive an acceleration of 7 mm/year, thresholds chosen based on predictions from the IPCC (2007).

The loss of tidal wetlands or an increase in tidal exchange as inundation increases may have a dramatic effect on the barriers and tidal inlets that front the system. Relationships between the size of a coastal embayment, the volume of water needed to fill it at each tide (tidal prism) and the size and shape of tidal inlets will cause feedbacks that lead to the enlargement of the inlets and the loss

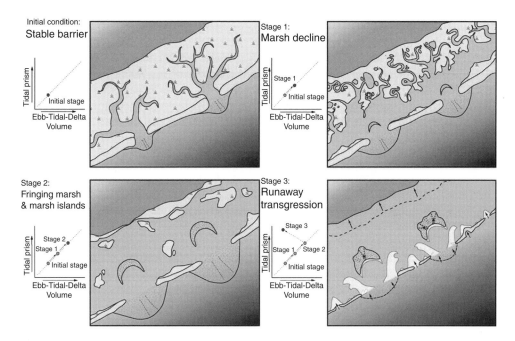

Fig. 12.3. The runaway deterioration of a back-barrier system (conceptualized by FitzGerald *et al.*, 2007).

of sediment from the barrier islands to the ebb and flood deltas (FitzGerald *et al.*, 2006, 2008; Fig. 12.3). Wetlands may also respond to changing sea level and inundation by expanding their drainage network, initially keeping pace with sea level, although ultimately this could lead to the dissection and erosion of the marsh platform (Hughes *et al.*, 2009).

Changes in ecosystems, species composition and diversity would be expected in response to both SLR and changes in temperature or precipitation. Lobsters, a favourite with the tourists in New England, are found in cooler waters, which would be moved northwards. As the water temperature changes the lobster will be found farther north as well, potentially removing them from the waters off Rhode Island and Massachusetts. The dominant species of tree in New England would be likely to change, the colourful maples that are responsible for a thriving tourist industry in autumn (known as 'leafing') are likely to be replaced by other species. Shore protection and development now prevents landward migration of coastal habitats in many areas. The loss of wetlands will remove valuable ecosystem services such as water filtering and spawning grounds for commercially important fisheries. Vulnerable species that rely on these habitats range from endangered beetles to fish and shellfish, and include migratory birds, marsh plants and aquatic vegetation.

For further details of coastal response to climate change and sea level rise, the reader is referred to the reviews by FitzGerald *et al.* (2008) and within the CCSP report (2009).

Feedbacks Between Human and Coastal Response

Over the next century, the impact of global climate change on both coastlines and mankind is likely to be significant (Nicholls *et al.*, 2007; FitzGerald *et al.*, 2008; CCSP, 2009). However, the actual extent of this impact is subject to uncertainty, mostly stemming from human-controlled factors. These include potential changes in management approach and dominant coastal land use (Nicholls, 2003). The impacts will include (NAST, 2000; FitzGerald *et al.*, 2006, 2008; CCSP, 2009):

- increased loss of property and coastal habitats;
- increased flood risk and potential loss of life;
- damage to coastal protection works and other infrastructure;
- loss of renewable and subsistence resources;
- loss of tourism and recreation;
- impacts to human health, through, for example, lowering of air quality due to increased temperatures;
- impacts on agriculture and aquaculture through decline in soil and water quality;
- disruption of transportation systems, infrastructure and culturally important sites.

Ports provide gateways for transport of goods domestically and abroad and coastal resorts and beaches are central to the US economy (CCSP, 2009). As a result, their loss would be significant financially. Societal response to SLR will potentially have huge ramifications in terms of the economy and the environment.

Societies are able to respond to changes in circumstance, especially if valuable resources are threatened. However, human reactions will be influenced not just by the physical setting, but also by the nature of the existing assets, laws, economics and, ultimately, human aspirations (CCSP, 2009). Mankind will gladly exploit advantageous changes, but will also adapt to the negative. Consequently, actual impacts tend to be much less than the potential impacts in the absence of adaptation (Nicholls, 2003; Fig. 12.4).

In terms of coastal response to global warming, the ability to adapt to future changes needs to be included in management policies now, in order to make it possible when the need arises (Cicin-Sain and Knecht, 1998). There is a need to develop adaptive capacity. Recent reports have concluded that management plans concerning the impacts of climate change are presently lacking (Nicholls, 2003; CCSP, 2009). In most countries, SLR is not addressed in coastal management despite the wide acceptance of the phenomenon, illustrating the poor basis to plan for future rise (Nicholls, 2003; CCSP, 2009). Policy adoption occurs in four stages: (i) information and awareness building; (ii) planning and design; (iii) evaluation; and (iv) monitoring and evaluation (Nicholls, 2003). These stages can be embedded within multiple policy cycles. Thus dissemination of scientific knowledge and concern, being part of the first stage, is vital in initiating the process.

Adaptation to SLR will most likely involve compromise, particularly in terms of cost–benefit. For example, while a seawall protects a community from SLR,

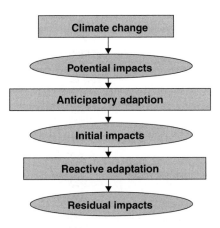

Fig. 12.4. Model of impacts of climate change (from Nicholls, 2003).

the long-term economic and ecological costs need to be considered. Increasing population density, development of residential or recreational property (and related infrastructure) conflict directly with the desire to maintain the natural sustainable ecosystems.

A balance between management and retreat is often necessary. The use of structural devices and beach replenishment projects to protect the current shoreline may protect the high value coastal property and tourism revenues, but will result in increased maintenance costs and environmental damage in the long term. Thus, while retreat is often socially disruptive in the short term, shore protection may be either unsustainable or disruptive in the long term. The environmental impacts of shore protection are likely to be the greater of the two choices and, in fact, may result in the elimination of wetlands (which require some sediment input) and natural beaches in most developed regions (CCSP, 2009). Beach nourishment schemes are the most common engineering response to the impacts of SLR on the Eastern Seaboard (CCSP, 2009). The state of New Jersey, for example, has responded to the SLR threat with both structural and non-structural approaches, but with a particular focus on beach nourishment (Cooper *et al.*, 2005). Beach nourishment may ultimately be too costly to sustain and may prevent overwash, which acts to maintain marshes in the back-barrier.

Implications for Tourism and Recreation

Given the potential for change in societal attitudes and management policy, it is difficult to predict the impact of climate change on tourism on the Eastern Coast. However, assuming a 'business as usual' scenario, certain conclusions can be drawn. As temperatures change, the north-east will experience extended periods of warm weather, during which beaches and shorelines can be enjoyed. This extended opportunity for outside recreation may be impacted by changes in precipitation patterns, if the climate does become increasingly rainy. The adverse impacts of temperature change will include a reduced snow pack and, thus, a potential decrease in recreational skiing during the winter. The saddest change may be the loss of the famous New England 'leafers' as the autumn foliage colours are muted by species composition changes. Some losses are subtler, for example, the decline of the lobster catch in Massachusetts or a reduction in maple syrup production in Vermont, but the impact on tourism may be significant because they are associated with tradition and local culture. In terms of human health, increases in insect populations are likely as the temperature and precipitation increase, threatening a rise in the occurrence of illnesses such as West Nile virus and Eastern Equine Encephalitis. In the south, heatwaves and droughts during summer may threaten the tourist industry. A notable heatwave in 1998 was estimated to have caused US$6 billion in damages and caused 200 deaths in the southern states (NAST, 2000).

Sea level rise threatens the entire coastline, particularly barrier shorelines and wetlands. This presents a hazard to existing waterline vacation homes and tourist accommodations. The greatest land loss is predicted in the Mid-Atlantic, but all regions are subject to the threat of saltwater intrusion into freshwater aquifers and increased storm damage and flooding to various extents. This pushes both coastal ecosystems and development inland, which may ultimately result in competition between the two.

New Jersey coastal tourism generates US$16 billion tourism annually, supporting hundreds of thousands of jobs with Atlantic City attracting over 37 million visitors each year. Ecotourism in coastal natural areas is flourishing. However, assuming a 'business as usual' scenario, there is a 50% chance that close to $20 km^2$ of developed shoreline will be impacted by permanent inundation over the next century (Cooper *et al.*, 2005). The US$2.6 billion coastal tourism industry in North Carolina is equally threatened (Poulter *et al.*, 2009).

Cicin-Sain and Knecht (1998) are clear in their conclusions that the survival and prosperity of coastal tourism in the USA requires good coastal management practices relating to:

- location of infrastructure and provision of public access;
- clean air and water, and healthy ecosystems;
- maintenance of a safe and secure recreational environment, specifically relating to management of hazards;
- provision of adequate levels of safety for boaters, swimmers and other recreational users;
- beach restoration, including beach nourishment and other efforts that maintain and enhance the recreational and amenity values of beaches; but with
- sound policies for coastal wildlife and habitat protection.

Yet, at the time that they drew these conclusions, little guidance was available from the federal government to steer either states or local communities in the development of sustainable coastal tourism development (Cicin-Sain and Knecht, 1998).

While individual states are becoming more aware of the need for sustainable tourism in coastal regions (for example, the document 'Improving Maine's Beaches' released by the Maine State Planning Office, 1998), there is still a general lack of management policy, leading the CCSP (2009) to conclude that most organizations are not yet taking specific measures to prepare for rising sea level. With the potential for dramatic land loss and ecosystem alteration on the East

Coast as our climate changes, it seems there is still a need to adapt our management policies and preserve the valuable assets, which support the billion-dollar tourist industry.

References

Adams M. and Giese, G. (2008) *Nauset Beach Breach and Inlet Formation, 2007–2008.* National Park Service, US Department of the Interior, Cape Cod National Seashore, Wellfleet, Massachusetts.

Bamber, J.L., Ekholm, S. and Krabill, W.B. (2001) A new, high-resolution digital elevation model of Greenland fully validated with airborne laser altimeter data. *Journal of Geophysical Research* 106(B4), 6733–6745.

CCSP (2009) *Coastal Sensitivity to Sea-Level Rise: A Focus on the Mid-Atlantic Region.* Report by the US Climate Change Science Program and the Subcommittee on Global Change Research. (Titus, J.G. (Coordinating Lead Author), Anderson, K.E., Cahoon, D.R., Gesch, D.B., Gill, S.K., Gutierrez, B.T., Thieler, E.R. and Williams, S.J. (Lead Authors)), US Environmental Protection Agency, Washington DC, USA.

Cicin-Sain, B. and Knecht, R.W. (1998) *Integrated Coastal and Ocean Management: Concepts and Practices.* Island Press, Washington, DC, 517pp.

Cooper, J.A.G. and Pilkey, O.H. (2004) Sea-level rise and shoreline retreat: time to abandon the Bruun Rule. *Global and Planetary Change* 43(3-4), 157–171.

Cooper, M.J.P., Beever, M.D. and Oppenheimer, M. (2005) Future sea level rise and the New Jersey coast: assessing potential impacts and opportunities. Working Paper, Woodrow Wilson School of Public and International Affairs, Princeton University.

Crossett, K., Culliton, T.J., Wiley, P.C. and Goodspeed, T.R. (2004) *Population Trends along the Coastal United States, 1980–2008.* NOAA National Ocean Service Special Projects Office, Silver Spring, Maryland, USA, 47pp.

Crowell, M., Coulton, K., Johnson, C., Westcott, J., Bellomo, D., Edelman, S. and Hirsch, E. (2010) An estimate of the US population living in 100-year coastal flood hazard areas. *Journal of Coastal Research* 26(2), 201–211.

Culliton, T. (1998) *Population: Distribution, Density, and Growth. NOAA's State of the Coast Report.* National Oceanic and Atmospheric Administration, Silver Spring, Maryland, 33pp.

Culver, S.J., Grand Pre, C.A., Mallinson, D.J., Riggs, S.R., Corbett, D.R., Foley, J., Hale, M., Metger, L., Ricardo, J., Rosenberger, J., Smith, C.G., Smith, C.W., Synder, S.W., Twamley, D., Farrell, K. and Horton, B. (2007) Late Holocene barrier island collapse: Outer Banks, North Carolina, USA. *The Sedimentary Record* 5(4), 4–8.

Culver, S.J., Farrell, K.M., Mallinson, D.J., Horton, B.P., Willard, D.A., Thieler, E.R., Riggs, S.R., Snyder, S.W., Wehmiller, J.F., Bernhardt, C.E. and Hillier, C. (2008) Micropaleontologic record of late Pliocene and Quaternary paleoenvironments in the northern Albemarle Embayment, North Carolina, USA. *Paleogeography, Paleoclimatology, Paleoecology* 264(1–2), 54–77.

Day, J.W., Gunn, J.D., Folan, J., Yáñez-Arancibia, A. and Horton, B.P. (2007) Emergence of complex societies after sea level stabilized. *EOS Transactions of the American Geophysical Union* 88(15), 169, 170.

Donnelly, J.P. (2006) A revised late Holocene sea-level record for northern Massachusetts, USA. *Journal of Coastal Research* 22, 1051–1061.

Douglas, B.C. (1991) Global sea-level rise. *Journal of Geophysical Research* 96(C4), 6981–6992.

Douglas, B.C. (2001) Sea level change in the era of the recording tide gauges. In: Douglas, B.C., Kearney, M.S. and Leatherman, S.P. (eds) *Sea Level Rise: History and Consequences.* International geophysics series v. 75. Academic Press, San Diego, pp. 37–64.

Elsner, J.B., Kossin, J.P. and Jagger, T.H. (2008) The increasing intensity of the strongest tropical cyclones. *Nature* 455(7209), 92–95.

Emanuel, K.A. (2005) Increasing destructiveness of tropical cyclones over the past 30 years. *Nature* 436(7051), 686–688.

Emanuel, K. (2008) The hurricane–climate connection. *Bulletin of the American Meteorological Society* 89(5), ES10–ES20.

Emanuel, K., DesAutels, C., Holloway, C. and Korty, R. (2004) Environmental control of tropical cyclone intensity. *Journal of the Atmospheric Sciences* 61(7), 843–858.

Emanuel, K., Sundararajan, R. and Williams, J. (2008) Hurricanes and global warming: results from downscaling IPCC AR4 simulations. *Bulletin of the American Meteorological Society* 89(3), 347–367.

Evans, R.L. (2004) Pinning down the moving shoreline. *Oceanus* 42, 1–6.

Fairbanks, R.G. (1989) A 17,000-year glacio-eustatic sea level record – influence of glacial melting rates on the Younger Dryas event and deep-sea circulation. *Nature* 342(6250), 637–642.

FEMA (Federal Emergency Management Agency) (1991) *Projected Impact of Relative Sea Level Rise on the National Flood Insurance Program: Report to Congress.* Federal Insurance Administration, Washington, DC, 61pp, www.epa.gov/climatechange/effects/downloads/flood_insurance.pdf (Accessed: 30 August 2009).

Fenster, M.S. and Dolan, R. (1994) Large-scale reversals in shoreline trends along the US mid-Atlantic coast. *Geology* 22, 543–546.

Field, C.B., Mortsch, L.D., Brklacich, M., Forbes, D.L., Kovacs, P., Patz, J.A., Running, S.W. and Scott, M.J. (2007) North America. In: Parry, M.L., Canziani, O.F., Palutikof, J.P., van der Linden, P.J. and Hanson, C.E. (eds) *Climate Change 2007: Impacts, Adaptation and Vulnerability.* Contribution of Working Group II to the Fourth Assessment Report of the Intergovernmental Panel on Climate Change Final Report. Cambridge University Press, Cambridge, UK, and New York, pp. 617–652.

FitzGerald, D.M., Rosen, P.S. and van Heteren, S. (1994) New England barriers. In: Davis, R.A. (ed.) *Geology of Holocene Barrier Island Systems.* Springer-Verlag, Berlin, Germany, pp. 305–394.

FitzGerald, D.M., Buynevich, I.V. and Argow, B.A. (2006) Model of tidal inlet and barrier island dynamics in a regime of accelerated sea-level rise. *Journal of Coastal Research* (Special Issue) 39, 789–795.

FitzGerald, D.M., Fenster, M.S., Argow, B.A. and Buynevich, I.V. (2008) Coastal impacts due to sea-level rise. *Annual Review of Earth and Planetary Sciences* 36, 601–647.

Galgano, F.A., Douglas, B.C. and Leatherman, S.P. (1998) Trends and variability of shoreline position. *Journal of Coastal Research* 26, 282–291.

Gornitz, V., Couch, S. and Hartig, E.K. (2002) Impacts of sea level rise in the New York City metropolitan area. *Global and Planetary Change* 32(1), 61–88.

Gutowski, W.J., Hegerl, G.C., Holland, G.J., Knutson, T.R., Mearns, L.O., Stouffer, R.J., Webster, P.J., Wehner, M.F. and Zwiers, F.W. (2008) Causes of observed changes in extremes and projections of future changes. In: Karl, T.R., Meehl, G.A., Miller, C.D., Hassol, S.J., Waple, A.M. and Murray, W.L. (eds) *Weather and Climate Extremes in a Changing Climate: Regions of Focus: North America, Hawaii, Caribbean, and US Pacific Islands.* Synthesis and Assessment Product 3.3. US Climate Change Science Program, Washington, DC, pp. 81–116.

Houston, J.R. (1995) *The Economic Value of Beaches*. CERCular, Coastal Engineering Research Center, Vol. CERC-95-4, December.

Hughes, Z.J., FitzGerald, D.M., Wilson, C.A., Pennings, S.C., Więski, K. and Mahadevan, A. (2009) Rapid headward erosion of marsh creeks in response to relative sea level rise. *Geophysical Research Letters* 36, L03602, doi:10.1029/2008GL036000.

IPCC (2007) Climate change 2007: the physical science basis, summary for policymakers. *Contribution of the Working Group I to the Fourth Assessment Report of the Intergovernmental Panel on Climate Change.* Cambridge, UK.

Jevrejeva, S., Moore, J.C., Grinsted, A. and Woodworth, P.L. (2008) Recent global sea level acceleration started over 200 years ago? *Geophysical Research Letters* 35, L08715, doi:10.1029/2008GL033611.

Karetinkov, D., Lakhey, S., Horin, C., Bell, B., Ruth, M., Ross, K. and Irani, D. (2008) *Report: Economic Impacts of Climate Change on North Carolina*. The Center for Integrative Environmental Research, University of Maryland, College Park, Maryland, 18pp, www.cier.umd.edu/climateadaptation (Accessed: 30 August 2009).

Karl, T.R., Meehl, G.A., Peterson, T.C., Kunkel, K.E., Gutowski, W.J. Jr and Easterling, D.R. (2008) Executive summary. In: Karl, T.R., Meehl, G.A., Miller, C.D., Hassol, S.J., Waple, A.M. and Murray, W.L. (eds) *Weather and Climate Extremes in a Changing Climate: Regions of Focus: North America, Hawaii, Caribbean, and US Pacific Islands.* Synthesis and Assessment Product 3.3. US Climate Change Science Program, Washington, DC, pp. 1–9.

Kirwan, M.L. and Murray, A.B. (2007) A coupled geomorphic and ecological model of tidal marsh evolution. *Proceedings of the National Academy of Sciences* 104(15), 6118–6122.

Komar, P.D. and Allan, J.C. (2008) Increasing hurricane-generated wave heights along the US East Coast and their climate controls. *Journal of Coastal Research* 24(2), 479–488.

Langley, J.A., McKee, K.L., Cahoon, D.R., Cherry, J.A. and Megonigal, J.P. (2009) Elevated CO_2 stimulates marsh elevation gain, counterbalancing sea-level rise. *Proceedings of the National Academy of Sciences* 106(15), 6182–6186.

Lythe, M.B. and Vaughan, D.G. (2001) BEDMAP: a new ice thickness and subglacial topographic model of Antarctica. *Journal of Geophysical Research – Solid Earth* 106(B6), 11335–11352.

Maine State Planning Office (1998) Improving Maine's Beaches: Recommendations of the Southern Maine Beach Stakeholder Group. Report by the Maine State Planning Office, Department of Conservation, Augusta, Maine, 18pp.

Meade, R.H. (1972) Transport and deposition of sediments in estuaries. *Geological Society of America* 133(1), 91–120.

Morris, J.T., Sundareshwar, P.V., Nietch, C.T., Kjerfve, B. and Cahoon, D.R. (2002) Responses of coastal wetlands to rising sea level. *Ecology* 83, 2869–2877.

National Assessment Synthesis Team (NAST) (2000) *Climate Change Impacts on the United States: The Potential Consequences of Climate Variability and Change.* US Global Change Research Program, Washington, DC.

Nicholls, R.J. (2003) *Case Study on Sea Level Rise Impacts*. Prepared for OECD workshop on the Benefits of Climate Policy: Improving Information for Policy Makers: 12–13 December 2002, Working Party on Global and Structural Policies, Organization for Economic Cooperation and Development, Paris.

Nicholls, R.J., Wong, P.P., Burkett, V.R., Codignotto, J.O., Hay, J.E., McLean, R.F., Ragoonaden, S. and Woodroffe, C.D. (2007) Coastal systems and low-lying areas. *Climate Change 2007: Impacts, Adaptation and Vulnerability*. Contribution of Working Group II to the Fourth Assessment Report of the Intergovernmental Panel on

Climate Change (Parry, M.L., Canziani, O.F., Palutikof, J.P., van der Linden, P.J. and Hanson, C.E. (eds)). Cambridge University Press, Cambridge, UK, and New York, pp. 315–356.

Pilkey, O.H. and Cooper, J.A.G. (2004) Society and sea level rise. *Science* 303(5665), 1781–1782.

Poulter, B., Feldman, R., Brinson, M.M., Horton, B.P., Pearsall, S.H., Reyes, E., Riggs, S.R. and Whitehead, J.C. (2009) Sea-level rise research and dialogue in North Carolina: creating windows for policy change. *Ocean and Coastal Management* 52(3–4), 147–153.

Psuty, N.P. and Ofiara, D.D. (2002) *Coastal Hazard Management: Lessons and Future Directions from New Jersey.* Rutgers University Press, New Brunswick, New Jersey, 429pp.

Rahmstorf, S. (2007) A semi-empirical approach to projecting future sea-level rise. *Science* 315(5810), 368–370.

Redfield, A.C. (1972) Development of a New England salt marsh. *Ecological Monographs* 42, 201–237.

Reed, D.J., Bishara, D., Cahoon, D., Donnelly, J., Kearney, M., Kolker, A., Leonard, L., Orson, R.A. and Stevenson, J.C. (2008) Site-specific scenarios for wetlands accretion as sea level rises in the mid-Atlantic region. In: Titus, J.G. and Strange, E.M. (eds) *Background Documents Supporting Climate Change Science Program Synthesis and Assessment Product 4.1: Coastal Elevations and Sensitivity to Sea Level Rise.* EPA 430R07004. US Environmental Protection Agency, Washington, DC, pp. 134–174. http://epa.gov/climatechange/effects/coastal/background.html (Accessed: 30 August 2009).

Rowley, R.J., Kostelnick, J.C., Braaten, D., Li, X. and Meisel, J. (2007) Risk of rising sea level to population and land area. *Eos, Transactions of the American Geophysical Union* 88(9), 105, 107.

Stive, M.J.F. (2004) How important is global warming for coastal erosion? An editorial comment. *Climatic Change* 64(1–2), 27–39.

Thieler, E.R. and Hammer-Klose, E.S. (1999) National Assessment of Coastal Vulnerability to Future Sea Level Rise: Preliminary Results for the US Atlantic Coast. *US Geological Survey Open-File Report 99-593*.

Titus, J.G. and Richman, C. (2001) Maps of lands vulnerable to sea level rise: modeled elevations along the US Atlantic and Gulf coasts. *Climate Research* 18(3), 205–228.

Titus, J.G. and Wang, J. (2008) Maps of lands close to sea level along the middle Atlantic coast of the United States: an elevation data set to use while waiting for LIDAR. In: Titus, J.G. and Strange, E.M. (eds) *Background Documents Supporting Climate Change Science Program Synthesis and Assessment Product 4.1: Coastal Elevations and Sensitivity to Sea Level Rise.* EPA 430R07004. US Environmental Protection Agency, Washington, DC, pp. 2–44.

Titus, J.G., Park, R.A., Leatherman, S.P., Weggel, J.R., Greene, M.S., Mausel, P.W., Brown, S., Gaunt, G., Threhan, M. and Yohe, G. (1991) Greenhouse effect and sea level rise: the cost of holding back the sea. *Coastal Management* 19(2), 171–204.

UNTWO (2008) *World Tourism Barometer*, 6(2) June 2008, p.55.

US Department of Commerce, ITA, Office of Travel & Tourism Industries (2009) *Summary of International Travel to the US.* (I-94) report, May 2009.

Zhang, K., Douglas, B.C. and Leatherman, S.P. (2004) Global warming and coastal erosion. *Climatic Change* 64(1–2), 41–58.

13 Would You Like Ice With That? Antarctic Tourism and Climate Change

JULIA JABOUR

Introduction

The Antarctic has lured explorers, adventurers, fishers, scientists and tourists to its icy landscape for nearly two centuries. There was a time in history when the actual existence of the continent was disputed, and times when people thought they would never *know* Antarctica because of the seemingly impenetrable barrier of ice excluding them. Today scientists have unlocked many of its secrets, and it seems that the more people know about the Antarctic, the more they want to know; its magic has entered their bones. There is no other way of explaining the curious attraction people have to the Antarctic wilderness (Tin *et al.*, 2008). Consequently, its exposure, through gallant tales of adventure and endeavour, has spawned a tourism industry that began modestly in the 1960s and has grown exponentially since, but especially during the last decade (Table 13. 1).

Using figures collated by the International Association of Antarctica Tour Operators (IAATO, 2008) for the 2007/08 season, actual landings by these 50,000 tourists on Antarctic islands and the continent were calculated to be 197,286, representing 17,263 person-days ashore. The latter calculation is based on the assumption that there were, in addition to the tourist landings, 9864 staff landings (calculated using the industry determined ratio of 20:1 passengers to staff), and each for at least 2 h duration (Jabour, 2009). It is clear, however, that actual tourist numbers are very modest in global terms, and visitor impact is more appropriately measured by comparing this number to scientific effort in Antarctica, which is 16 times greater. The estimated person-days ashore for scientific summer-only personnel for the same period were 282,690. Here it was assumed that the number of staff was 3141 (based on the reported peak station capacity of 4229 minus 1088 year-round positions) and that each national science programme summer-only position was occupied at a base in Antarctica for an average of 90 days per year (Table 13.2; Jabour, 2009).

Table 13.1. Comparison of approximate numbers of voyages and landed tourists for reporting seasons 2001 and 2008 (From: International Association of Antarctica Tour Operators, 2001, 2008).

Year	Voyages (all)	Landed tourists
2001	134	12,000
2008	309	50,000

Table 13.2. Comparison of approximate person-days ashore for scientific summer-only personnel and landed tourists in 2008 (Jabour, 2009).

	Scientific summer-only personnel	Landed tourists
Person-days ashore	282,690	17,263

Put like this, it is easy to imagine that human impact is likely to come from Antarctica's extraordinary scientific importance, more so than from its touristic values (historic, wilderness or aesthetic). Notwithstanding, all values must co-exist harmoniously and herein lies the great Antarctic paradox: there is considerable competition for Antarctica's prime coastal real estate, with the major tourism effort occurring along the coastline of the Antarctic Peninsula and its close offshore islands – the same places where a significant cluster of research stations have been built (COMNAP, 2009) and where large numbers of wildlife congregate to breed and feed, the objects of the gaze of scientists and tourists alike (Fig. 13.1). Add to this the usual commercial demons associated with tourism operations anywhere in the world, and Antarctic tourism is indeed a complex beast. However, it is further plagued by problems of uncertain jurisdiction, localized extreme weather, sea ice and icebergs, high operating costs, minimal or no infrastructure, problematic search and rescue capability and the disproportionate expectations of high-end clients. Today this is played out in conditions of rapid climate warming, which have accelerated in recent years and now threaten to have considerable impact on the tourism destination and ultimately the industry.

Antarctic tourism is unique, the distinguishing feature being the lack of legally proven, and in some cases disputed, sovereignty over the continental destination. Specifically, there is not one single government that can make and enforce a uniform set of laws relating to tourism activities in, or affecting, its territory in Antarctica that can be universally applied to every tourism operator, or tourist, or vessel. Article IV of the 1959 Antarctic Treaty proscribes such an approach by indefinitely freezing claims to territory as they were in 1959, meaning that the seven claimants maintained their claim, the two who reserved their right to claim maintained that right, and the rest could do nothing while the Treaty was in force. The search for a new or more efficient system to regulate tourism and manage growth in these changing climatic conditions is, therefore, more

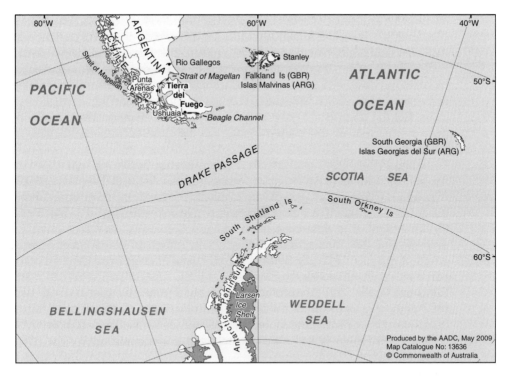

Fig. 13.1. The Peninsula (west Antarctic) region and major gateway ports (From: AADC, 2009).

complicated because precedents simply do not exist. This chapter examines how changing climatic conditions may affect the current tourism product and destination. Tourism is a poor cousin to scientific research in Antarctica, therefore tourists are likely to have more stringent regulation applied to them than the scientists. But tourism is also a legitimate peaceful activity that cannot be stopped. The key will be to manage tourism growth under these dynamic circumstances without disenfranchising operators or worse, isolating them to the point where tourism is driven underground and becomes largely unregulated.

Tourism Product and Destination

The way visitors (scientists and tourists) perceive the Antarctic is different to anywhere else on the planet, for some curious reason. The Antarctic is suffused in a mythology of romance and adventure, until you travel there. Then the myth becomes reality! A voyage south can be a life-changing journey, awakening a sense of Antarctica's special appeal and an obligation to protect it for future generations. Some visitors are there to do science, others to provide support for them. The tourism literature reports that some just want to see what all the fuss is about, to check off their seventh continent, to fulfil a life-long dream, or to follow in the footsteps of the famous explorers – Amundsen, Scott and Shackleton (Bauer, 2001; Powell *et al.*, 2008). Most are glassy-eyed with expectation, and they are rarely disappointed, despite the challenging physical and mental conditions of getting there. It's cold; it's a long way by sea; it can be extremely uncomfortable if you are not a good sailor, and sometimes even if you are! The pitching and rolling are relentless; the routine can be monotonous; and the weather, atrocious. But the rewards are good and the visitors keep coming. The majority of them are fare-paying tourists participating in the largest commercial activity in the Antarctic.

Greater than 90% of Antarctic tourism is ship borne, operating out of the port of Ushuaia in Argentina to locations in the Antarctic Peninsula region (Fig. 13.1). Other gateway ports with relatively less traffic include Punta Arenas (Chile) and Hobart (Tasmania), Lyttelton (New Zealand) and Cape Town (South Africa). The difference between west (Peninsula) and east Antarctic tourism, and the primary reason why South American embarkation is preferred, is distance: it is only 800 km across Drake Passage from Ushuaia compared with 2600 km across the Southern Ocean to East Antarctica from Hobart. Either sea voyage can be extremely rough, but a force 10 storm is not so bad for 2 days; any longer, and it would be almost unbearable for all but a hardy few! Antarctic tourism is, therefore, a significant seasonal economic activity for Ushuaia particularly, but also Punta Arenas; it is less important for the other ports (Muir *et al.*, 2007).

The industry body, IAATO, collects, collates and publishes tourism figures (not verified by any independent source other than, occasionally, the port of Ushuaia). Industry statistics are in the public domain (at www.iaato.org), however. IAATO (2009a) describes a typical tourism product thus:

> Antarctic visits are mainly concentrated at ice-free coastal zones over the five-month period from November to March. Visits ashore are generally of short duration (+/– 3 hours), of moderate intensity (<100 people), and of variable frequency. Typically there are 1-3 landings per day. Landings are made using Zodiacs (Jacques Cousteau type rubber inflatable crafts) or, in the case of Russian icebreakers, also by helicopter. Other activities by visitors to Antarctica include mountain climbing, camping, kayaking and scuba diving from tourist vessels.

November to March is the short window of opportunity for tourism, coinciding with the peak summer research effort and the breeding season of charismatic penguins, seals and albatrosses. The paradox, of course, is that the wellbeing of the very creatures that lure more than 90% of tourists to Antarctica (Powell *et al.*, 2008:236) may actually be put in jeopardy by the presence of tourists. It is a balancing act requiring great precision, to maintain the integrity of the destination and still provide a unique wilderness experience.

Tour vessels sometimes operate for longer periods than this, and in the latest reporting season, the port of Ushuaia recorded the first vessel departing for Antarctica on 9 October 2008 and the last vessel returning from Antarctica on 5 April 2009 (Government of Argentina, 2009), in total nearly 6 months of operating time. Official port records indicate that 36 vessels departed Ushuaia on 233 voyages, and carried an estimated 35,687 tourists.

From crew lists supplied to port authorities, it was determined that as few as five of the 36 vessels declared having an ice master or ice pilot as part of the crew for any or all of the season (Government of Argentina, 2009). This becomes an important statistic in light of the changing nature of sea ice and the matter has received greater scrutiny since the sinking of MS *Explorer* in November 2007, which will be discussed later.

IAATO publicizes a membership directory (IAATO, 2009b) and annual updates of tourism statistics. The latest figures are an estimation only of the 2008/09 season (at the time of publication, for some unknown reason the 2008/09 statistics had not been released publicly). An estimate of 38,900 tourists was offered, which represents an 8% drop in the number estimated the previous year (IAATO, 2009c). One experienced operator has proffered an anticipated 20% decrease in numbers across the board in the 2009/10 season because of global financial constraints (Greg Mortimer, Aurora Expeditions, 2009, personal communication). If this does occur, it should ease the minds of the Antarctic Treaty Parties – the group of 48 countries that manage all human activities in the Antarctic south of 60°S. While they have been actively challenging and criticizing tourism for many years now, they have both accepted it as a legitimate Antarctic activity and imposed, to date, no regulation on industry members that the operators themselves did not inspire or could not live with.

Tourism Regulation and Management

Tourism is regulated and managed under a three-tiered system: the Antarctic Treaty System, state governments that are contracting parties to the Antarctic Treaty, and the bylaws and rules of the industry body, IAATO. The groups work both independently, and together through the Antarctic Treaty Consultative Meeting (ATCM) forum, to try to overlay some order on the activities of tour operators. Collaboration will be crucial if they are to face the challenges of climate change with competence.

Regulation through the Antarctic Treaty System

The 1959 Antarctic Treaty is an elegantly simple instrument gimballed by its Article IV to keep the region steady in a dynamic world. It contains only 14 articles that prescribe how the Antarctic can remain a continent devoted to peace and science by avoiding international disharmony. Its Article IV creatively resolves irreconcilable claims to sovereignty by not making the legitimacy or efficacy of the Treaty contingent on any such resolution. While this has worked well for all other aspects of Antarctic activity, it has not necessarily worked well in regard to the management of tourism.

When the Treaty was adopted in 1959, peace and science were paramount and tourism was not even on the radar; accordingly the Treaty contained no words that referred directly to tourism. In the subsequent 50 years, however, a system of rules and laws for the administration of the Antarctic and the control of all human activities there evolved and is known collectively as the 'Antarctic Treaty System'. The system includes rules about sealing, fishing, and environmental expectations. Tourism, although lacking a precise definition, is none the less acknowledged as a legitimate ('authorized') activity and is expressly mentioned in the Protocol on Environmental Protection to the Antarctic Treaty (the 1991 Madrid Protocol) that deals with, *inter alia*, environmental evaluation (Murray and Jabour, 2004).

Each year the contracting parties to the Treaty meet to discuss matters and recommend actions to their governments. An inner core, known as the Consultative Parties (currently 28 of the 48 signatories), participates fully in decision making, based on their scientific endeavours in the Antarctic. The remainder participate but do not vote. Decisions are made by consensus, which the parties interpret as the absence of formal objection. This means that all decisions are considered and deliberate and are not necessarily watered down to reach the lowest common denominator; often discussion and negotiation continue over a number of years until consensus is reached.

The Parties could regulate tourism by adopting legally binding measures at their ATCMs, or by environmental evaluation ruling out some activities and condoning others. However, the parties have only made two rules that will be binding on tour operators in their 50-year history! At the 2004 ATCM in Cape Town, the Parties adopted a legally binding Measure (#4 of 2004) that, once implemented into domestic legislation, would require tourism operators to carry adequate insurance for emergency search and rescue before entering the Antarctic. The intent of the Measure was to encourage compliance with tourism best practice and self-sufficiency (Jabour, 2007), however, governments are having great difficulty transforming this into domestic law because of potential conflict with overlapping obligations under the 1979 International Convention on Maritime Search and Rescue (IMO, 2009). This Convention deems that rescue at sea of vessels in distress is a maritime community service not contingent upon insurance status. To date, Measure 4 is not in force because only nine of the requisite 27 ratifications have been received (in 2004 there were only 27 Consultative Parties; ATS, 2010).

The second Measure (#15 of 2009) was adopted by the Parties at ATCM XXXII in Baltimore. The industry Bylaws already contained obligations to not land passengers from vessels carrying more than 500 persons (IAATO Bylaw Article X-A.3), to restrict the number of passengers ashore at any one time to 100 or less (IAATO Bylaw Article II-F), and to only allow one tourist vessel to visit a site at one time (IAATO Bylaw Article X-B). These three bylaws became the substantive obligations of Measure 15, which – once in force – will become legally binding on tourism operators through States Parties to the Treaty in which the tourism is organized.

Rules and procedures for evaluating the environmental impact of authorized activities, including tourism, are found in the Madrid Protocol. The framework ideology is contained within Article 8, and the responsibility for implementation rests with individual States Parties: the flag state of the ship, the aircraft, the company, the charterer and/or the tourist. The processes and standards (such as they are) are elaborated in Annex 1. The Madrid Protocol and its annexes contain complex arrangements subject to various jurisdictions that do not always provide an unambiguous, wholly satisfactory standard of environmental accounting. For example, while guidelines do exist, there are no indicative lists prescribing actions that trigger the next level of evaluation; and interpretation is at the discretion of the beholder. Notwithstanding, some Parties have quite substantial domestic environmental arrangements they might invoke in the planning stage of tourism carried out under their flag.

Regulation and management through state governments

Tourism today is viewed through the environmental lens articulated in the Madrid Protocol. Much of the early development of Antarctic tourism centred on the peri-, sub-Antarctic and Antarctic Islands (Headland, 1994) and they are still an essential component of the Antarctic experience today. Some islands are the undisputed sovereign territory of Antarctic Treaty Parties such as Australia, New Zealand, France or Norway, thus the regulation and management of tourism there is relatively problem-free. In other cases – the Falkland Islands/Islas Malvinas and South Georgia/Islas Georgias del Sur for example (Fig. 13.1) – Great Britain and Argentina are in dispute over sovereignty, making jurisdiction unclear for operators and creating potential lacunae in the regulatory system. Considering also the peculiar unresolved jurisdiction over the Antarctic continent itself, regulation and management of tourism is complicated even at state level.

Risks such as the accidental introduction of alien species to the naïve Antarctic environment are becoming more prominent as generalized warming provides a more receptive host. This is best dealt with at state level because the services of agencies such as quarantine and inspection are usually located at or near ports of embarkation to the Antarctic. In cases of sub-Antarctic islands where sovereignty is not in dispute, the law of the country that has possession of the island prevails. Australia, for example, has undisputed sovereignty over Macquarie Island, which is an essential stopping off point for the long cruises departing from Hobart to the East Antarctic region. Macquarie is subject to a mixture of Tasmanian regulation (regarding site permits and quotas, and the requirement for Parks Rangers to act as guides, as Macquarie is a Tasmanian Nature Reserve) and Federal laws (regarding environmental evaluation of tourist activities, for example, as Macquarie is also a World Heritage Area). Furthermore, jurisdiction is assured over those nationals and flagged vessels or aircraft belonging to an Antarctic Treaty State party (signatory). Most Australian law applies to Australian nationals anywhere in Antarctica, for example, and not just the Australian Antarctic Territory.

In such cases, dealing with tourism in a changing climate may simply be a matter of adopting and enforcing appropriate regulations at state level. In other cases, however, uncertainty is transferred to tour operators as the ship or aircraft may well be flagged to a state outside the Antarctic Treaty System and be chartered or operated by a company 'flagged' outside as well. Of the 36 vessels using the port of Ushuaia in the 2008/09 season, less than half (14) were flagged to

Antarctic Treaty Parties (Government of Argentina, 2009). In these cases, there is virtually no Antarctic-specific legal regime that covers their activities, as all international law that applies in the region is consent-based and cannot easily be applied to non-signatory states.

An alternative, in these cases, is to implement strict standards through the port State. Quarantine, inspection, remedial protocols and other biosecurity measures for personal effects, vessels and equipment can most efficiently be carried out on the dock. However, capacity and political will vary, and this makes the involvement of the International Association of Antarctica Tour Operators (IAATO) even more crucial to filling in the regulatory gaps. Ultimately it is, in fact, IAATO that manages – and to a softer degree, regulates – Antarctic tourism.

Management through IAATO

IAATO (2009b) describes its membership thus:

> Currently, more than 100 Antarctica-bound outfitters are voluntary members of our organization ... Together we have established extensive procedures and guidelines that ensure appropriate, safe and environmentally sound private sector travel to the Antarctic.

IAATO manages its various categories of members through its Bylaws, which prescribe membership requirements and industry expectations (ByLaw Article III). For example, Section F warns that any category of member not in good standing will be reprimanded or have their membership status downgraded. They may even be expelled for non-compliance with the rules. The rules are conditional upon the operator's category, which may, for example, be the operator of a vessel carrying 13–200 passengers and making landings; a vessel that carries 201–500 passengers and makes landings; or a vessel making no landings (cruise only, including all vessels carrying more than 500 passengers) (IAATO, 2009b).

IAATO operators have a range of rules to abide by including the following: vessels that carry more than 500 passengers are not permitted to allow landings; no more than 100 visitors (excluding expedition staff) ashore at any one site at the same time; must abide by stringent restrictions on time and place of landing activities (i.e. obey site guidelines); must coordinate landings via the IAATO Ship Scheduler and the agreed ship-to-ship communication procedures so that not more than one vessel is at one site at the same time; minimum expedition staff-to-visitor ratio of 1:20 while ashore; to have sufficient number of experienced expedition staff, with at least 75% having previous Antarctic experience; and should have a captain, ice master or bridge officers with polar experience (IAATO, 2009b). The latter is an important point in view of the recent MV *Explorer* sinking. The 2009 ATCM in Baltimore received a report from Liberia, the flag state of the *Explorer*, in which the cause of the accident was attributed to Master error in misjudging the type of ice field he was entering (Government of Belguim, 2009:74).

It is this latter point that is crucial to the discussion of Antarctic tourism and climate change. Because there are virtually no substantive provisions applicable to Antarctic ship-borne tour operators other than the general corpus of maritime law, which itself is complex, the soft line approach taken in the Antarctic regime briefly described here may turn out to be inadequate in the changing climate of a warming Antarctica unless a unified position can be adopted and some appropriate regulatory controls established.

Climate Change Projections

> If all the freshwater currently locked up as ice in the polar ice sheets was melted, global sea level would rise by more than 60 metres.
>
> (ACE CRC, 2009a)

As the polar ice sheets disintegrate in the warming climate, changes in ocean temperature and salinity will alter the nature of icebergs and sea ice. It is the latter that we are more concerned with here, as this is the working environment of tourist vessels. The Liberian report alludes to how ice conditions have already become unexpectedly different.

> Climate models predict, on average, that Antarctic sea ice will, by the end of this century, reduce by 24% in extent and 34% in volume.
>
> (ACE CRC, 2009b)

These predictions represent prospective climate change scenarios but they are by no means conclusive. Changes due to warming are predicted to, among other things, alter local weather patterns, increase climate variability and change marine ecosystems (McClintock *et al.*, 2008; Jenouvrier *et al.*, 2009). For example, there may be local sub-Antarctic extinctions and species invasion further south into the Southern Ocean as a result of a climate-induced range shift (Cheung *et al.*, 2009). What this may do is change the tourism product. It is not yet possible to predict how the combined impacts of changing conditions will affect marine biodiversity, however, it is known that 'sea ice plays a pivotal role in structuring Antarctic marine ecosystems ... one of the major factors that make this region of the ocean so productive' (ACE CRC, 2009b). It is also known that changes in sea ice characteristics will impact on all trophic levels from sea ice algae to the tourism draw-cards – whales, seals and penguins.

What is not known, however, is how serious the impacts will be, over what timeframe, and which species will thrive and which will not. There is no realistic barometer to warn us when to push the panic button or how to gauge the extent of feedbacks, risks or benefits of a warming climate in specific areas. In fact, there is strong evidence to suggest that the effects will be uneven, with the more conducive climate of the Antarctic Peninsula region warming quicker than East Antarctica, which is heavily glaciated and has less ice-free exposed rock.

The problem, then, can be reduced to that of not knowing whether Antarctic tourism pathways and destinations can safely continue to absorb, indefinitely, more visitors in more ships or aircraft over a longer season (Wolters, 1991) and what, exactly, the tourism experience will consist of when they arrive. The experience has already been altered in places by the presence of large numbers of aggressive juvenile fur seals, which make landings or transit to and from the beach unsafe (Jabour, 2008). This situation has resulted from the successful conservation of fur seals, which has had unintended consequences. However, there have been no moves to recommend culling the seals, which would in this case be the ultimate irony, and tourist operators routinely seek alternative landing sites to those places where seals might compromise safety.

The diversity of potential regulators and managers, together with the unknown characteristics of the changing environment, mean that dialogue and collaboration between all stakeholders will be essential to the competent handling of future scenarios.

Discussion

There are no restrictions on what kinds of vessels can operate in ice-infested waters and increasingly, vessels that are cruise ships rather than icebreakers or ice-strengthened ships are undertaking Antarctic cruise tourism (Fig. 13.2). Some carry large numbers of people (in one case about 4500), although most do not. In the past two summer seasons there have been four tourist ship groundings in the Antarctic Peninsula (IAATO, 2009c). In the *Explorer* incident, the 30-year veteran of polar tourism sank after hitting a submerged object in the twilight of a late Antarctic summer evening. It is now known that the ice object was very hard

Fig. 13.2. The tourist vessel, MV *Orion* (with a strengthened hull) encounters sea ice in near blizzard conditions on departing Commonwealth Bay, January 2006. (Image © J. Jabour.)

'land' (glacial) ice, which was in a field of softer, first-year sea ice (Government of Belguim, 2009:59). No doubt this was a product of additional disintegration of the Antarctic ice cap. All on board the *Explorer* were rescued safely, with a significant degree of luck regarding calm conditions and mild weather contributing to what might otherwise have been a tragedy (Government of Belguim, 2009: 29). There are no specific vessel construction, navigational or operation regulations or standards applied to Antarctic cruise tourism beyond those expected of cruise ships operating anywhere in the world (Jensen, 2008). This is in spite of the ships operating in waters beset with sea ice and subject to changing ice conditions, prone to extreme and unpredictable weather (now, and possibly more so in the future), and as remote from search and rescue services as anywhere on the planet (Jabour, 2007; ACE CRC, 2009b). The Liberian flag state report into the *Explorer* accident recommended, among other things, 'The Republic of Liberia should use its influence at the IMO to recommend that the IMO establish competency training requirements for ice navigators pursuant to STCW 1978 as Amended' (Government of Belguim, 2009: 74). Currently no formal qualifications are required, although training is available in several northern European centres. An ice pilot's training is usually experiential, from discussions in navigation school through to experience in the field as an understudy to a more experienced person (Dag Hareide, personal communication).

Because the majority of Antarctic tourism is ship-borne out of Ushuaia in Argentina to the Antarctic Peninsula, which is the location of overlapping claims between Britain, Chile and Argentina and therefore subject to uncertain jurisdiction, the future challenge will be to manage and regulate tourism in such a way that no harm is done to either the environment or the platforms and people on them. In addition to increasing human impact on the Antarctic environment by increasing numbers of visitors, other principal concerns will be about: inappropriate vessels (i.e. ones that are not ice classed); the absence of necessity for ice pilot certification; and the absence of formal regulations on passage through ice-prone areas (e.g. speed limits, pilotage, no-go zones). These concerns are driven primarily by two potential impacts: the inability of authorities to guarantee appropriate and timely SAR services in the event of an emergency, and environmental degradation from particularly, but not solely, oil spills. (Another matter not discussed here for reasons of space is the potential for unintentional introduction of alien species, which could thrive in a more conducive environment and in the case of microorganisms (diseases), decimate naïve populations of native fauna.)

The International Maritime Organization (IMO) does have guidelines that can be of assistance here. One, the *Enhanced Contingency Planning Guidance for Passenger Ships Operating in Areas Remote from SAR Facilities*, relies on vessel operators voluntarily complying with strengthened emergency contingency plans (IMO, 2006). It does not preclude Southern Ocean travel for any tourist vessel, however. Neither do the *Guidelines on Voyage Planning for Passenger Ships Operating in Remote Areas*, which recommend only that voyage plans specifically include high-level professional knowledge about ice and other environmental conditions that will help contribute to safe passage (IMO, 2008). Implementation of these guidelines is voluntary, and a State party responsibility.

In the growing unease about Antarctic tourism, operators may find themselves subject to additional restrictions imposed on them by the Antarctic Treaty Parties, such as an obligation to comply with a concept such as a sponsoring state. This was adopted by the Treaty Parties and incorporated into the now invalid 1988 Convention on the Regulation of Antarctic Mineral Resource Activities (CRAMRA). Extrapolating from the CRAMRA context, this would mean that Antarctic Treaty Parties that have a genuine and substantial link with a tourism operator would be eligible to sponsor that operator (see CRAMRA Art.1.12) but would be held strictly liable for its actions (see CRAMRA Article 8). Sponsoring states would be required to transform any future international legal obligations from ATCMs into their domestic law and have the means to ensure compliance or to punish breaches by their operators. However, this does not deny vessels or operators flagged to non-Treaty Parties access to the Antarctic destination because there are no polar police to monitor and enforce the rules.

Other regulation options available to the Consultative Parties include: specific legal and operational requirements for all vessels (e.g. a shipping code analogous to the Arctic guidelines; Jensen, 2008); open and closed seasons and areas (through the Specially Protected Area provisions of the Protocol, Parties could effectively ban tourists visiting any designated SPA without a permit, for example); quotas for specific sites and perhaps a quota trading system; centralized reporting to the Antarctic Treaty Secretariat in addition to IAATO; independent accreditation; and independent observers with the mandate to conduct compliance audits. It is not speculated which, if any, of these options the Parties might consider (although rudimentary site guidelines do exist now and the IMO is drafting a shipping code), or under what circumstances they may be prompted to consider any at all. Nevertheless, it will be incumbent on the operators to ensure they play a lead role in any discussions about a new or more efficient regulatory system.

Conclusions

Regulation of Antarctic tourism *is* necessary and growth *does* need managing. Although tourism is an increasingly popular activity, this is not a problem per se. Antarctica is huge – over 14 million km^2 – and the number of person days ashore is modest: ~17,000 for landed ship-borne tourists compared with a staggering 283,000 for summer-only national science programme personnel (Table 13.1). The problem, rather, is that significant growth in tourist numbers is occurring during a period of major uncertainty: the Antarctic environment is vulnerable because of climate warming; parts of the polar ice cap are melting and disintegrating, contributing to sea level rise and increasing storm surges, freshening the ocean, slowing ocean circulation, and altering marine biological diversity. Secondly, there is unequivocal agreement that the Antarctic Peninsula is warming and the extent, thickness and duration of sea ice on the western side is reducing. The western Peninsula is the focus of most current sea-borne tourism activity and there is no reason to believe that it will not continue to be so in the future. Even if the focus was to turn to East Antarctica, the product would be very different (an expedition rather than cruise market) and the destination wilder and more isolated, though no less spectacular. It is even possible that there will be more ships of greater capacity attracted to the Peninsula by a reduction in sea ice lengthening the visiting season. If these ships are not ice-strengthened, as many are not now, and they continue to travel into poorly charted areas, risk will be exacerbated. Localized extreme weather, especially during the summer cruising season, makes high latitude navigation increasingly dangerous when considered in combination with the presence of less predictable sea ice and icebergs and changing local weather conditions (e.g. strengthening westerly winds).

In its simplest form, any new or more efficient system to regulate tourism and manage growth will need to balance the pressure of increasing activity with the capacity of the resource – the Antarctic environment – to absorb the pressure under rapidly changing and stressful environmental circumstances. This will not be easy. Chances of success will be complicated by the fact that the Antarctic tourism industry is, first and foremost, commercial in nature and secondly, that it is in competition with scientific research in locations that have the highest density of charismatic wildlife of the continent.

References

AADC (Australian Antarctic Data Centre) (2009) Map 13636.

ACE CRC (Antarctic Climate and Ecosystems Cooperative Research Centre) (2009a) Position Analysis: Polar ice sheets and climate change. Position Analyses, at: www. acecrc.org.au/drawpage.cgi?pid=publications&aid=797037.

ACE CRC (Antarctic Climate and Ecosystems Cooperative Research Centre) (2009b) Position Analysis: Changes to Antarctic sea ice: Impacts. Position Analyses, at: www. acecrc.org.au/drawpage.cgi?pid=publications&aid=797037 (in press).

ATS (Antarctic Treaty Secretariat) (2009) Measure 4 (2004) – ATCM XXVII–CEP VII, Cape Town Approval Details, at: www.ats.aq/devAS/info_measures_approval. aspx?id=321&title=Measure%204%20(2004)%20-%20ATCM%20XXVII %20-%20CEP%20VII,%20Capetown&fecharec=06/04/2004&fa=0&lang=e (Accessed: 23 September 2010).

Bauer, T.G. (2001) *Tourism in the Antarctic: Opportunities, Constraints, and Future Prospects*. Haworth Hospitality Press, New York.

Cheung, W.L., Lam, V.W.Y., Sarmiento, J.L., Kearney, K., Watson, R. and Pauly, D. (2009) Projecting global marine biodiversity impacts under climate change scenarios. *Fish and Fisheries* 10(3), 235–251.

COMNAP (Council of Managers of National Antarctic Programs) (2009) COMNAP Antarctic Facilities Map, Edition 4 (26 March 2009), downloadable from: www. comnap.aq/publications/maps/COMNAP_Map_Edition4_A0_2009-03-26.pdf/view (Accessed: 29 May 2009).

Government of Argentina (2009) Report of activities of Antarctic tourism cruise ships operating from Ushuaia during austral summer season 2008/2009. Information Paper 119 submitted to ATCM XXXII, at Antarctic Treaty Secretariat, Meeting Documents, www.ats.aq/devAS/ats_meetings_documents.aspx?lang=e (Accessed: 23 April 2009).

Government of Belgium (2009) Report by Liberia on Sinking of MS Explorer. Information Paper 120 submitted to ATCM XXXII, at Antarctic Treaty Secretariat, Meeting

Documents, www.ats.aq/devAS/ats_meetings_documents.aspx?lang=e (Accessed: 23 April 2009).

Headland, R. (1994) Historical development of Antarctic tourism. *Annals of Tourism Research* 21(2), 269–280.

IAATO (International Association of Antarctica Tour Operators) (2001) 2000–2001 Summary of Sea-borne and Land based Antarctic Tourism. IAATO, Tourism Statistics, at www.iaato.org/tourism_stats.html (Accessed: 27 January 2009).

IAATO (International Association of Antarctica Tour Operators) (2008) 2007–2008 Tourism Summary. IAATO, Tourism Statistics, at: www.iaato.org/tourism_stats.html (Accessed: 27 January 2009).

IAATO (International Association of Antarctica Tour Operators) (2009a) About IAATO: Tourism Overview, at: www.iaato.org/tourism_overview.html (Accessed: 22 April 2009).

IAATO (International Association of Antarctica Tour Operators) (2009b) at IAATO Membership Directory 2008–2009, at: www.iaato.org/directory (Accessed: 22 April 2009).

IAATO (International Association of Antarctica Tour Operators) (2009c) IAATO Overview of Antarctic Tourism: 2008-2009 Antarctic Season and Preliminary Estimates for 2009-2010 Antarctic Season. Information Paper 86 rev.1 submitted to ATCM XXXII, at Antarctic Treaty Secretariat, Meeting Documents: www.ats.aq/devAS/ats_meetings_documents.aspx?lang=e (Accessed: 23 April 2009).

IMO (International Maritime Organization) (2006) Enhanced Contingency Planning Guidance for Passenger Ships Operating in Areas Remote from SAR Facilities. MSC.1/Circ.1184, 31 May 2006.

IMO (International Maritime Organization) (2008) Guidelines on Voyage Planning for Passenger Ships Operating in Remote Areas. A25/Res.999, 2 January 2008.

IMO (International Maritime Organization) (2009) at IMO Conventions, SAR, at: www.imo.org/home.asp?topic_id=161 (Accessed: 27 January 2009).

Jabour, J. (2007) Underneath the Radar: Emergency search and rescue insurance for East Antarctic tourism. *Tourism in Marine Environments* 4(2), 203–220.

Jabour, J. (2008) Successful conservation – then what? The de-listing of *Arctocephalus* fur seal species in Antarctica. *Journal of International Wildlife Law and Policy* 11(1), 1–29.

Jabour, J. (2009) National Antarctic programs and their impact on the environment. In: Kerry, K.R. and Riddle, M.J. (eds) *Health of Antarctic Wildlife: A Challenge for Science and Policy*. Springer-Verlag, Heidelburg, pp.211–230.

Jenouvrier, S., Caswell, H., Barbraud, C., Holland, M. and Stroeve, J. (2009) Demographic models and IPCC climate projections predict the decline of an emperor penguin population. National Academy of Sciences, at: www.pnas.org/cfi/doi/10.1073/pnas.0806638106 (Accessed: 27 January 2009).

Jensen, O. (2008) Arctic shipping guidelines: towards a legal regime for navigation safety and environmental protection? *Polar Record* 44(2), 107–114.

McClintock, J., Ducklow, H. and Fraser, W. (2008) Ecological responses to climate change on the Antarctic Peninsula. *American Scientist* 96, 302–310.

Muir, S., Jabour, J. and Carlsen, J. (2007) Antarctic gateway ports: opening tourism to Macquarie Island in the East Antarctic from Hobart. *Tourism in Marine Environments* 4(2), 135.

Murray, C. and Jabour, J. (2004) Independent expeditions and Antarctic tourism policy. *Polar Record* 40(4), 309–317.

Powell, R.B., Kellert, S.R. and Ham, S.H. (2008) Antarctic tourists: ambassadors or consumers? *Polar Record* 44(3), 233–241.

Tin, T., Hemmings, A.D. and Roura, R. (2008) Pressures on the wilderness values of the Antarctic continent. *International Journal of Wilderness* 14(3), 7–12.

Wolters, T.M. (1991) *Tourism Carrying Capacity*. WTO/UNEP, Paris.

14 UK Coastal Tourism Destinations – Assessment of Perceived Climate Impacts: Issues for Destination Management, Local Governance and Public Policy Making

ANDREW JONES

Introduction: the British Seaside Resorts and Tourism

Britain's coastlines are a prime destination for both international and domestic tourism. The British resorts and Destination Association (BRADA) provides key information on Britain's coastline resorts. As a whole, mainland Britain has a coastline of 9040 miles (14,549 km). For example, England and Wales have a coastline of 3240 miles (5214 km) and Scotland has a coastline of 5800 miles (9335 km). Associated with this there are five coastal National Parks, 26 coastal Areas of Outstanding Natural Beauty and 45 Heritage Coasts measuring 950 miles (1,520 km); Scotland has no Heritage Coasts. The National Trust owns 555 miles (888 km) of coastline and 74% of their coastline is designated Heritage Coast (BRADA, 2009).

In terms of economies the resident population of the 43 principal seaside resort towns in England, Scotland and Wales totals 3.1 million, marginally more than the total population of Wales (2.9 million). The adult resident population of working age in the same 43 principal resorts was some 366,000 greater in 2001 than it was in the heyday of traditional seaside resort holidays of 1971. Over the same period, the total number of jobs available in these towns had also increased by a massive 320,000 (BRADA, 2009).

In this context Visit Britain (2009) states that tourism is one of the largest industries in the UK, with direct tourism spending accounting for 2.7% of UK Gross Value Added, or approximately £86.3 billion in 2007 (Visit Britain, 2009). In addition a recent Deloitte study 'The Economic Case for the Visitor Economy' estimated that the industry was worth £114.4 billion in 2007, equivalent to 8.2% of UK GDP (Deloitte, 2008).

Within these general statistics, the UK Tourism Survey 2007 highlights that the largest single element (particularly for domestic tourism) remains the coastal sector, including within it, the larger traditional seaside resorts and popular rural coastal destinations. The economic impact is thus substantial. In 2007 UK residents took a total of 26.4 million seaside trips involving one or more overnight stays. Within the 26.4 million figure, 22 million trips were made purely for seaside holidays, generating a tourism spend of £4.5 billion. England accounted for 17.0 million of these seaside holidays and £3.5 billion of the total spend. In Wales the equivalent figures were 2.8 million seaside holidays and £0.48 billion spend, and in Northern Ireland 0.5 million seaside holidays and £0.072 billion. In Scotland 1.42 million seaside holidays generated £0.28 billion (UKTS, 2007).

Of the top ten English towns and cities visited for a holiday trip in 2007, four were coastal resorts, including Scarborough, Skegness, Bournemouth and Blackpool. In addition to these overnight trips there were almost 270 million day visits made to the British coast, generating a further £3.1 billion spend (UK Day Visits Survey 2002–2003).

Despite such figures, there has been much literature associated with British 'seaside' resorts, especially, latterly, research associated with the challenges confronting many seaside holiday towns and resorts. A recent government report and associated Parliamentary Committee has raised such challenges (Department for Communities and Local Government, 2008). This is not just a recent phenomenon however. Since the early 1980s, evidence from many such destinations has tended to show a slow but continued decline. For example, Llandudno in North Wales, Skegness and Paignton in England are well documented. Walton (2005:223) succinctly states the contemporary situation by describing many resorts as showing signs of:

> degradation of the built environment with architecture losing its distinctiveness, emblems of seaside pleasures demolished or allowed to decay, – shopping precincts and sea-front flats typical of 'up-market south-eastern retirement resorts … reducing the visual sense of seaside place identity'.

However, not all have undergone these negative experiences. There have been a few resorts that have contravened such trends and have developed innovative and unique contemporary tourism experiences as for example the 'gastronomy' resort of Padstow or the 'surf culture capital' of Newquay, both located in Cornwall. Statistics supplied by UKTS (2007) and BRADA (2009) also suggest positive futures. Despite such examples, however, many British tourism resorts have undergone fundamental changes over the last two decades, often with local/regional government authorities, local tourism professionals and the wider tourism business community trying to respond and react to changing social, environmental and economic pressures and needs. Added to this, in recent years, has been the growing debate on climate change and the UK responses to this.

UK Coastal Tourism and Current Responses to Climate Change

Albeit small in global tourism contexts, UK tourism is also set to witness the many predicted effects from climate change. In this respect, the UK's tourism industry is particularly vulnerable. Britain, as already outlined, has many coastal areas, most of which attract many tourists each year, particularly to established coastal 'seaside' resorts. With global warming and consequent predictions of rising sea levels, coastal tourism resorts along with many other coastal destinations in the UK are increasingly susceptible to flooding and other adverse climate impacts. Already authors such as Tsimplis (2004), Gössling and Hall (2006), Pearson (2008), Hampson (2008) and the National Trust (2008) have begun to raise such issues. A recent Royal Geographic Society forum (2008) titled 'Tourism & the British Coastline' provide other examples of the growing debate within this field. The economic, social and environmental consequences are thus critical.

Despite these growing concerns however, there still remains little focused literature or empirical research related to British holiday resorts, particularly those in coastal locations, and the current ongoing debates centred upon and concerning climate change and predicted impacts.

As a parallel issue, Britain was one of the first countries to develop policies for tackling climate change (Environment Agency, 2008). Britain joined the UN's 1997 Kyoto Protocol and the new Labour government, at that time, came to office promising to go beyond its Kyoto target of a 12.5% cut in emissions and make a 20% cut between 1990 and 2010. A target of a 60% emissions cut by mid-century was subsequently set. By and large, British emissions of greenhouse gases covered by the Kyoto Protocol have fallen since 1990, but largely as a result of the replacement of coal with natural gas in many of the nation's power stations. Progress in recent years has, at best, been faltering and the downturn in global economies in 2008 does not bode well in the near to mid term.

Ambitions nevertheless remain firm. The Climate Change Bill, introduced by the UK Government in 2007 and receiving royal assent in November 2008, puts in place a statutory goal of at least a 60% reduction in CO_2 emissions by 2050, with real progress required by 2020 (Defra, 2008). The targets, although not specifically tourism focused, will be supported by a new system of 5-yearly 'carbon budgets', set at least 15 years ahead, with progress reported annually to Parliament. The Government has suggested that other countries have been following the progress of the draft Bill with interest, and hopes it will encourage a global response to tackle the real threats from climate change (Brown, 2007).

In association with this, the recent climate change projection statistics published by the UK Government in June 2009 consider the effect of climate change on each region in the UK using advanced climate change modelling. Predictions suggest that sea levels will rise by approximately 18 cm by the 2040s with the North-West possibly having 35% more rain in the winter while across the rest of the country rainfall could increase by more than 20%. By the end of the century, predictions also suggest that there could be 1 m of additional storm surges along coastlines (Met Office, 2009).

As a result there have also been some relatively new policy responses and research from UK NGOs, research centres and National Tourist Boards (Tsimplis, 2004; WAG, 2007a), which target initiatives to combat climate change through mitigation and adaptation. The Wales Coastal Tourism Strategy is a case in point (WAG, 2007b). Such reports start to raise issues on the implications of coastal change for coastal resources and assess social and economic impacts. A wide range of adaptation options including flood risk management systems and planned retreat are often explored and alternatives for improving coastal governance between coastal communities, coastal managers and governments discussed.

It is clear from such evidence, thus far, that climate change is one of the largest long-term issues facing the tourist industry, leading potentially to the loss of many destinations whose appeal depends on their natural environment, particularly coastlines. Many low-lying UK coastal regions are at risk from rising sea levels, as is already evident from authors such as Tsimplis (2004), Churchill (2006), Allen (2008), the National Trust (2008) and WAG (2007b). As already stated in earlier chapters, the wider implications of climate change and its impact on tourism have been reviewed by such authors as Becken and Hay (2007).

With UK tourism industries currently worth approximately £114.4 billion in 2007, equivalent to 8.2% of UK GDP (Deloitte, 2008), and coastal sectors comprising substantial proportion of this figure, the issue of adverse climate impact has potential dire economic, environmental and social outcomes.

Thus a paradox is emerging, which on the one hand highlights the current threats from climate change and on the other shows a continued drive and effort from tourism destination managers, local municipalities, regional marketing organizations and the broader tourism industry in general, in trying to sustain, regenerate and develop existing tourism infrastructure and facilities. At this moment in time, however, there seems very little common ground or dialogue, especially in published research, that starts the process of linking these two phenomena together, especially in recognizing common synergies or solutions to the challenges perceived on the one hand for sustained tourism development and on the other combating threats from climate change. The situation remains that tourism policy makers, tourism entrepreneurs, marketers, destination managers etc., get on with the job of promoting and developing tourism facilities within their destinations while, for example, 'remoter' government officials, politicians and environmental advocates get on with the job of assessing the perceived threats of climate change and evolving policy to address this.

At present there exists very little common ground between the two. The threats from climate change, although still largely unpredictable, are fairly clear to the UK tourism industry. Despite this, however, the policy and institutional frameworks of who takes responsibility for policy and action, who enacts mitigation or adaptation measures, and who pays, all remain unanswered questions that at best are ambiguous and at worst institutionally irresponsible and negligent. These issues have already been highlighted by Jones and Phillips (2008) and Okonski (2003), and are unresolved critical concerns for ensuring proper coordinated responses for adaptation and mitigation to combat the predicted effects of climate change.

In this respect local, regional and national governmental frameworks and structures particularly within the UK are quite critical. The divided responsibilities between local authority, regional and national governments and their relationship with tourism business, as well as European Union responsibilities, remain at best clouded and at worst over complex, which belies the underlying issue of problem perception, problem recognition and problem actions. The focus of this particular chapter thus aims to raise some debate and present some factual findings of the current thinking from tourism professionals within UK tourism resorts on this pertinent subject matter and highlight thoughts from such individuals on perceived current challenges and perceived solutions.

Developing a Research Agenda: Perceptions of Governance and Policy Making

The aim of the research was to investigate the awareness of key stakeholder groups on the possible impacts climate change may have on coastal tourism destinations. The study aims to meet four objectives:

- to investigate current reflections of climate change on tourism destinations;
- to analyse the short term and long term perceived threats of climate change at each destination;
- to assess responses to the effects of climate change; and
- to evaluate future repercussions and priorities for such destinations.

Secondary data were gathered for the contextual underpinning for this research. As Dunsmuir and Williams and Dunsmuir (1990) suggest, such secondary research provides an important literature base, which provides a benchmark from which to evaluate and synthesize primary data sources. The secondary data were thus gathered from a range of existing climate change data sources including academic reports and articles, government and inter-governmental reports, newspaper articles and journals, which, thus, provided the 'backdrop' for the study.

To supplement the secondary data, primary data, in the form of survey work, were obtained. This was carried out by undertaking a series of interviews with key stakeholders from eight UK coastal tourism destinations. The survey methodology was based upon a qualitative approach, which, as Phillimore and Goodson (2004) suggest, collects data about activities, events, occurrences and behaviours and seek an understanding of actions, problems and processes in their social context. In short, the research thus aimed to investigate in-depth attitudes of professional opinion. This was based primarily upon current reflections of climate change, professional reactions to climate change and, as a consequence, the perceived repercussions of climate change impacts. The key stakeholders were comprised primarily of individual tourism professionals based at each of the tourism destinations across the UK.

Albeit a small sample, eight individual interviews of professionals were undertaken. The sample comprised key interviews with public sector tourism professionals from the following coastal tourism destinations: Pembrokeshire, Wales; West Somerset, England; Torbay, Devon, England; Skegness, Yorkshire, England; Scarborough, Yorkshire, England; Rhyl, Clwyd, Wales; West Devon, England; and Blackpool, England.

The choice of such key stakeholders was based on the premise that public body tourism professionals who are 'engaged' with tourism decision making and policy making responsibilities at regional governmental level would have reasonable 'expert' opinion on challenges confronting their respective tourism destinations, including issues and challenges from predicted climate change. To ensure reliability of responses, the same set of questions were given to each interviewee in order to ensure that the aims and objectives set were matched against the responses and answers ascertained. In this respect the aim was to achieve, as far as possible, a valid and meaningful dialogue, which ultimately, as Silverman (2004) suggests, arrives at the real 'truth' of the questions asked and answers offered.

Following the completion of the interviews, a synopsis or précis of the data was transferred into matrix tables, which allowed a synthesis of the results, thereby enabling common patterns and trends from each of the interviews to be highlighted. As McNeill (1990) cited by Finn *et al.* (2000:112) suggests, such a process provides a useful method of analysing the contents of non-statistical material in such a way that it is possible to make comparisons between them.

In such methodological approaches there are, of course, a number of limitations, these include appropriateness of the sample selection and size, limited time for the interview process, willingness of interviewees to participate and to answer questions thoroughly and ultimately the extent and level of professional and technical expertise of each interviewee. Such limitations are explored by authors such as Collis and Hussey (2003) and Corbin and Strauss (2008). In this respect, the selection process for each interviewee was against a set of criteria that aimed to obtain a pre-selected purposeful sample, which ensured: (i) regional knowledge; (ii) an understanding of strategic tourism management responsibilities; (iii) representation from regional authorities; (iv) local professional tourism management experience; and (v) visitor coastal destination experiences. The limitations on time and financial resources obviously constrained the extent to which survey work could be undertaken and therefore results gained should be considered in such light. The sample size was obviously somewhat small. However, the results do provide an interesting insight into both local and regional perceptions of tourism management issues associated with coastal tourism management needs and current assessments of climate change. In this respect, the case study should be considered as an informative pilot study that, with broader application, could be developed into a wider research project.

Professional Perception: Problem Recognition, Policy Empowerment and Strategic Actions

Current perceptions of climate change and tourism

From the secondary data, it is quite evident that climate change is one of the most significant long-term issues facing the tourist industry today. It is not just the issue of global warming that is affecting the industry, but the impacts that climate change is having more broadly upon such issues as rising sea levels, temperamental weather patterns, landscape and ecological disaster, and on travel risks, health, safety and security. Much of the existing literature relates to such phenomena, for example Becken and Hay (2007), Allen (2008) and the National Trust (2008).

Although such issues are now widely published as part of daily news bulletins, the results from key tourism personnel on this particular issue seemed to be rather varied. Although such issues of perceived climate change are now widely accepted, each of the respondents had a very different level of awareness or reflection on the issue. With respect to general perceptions, at best each of the interviewees demonstrated a reasonable awareness of environmental concern linked to changing climate but at worst had a poor understanding of specific impacts that climate change can have on tourism. Most lacked sufficient technical or professional knowledge and most perceptions were very much based upon basic knowledge gained through the press and general media sources. None reflected detailed specialist knowledge or expertise on the real challenges of climate change confronting the tourism industry at each of their respective tourism destinations. Indeed, some thought of climate change in only a positive light.

Perceived short-term and long-term threats of climate change

It is evident from the secondary data that there are many different threats from climate change, both short term and long term, that face tourist destinations. Again, Churchill (2006), Allen (2008), the National Trust (2008), UNWTO (2007) and Becken and Hay (2007) address such issues. The responses on such issues were again very general and based upon the long-term general issues surrounding climate change. Specific short-term and long-term issues were not articulated particularly well especially with respect to specific climate issues or specific long term–short term time frames. Again, most opinion was based on a general knowledge of the climate change debate with little professional or technical knowledge of specific agendas. Opinions largely reflected media-led issues. Complacency and cynicism, in recognizing general climate change issues, seemed to be the common denominator in all responses.

Policy empowerment to offset the effects of climate change

To offset the impact of climate change there are several strategic policy responses linked to mitigation and adaptation to ameliorate impact. These have been alluded to in much of the secondary data. Clearly this is an issue now confronting many coastal tourism destinations as destination managers and policy makers have to recognize and react to the realities of climate change impact in both the short and long term (Okonski, 2003; Tsimplis, 2004; Phillips and Jones, 2006; Jones and Phillips, 2008).

The responses from the interviewees seemed even more complacent in this context. In summary, the responses to the general questions on responses to climate change based upon mitigation and adaptation were again very varied. Again most of the interviewees lacked a detailed technical understanding of mitigation and adaptive measures, that are, or could be undertaken. There was also some confusion by each respondent on the definition of each and the terms of reference for mitigation and adaptation. Some respondents had clearer definitions than others. The responses to specific questions where however quite in depth with a variety of answers being given. Most respondents were able to give examples of policies that aimed to promote 'greener' solutions to tourism (and thus indirectly help mitigate against climate change). Such initiatives generally included promoting greening business practices, promoting alternative transport and engendering general sustainable tourism policies. Answers to adaptation received less detailed responses and, where discussed, remained largely on the issue of new flood defences. Only one response demonstrated a clear understanding of the strategic approaches required.

The answers given therefore remained quite general and thus generally illustrate quite a 'patchwork' of initiatives that vary quite considerably from one destination to another. In this respect there appears to be little national strategic response to the issues of climate impact despite national government apparatus promoting the issue of climate change quite vociferously. Mitigation measures seem to be adequate in respect to promoting sustainable tourism but there is little evidence to suggest that these are directly a response to climate change threats. All policy responses tended to be fairly local with little reference to broader national or international policy frameworks. This was also the case for adaptive measures. These would appear to be a more difficult concept to grasp, especially as many adaptive measures are considered to require more capital funding and strategic responsibility from 'higher up' organizations. In this context, most respondents saw adaptation as a responsibility for others.

Future reflections: strategic actions

In summary, the variety of responses that discussed strategic actions appeared to be rather piecemeal in terms of tackling the effects of climate change in the future. Very little strategic guidance is offered or even desired on behalf of the destinations. Destination management priorities appear to remain largely focused upon economic development objectives with little or no references to climate change. The responses from each of the interviewees tended to be rather myopic and concentrate on rather short-term policy agendas rather than longer term strategic goals. In this respect the tourism departments at each destination, at best appear to be rather powerless to influence the policy agendas that might help promote strategic sustained responses to the threat of climate change and at worst completely disenfranchised. As such, local authority tourism policies would appear to generally ignore climate change issues and focus largely on short-term business strategies that aim to sustain the growth of their respective tourism markets and promote their destinations.

Moving Forward: Lessons for the Future

In some ways the results, albeit disappointing, are also somewhat predictable. In this respect there did not appear to be any unusual trends in the results. Responses from the survey results were very mixed. On general reflection it was interesting to see that the results demonstrated lack of sufficient knowledge about climate change and how it affects tourism. In general, the basic issues of climate change are now common knowledge to most people, although one would believe that 'so-called' professional stakeholders with tourism management and destination management experiences would have more specialist knowledge on such concerns. To be fair, the results show that each of the interviewees was aware of climate change impact to some degree. Respondents were generally aware that climate change is and will continue to affect tourism but none could speculate specifically to what extent. It was also interesting to see the different levels of awareness on the subject between each of the interviewees. When reviewing the secondary data on climate change and its effects on the natural environment the rise in sea level was highlighted as one of the main concerns together with extreme temperature variations and increased storm incidences (IPCC, 2007; WWF, 2007; Allen, 2008; National Trust, 2008). In this respect, issues such as sea level rise was mentioned by most of the interviewees along with weather patterns, although no detailed figures were quoted.

The secondary data also highlighted both the short- and long-term effects of climate change on tourism destinations (e.g. Becken and Hay, 2007; IPCC, 2007). Each of the interviewees was marginally aware of the threats that climate change may cause to their destination in the short term and long term, although most responses remained ambiguous. Primarily, destruction of the environment, flooding due to the rise in sea level, the effects on the economy, and changing patterns to tourist flows were highlighted. However, little in the way of strategic recognition or detailed technical outcomes where discussed or mentioned. This suggests a malaise in recognition of climate change threats and as a consequence rather mixed or limited strategic policy or management responses to such threats.

Professional responses to the threats of climate change also showed a similar pattern of answers. From the interviewee responses there did not appear to be any strategic initiatives being implemented or considered at any of the destinations. This was in quite stark contrast to global and national government initiatives and policy responses such as the IPCC (2007) fourth assessment and the UK government's own blueprint for tackling climate change, which sets out a framework for moving the UK to a low-carbon economy (Defra, 2008). Having said this, there was evidence that there are green initiative schemes underway in some of the destinations, which do comply with the government's climate change bill. This involves the local authorities promoting sustainable practices to local businesses and encouraging them to join schemes such as green tourism business schemes. Though evidence shows that this is happening at most destinations, the initiatives largely remain sustainable management tools that promote green business rather than strategic tools to offset the threats from climate change. The initiatives taken are thus, largely piecemeal, ad hoc and remain a patchwork of idiosyncrasy. More strategic and, in most cases, costlier alternative policy responses that aim to adapt rather than mitigate to change are generally considered to be the responsibility of 'others'. In this respect solutions or responses to climate change remain, at best, ambiguous and laissez-faire and, at worst, ill informed, parochial and myopic.

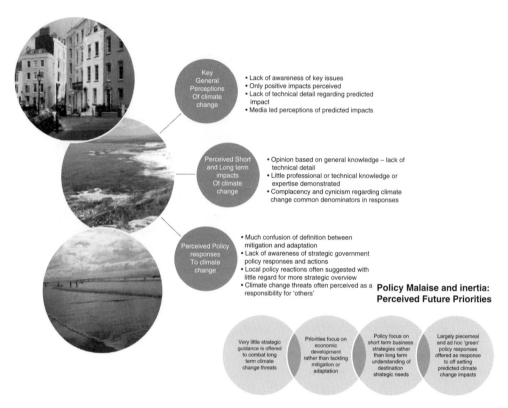

Fig. 14.1. Perceptions of climate change – views from UK coastal tourism resorts.

It seems that answers from interviewee reflections and responses also set the scene and tone for the final assessments on repercussions and future priorities for tackling climate change. Over half the respondents were able to discuss sustainable tourism strategies being undertaken or underway within their respective destinations. None mentioned strategic government strategies. There were also limited references to other future priorities, particularly reference to longer term strategic projects, at any of the destinations surveyed.

In conclusion it seems reasonable to assume that from the results most respondents do not view climate change as a major threat to their respective tourism destinations at this moment in time. Professional opinion and management perceptions demonstrate some awareness of climate change threats but do not seem to promote effective mitigation or adaptive measures to confront them. At best, professional attitudes to climate change and implications for coastal destination management are muddled. There still appears to be much confusion on the realities, or not, of climate change and its potential impacts. Professional awareness and in turn professional responses are piecemeal and reflect a lack of strategic vision. Technical and professional understanding also remains minimal with little desire, or need, to initiate longer term policy or management responses to offset the impacts of perceived climate change on coastal tourism destinations. Technical understanding of, and the ability to differentiate between, mitigation and adaptation policies also remained somewhat ambiguous. Ultimately, evidence and lessons from the survey suggest that communications and actions between intra-governmental, national government, NGOs and municipal government will need to be strengthened in order to effect proper responses to ongoing and ultimately growing threats from climate change processes on Britain's coastal resorts and environments. A summary of these issues can be seen in Fig. 14.1.

Clearly, issues remain concerning recognition of climate change and predicted impacts at UK coastal tourism destinations. This in turn will require more effective measures that facilitate strategic actions to tackle better the threats that climate change now poses. Such measures should, for example, aim to: (i) provide improved governance and effective coordination of stakeholder groups; (ii) aim to ensure stakeholder empowerment and capacity building within coastal communities; (iii) aim to provide and allow for longer term policy formulation to tackle risk, public liability and risk adverse measures; and ultimately, (iv) aim to provide adequate access to affordable private and public funding streams for medium- and long-term infrastructure initiatives. The coordination of such measures will become increasingly critical in order to sustain Britain's coastal environments from the long-term threats of climate change, now clearly identifiable within the not too distant future.

References

Allen, N. (2008) Landmarks will be lost to the sea. *Daily Telegraph*, 27 August, p.3, The Daily Telegraph Group, London, UK.

Becken, S. and Hay, J.E. (2007) *Tourism and Climate Change: Risks and Opportunities*. Channel View Publications, UK.

BRADA (British Resorts and Destinations Association) (2009) *Facts about UK Domestic Tourism*. Available at: www.britishresorts.co.uk/tourismfacts.aspx (Accessed: 30 October 2009).

Brown, G. (2007) *Speech on Climate Change*. HMSO, 19 November. Available at: www.number10.gov.uk/output/Page13791 (Accessed: 30 October 2009).

Churchill Insurance Group (2006) *Report into the Future of Travel*. The Centre for Future Studies, Churchill Insurance, London, UK.

Collis, J. and Hussey, B. (2003) *Business Research*. Palgrave Macmillan, Basingstoke, Hampshire, UK.

Corbin, J. and Strauss, A. (2008) *Basics of Qualitative Research 3e*. Sage Publications, California.

Defra (Department for Environment, Food and Rural Affairs) (2008) *Climate Change Act 2008*. Defra, HMSO, London, UK.

Deloitte (2008) *The Economic Case for the Visitor Economy*. Deloitte, London, UK.

Department for Communities and Local Government (2008) *England's Seaside Towns: A Benchmarking Study*. Christina Beatty, Steve Fothergill and Ian Wilson, Centre for Regional Economic and Social Research, November 2008, Sheffield Hallam University. HMSO, UK.

Environment Agency (2008) *Climate Change Adaptation Strategy 2008–11*. HMSO, London, UK.

Finn, M., Elliott-White, M. and Walton, M. (2000) *Tourism and Leisure Research Methods: Data Collection, Analysis and Interpretation*. Pearson Education, UK.

Gössling, S. and Hall, C.M. (2006) *Tourism and Global Environmental Change: Ecological, Social, Economic and Political Interrelationships*. Routledge, London, UK.

Hampson, P. (2008) British resorts and destinations. *Proceedings from Tourism and the British Coastline*. Royal Geographical Society with IBG, Conference, 1 October.

IPCC Intergovernmental Panel on Climate Change (2007) *Climate Change 2007, the Fourth IPCC Assessment Report*. UNEP, Cambridge University Press, UK.

Jones, A. and Phillips, P. (2008) Tourism infrastructure and the coastal Zone: Management change. In: Krishnamoorthty, R. (ed.) *Global Integrated Coastal Zone Management: Current Scenarios*. CH 40, New Delhi, India.

Met Office (2009) *UK Climate Projections 2009*. Met Office, HMSO. Also available online UKCP09 at: http://ukcp09.defra.gov.uk/index.html.

National Trust (2008) *Shifting Shores Report*. National Trust, London, UK.

Okonski, K. (2003) *Adapt or Die: The Science, Politics and Economics of Climate Change*. Profile Books Ltd, UK.

Pearson, A. (2008) The New English Riviera. In: *Proceedings from Tourism and the British Coastline*, Royal Geographical Society with IBG, Conference, 1 October.

Phillimore, J. and Goodson, L. (2004) *Qualitative Research in Tourism: Ontologies, Epistemologies and Methodologies*. Routledge, London.

Phillips, M. and Jones, A. (2006) Erosion and tourism infrastructure in the coastal zone: problems, consequences and management. *Tourism Management* 27(3), June, 517–524.

Royal Geographic Society (2008) *Proceedings from: Tourism and the British Coastline Forum*, 1 October 2008. RGS/Tourism Society, London, UK.

Silverman, D. (2004) *Doing Qualitative Research: A Practical Handbook*. SAGE Publications, London.

Tsimplis, M. (2004) *Towards a vulnerability assessment for the UK coastline – Technical Report 10*. Tyndall Centre for Climate Change Research, Tyndall Centre, University of East Anglia, UK.

UKTS (UK Tourism Survey) (2007) *Tourism Statstics*. Visit England, Visit Scotland, Visit Wales, Northern Ireland Tourist Board, TNS Research International, Edinburgh.

UNWTO (United Nations World Tourism Organization) (2007) *Davos Declaration*. Second International conference on climate change and tourism – climate change and tourism responding to global challenges. Davos, Switzerland, 3 October.

Visit Britain (2009) Key Tourism Facts. Online at: www.tourismtrade.org.uk/Market-IntelligenceResearch/KeyTourismFacts.asp (Accessed: 30 October 2009).

WAG (Welsh Assembly Government) (2007a) *Sustainable Tourism Framework*. WAG, Cardiff, UK.

WAG (Welsh Assembly Government) (2007b) *Wales Coastal Tourism Strategy*. WAG, Cardiff, UK.

Walton, J.K. (2005) *The British Seaside: Holidays and Resorts in the Twentieth Century*. Manchester University Press, UK, 223pp.

Williams, L. and Dunsmuir, A. (1990) *How To Do Social Research (Sociology in action)*. Collins Educational, London.

WWF (World Wide Fund For Nature) (2007) *Environmental Report 2007*. WWF UK, London, UK.

15

Grand Isle, Louisiana: a Historic US Gulf Coast Resort Adapts to Hurricanes, Subsidence and Sea Level Rise

Klaus J. Meyer-Arendt

Introduction

The shorelines of the eastern USA and the Gulf of Mexico are under attack by rising sea level and increasingly severe storms, both of which are linked directly to atmospheric and oceanic temperature rise (Elsner *et al.*, 2008). Along resort and other urbanized coastlines, storm destruction and shoreline erosion have been countered by reinforced reconstruction of beachfront housing and increased 'shore protection' measures such as seawalls and beach nourishment (Pilkey and Cooper, 2004).

The US Gulf Coast in particular has experienced increased shoreline erosion since the mid-1990s because of hurricanes and elevated Gulf of Mexico waters. Along the Florida Panhandle (north-west Florida), for example, beaches that had never been nourished (Destin, Ft Walton Beach, Navarre Beach, Pensacola Beach, Perdido Key) prior to 1990 all saw their virgin white-sand beaches succumb to post-storm dredged-material disposal in the 1990s and early 2000s. While care was taken that the nourishment sands approximated the colour and texture of the natural sands (colour according to the Munsell soil charts), it was clear to many that a new era had begun. Long-term Gulf Coast resorts had been put into a position of fighting (or at least working with Mother Nature) to preserve the natural resource that attracted the tourists and residents to the sites to begin with. In Walton County, Florida, Hurricane Dennis in 2005 caused so much bluff erosion that dozens of permit waivers were granted to allow property owners to sink sheetpile buffers into the sand to preclude loss of structures to the surf.

While resorts across the Atlantic and Gulf Coasts of the USA fight to preserve their attractions and their existence, probably the most vulnerable of resorts is Grand Isle, Louisiana, 80 km (50 miles) due south of New Orleans (Fig. 15.1). A resort destination for two centuries, Grand Isle is slowly succumbing to the combined effects of subsidence, sea level rise, shoreline

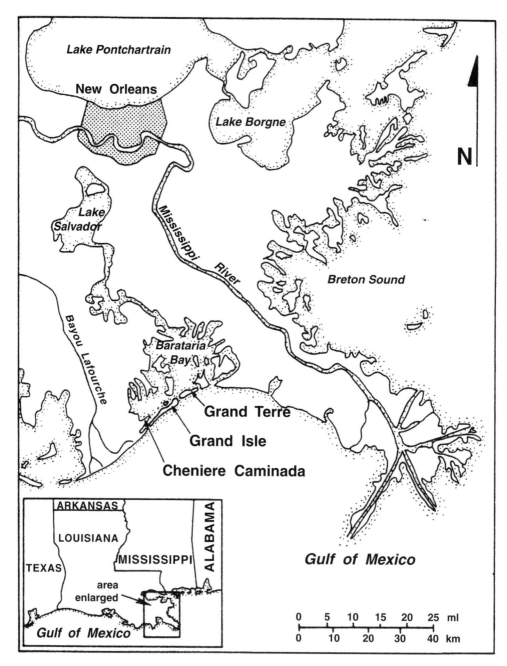

Fig. 15.1. Regional setting of Grand Isle (Meyer-Arendt, 1987b).

erosion and the onslaught of frequent hurricanes. This chapter examines the physical setting, the historical touristic evolution, the physical degradation, human adaptation and the current role of the sinking fishing destination of Grand Isle.

The Study Area

Grand Isle is a barrier island, 10 km (6 miles) long and about 1 km (0.6 miles) wide (Fig. 15.2). It formed by erosion of a former Mississippi River delta at the mouth of Bayou Lafourche and subsequent north-eastward transport of eroded sands. A sand spit formed, and after it broke off from the mainland, Grand Isle was formed. The island has followed a pattern of realignment characterized by natural erosion along its western half and accretion on its eastern half. The west end of the island is barely above sea level and thus frequently subject to over-wash in which extensive silty sand deposits wash across the island (most recently following hurricanes Gustav and Ike in 2008). A complex of low beach ridges forms much of the island, along with higher (up to 2 m, or 6 ft) ridges (*cheniers*) that are colonized by live oak trees (*Quercus virginiana*). The back-barrier zone is dominated by frequently inundated saltmarshes. A fishing community became established on the island in the late 1700s, right at that nodal point between reaches of shoreline erosion and shoreline accretion (Stielow, 1977; Meyer-Arendt, 1987a, b).

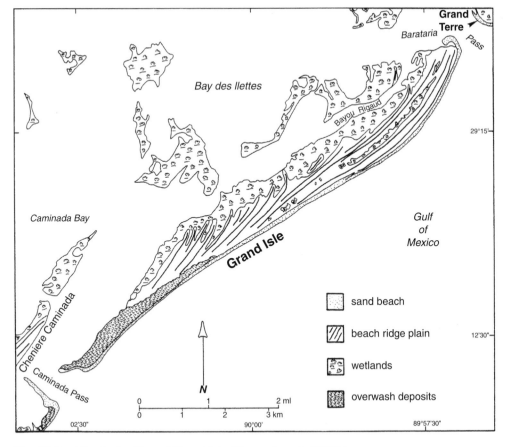

Fig. 15.2. Physical setting of Grand Isle (Meyer-Arendt, 1987b).

Historic Tourism Development

Grand Isle became a tourist destination in the early 19th century, primarily for wealthy south Louisiana planters and the New Orleans elite. Its tourism evolution has been described in terms of a resort cycle model by Meyer-Arendt (1985) and is briefly summarized here (Fig. 15.3).

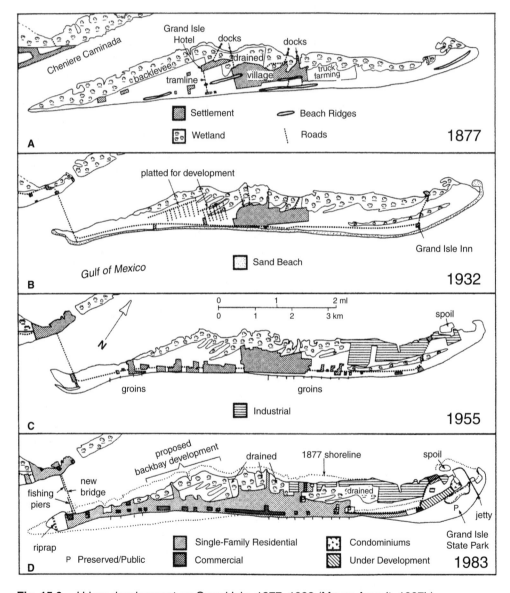

Fig. 15.3.   Urban development on Grand Isle, 1877–1983 (Meyer-Arendt, 1987b).

Grand Isle's tourism exploration stage began in the early 19th century, as its economy progressed from fishing and smuggling to one of sugarcane and cotton cultivation. The island's summer visitors were primarily wealthy New Orleanians and South Louisiana planters who were the occasional guests of Grand Isle plantation owners. By the 1850s, the first summer cottages had been built, as well as a small boarding house (Evans *et al.*, 1979).

During this early period, building on the island was designed to accommodate the recurring problems of shoreline erosion and storms. Houses and village shops, usually built of imported cypress with their floors elevated 2–3 feet (0.6–0.9 m) off the ground, were located behind the cheniers that offered protection from wind and waves. Residents were forbidden to cut the oaks that grew on these ridges and new trees were planted regularly. Driftwood was left on the beach to discourage erosion and residents gathered only enough wood to meet basic needs for fuel. Boat docks were located on the protected backside, where levees and drainage ditches controlled bayside flooding.

The Civil War and salinization of the soil put an end to the island's plantation economy. The old Barataria Plantation was converted to the Grand Isle Hotel and 38 slave quarters became guest cottages (Fig. 15.3A). A mule-drawn tram carried sea-bathers to the beach, where they could change in bathhouses. Visitors could reach the island in 8 h by steamship from New Orleans, and by the 1880s many well-to-do south Louisianians were glad to escape the stifling summer heat and humidity to this 'idyllic subtropical isle', as author Kate Chopin (1899) called it.

It was during this time that the pattern of touristic settlement began to change, shifting away from the bay and interior portions of the island toward the beach. But fear of storms discouraged tourists from staying in the beach cottages past the beginning of the hurricane season and the driftwood remained in place to help retard shoreline erosion.

The development stage of Grand Isle's resort cycle lasted about 70 years. The first phase saw the construction of the luxurious Ocean View Hotel (over 400 feet/120 m long and 'two blocks from the beach'), 60 new bathhouses, and a new railroad on the lower Mississippi River that, with steamship connections, shortened the trip from New Orleans to 4 h. Hotel and cottage construction began to concentrate along the shorefront. This phase lasted until 1893, when an October hurricane destroyed the Ocean View Hotel and most tourism infrastructure and took 12 lives. This was the most severe hurricane ever to hit Louisiana; at nearby Cheniere Caminada, where the hurricane made landfall, 700 lives were lost and only four of 400 buildings were left standing. The damage on Grand Isle was so devastating that the island was unable to recover for many years.

The second phase of development, from 1893–1945, was marked by ephemeral spurts of recreational development, but also more hurricanes, two world wars and the stock market crash of 1929. Severe hurricanes in 1909 and 1915 again destroyed incipient tourism redevelopment. Real-estate moguls from New York and Florida proposed various schemes, including a seawall for hurricane protection and even a monorail to New Orleans, but interest languished in the face of the nation's preoccupation with World War I. During the Roaring

Twenties the Grand Isle Tarpon Rodeo was established, and new beach cottages were built. But in the 1930s, many islanders were forced by the Depression to sell their property to real-estate speculators who had Florida-style development on their minds. About 1500 acres (600 ha) were subdivided into holiday home sites, and a network of streets was laid (Fig. 15.3B). A large beachfront hotel, the Grand Isle Inn, was built at the island's east end, and many additional beach cottages went up.

A highway to the island was completed in 1934, which allowed visitors easy automobile access to the beach. Soon all recreational activity focused on the beachfront (Fig. 15.3C). The beach was cleaned of driftwood, which was burned, and beach ridges were levelled to provide more home sites and a better view of the sea (Conatser, 1969). From 1945–1960, the beachfront became crowded with summer beachfront homes (known as 'camps' in Louisiana). Several large hotels and numerous rental cottages provided accommodation for tourists. An information centre promoting the island was established in New Orleans, and lobbying for a state park on the beach began. On weekends as many as 10,000 tourists came to the island (Stielow, 1977).

Tourism vis-à-vis the environment

As post-war tourism increased at Grand Isle, so did shoreline erosion. The removal of driftwood and the levelling of beach ridges had increased the rate of erosion. In the early 1950s, as recreational development boomed, the problem became even worse, and public pressure for erosion control measures increased (Coleman, 1985).

In response, the state built a series of 14 timber groins along the beachfront where erosion threatened the highway. Unfortunately, the groin field proved to be even more damaging. The groins increased downdrift erosion, so that there was no net accretion of sand in those areas under normal conditions, and during storms, the intense scouring of sand around the groins worsened beach erosion. Over a million cubic yards of sand were pumped in from offshore to augment the beach in the mid-1950s, but in less than a year, almost half of it was lost via littoral drift to the eastern end of the island, which gained markedly in width and volume as result. In 1956, Hurricane Flossy carried most of the rest of the fill into the back-bay area or offshore. In 1958 and 1959, a jetty constructed at the east end of the island successfully trapped sand, but the built-up beach here did not benefit the western and central parts of the island where touristic development was most concentrated.

Grand Isle's tourism development began to slow in the early 1960s, primarily because of severe beach deterioration, the ramshackle quality of its tourism infrastructure and improved highway access to the more attractive seaside resorts of Mississippi, Alabama and Florida. When Grand Isle incorporated in 1963, a comprehensive city plan recommended land-use guidelines and erosion control. But the land-use proposal was ignored and available funds allowed only periodic beach renourishment.

Category-3 Hurricane Betsy struck Grand Isle in 1965, causing a 3 m (10 ft) storm surge that crossed the island and destroyed nearly everything in its path. The western beach was severely eroded up to the coastal highway, sand several feet thick washed across the island, and the business district was destroyed. Many hundreds of people were left homeless.

The hurricane's impact wasn't all negative, however: low-interest loans and insurance payments encouraged quick reconstruction, the small recreational business district sprouted new motels, and the beach was augmented with sand for the eastern end of the island. The 'facelift' given the island by Betsy revitalized its tourist industry for a few years, but by 1975, Grand Isle had again slipped into equilibrium. A concrete revetment built by the Corps of Engineers in 1971 stabilized the coastal highway at the western end but also caused erosion to homes downdrift of the project. Mobile homes that had been brought to the island as temporary post-Betsy shelters became permanent housing and gave the island a makeshift appearance. When Grand Isle was damaged by another hurricane in 1974, its future as a resort looked bleak.

A mid-1980s resort rejuvenation?

In the mid-1980s it briefly appeared that a rejuvenation of sorts was going to offset the serious environmental degradation caused by relative sea level rise and shoreline erosion. In 1984, using sand dredged from offshore, the US Army Corps of Engineers undertook a major beach restoration project at Grand Isle. A sand levee was created – an artificial dune 11 ft (3.3 m) above sea level, stabilized with vegetation. The levee was fronted by a wide beach, 225 ft (68 m) deep and running the length of the island. Grand Isle State Park facilities were expanded with an observation tower, a concession shop and a 400-ft (122 m) fishing pier. The project was completed in early 1985 (Meyer-Arendt, 1987a).

As a result of the touted benefits of this project, interest in Grand Isle perked even before construction began. The island's first condominiums and a modern marina were built, summer camp construction increased, and plans were made to build a major new hotel and to expand recreational development into the back-barrier wetlands (Coastal Environments, Inc., 1986). Various newspapers throughout the state carried stories about the 'new' Grand Isle, with such titles as 'The Cajun Riviera' and 'Grand Isle is Back and Ready for Boom'.

Unfortunately for Grand Isle, 1985 was a record hurricane season, as Danny, Elena and Juan all caused major damage to the island. Winds and storm surges flattened the new levee (in places) and scoured the beach, sending tonnes of sand sprawling across the island. Some agreed that the beach nourishment and levee construction project minimized property damage, but it was clear that Grand Isle's hopes for tourism rejuvenation had been dashed (Gill, 1986).

Whether this rejuvenation would have been a flash in the pan, a brief renewal after Hurricane Betsy, or a genuine renaissance, in which wise management would have forestalled resort decline indefinitely is unfortunately now a moot question.

Grand Isle 1985–2010

Since 1985 conditions at Grand Isle have deteriorated both physically and touristically. Elevated water levels in the Gulf of Mexico and periodic hurricanes (including Katrina in 2005 and Gustav in 2008 and their associated storm surges), coupled with land subsidence, have taken a severe toll on the resort.

Since 1985, there has been great public (and political) awareness of land loss and shoreline erosion in Louisiana, and the little resort of Grand Isle lies at the epicentre of environmental problems. Whereas New Orleans may command the attention of the international media after an event such as Hurricane Katrina (2005), Grand Isle may be seen more as a bellwether of the environmental condition of south Louisiana. Indirectly the causes for environmental degradation may be deltaic subsidence and global warming, but direct causes include (relative) sea level rise, erosion (along both the Gulf and the bay sides), increased hurricane activity and human-induced physical changes (Gonzalez and Törnqvist, 2006). A survey of elevation benchmarks by the National Geodetic Survey found that Highway 1 (the main highway leading to Grand Isle) had subsided as much as 1 foot (0.3 m) between 1982 and 2002 (NOAA, 2003).

In the early 2000s, Louisiana has moved beyond producing studies of the problems and disseminating information to the general public. The state is moving toward implementing various sorts of restoration projects, including diverting sediments into regions of wetland loss and combating erosion via breakwaters, riprap revetments and beach nourishment. In 2009, the US Army Corps of Engineers presented its draft Louisiana Coastal Protection and Restoration (LACPR) plan, although that has already been criticized for not offering a 'comprehensive long-term plan for structural, nonstructural, and restoration measures across coastal Louisiana' (NRC, 2009). Rosati and Stone (2009) outline design guidelines for major portions of the Louisiana shoreline. Most of these restoration efforts are targeted for unpopulated areas, but Grand Isle holds a special place in the hearts of south Louisianians.

Grand Isle has had various beachfront 'makeovers' since the hurricane season of 1985, and in most cases it was a generous infusion of federal funds that made this possible. Renourishment of the beach and patching of the broken sand levee has been undertaken numerous times, most recently in 2008 following Hurricane Gustav (Fig. 15.4). Although few, if any, scientific studies touted the benefits of rocks on the beach, in the 1990s several barge-loads of rocks were placed both offshore and on the beach, giving the visage of Grand Isle an almost-Zenlike appearance, especially when the surrounding beach is freshly raked (Fig. 15.5). Extensive offshore breakwaters have been placed along the north-east Gulf side of the island as well as along much of the bayside (Fig. 15.6). Bencaz and Birdseye (1990) found that Grand Isle had actually increased in area since 1945 because of the extensive beach nourishment and also that bayside erosion was much worse than Gulf-side erosion. In any case, Grand Isle is environmentally vulnerable to sea level rise and shoreline erosion, and engineering works may just be stopgap measures to offset a natural decline (Fig. 15.7).

Fig. 15.4. Post-Hurricane Gustav sand levee, Grand Isle (photo by author, 2009).

Fig. 15.5. Rocks on beach, central Grand Isle (photo by author, 2009).

Fig. 15.6. Offshore breakwater, bayside of Grand Isle (photo by author, 2009).

Fig. 15.7. Recreation on a shrinking beach, Grand Isle (photo by author, 1991).

In terms of tourism, Grand Isle does not appear that much different today than it did in the past. The landscape of 2010 is eerily similar to that of the post-hurricane season of 1986. Periodic levelling of the island by hurricanes ensures – thanks to federally-subsidized insurance payouts – continuous new post-storm construction (Fig. 15.8). In the mid-1980s, there were plans to construct an elaborate resort complex in the back-barrier wetlands, on the property of the antebellum Barataria Plantation (Coastal Environments, Inc., 1986), but a recession and difficulty in obtaining wetlands construction permits halted this development (Fig. 15.3D). In 2010, a smaller-scale version of this back-barrier development (a residential canal subdivision named Queen Bess Bay) was under construction.

But the built environment masks the true human landscape beneath. The beach-goers are now rare on Grand Isle, having moved to nicer Gulf Coast beaches east of Louisiana (notably in the Florida panhandle). Grand Isle State Park has experienced steady declines in visitation, and even its closing (following Hurricane Gustav in August 2008) has not impacted island tourism revenues significantly (Fig. 15.9). A sociological study of local residents in 2004 found that in spite of strong place attachment to Grand Isle, many were resigned to abandoning the island in view of continued sea level rise and related environmental degradation (Burley *et al.*, 2004).

It has been suggested that coastal communities that face inundation due to climate change (e.g. rising sea level) have three options: protection, accommodation and retreat (Few *et al.*, 2007). Grand Isle has shifted from a strategy of protection to one of accommodation. Hard and soft structural protection has

Fig. 15.8. A typical recreational stilt camp, Grand Isle (photo by author, 2009).

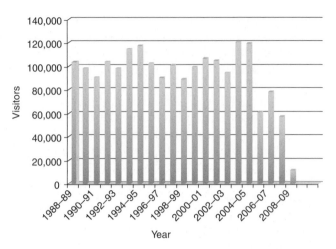

Fig. 15.9. Grand Isle State Park visitation, 1988–2009 (Louisiana State Parks, 2009).

proven to be stopgap at best, and although it may always remain a political priority, its effectiveness cannot be guaranteed. Accommodation via home-raising, roof-fastening and other defence mechanisms against water and wind – as well as rebuilding after every storm – appears to be the dominant adaptation strategy. Retreat – in the sense of moving buildings and roads back from the shorefront – is not an option because of the low (and sinking) physical setting (although individual residents are abandoning the island and retreating to higher ground further inland in Louisiana).

What may become left behind on Grand Isle is a fishing destination. Fishermen are concerned less about resort aesthetics than they are about good fishing (Fig. 15.10). Grand Isle has always been a destination for fishermen, and the Grand Isle Tarpon Rodeo is billed as the 'oldest deep-sea fishing rodeo in the USA' (Meyer-Arendt, 1985). But over time, and definitely since 1985, the non-fishing resort functions have gradually dwindled away to but a tiny portion of the overall resort economy. There are few restaurants (why would fishermen order fish in a restaurant, anyway?), and the most popular was for sale in 2009. The few modest motels on the island mostly cater to fishermen and proudly display fishing emblems on their façades. There are elevated stilt-trailer camps geared almost exclusively to fishermen. Most residential properties, many of which are mobile homes (caravans) or pre-manufactured housing raised on pilings as high as 14 ft (4.3 m) or more above sea level, are owned by fishermen. Even the fancier vacation homes are owned by wealthier recreationists attracted to fishing. The only vacant areas upon which to develop new housing on Grand Isle are in the back-barrier, where the residential-canal subdivision is currently being developed. While lots are being pre-sold for this 'gated waterfront community' in the 'heart of Grand Isle', it is hard to imagine this neighbourhood catering to anyone other than seasonal recreational fishermen.

Fig. 15.10. Fishing off the old Grand Isle–Cheniere Caminada Bridge, an enduring past-time (photo by author, 2009).

Summary

Grand Isle is an old seaside settlement with a resort tradition dating back over two centuries. This long tradition of tourism may be traced to the island's relative proximity to New Orleans, at one time the second most populous city in the USA. But Grand Isle's location in the heart of a subsiding Mississippi River deltaic plain has made it vulnerable to sea level inundation and tropical storms and hurricanes. Its tourism economy long characterized by cycles of boom and bust (related both to economic as well as environmental factors), Grand Isle has declined ever since a brief boom in the mid-1980s when a protective sand levee and wide beach were built. But structural protection alone is not ensuring the survival of the resort community. Beach tourists have shifted their sun–sand–sea–surf attentions elsewhere, and long-term residents are abandoning their multi-generational home island. Some residents and recreational fishermen are adapting to the environmental degradation by living with periodic onslaught of hurricanes and storm surge and rebuilding anew after every catastrophe. Whether this pattern can be sustained forever – or even until 2100 – remains to be seen.

Postscript

To compound the environmental problems that Grand Isle faces, on 20 April 2010 the BP-owned Deepwater Horizon mobile offshore drilling unit exploded – less than 70 miles (110 km) from the island – and the ruptured pipe sent millions of gallons of oil and gas into the Gulf of Mexico. By the end of May, the oil had washed ashore on the beaches and in the wetlands surrounding Grand Isle, effectively ruining the summer tourist season, the fishing industry and the island economy in general. In summer 2010, as the oil continued to flow, the only bright spot in the economy was the BP-funded cleanup and remediation effort. While this appears to be the 'nail in the coffin' for Grand Isle, the resort island has been resilient in the past. I suspect it will slowly recover from this disaster, even as it slowly sinks into the Gulf.

References

Bencaz, C.A. and Birdseye, R.U. (1990) Shoreline Evolution from 1945 to 1988 at Grand Isle, Louisiana. *Transactions, Gulf Coast Association of Geological Societies* 40, 147–159.

Burley, D.M., Jenkins, P., Darlington, J. and Laska, S. (2004) Loss, Attachment, and Place: A Case Study of Grand Isle, Louisiana. Paper presented at the annual meeting of the American Sociological Association, San Francisco, California, USA. Available online at: www.allacademic.com/meta/p109359_index.html (Accessed: 12 June 2010).

Chopin, K. (1899, 1976) *The Awakening*. New American Library, New York, USA.

Coastal Environments, Inc. (1986) Plantation Landing, A Proposed Development on Grand Isle. Unpublished Environmental Assessment, Baton Rouge, Louisiana, USA.

Coleman, E. (1985) Grand Isle: A Renewable Resource. *Aquanotes* 14(4), 1–5.

Conatser, W.E. (1969) The Grand Isle Barrier Complex. PhD dissertation, Tulane University, New Orleans, Louisiana, USA.

Elsner, J.B., Kossin, J.P. and Jagger, T.H. (2008) The increasing intensity of the strongest tropical cyclones. *Nature* 455, 92–95.

Evans, S.K., Stielow, F. and Swanson, B. (1979) *Grand Isle on the Gulf – An Early History*. Jefferson Parish Historical Commission, Metairie, Louisiana, USA.

Few, R., Brown, K. and Tompkins, E.L. (2007) Climate change and coastal management decisions: insights from Christchurch Bay, UK. *Coastal Management* 35, 255–270.

Gill, J. (1986) Our Grand Isle: Paradise found? *New Orleans Times-Picayune*, 10 August.

Gonzalez, J.L. and Törnqvist, T.E. (2006) Coastal Louisiana in crisis: subsidence or sea level rise? *EOS* 87, 493–508.

Louisiana State Parks (2009) Monthly Visitor Records of Grand Isle, La. 1986–2009. Provided by Sharon Broussard, Public Information Officer, Baton Rouge, Louisiana, USA.

Meyer-Arendt, K.J. (1985) The Grand Isle, Louisiana Resort Cycle. *Annals of Tourism Research* 12, 449–465.

Meyer-Arendt, K.J. (1987a) Grand Isle – the evolution of a Louisiana seaside resort. In: Penland, S. and Suter, J. (eds) Barrier Shoreline Geology, Erosion, and Protection in Louisiana. Coastal Sediments '87, ASCE, New Orleans, 11–16 May, pp. 10/3–10/18.

Meyer-Arendt, K.J. (1987b) Resort Evolution along the Gulf of Mexico Littoral: Historical, Morphological, and Environmental Aspects. PhD dissertation, Dept of Geography and Anthropology, Louisiana State University, Baton Rouge, Louisiana, USA.

National Oceanographic and Atmospheric Administration (NOAA) (2003) Subsidence and Sea Level Rise in Louisiana: A Study in Disappearing Land. NOAA Magazine Online (Story 101), www.magazine.noaa.gov/stories/mag101.htm (Accessed: 16 May 2009).

National Research Council of the National Academies (NRC) (2009) Final Report from the NRC Committee on the Review of the Louisiana Coastal Protection and Restoration (LACPR) Program. National Academies Press, Washington, DC. Available at: www.nap.edu (Accessed: 12 June 2010).

Pilkey, O.H. and Cooper, J.A.G. (2004) Society and sea level rise. *Science* 303, 1781–1782.

Rosati, J.D. and Stone, G.W. (2009) Geomorphologic evolution of barrier islands along the Northern US Gulf of Mexico and implications for engineering design in barrier restoration. *Journal of Coastal Research* 25(1), 8–22.

Stielow, F.J. (1977) Isolation and development on a Louisiana Gulfcoast island, 1781–1962. PhD dissertation, Indiana University, Bloomington, Indiana, USA.

16 Impact of Climate Change on Island Tourism – the Balearic Islands: Impacts, Vulnerability and Critical Management Issues

ALVARO MORENO

Historic Growth of the Destination

The Balearic Islands autonomous community is situated off the east coast of mainland Spain, in the Mediterranean Sea. The capital of the region, Palma, is located on the biggest island – Mallorca – about 130 km east of Valencia. There are another two major islands called Menorca and Ibiza and three smaller ones – Formentera, Cabrera and Dragonera (Fig. 16.1).

The history of the Balearic Islands as a tourist destination goes back more than 100 years (Bayón Marine *et al.*, 1999). In 1905 the Fomento de Turismo de Mallorca was created, the first institution of its kind, that aimed to attract and entertain visitors to the islands. During the first 30 years of the 20th century, the first hotels were built and tourism activities started to have relevance, particularly in Mallorca between 1925 and 1930. In 1935, Mallorca received more than 40,000 tourists, mainly upper-class visitors from other Spanish regions. This tourism evolution was interrupted by the occurrence of the two World Wars and the Spanish Civil War. It was not until the 1950s that the Balearics start their race to become one of the major tourism destinations in Europe. Several reasons explain the growth that started in the 1950s. At the global scale, the improvement of workers' rights, including the introduction of paid holidays, together with technological development and improvements in the means of transport made the islands more accessible than ever to the main international source markets. The decision of the United Nations to remove the economic restrictions on Spain (put in place as a mean of pressure to the dictatorship of General Franco) and the policies and infrastructure development during these years opened the borders to international tourism.

The rapid growth during the 1950s, 1960s and 1970s coincided with the emergence of package holidays from western and northern European markets and the development of mass tourism. In this period the islands, and especially

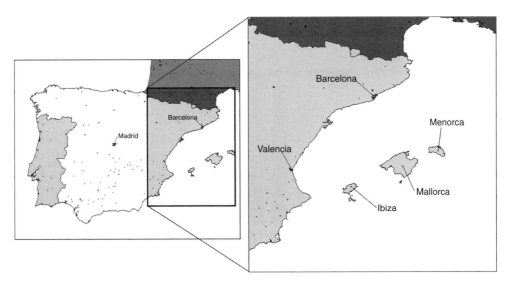

Fig. 16.1.   Location of the Balearic Islands.

Mallorca, experienced a process of homogenization, uncontrolled development with lack of planning and poor quality construction, a phenomenon that has received the name of 'balearization' and a concept that explains some of the challenges the tourism industry faces today (Robledo and Batle, 2002; Bramwell, 2004). To give an idea of the exponential growth of arrivals the Balearic Islands experienced during this period, it is worth mentioning that the milestone of one million arrivals per year was reached in 1965; in just 15 years the ratio changed from 1 tourist per 5 inhabitants to 2 tourists per inhabitant (Bayón Marine *et al.*, 1999): a ten-fold increase. In the 1980s, problems associated with this unrestrained growth became apparent, with environmental degradation becoming a serious issue and the whole destination receiving lower-income visitors and an image of downmarket and poor standards (Essex *et al.*, 2004). Following the terminology coined by Butler (1980), the destination was entering the 'stagnation' and 'decline' phases and required management intervention if its 'rejuvenation' was to be ensured. This intervention of the local authorities and industry started in the 1990s in an effort to control tourism development, and improve standards and the overall quality of the sector, focusing on product diversification and the attraction of higher-income tourists. The consequences of this intervention have been diverse and are discussed in some more detail below.

Current Tourism Trends

The most up-to-date and complete overview of the state of tourism in the Balearic Islands is published every year by the Conselleria de Turisme (Balearic Tourism Ministry). The evolution of arrivals by air shows a clear increase of approximately

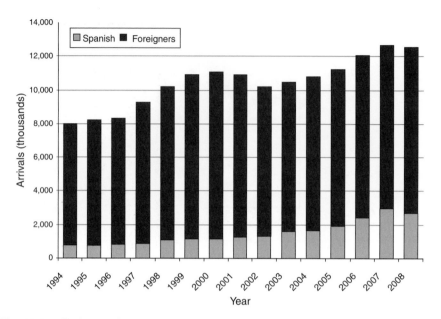

Fig. 16.2. Evolution of tourist arrivals by air 1994–2008 (Conselleria de Turisme, 2009).

57% between 1994 and 2008 (Fig. 16.2). The positive trend in arrivals halted in 2000, when a negative tendency started that lasted until 2003, mainly due to the economic crisis in Germany (Aguiló *et al.*, 2005). Since then, and with the exception of 2008, arrivals have increased yearly. According to the latest report available from the Conselleria de Turisme (2009), the Balearics received in 2008 a total of 13.1 million tourists arrivals, of which 96% arrived by air and 4% by sea. Foreign visitors outnumber domestic tourists (76% against 24%, respectively), and the international markets are dominated by Germany (32%) and the UK (27%). In 2008, as compared to 2007, there has been a drop of 1% in the total number of arrivals: while the number of foreign visitors increased by 0.9%, the number of Spanish tourists decreased by 6.5%. A trend towards shorter stays has also been observed: from 11.1 days on average in 2005 to 9.9 days in 2008. The economic significance of the sector can be easily envisaged. In the Balearic Islands, tourism is responsible for 44.2% of the GDP and employs directly and indirectly 30.8% of the active population. Tourism is also a major source of revenues for the regional government, generating 42.5% of the total earnings by means of taxes (Conselleria de Turisme, 2008).

Seasonally, the distribution of arrivals is characterized by a clear summer peak: 46.9% of the tourists visit the islands in the months of July, August and September, and 79% if the period is extended to include May, June and October (Fig. 16.3). Two elements explain this seasonal concentration: the profile of the tourists and their motivations for choosing this destination. Roughly 40% of the visitors to the islands are between 25 and 44 years old; 92% of them come with their families for leisure (Conselleria de Turisme, 2009). This implies that, to a

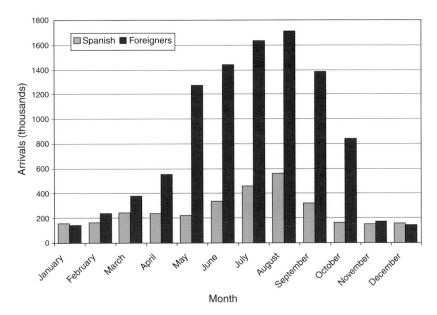

Fig. 16.3. Monthly tourists arrivals in the Balearic Islands in 2008 (Conselleria de Turisme, 2009).

great extent, these tourists are limited in their choice of the holiday period by the school and work holidays. Senior citizens (age above 64), the market often associated with higher flexibility in choosing their vacation time, represent only 13.2% of total arrivals and the smallest group of all recorded.

The motivations of tourists to choose the Balearic Islands are a second and very important factor explaining the marked seasonality. Research by Kozak (2002) among German and British tourists found out that weather is the most powerful destination attribute for a summer vacation on the Balearic Islands. Similar results were also presented by Lohmann and Kaim (1999) and Aguiló *et al.* (2005). This preference for climatic attributes is therefore another factor determining the summer concentration of tourists. Based on the data presented before, and according to Aguiló *et al.* (2005), it can be argued that 'sun and sea' is the main tourist product attracting tourists to the islands. However, and due to the intervention of the Balearic government and businesses to curve the declining arrivals during the 1980s, there has been an important effort to diversify the activities offered to tourists besides the typical beach tourism. The evolution in recent years of nautical, cruise and golf tourism is summarized in Fig. 16.4.

Motivations, together with the activities that tourists carry out during their stay, play a major role in understanding the potential climate change impacts on tourism; when motivations and activities are heavily dependent on the weather of the destination, climate change impacts can be expected to be greater (Moreno and Becken, 2009). The combination of weather-driven pull factors and highly sensitive tourism products – beach tourism – imply the Balearics will be very vulnerable to the impacts of climate change.

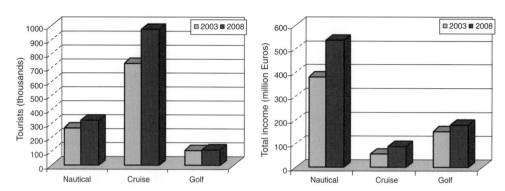

Fig. 16.4. Evolution of nautical, cruise and golf tourism 2003–2008 (Conselleria de Turisme, 2009).

Current Tourism Issues and Challenges

Some of the major management issues and challenges that the Balearic Islands are facing at present are rooted in the mass tourism model the islands experienced during the 1950s and 1960s. Overdevelopment of infrastructures and residential areas (unplanned to a great extent), deterioration and disappearance of environmental attributes and dependence on northern European tour operators and markets are some of the major weaknesses of this clearly unsustainable model. The decline in arrivals during some periods and the negative tendency of other variables such as the declining expenditure per tourist, made some authors suggest that any rejuvenation strategy of these mass market resorts was condemned to fail (Knowles and Curtis, 1999). On the other hand, Aguiló *et al.* (2005) suggest that the market reality does not support this view as recent trends indicate that there is still ample demand for 'sun and sand' tourism in the Balearics. In addition, there has been a profound restructuring process based on quality-based measures and the application of sustainable development-guiding principles. Current tourism plans are precisely focused on this commitment to rejuvenation strategies and environmental protection to halt the decreasing arrivals. Sustainable development principles have become a fundamental component in the new tourism planning. The district of Calvià – once a major tourist area that experienced severe degradation due to unplanned tourism development – is a good example of successful rejuvenation related to the implementation of the Agenda 21 for sustainable tourism (EC, 2000). However, not all measures have obtained the expected support and results. A good example of this is the case of the 'ecotax', which was agreed upon by the parliament in 2001 as a response to the increasing environmental degradation related to tourism. The 'ecotax' was contentious from the beginning and found a strong opposition both from hoteliers (who were supposed to collect the tax from tourists) as well as from tour operators. Introduced in May 2002, the polemic tax was abolished in November 2003 (Palmer and Riera, 2003; Essex *et al.*, 2004).

Some major challenges remain for the islands, with resource availability, especially water, needing special attention as it is already a major issue and is likely to be significantly affected by climate change, threatening the short- and long-term sustainability of the Balearic tourism industry. Several elements play a role in determining the pressure of tourism on water resources, including the volume of tourists, the type of activities offered and their geographical and temporal concentration. Water consumption by tourists is known to be higher than that of the resident population and the type of amenities developed for tourists are in many cases water intensive (Essex *et al.*, 2004). In addition, temporal concentration of visitors during the drier months of the year (almost 50% of arrivals occur between July and September) adds extra pressure over the water resources of destinations. During the 1980s and 1990s, the continuous growth in the housing and tourist sector (more than 100,000 beds between 1995 and 2000 in Mallorca alone (Consell de Mallorca, 2004)) and the efforts made to revitalize and diversify the sector were associated with important increases in water demand; in 1999, the gross average consumption in Mallorca was 367 l/day (Garcia and Servera, 2003; Essex *et al.*, 2004). These elements, combined with the use of irrigation in farmlands (62% of total water demand), the natural seasonal and annual variability and the geophysical characteristics of the islands have had important consequences on the water resources. Between 1973 and 1994, the water table of the main aquifer in Mallorca had been lowered by 110 m and saltwater contamination of the aquifers due to saline intrusion (rendering them useless for irrigation or human consumption) has become a major problem for the water supply of the island and consequently for the tourism sector (Essex *et al.*, 2004). In Mallorca, three-quarters of water requirements are covered by groundwater, a major source of vulnerability given the fact that already in 1998 eight of the 21 hydrological units were over-exploited, six of them suffering problems of saline intrusion (Kent *et al.*, 2002).

Existing and Perceived Climate Change Impacts

The Mediterranean region has been identified as being highly vulnerable to the impacts of climate change. In the Balearic Islands, the historical climate records for temperature (1976–2006) and precipitation (1951–2006) available provide information of the observed changes during the last decades. An increase of the maximum temperatures has been recorded at a rate of 4.83°C/100 years, much higher than the global average increase. As a matter of fact, the mean warming in Europe in the past has been approximately twice as rapid as the global average, a trend that can also be observed on the Balearics. As for rainfall, the average annual precipitation has shown a negative linear trend of −170mm/100 years (30% reduction per 100 years compared to the 550 mm reference value) (Conselleria de Medi Ambient, 2008). These trends constitute a remarkable example that supports the projections of a warmer and drier Mediterranean as projected by the IPCC (2007).

According to the study by Moreno *et al.* (2005) for the Spanish Environmental Ministry, the potential climate change impacts in Spain and in the Balearic Islands specifically are:

- Mean temperatures: increases in mean temperature in the Balearics during the 21st century of 3–4°C in winter and up to 5°C in the summer (A2 scenario);
- Accumulated precipitation: overall, a greater variability in the temporal and spatial distribution of precipitation can be expected, with a generalized trend to less annual precipitation during the summer months and without appreciable changes in the rest of the year (A2 scenario);
- Sea level rise: for the Balearics, a realistic scenario points towards a rise of 50 cm. In the face of this rise, beaches (especially those that are confined by human infrastructures) are expected to be the most vulnerable to processes of inundation and erosion. Combined with the increasing extraction of water for human consumption and the reduction of precipitation, sea level rise may lead to processes of saltwater intrusion into aquifers and their deterioration and unsuitability for human and ecosystem services;
- Impacts on biodiversity and ecosystems: severe impacts on wetlands and animal and plant communities (both terrestrial and marine), favouring the expansion of invading species and plagues, the frequency of forest fires, processes of land degradation and desertification and the loss of fertility;
- Interannual variability of monthly values: increase in the range (+20%) and frequency of monthly thermal anomalies (i.e. in the anomalous hottest months in the future climate, the temperature increases will be around 20% higher than the projected values for average warming);
- Frequency of extreme events: the occurrence of flash floods, droughts and heat-waves are not new in the Balearics. Although climate models provide very limited information about the trend of these phenomena, it can be assumed that any increase in the frequency or intensity will have severe implications for the tourism industry.

The way in which tourism in the Balearic Islands will be affected by these climate change impacts has not been systematically assessed, although several studies exist that explore the implications of some of these impacts for tourism in the Mediterranean as a whole (Amelung and Viner, 2006; Perry, 2006; UNWTO, 2008). The decreasing climate suitability for summer tourism in the Mediterranean due to heat stress associated with high temperatures is recurrent in these studies. Overall, the tourist season is projected to extend over the spring and autumn, while the summer loses part of its attractiveness due to excessive heat. However, most of these studies are based either on qualitative hypothetical descriptions (e.g. Perry, 2005, 2006) or on models that were not specifically designed for sun and sea tourism and therefore of limited application to the case of the Balearic Islands (Amelung and Viner, 2006). Little is known about the existence of thresholds – especially related to temperature – affecting the perception of comfort or safety of beach users and beyond which tourists might not be willing to stay at a destination. Although some studies exist about the stated preferred temperature for beach tourism, they must be considered with caution as they have not been validated with on-site data or compared to real behaviour (e.g. Morgan *et al.*, 2000; Scott *et al.*, 2008; UNWTO, 2008). Other studies have attempted to observe behaviour and compare it to weather conditions and no upper threshold could be found, suggesting that previous studies might have overstated the impact of heat events on beach tourism (Martínez Ibarra, 2006; Moreno *et al.*, 2009). Regardless of the lack of certainty about exact temperature thresholds, it is possible that the increase of several degrees during the summer season as projected by climate models will have important consequences on tourists' comfort.

The Vulnerability of the Balearic Tourism Sector to Climate Change

This section aims at filling the gap in the lack of knowledge about climate change impacts on Balearic tourism by providing a guiding framework for the assessment of vulnerability. Vulnerability is a concept commonly used in climate change studies and it represents the degree to which a system is able to cope with or is susceptible to the adverse effects of climate change. Vulnerability is a function of the exposure to climate impacts, the sensitivity to these changes and the capacity to adapt to, avoid, or reduce the impacts. Although broad world regions, ecosystems or sectors are regularly used as the units of analysis of vulnerability assessments, it has been recognized that there is a need to switch this approach towards coupled human–environment systems (Turner *et al.*, 2003; Schröter *et al.*, 2005; Füssel, 2007; Polsky *et al.*, 2007). Based on these concepts, Moreno and Becken (2009) have developed a methodology to facilitate the assessment of tourism vulnerability to climate change. The assessment is rooted in strong stakeholder participation and comprises five steps: (i) description of the economic, environmental and social context of the destination and key tourism activities; (ii) characterization of the climate and identification of key hazards and selection of tourism component–climate hazard subsystems (human–environment systems); (iii) operationalization of vulnerability by identifying the components and indicators to define the exposure, sensitivity and adaptive capacity of each tourism-hazard subsystem; (iv) integration of individual assessments from (iii) and analysis of non-linearities, interdependencies, future scenarios and overall vulnerability of the tourism destination; and (v) communication of results. Derived from the information presented in the previous section, three key tourism-hazard subsystems of the Balearic Islands (step ii) could be proposed (this analysis is elaborated for illustration purposes and is not derived from stakeholder consultation):

1. *Tourists' comfort–temperatures change leading to heat stress.* As explained previously, it is possible that an increase in temperatures may lead to increasing tourists' discomfort. Although not formulated for beach tourism, analysis of the climatic suitability for tourism in the Balearics by means of the Tourism Climatic Index (Mieczkowski, 1985) shows that by 2080 summer months could reduce their attractiveness due to heat stress (Amelung and Viner, 2006).

2. *Water availability for tourism – precipitation patterns.* The IPCC technical report on water and climate change projects that annual runoff in southern Europe may be up to 23% lower in the 2020s, and 36% lower in the 2070s according to the different model calculations. The same report also predicts an increasing drought risk: in parts of Spain, today's 100-year droughts are projected to return every 10 years (or fewer) on average by the 2070s (Bates *et al.*, 2008). Groundwater exploitation and sea level rise are likely to intensify the contamination of freshwater resources, reducing even further the water availability for human uses and ecosystem services (Kent *et al.*, 2002).

3. *Beach conditions – change on coastal dynamics.* The unplanned urban development and modification of the coast has led to degradation processes over the beach-dune system and the implementation of renourishment plans, although the result seems to be an acceleration of the beach erosion processes (Garcia and Servera, 2003). 'Urban beaches' – surrounded by architectural elements, disconnected from the dune field and requiring artificial nourishment due to the absence of sediments – are therefore more vulnerable to sea level rise and beach erosion processes. According to the European Commission, the Balearic Islands have 'high exposure' to coastal erosion, including the effect of sea level rise (EC, 2004).

The operationalization of the tourists' comfort–temperature changes subsystem is represented in Fig. 16.5 as an example. The exposure of the system to this hazard includes components such as 'temperature changes' or the changes in the 'climate suitability' for tourism. Temperature changes could be measured by monitoring the 'temperature variation' for the different seasons and the 'number of days in the year with maximum temperatures above *x* degrees', with *x* representing a certain threshold found to cause heat stress for beach tourism. Climate suitability is measured by 'changes in tourists' comfort' as measured by some indicator like the Tourism Climatic Index adapted to beach tourism ((TCI) Mieczkowski, 1985). Sensitivity can be described through the characteristics of the 'infrastructures' and the 'tourists' perceptions'. The sensitivity of the infrastructures is measured by the 'number of hotels which are air-conditioned', and 'tourists' climatic preferences' and 'country of origin' function as indicators of the sensitivity of tourists. Finally, adaptive capacity is determined by the 'institutional', 'financial' and 'managerial' components. Institutional support is reflected on the existence of 'early warning systems' in case of heat-wave periods and by 'monitoring and enforcing' construction standards that deal better with new climate conditions. The 'investment into adaptation' is used as indicator of the financial support. Finally, management strategies is monitored by the 'diversification' and 'marketing' programmes and the implementation of 'building standards' on all new tourism developments.

Overview of Current Management and Policy Strategies

Throughout the more than 50 years of tourism expansion, the Balearic Islands have developed an elaborate set of norms and laws to control and regulate the

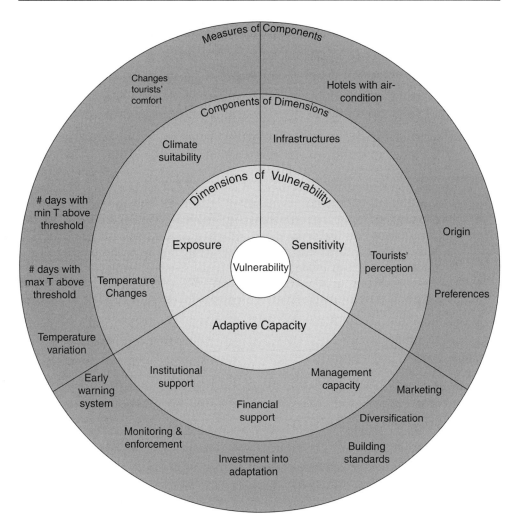

Fig. 16.5. Hypothetical operationalization of the tourists' comfort-temperatures changes subsystem (adapted from Moreno and Becken, 2009).

growth of tourism. It has been acknowledged many times that the continuous development of new tourist infrastructures generates a negative image of over-development of the islands. In practice, however, tourism laws have not only been unable to stop growth, they have stimulated growth in many cases.

Clearly, tourism is not only regulated by tourism plans and the Balearic Tourism Ministry; it is also affected by general spatial planning and coastal management plans among others. In other words, the division by sector or areas within the regional government has an effect on the high fragmentation of information, where for example tourism management and climate change plans affecting tourism are coordinated by different governmental divisions and not integrated.

Legislation at different levels – from local to international – often has an effect on regional destination management as well.

To illustrate this data fragmentation and regulation overlap, three documents are briefly described, the first two setting the basic regulatory framework of tourism management and the last one showing the initiatives that the Balearic Islands are taking in the field of climate change. The first of these documents is the sectorial plan regulating tourism (Plan de Ordenación de la Oferta Turística (POOT), Consell de Mallorca, 1995), which identifies tourism as the main economic driver of the island of Mallorca and includes among its objectives the improvement of the tourism offering, the determination of the carrying capacity, the promotion of measures to control excessive urban development of the coast and the renovation of obsolete tourism accommodation. The second legal text relevant to tourism management is the territorial plan of Mallorca (Plan Territorial de Mallorca (PTM), Consell de Mallorca, 2004), which analyses the current situation of aspects as diverse as education centres or energy resources and proposes guiding principles for their management and future development. In terms of tourism, this plan aims at adapting the tourism offering to the new motivations of demand, valuing the environmental aspects of tourist destinations and fostering the quality of the products. It is remarkable that despite the recognition of controlling excessive development in urban and coastal areas and the associated environmental degradation, the goals marked by the plan are to be achieved by making terrain available for the construction of 183,000 houses, which will increase substantially the pressures on the territory and its resources (Exceltur, 2007). These two documents (POOP and PTM) are specific for the island of Mallorca, although similar documents exist for the other islands. Despite the recognition of tourism as the main driver of the economy on the islands, none of the reports makes any reference or proposes any policy or management plan in relation to climate change and therefore to the vulnerability of the sector to its impacts. Some local governments are taking initiatives to compensate for the absence of a common strategy for the whole autonomous community. Ibiza is probably one of the most active ones at addressing the issue of climate change and tourism. It has taken several initiatives, such as the organization of the international conference 'World Heritage, Tourism and Climate Change – Sharing knowledge & good practices' in May 2008.

The lack of a common climate change and tourism strategy does not mean climate change is not seen as an important issue by the regional government. In 2005, the Government of the Balearic Islands created the general climate change office (Direcció General de l'Oficina del Canvi Climàtic) with the role of coordinating the measures of the region on climate change and which belongs to the Balearics' environmental ministry. In the same year, the first Balearic strategy against climate change was approved, and in 2008 the action plan (Pla d'Acció) was presented, including the mitigation measures the Balearic Islands will implement in the period 2008–2012. This action plan is structured around six sectors, including tourism and commerce, and provides specific measures to reduce greenhouse gases emission and indicators to monitor their development over time. It also includes a number of generic measures, which are not specific for any sector, and that aim at changing the frame of reference in which the policies

Table 16.1. Mitigation measures for tourism and commerce included in the Balearic action plan to fight climate change (Conselleria de Medi Ambient, 2008).

Component	Measure	Indicator
Energy efficiency and saving	Development of entrepreneurial policies of efficient use of energy (e.g. lighting, air conditioning, heating, etc.)	Number and cost of grants
	Incorporate an assessment of GHG emissions and corrective measures on the application of licences for tourism activities	Number of projects that include the assessment of GHG emissions Number of correcting measures per project
Good practices and technological improvements	Promotion of the use of more energy-efficient technologies and their monitoring on tourism accommodation	Number of accommodations that installed these mechanisms Energy consumption of the sector
	Promotion of good practices by medium and small businesses and certificate of best practices	Number of businesses with quality certificate
	Advice to the Balearic Islands and chamber of commerce for a sustainable entrepreneurial activity	Consumption of companies Number of companies with certificate of environmental management Number of environmental audits carried out
	Promotion of good practices in the field of environment by the tourist sector	Number of establishments with Environmental Management Systems (e.g. Ecolabel)
Development of regulations	Creation of a law to promote energy savings on tourism establishments	Energy consumption by the tourism sector

and sector programmes are developed (e.g. education). The mitigation measures specific for the tourism sector are included in Table 16.1. Adaptation to climate change is an issue that still has not been addressed by the regional authorities.

Summary and Conclusions

The Balearic Islands are one of the oldest and most important tourism destinations in the Mediterranean. Their success is based on a model of package holidays with highly competitive prices and rooted in the intrinsic beauty of the islands combined with the pleasant weather. Tourism is now the main economic activity, and therefore the islands rely heavily on tourists' flows, mainly linked to beach tourism. The geographical location of the Balearic Islands (west Mediterranean) and the high dependency on weather conditions of beach tourism, make the destination highly vulnerable to climate change. Increasing temperatures might lead to heat stress during the summer months, whereas changes in precipitation patterns might reduce the availability of water for tourism and other activities. Sea level rise might have severe implications for tourism activity, exacerbating current issues such as saltwater intrusion in aquifers and important problems of beach erosion and degradation due to the high degree of anthropogenization of the coast.

Past efforts to revitalize the tourism sector in this mature destination have focused on product diversification and environmental protection; climate change has been neglected so far. Despite the interest the regional government shows for the issue (e.g. with the creation of a specialized office within the regional environmental department), this interest has not been reflected yet in any legal document on tourism management: future tourism planning is still completely unconnected to climate change from a legal point of view, particularly regarding adaptation. In this sense, authorities and businesses should realize that current tourism management strategies will be insufficient to deal effectively with future climate change.

Our lack of understanding of how tourism is affected by climate change is a major source of uncertainty that needs to be tackled. To help increase the knowledge base on climate change impacts on the islands, a vulnerability methodology has been proposed. This methodology should provide a framework for the systematic assessment of major hazards and possibilities for adaptation in the tourism sector. However, to gain an integrated view guiding adequate management of the destination, climate change knowledge must be combined with other components, including the sensitivity to the costs of transport and oil prices, weather anomalies, change in tourists' preferences and market trends and the appearance of new competitors. The combination of these elements in tourism management plans is likely to improve the sector's awareness and its resilience to climate change and other shocks.

References

Aguiló, E., Alegre, J. and Sard, M. (2005) The persistence of the sun and sand tourism model. *Tourism Management* 26, 219–231.

Amelung, B. and Viner, D. (2006) Mediterranean tourism: exploring the future with the Tourism Climate Index. *Journal of Sustainable Tourism* 14, 349–366.

Bates, B.C., Kundzewicz, Z.W., Wu, S. and Palutikof, J.P. (2008) Climate change and water. Technical paper of the Intergovernmental Panel on Climate Change, IPCC Secretariat, Geneva.

Bayón Marine, F., Gonzalez de Souza, M.A., Marcos Valdueza, H., Alonso Sutil, M.C., Vogeler Ruiz, C. and Gomez-Luengo San Roman, E. (1999) *50 años del turismo español: Un análisis histórico y estructural.* Editorial Ramon Areces, Madrid.

Bramwell, B. (ed.) (2004) *Coastal Mass Tourism. Diversification and Sustainable Development in Southern Europe.* Channel View Publications, Clevedon, UK.

Butler, R. (1980) The concept of a tourist area cycle of evolution: implications for the management of resources. *Canadian Geographer* 24, 5–12.

Consell de Mallorca (1995) Pla d'ordenació de l'oferta turística (POOT). Palma. Available at: www.conselldemallorca.net/?id_section=1518&id_son=1519&id_parent=493 (Accessed: 27 February 2009).

Consell de Mallorca (2004) Plan territorial de Mallorca. Palma. Available at: www. conselldemallorca.cat/platerritorial (Accessed: 27 February 2009).

Conselleria de Medi Ambient (2008) Pla d'acció per la lluita contra el canvi climatic. Palma. Available at: www.caib.es/sacmicrofront/archivopub.do?ctrl=MCRST297ZI4 1685&id=41685 (Accessed: 5 March 2009).

Conselleria de Turisme (2008) Principales conclusiones del informe IMPACTUR Illes Balears 2007, Palma. Available at: http://exceltur.org/excel01/contenido/portal/files/Resumen%20IMPACTUR%20Illes%20Baleares%202007.pdf (Accessed: 28 February 2009).

Conselleria de Turisme (2009) El turisme a les Illes Balears. Dades informatives 2008. Palma.

EC (2000) *Towards quality coastal tourism*. European Commission, Brussels.

EC (2004) Living with coastal erosion in Europe – sediment and space for sustainability. Results from the Eurosion study. European Commission, Luxemburg.

Essex, S., Kent, M. and Newnham, R. (2004) Tourism development in Mallorca: is water supply a constraint? *Journal of Sustainable Tourism* 12, 4–25.

Exceltur (2007) Estrategias turistícas integradas en los vigentes planes de ordenación del territorio, en zonas del litoral mediterraneo, Baleares y Canarias. Exceltur.

Füssel, H.M. (2007) Vulnerability: a generally applicable conceptual framework for climate change research. *Global Environmental Change* 17, 155–167.

Garcia, C. and Servera, J. (2003) Impacts of tourism development on water demand and beach degradation on the island of Mallorca (Spain). *Geografiska Annaler* 85A, 287–300.

IPCC (2007) Climate Change 2007: Impacts, Adaptation and Vulnerability. Contribution of Working Group II to the Fourth Assessment Report of the Intergovernmental Panel on Climate Change. Parry, M.L., Canziani, O.F., Palutikof, J.P., van der Linden, P.J. and Hanson, C.E. (eds). Cambridge, UK.

Kent, M., Newnham, R. and Essex, S. (2002) Tourism and sustainable water supply in Mallorca: a geographical analysis. *Applied Geography* 22, 351–374.

Knowles, T. and Curtis, S. (1999) The market viability of European mass tourist destinations. A post-stagnation life-cycle analysis. *International Journal of Tourism Research* 1, 87–96.

Kozak, M. (2002) Comparative analysis of tourist motivations by nationality and destinations. *Tourism Management* 23, 221–232.

Lohmann, M. and Kaim, E. (1999) Weather and holiday destination preferences: image, attitude and experience. *The Tourist Review* 2, 54–63.

Martínez Ibarra, E. (2006) Consideraciones geográficas en torno al binomio clima-turismo: aplicación al litoral alicantino. Universidad de Alicante, Alicante.

Mieczkowski, Z. (1985) The Tourism Climate Index: a method of evaluating world climates for tourism. *The Canadian Geographer* 29, 220–233.

Moreno, A. and Becken, S. (2009) A climate change vulnerability assessment methodology for coastal tourism. *Journal of Sustainable Tourism* 17(4), 473–478.

Moreno, J.M., Aguiló, E., Alonso, S., Cobelas, M.Á., Anadón, R., Ballester, F., Benito, G., Catalán, J., Castro, M.d., Cendrero, A., Corominas, J., Díaz, J., Díaz-Fierros, F., Duarte, C.M., Talaya, A.E., Peña, A.E., Estrela, T., Fariña, A.C., González, F.F., Galante, E., Gallart, F., Jalón, L.D.G.d., Gil, L., Gracia, C., Iglesias, A., Lapieza, R., Loidi, J., Palomeque, F.L., López-Vélez, R., Zafra, J.M.L., Calabuig, E.d.L., Martín-Vide, J., Meneu, V., Tudela, M.I.M., Montero, G., Moreno, J., Saiz, J.C.M., Nájera, A.,

Peñuelas, J., Piserra, M.T., Ramos, M.A., Rosa, D.d.l., Mantecón, A.R., Sánchez-Arcilla, A., Tembleque, L.J.S.d., Valladares, F., Vallejo, V.R. and Zazo, C. (2005) A preliminary assessment of the impacts in Spain due to the effects of climate change. Ministry of Environment, Madrid, Spain.

Moreno, A., Amelung, B. and Santamarta, L. (2009) Linking beach recreation to weather conditions. A case study in Zandvoort, Netherlands. *Tourism in Marine Environments* 5(2–3), 111–119.

Morgan, R., Gatell, E., Junyent, R., Micallef, A., Ozhan, E. and Williams, A.T. (2000) An improved user-based beach climate index. *Journal of Coastal Conservation* 6, 41–50.

Palmer, T. and Riera, A. (2003) Tourism and environmental taxes. With special reference to the 'Balearic ecotax'. *Tourism Management* 24, 665–674.

Perry, A. (2005) The Mediterranean: how can the world´s most popular and successful tourist destination adapt to a changing climate? In: Hall, M. and Higham, J. (eds) *Tourism, Recreation and Climate Change.* Channel View Press, Clevedon, UK, pp.86–97.

Perry, A. (2006) Will predicted climate change compromise the sustainability of Mediterranean tourism? *Journal of Sustainable Tourism* 14, 367–375.

Polsky, C., Neff, R. and Yarnal, B. (2007) Building comparable global change vulnerability assessments: the vulnerability scoping diagram. *Global Environmental Change* 17, 472–485.

Robledo, M.A. and Batle, J. (2002) Re-planning for tourism in a mature destination: a note on Mallorca. In: Voase, R.N. (ed.) *Tourism in Western Europe: a Collection of Case Histories.* CAB International, Wallingford, pp.85–94.

Schröter, D., Polsky, C. and Patt, A.G. (2005) Assessing vulnerabilities to the effects of global environmental change: an eight step approach. *Mitigation and Adaptation Strategies for Global Change* 10, 573–596.

Scott, D., Gossling, S. and De Freitas, C.R. (2008) Preferred climates for tourism: case studies from Canada, New Zealand and Sweden. *Climate Research* 38, 61–73.

Turner, B.L., Kasperson, R.E., Matson, P.A., McCarthy, J.J., Corell, R.W., Christensen, L., Eckley, N., Kasperson, J.X., Luers, A., Martello, M.L., Polsky, C., Pulsipher, A. and Schiller, A. (2003) Science and technology for sustainable development special feature: A framework for vulnerability analysis in sustainability science. *Proceedings of the National Academy of Sciences* 100, 8074–8079.

UNWTO (2008) Climate change and tourism. Responding to global challenges. World Tourism Organization, Madrid, Spain.

17 The Impact of Climate Change on Reef-based Tourism in Cairns, Australia – Adaptation and Response Strategies for a Highly Vulnerable Destination

Robyn F. Wilson and Stephen M. Turton

Introduction

Australia's Great Barrier Reef (GBR) is the world's most spectacular coral reef ecosystem and is a major international and domestic tourist destination. It is recognized by UNESCO as a World Heritage Site and is frequently cited as one of the seven wonders of the natural world. However, despite the level of protection afforded by its World Heritage status and high level of management through its status as a marine park, it is not immune to the impacts of climate change. It is recognized as a critical tourist destination under threat from anthropogenic induced climate change and other human pressures, including nutrient and sediment runoff from adjacent river catchments into the GBR lagoon (Lewis *et al.*, 2007; Scott *et al.*, 2007; UNESCO WHC, 2007).

In this chapter we present a synthesis of existing knowledge on anticipated biophysical changes to the GBR due to anthropogenic climate change over the next 10, 40 and 60 years with implications for the reef-based tourism industry based in the Cairns region. On the basis of the existing knowledge of likely biophysical impacts of climate change on the GBR, we present findings of stakeholder interviews and a social learning workshop used to identify and prioritize adaptation strategies and responses for the Cairns tourist industry for the three timeframes into the future.

The Cairns Tourism Region

The Cairns tourism region (Fig. 17.1), which encompasses the land and reef areas from Cape Tribulation in the north to Cardwell in the south and extends west to the Atherton Tablelands (74,005 km²), has been identified by an Australian intergovernmental task force as one of Australia's most highly

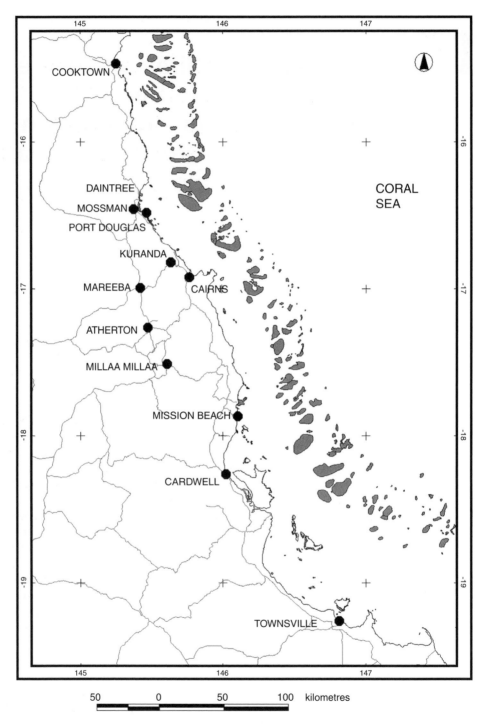

Fig. 17.1. Map of the north-east Queensland region of Australia. The Cairns case study region is depicted, together with main population centres referred to in this study.

vulnerable regions in terms of likely climate change impacts on its tourism industry. This region represents less than 20% of the coastline adjacent to the Great Barrier Reef World Heritage Area (GBRWHA) but attracts approximately half of the tourists to the GBRWHA each year. The population in the GBR catchment is almost 850,000 people and expected to reach 1 million by 2026 (Fenton *et al.*, 2007). Approximately 21% of the population is in the Cairns region. Of the two major regions supporting tourism to the GBR, that is Cairns and the Whitsundays to the south, Cairns has the greater number of trips to reef pontoons (Moscardo *et al.*, 2003). The reef is closest to the shore in the Cairns region, becoming progressively further offshore to the south.

There were 2,430,000 visitors to the Cairns region in the year ending June 2007 (four year average to June 2007: Tourism Research Australia, www. tra.australia.com). Approximately 75% of visitors to the region visited the GBR, comprising 1,831,609 visitors in 2006 (GBRMPA, 2007). Domestic tourists comprise the majority of the visitors (59% domestic and 41% international) to the region, however, they stay for a shorter periods than international visitors (average number nights of domestic 3.83 and international 5.53 per annum). As a consequence, the time spent in the region by domestic and international tourists is similar (visitor nights domestic 6,514,000 and international 6,297,000 per annum).

The importance of tourism to the overall GBR region is evidenced by the size of the economic contribution it makes to the economy. In 2005–2006 the total (combined direct and indirect) economic contribution of tourism, including commercial fishing and recreational activity, was AU$6.9 billion (Fenton *et al.*, 2007; GBRMPA, 2007). Visitation, excluding commercial fishing and recreational activity, represented approximately 87% of the gross product of AU$6.9 billion for the region (GBRMPA, 2007). Tourism associated with the GBR employs about 66,000 full-time equivalent persons with 30,000 of those positions in the Cairns region (Cairns Chamber of Commerce, 2007; Fenton *et al.*, 2007; Hennessey *et al.*, 2007).

Total expenditure of domestic (overnight and day visitors) and international visitors in the Cairns Region (four year average to June 2007, Tourism Research Australia database, www.tra.australia.com) was slightly higher for domestic than international travellers (domestic AU$1,244 million and international AU$1,068 million). International visitors spent more per trip than domestic overnight and day visitors (domestic overnight AU$832, domestic day AU$143 and international AU$1252).

The Cairns region (Fig. 17.1) includes three local government areas as of 2008. There are a range of different sized businesses in the region, from non-employing to large companies employing 20 or more people. In the region almost half of the 6678 businesses are non-employing and many support the tourist industry. Two-thirds, that is 2115 businesses, are based in the Cairns area and the remainder is spread across the other regional towns of Innisfail, Mareea, Port Douglas and Cardwell, respectively (four year average to June 2007, www. tra.australia.com).

Great Barrier Reef World Heritage Area

Reef tourism activities

Climate affects the timing of visits, length of stay and quality of experience to the GBR (Shafer et al., 1998), as well as impacting on the condition of the natural asset. On the GBR, climate affects water temperature, ocean acidification, sea level, water quality and intensity and frequency of cyclones, all of which affect the quality of the reef and hence the tourist experience (Johnson and Marshall, 2007). Climate is also known to affect the arrival and departure times and the tourists' experience in the Cairns region (Prideaux et al., 2006).

Tourist revenue comes from many reef-based activities. These include commercial boat trips offering snorkelling, birdwatching, whale watching, glass bottom boats, semi-submersibles and diving, to boat hire and fishing charters, kayaking, water sports, sailing, island resort accommodation and restaurants (Norris and McCoy, 2003; Norris and Murphy, 2004; Wachenfeld et al., 2007). Cruise ships are also an important source of revenue. Most of the commercial boat trips to the reef are operated by large companies employing many staff from the region.

Contemporary human impacts on the GBR

Human pressures on coral reefs at a global scale, independent of climate change, are having major negative impacts on the sustainability of these ecosystems. These impacts include overfishing, destructive fishing, mining, coastal development (dredging and land clearing), degradation of water quality due to high sediment loads and nutrient and chemical pollution from agricultural runoff (Jackson et al., 2001; Lough, 2008). Anthropogenic climate change is an added factor that is likely to have negative synergistic effects on the health of coral reef ecosystems.

The GBR is in better condition than most of the reefs in the world. This is due to its immense size, its wide latitudinal range (approximately 14°) allowing it to cope with a wide range of temperatures, its location abutting another World Heritage Area (Wet Tropics of Queensland), relatively low population densities along most of the coast adjacent to it, monitoring programmes permitting early intervention or response to detrimental impacts, and being located in a developed country with a well structured management system (Great Barrier Reef Marine Park Authority) with input from numerous experts (Johnson and Marshall, 2007). However, in the last decade the reef has exhibited signs that it is highly vulnerable to climate change despite its high level of protection and highly regarded management systems (Hoegh-Guldberg, 1999).

Types of threatening biophysical processes on the GBR, associated with anthropogenic climate change, that have important implications for the quality of the reef and hence tourism are:

• Warming of the oceans associated with extended El Niño Southern Oscillation (ENSO) episodes to an extent that abnormal heated pulses of water are now being experienced on the GBR during El Niño years (Veron, 2008);

- Acidification of the ocean as CO_2 from the atmosphere is absorbed and consequential reduced calcification rates of reef organisms (Orr *et al.*, 2005; De'ath *et al.*, 2009);
- Increased discharge from rivers during intense rainfall events resulting in increased turbidity and high nutrient inputs from agriculture and decreased salinity further out on to the reef (Lough, 2008);
- Disease resulting from stressed environments (Bruno *et al.*, 2007; Webster and Hill, 2007); and
- Outbreaks of crown of thorns starfish (Engelhardt *et al.*, 2001; Brodie *et al.*, 2005).

Climate change is also expected to affect key processes such as ocean currents, connectivity, dispersal and settlement patterns of larvae (Kingsford and Welch, 2007; Steinberg, 2007). These changes will impact on all reef biota including invertebrates such as corals, echinodermata and molluscs, and marine vertebrates such as whales, turtles and fish, affecting the attractiveness and suitability of the GBR for tourism (Kingsford and Welch, 2007).

As stated above, the two most threatening processes due to climate change are increased sea temperature and ocean acidification (Hoegh-Guldberg, 1999; Hennessy *et al.*, 2007; Webster and Hill, 2007). Other physical factors include sea-level rise, storm and cyclone damage, and discharge from floods on land (Anderson-Berry and King, 2005; Webster and Hill, 2007). Biological impacts include stress, disease, and outbreaks of crown of thorn starfish (Brodie *et al.*, 2005; Webster and Hill, 2007).

An increase in sea temperature is the biggest threat to the reef in the short to medium term. It is associated with coral bleaching, a reduction in plankton, pelagic fish and a decline of seabird colonies (Hoegh-Guldberg, 1999; Congdon *et al.*, 2007; Johnson and Marshall, 2007). Recent warming on the GBR this decade has resulted in two major mass coral bleaching events (Berkelmans *et al.*, 2004). Importantly for tourism and the recovery of the reef was that the intensity of the bleaching was variable and not all reefs were impacted to the same degree (Hughes *et al.*, 2003; Berkelmans *et al.*, 2004). Interestingly, some corals have shown resilience to warming leading some scientists to predict that there will be coral reefs in the future although they may not be as diverse as they are today (Berkelmans and van Oppen, 2006; McCook *et al.*, 2007a, b). Few scientists are willing to predict the extent of loss of coral from climate change although most agree that the risk of extinction of many species is high (Carpenter *et al.*, 2008). As a guide, a rise of sea surface temperature of 0.8°C will result in more frequent bleaching and a 2 to 3°C increase will kill most coral (Smithers *et al.*, 2007).

As CO_2 in the atmosphere continues to increase and the oceans absorb more of it there is a point at which ocean acidification will destroy corals and other calcium-based life-forms. This is predicted to occur by about 2050 (mid-to-longer term), when atmospheric CO_2 reaches about 500 ppmv. This will be catastrophic for the structure of the coral reefs and the crustaceans, molluscs and coralline algae.

A third environmental variable that is anticipated to increase with climate change is sea level. This change is expected in the short-to-medium term but it is

predicted that sea level change will not be uniform across the GBR. The implications for the GBR is greater depth of water over the reefs potentially affecting
light penetration and coral growth, surge and storm damage eroding the coast
and islands but also accretion on some islands and reshaping of their forms. The
rate of rise will be critical and will affect the expansion of coral into freshly submerged areas such as reef islands (Smithers *et al.*, 2007). The success of larval
settlement will also be influenced by potentially larger waves at reef island shores
(Smithers *et al.*, 2007) and their survival in warmer water in the shallows.

An adaptive response to human activities on the reef (that was first initiated
with the listing of the GBR as a World Heritage site in 1981) is the zoning of the
reef for different activities. The original zoning plan of the GBR was revised in
2003 to increase the level of its protection (Wachenfeld *et al.*, 2007). Tourist
groups such as the Association of Marine Park Tourism Operators (AMPTO) and
Tourism Queensland 'recognize that they will benefit from the new zoning
because it offers greater security for members, expands potential for sustainable
tourism and will enable them to offer higher quality destinations into the future'
and offer a broader range of products (Anon, 2003). New zoning has increased
the protection of marine turtle nesting sites from commercial fisheries (Dryden *et
al.*, 2008) and resulted in a rapid increase in fish stock in protected areas (Russ
et al., 2008). This is important for tourism as it aids in providing resilience to the
biodiversity of the region. It may also benefit recreational diving by providing
access to healthy reefs as the health of reefs around the world decline and bring
increased numbers of tourists to the region (Anon, 2003). It is envisaged that 'the
revised zoning plan also offers protection of prime tourism destinations, greater
incentives for site stewardship and, potentially, reduced incidence of conflicts of
use' (Anon, 2003), all of which benefit tourism in the Cairns region.

Anticipated biophysical changes to the Great Barrier Reef

There are large differences in the scale and level of confidence of climatic
variables derived from global climate models (GCMs). Changes in water, air
temperature and sea level rise have been modelled at a regional level with a high
level of confidence. In contrast, ocean circulation, storm and tropical cyclone
genesis, ENSO and ocean acidification have been modelled at a global scale
with low confidence. As a consequence of the low confidence in the latter models
there is greater uncertainty as to how they will affect the GBR.

Climate predictions for the next 10, 40 and 60 years for the Cairns region of
the Great Barrier Reef, relative to the 1971–2000 climatology or baseline period,
were derived for this study (Table 17.1; Hennessy *et al.*, 2008). They predict that
annual average daily maximum and minimum temperatures are likely to increase
by about 0.6°C by 2020 for mid-range emissions scenarios of the IPPC, about
1.0°C for low emissions, 1.6°C for high emissions by 2050, and about 1.3°C for
low emissions or 2.5°C for high emissions by 2070. Sea surface temperatures are
likely to increase at a slightly slower rate but will more or less mirror increases in
air temperatures (Hennessy *et al.*, 2007; Carpenter *et al.*, 2008). Based on these
climate change scenarios and a critical review of the biophysical changes that are

linked to these conditions, together with features of the reef that are attracting tourists today, we have attempted to predict what the reef will look like in the future and how it might affect tourism to the GBR (Table 17.2). The information derived in Tables 17.1 and 17.2 forms the basis for our social learning workshop with GBR stakeholders, discussed below.

Stakeholder Interviews

In this section we report on the knowledge and awareness of climate change in the GBR tourist industry, based in Cairns, and the adaptive responses and strategies identified by stakeholders in the industry following individual semi-structured interviews. The adaptive strategies were prioritized for the climate change scenarios for 2020, 2050 and 2070 (refer to Tables 17.1 and 17.2) during a social learning workshop. Twenty-four leaders involved in policy and/or practice in the community and tourist industry were interviewed; 22 of these had lived in the region for greater than 10 years. We used a Visitor (V), Industry (I), Community (C) and Environment (E), VICE matrix to achieve maximum representation of the business and regional community (Table 17.3). Organizations included in the survey were Queensland Tourism Industry Council (QTIC, the State peak body for tourism), Great Barrier Reef Marine Park Authority (GBRMPA), Cairns Regional Council, Tourism Tropical North Queensland (TTNQ), Wet Tropics Management Authority (WTMA), Environmental Protection Agency/Queensland Parks and Wildlife Service (EPA/QPWS), State Emergency Services (SES), Hotel Managers, Cairns and Far North Environment Centre (CAFNEC), Association of Marine Parks Tourist Operators (AMPTO), board members of Rainforest Aboriginal Council, local member of state parliament, and managers of small and large tour companies (Table 17.3).

Table 17.1. Predicted climatic conditions in 2020, 2050 and 2070 for the Cairns region of the Great Barrier Reef, relative to 1971–2000 average (climate data from Hennessy *et al.*, 2008).

Climatic variable	Scenario 1 2020	Scenario 2 2050	Scenario 3 2070
Temperature (min. and max.)	0.6°C ↑	1–1.6°C ↑	1.3–2.5°C ↑
Sea level and storm surge risk	8–14 cm	19–37 cm	35–56 cm
Increase in days over 35°C	+1	+4–8	+5–28
Total rainfall (%)	−0.7	−1.9	−3.0
Number of rain days	0.0 Little change	−0.1 Little change	−0.1 Little change
Percentage increase in heavy rainfall	1.8	5.1	8.2
Cyclone intensity of category 3–5		60%	140% ↑
Atmospheric CO_2		500 ppm	
Sea surface temperature (°C)	0.5 ↑	1.3 ↑	2.1 ↑

Table 17.2. Anticipated environmental changes on the Great Barrier Reef and likely impacts on reef-based tourism activities for 2020, 2050 and 2070.

Variable	Scenario 1 2020	Scenario 2 2050	Scenario 3 2070
Disturbance from climate change	Minor	Moderate–severe	Severe
Bleaching	More frequent; some loss of coral diversity Bleaching <1 every 10 years	Reef bleached; 95% loss of coral reefs >once every 5 years	Reef bleached; 95% loss of coral reefs Annual event
Coral structure	No major damage	Structural damage; 50% decline in iconic coral species and shift to crusting forms	Rubble. Total loss of coral structure
Macro algal cover	Minor coverage – isolated	High coverage across reefs	Very high – extensive coverage
Invertebrates	Little change	Major decline	Few rubble inhabitants
Obligate reef fish (10% of total fish speciation; small colourful species)	Little change – decline on some reefs	Major decline	Total loss and 70% decline in pre-existing fish
Herbivorous species of fish	Little change	Increase	Dominant type but also a decline in species
Seabirds	Decline in nesting colonies	Major decline	Colonies crashed (loss of pelagic food source)
Impact on tourists	Some decline at some sites	Major loss of tourist sites, especially near shore and shallow reefs	Reef severely degraded; total loss of visual amenity. Possibly interest due to size of destruction and algae
Chance/likelihood for 'average tourist' of: seeing good coral; seeing turtles; seeing whales; catching fish	High	Very low	Extremely low

Understanding the impacts of climate change on the natural environment

Prior to the identification of adaptation strategies, stakeholders were asked to consider the level of acceptance and understanding of climate change and its impact on the region. Approximately half the respondents across the VICE matrix

Table 17.3. Populated Visitor, Industry, Community and Environment (VICE) matrix.

	Visitors (V)	Industry (I)	Community (C)	Environment (E)
Policy	Federal and regional tourism organizations	State and regional tourism organization: QTIC, TTNQ	Elected Member of Parliament Barron Electorate	Land and reef management agencies: WTMA, GBRMPA
Practice	Large tour companies	Large accommodation provider	Community board members	Land and reef management agencies: Marine Parks, EPA /QPWS
Practice	Small Tour Operators	Tourism consultants; Ecotourism peak body – Marine & Reef AMPTO	City Regional Planner; State Emergency Services	Non-governmental organization: CAFNEC

AMPTO, Association of Marine Parks Tourist Operators; CAFNEC, Cairns and Far North Environment Centre; EPA/QPWS, Environmental Protection Agency/Queensland Parks and Wildlife Service; GBRMP, Great Barrier Reef Marine Park Authority; QTIC, Queensland Tourism Industry Council; TTNQ, Tourism Tropical North Queensland; WTMA, Wet Tropics Management Authority.

reported that changes in climate and weather patterns were not being discussed in their organizations. They recognized that weather is changing but not everyone is convinced it is anthropogenic in origin. All respondents representing the environment sector reported that people in their sector were discussing weather as it affected short term management but it was not a major item on their agendas.

In contrast, climate change was being discussed across all sectors of the VICE matrix by policy makers and practitioners (21 of 24 respondents), the exception was industry. Most responded that people in their sector were aware of, talking about and some were planning and preparing for climate change. The general conception was there had been a massive shift in people's awareness of climate change but they are not really processing or understanding the potential consequences (V policy).

The majority of tourism operators have only come to believe climate change is happening in the last year or so and their knowledge of anticipated impact is varied (I practice). Some industry practitioners consider that climate change is only another cycle. Of greater concern to the tourist industry is the exchange rate, lack of skills, aviation costs, access, 'rogue' operators and externalities such as the sub-prime collapse in the USA, energy crisis and peak oil, health scares such as SARS, terrorists attacks and war (I policy).

Leaders in the tourism industry are seriously considering climate change at the state and national levels and are looking at how they can respond to any predicted changes. However, at a regional level climate change is considered too difficult and is not part of any planning measures. At a regional level, the business concern is specifically economic and directed at 'carbon' offsets. There was a feeling that we are being buffered from climate change in the Cairns region compared with the rest of Australia, which has recently experienced severe droughts and bushfires (I practice and C policy).

Few positive effects of climate change were identified by the visitor, industry and environmental sectors (Table 17.3). Industry considered if there were radical changes people will come up with innovations, e.g. shading reefs to keep light factors at the same level. The environmental sector suggested there may be a potential that water quality will improve if there are changed patterns of water use, e.g. 'we need to map the water patterns better and look at mangrove distribution and how the reef is affected' (E), and 'we also need to consider the rate of change and more extreme events, such as rising sea-level and ambient water temperature affect quality of water, flooding and more spikes on reef' (E).

The community sector identified several impacts of climate change that were neutral or could benefit the reef. Sea level rise was not necessarily considered as negative. Some of their comments were: 'the reef requires more coverage instead of being bleached; more depth of water over it. Reef will adjust. Slow down the process; corals spread not grow up. Reef will then do its job and build and come up. It depends on speed of climate change and how it will grow' (C). Others stated that 'there is a potential for change in the distribution of different ecosystems which will be positive for some species and negative for others' (C). The initial response of climate change on reef tourism may be positive according to the community group: 'it is possible there may be a rush to the region to see it before a change occurs in the environment that isn't positive' (C). This may spur the industry to work more closely with other agencies leading to a more resilient industry to see the GBR before it declines in quality/disappears (C). The community generally believe that there will always be some core areas of reef left in the future: 'if you believe the area is so large and still have habitat then the impact will affect the edges but there will still be core habitat' (C).

Numerous negative effects of climate change on tourism on the GBR were identified. All sectors (Table 17.3) identified rising sea temperature leading to increased coral bleaching as potentially 'wiping out' the reef. The community and environment sectors also identified the more serious problem of ocean acidification and also how more severe weather events may impact on the GBR in the future: 'severe weather will cause destruction and lead to a loss of tourism value of assets' (I, C). Many were aware that climate change might interact with other threatening processes, such as crown of thorns (COT) starfish outbreaks: 'outbreaks are cyclic and these starfish are never really destroyed' (I, C), and 'future recovery of the coral may be limited and infestations of COT more frequent under climate change' (I, C).

Algae infestations were also considered a negative impact that was likely in future due to poor water quality as well as interacting with other changes (I): 'sea level rise is associated with climate change which may impact the reef' (E), and 'if the Great Barrier Reef declines in quality it will be less attractive to tourists; the impact on the tourism is that people will need to travel further to less affected areas, i.e. penetration will have to shift to the core areas' (C). Many saw climate change as being a serious threat because it is impacting on 'resilience of the reef' (E). Impacts on land that stakeholders considered will negatively impact the GBR were associated with more intense rainfall events: 'if it causes flooding there will be washing of large amounts of fresh water and nutrients into GBR lagoon leading to elevated nutrient and other impacts' (C).

All sectors were concerned about how the region is portrayed in the media on a global scale and how we compare with the rest of the world, citing that 'publicity being driven by the climate change debate has convinced the European market that GBR is already dead' (V). Tropical cyclones are a big media event that have a ripple effect on tourism in the region both internally and internationally and has the potential to 'deter people from visiting Cairns' (C). For example, following Cyclone Larry there was misinformation to the rest of the world that 'the whole area was messed up, including Cairns' (E).

Climate change and impact on tourism infrastructure

Large operators have vessels to cope with a 1:50 year tropical cyclone but in the future the industry maintains they may need vessels to go further out requiring a different and more robust vessel (V, I). The industry states that 'intense cyclones will be a big issue for pontoons and may wipe out part of the business' (I, E), and Marine Parks may also want 'stronger designs to prevent legal action' (I).

On the positive side the industry has suggested that climate change may 'empower industry to improve building design of infrastructure and the shipping industry' (I). A further positive move may be boats also switching from 'diesel to biofuels' (V). The industry's take home message is 'design and construction of tourism infrastructure must be environmentally friendly' (E). However, costs to the industry are likely to be high due to damage to infrastructure from cyclones; in particular, infrastructure such as 'marinas and jetties are not designed for Category 4 or 5 cyclones' (V).

Impact of climate change on reef-based tourist activities

Given the predicted changes to the GBR as a consequence of climate change, will the Cairns region still attract tourists in the future? Many respondents felt 'it is unknown if coral can adapt, if they will show resilience or if the future reef will be dominated by algae' (V, C). They also considered the implications for tourist activities: 'if coral is bleached then less people will want to go to the reef as it will not be attractive for snorkelling or diving' (C, E), and 'if it dies then there will be no reef tour operators' (V, I).

A positive effect for the reef is a 'greater tourism investment in the natural product as operators want to retain quality or restore it to good quality'(C). To many respondents, rising sea level is not a great issue for the reef as there are 'different depths all the time and operators adapt' (I). Many felt that the 'reef will still be there as long as natural cycle exists' (C). Although there may be a decrease in reef coverage in one area there may also be an increase in another, which will result in shifting operations, with many seeing that as 'a gradual process i.e. 20–30 years at a time' (V).

A predicted change in seasonality, with wetter 'wet seasons' and drier 'dry seasons', may be positive as most visitation to the GBR takes place in the cooler drier season. For example, 'if wind drops in the dry season, and the dry season is longer then water is clearer and tourists should see more fish on reef' (E). Some respondents felt that 'there may be a reduction in reef tourism sites and an eventual cap on number of sites to visit' (C). It was suggested that 'extra vessels or people in area may be unsustainable because the points of attraction cannot take the numbers, i.e. only so many large operators to one reef pontoon' (C).

Finally, there was a universal concern that 'potential international tourists may hear about impact of climate change and may assume the reef is already degraded and make a decision to not visit' (I). In terms of domestic tourism, 'in the future if winters are warmer down south then no incentive to visit the north in that season for fun in the sun' (V).

Social learning workshops

Fifty adaptation strategies for tourism in the Cairns region were identified from the semi-structured interviews. These strategies were categorized into themes that developed during the interviews, e.g. natural environment, tourist, infrastructure, community and policy (Table 17.4). Some adaptation strategies were common to more than one theme and here we report on the high adaptation strategies for the GBR, and those on the land that directly impact the reef, for 2020, 2050 and 2070 as identified by mixed VICE groups (Table 17.3) and report on specific comments from the different sectors of the VICE model.

Most adaptation strategies that were considered high priority (Table 17.4) were also high priority for all three climate change scenarios (Tables 17.1 and 17.2). A caveat on all adaptation strategies was that extreme events may result in severe damage to infrastructure as early as 2020 and the community may be unable to adapt due to costs of repair and lack of or unaffordable insurance cover in the future. The visitor/industry sector felt that the most important thing to consider when talking about adaptations to any of the scenarios was costs.

Natural environment: water quality

An adaptation strategy considered of very high priority for the health of the GBR was to improve water quality on land. It was seen as of prime importance in building ecological resilience on both the land and the reef and applies to all three scenarios. It was also one of the adaptation strategies that are already being implemented by the state government. However, there is still scope for developing this strategy as identified by the community sector: 'despite very strong water quality legislation there are no legislative requirements for landowners to restore riparian zones; … there is a need for the provision of legislative power to enforce restoration'; 'If a system is more resilient it is better able to cope with climate change. By dealing with water quality on land you build resilience of other ecosystems and corals will be healthier' (E).

Table 17.4. High priority adaptation strategies and responses to climate change for the Great Barrier Reef identified by the VICE group participants based in the Cairns Region (x = high priority; o = medium–low priority).

2020	2050	2070	Adaptation strategies
Year			
Natural environment			
x	x	x	Deal with water quality on the land and corals will then be healthier, more resilient and better able to adapt to climate change
x	x	x	Build resilience of ecosystems by reducing or controlling other pressures, e.g. control weeds and feral animals and water quality
x	x	x	Zoning – reduction of area/sites we can interact with
x	x	o	Risk assessment of natural assets under climate change, develop strategies to minimize risk around these assets
x	o	x	Planting coral gardens and planting corals that are from areas adapted to higher temperatures
x	o	o	Shading of coral to reduce temperature on certain reefs; spraying of water on top to increase surface reflection
o	x	o	New ventures, e.g. aquaculture ventures such as clam farm – for education, commercial/restaurant and seeding new areas
Infrastructure			
x	x	x	Transport – alternative fuels; buses and boats move from diesel to biofuel
x	x	x	Research alternative energy technologies and identify what you can do to retrofit or, if new, what you need that is not in current design
x	o	x	Provide incentives (tax) to replace engines with more efficient technology
Tourist/community			
x	x	x	Low footprint tourism – offset and design, adapt attitudes; change advocacy. What can tourism provide to make the natural area resilient?
x	x	x	International 'families' and domestic tourism – market as 'energy conservative' accommodation and ground travel; promote planet safe partnership
x	x	x	Position ourselves as 'Green and Clean'; marketing positive changes as they arise. Rainforest visitation is for the aesthetics, greenery
x	x	x	Using climate change as a trigger to promote sustainable activities
x	o	x	Offer complementary experiences to pristine reef and rainforest in cultural, business, education and research; focus tourism in different areas, which take up different economic activities; more island-based activities and interpretation
x	o	x	Tourism workforce needs to be trained and valued in a way that ensures they can offer tourist a rewarding experience and where we are known as a place where exceptional service is provided
x	o	o	Politicians responding and working with researchers and operators: e.g. Crown of Thorns video, asked about presenting it to parliament but advised not to show it as if you show negative pictures you will not receive the money

(Continued)

Table 17.4. Continued.

	Year		
2020	2050	2070	Adaptation strategies
x	x	o	Identify why we are unique and how we adapt to climate change – build resilience and brand
o	x	x	Resource sharing among operators – to reduce carbon offsets, higher fuel costs and reduce 'C' emissions
o	o	x	Niche may be 'looking at change' – come and experience the impacts of climate change
o	o	x	Video-cam in natural setting – interpretive centre in the rainforest where you interpret the rainforest and the reef via a video link. Camera will be set up in different strategic places in the reef and rainforest to show different conditions
o	o	x	Cairns region compared with the rest of Australia – don't need warm clothes, still have lots of freshwater, no extreme heat, have a growing (agriculture) climate, all positives. Return to basics
Policy			
x	x	x	Good information from reputable scientists that give key points, e.g. research on wind, more on storms, hybrid transport, solar power. Not obvious what we need to plan for
x	x	x	Standardized system of calculating 'C' and ETS (emissions calculator; Green globe – auditing) and rigorous annual energy audit (Federal assessment)
x	x	x	Combat negative publicity promptly and effectively
x	x	x	Implement offsets or more efficient ways of travelling to reduce their contribution to Green House Gas Emissions; if international concern about long haul flights on climate change, then have an offset arrangement applied directly at reef and rainforest
x	x	x	A marketing strategy where travellers are attracted to the area because of approach to energy efficiency and reducing carbon emissions; changing marketing strategies that match tourist expectations with what is available on the reef and in the rainforest
x	x	-	Identify and sell benefits – only way to sell mitigation is to sell benefits
x	o	x	Emergency evacuation policy – risk assessment and plan for emergency events, and well-informed staff and community
x	o	o	Separate organization to manage climate change – parliamentary term too short for politicians to manage it
x	o	o	Price product so it is competitive domestically and internationally with comparable experiences
x	x	o	Fund research and have long term monitoring – have operators involved; smarter operators
x	x	o	Data storage and dissemination – system where you store information and it is readily available to everyone, not restricted to departments
o	x	o	Increase efficient way in which community and tourists live – reduce energy use, water use and recycle, reduce carbon footprint

Year			
2020	2050	2070	Adaptation strategies
o	x	o	Positioning: if no change here in extreme events, less extreme, or temperatures more amenable than elsewhere then turn it into a positive
			Land-based adaptation strategies that influence the reef
x	x	x	Research and build infrastructure to cope with climate change – roads, pipes, sewerage, sewage treatment plants
x	x	x	Build infrastructure that has low carbon emissions and use this in marketing. Tax people if they do not choose to use low emission infrastructure
x	x	x	No development or sale of land in flood-prone areas
x	x	x	CO_2 sequestration programmes – tree-planting – community revegetation programmes
x	x	o	Water availability – more tourists and residents, need more water or better use. This will have a flow-on effect on infrastructure services, schools and hospitals. Cap number of residents and tourists in response to climate change scenario
x	x	o	Recycling programme – hotels, houses, government buildings, community
x	x	o	Applying best practice in plant husbandry to reduce loss of habitat, land degradation and control exotic pests and diseases, bio-sequestration technologies and carbon accounting practices
x	o	x	Implementing a building code for all accommodation/infrastructure design to cope with extreme winds of cyclone Category 5
o	x	o	Engineering – ways to protect low lying areas; build bund/retaining walls

Zoning is a management strategy that is already in place on the GBR. However, in the future it is recognized that this will need to be redefined as conditions change and there may be a reduction in the reef area available for tourism.

Natural environment: corals

Strategies for 2020 to protect the coral from high temperatures were to shade or spray water on top to increase surface reflection. However, these strategies were not considered high priority in the longer term. Another approach to sustaining coral in an area that was seen as applicable to all three scenarios was to translocate coral with high thermal tolerance into disturbed (bleached) areas. The community sector, in particular, supported this but identified the need for research now, and planning and policy development before 2020. To enhance the success of this a risk assessment and monitoring of natural assets under climate change was also seen as high priority: 'There is also a strong need for monitoring resources to ensure that we monitor condition in response to adaptation strategies and can respond, or adapt, following assessment of progress or undesirable changes in condition' (C).

Tourism infrastructure

Several of the adaptation strategies identified under this theme, such as more water availability, water recycling, and building design and structure, are land based and have been included in the land-based strategies that influence the reef (Table 17.4). The high adaptation strategies directly related to the reef were adopting alternative fuel, developing new technologies and tax incentives. These were seen as applicable to all three climate change scenarios and important in protecting the environment, however, they would need policy to drive them. Incentives that are bonus-based to build a 'green and clean' image were seen as a positive. In contrast there was little support for additional taxes. Government was targeted to make this a priority so that funds are there from consolidated revenue to support an incentive-based programme.

Tourist/community

Most strategies related to 'tourism/community' focused on using climate change as a trigger to promote sustainable activities. These included developing low footprint tourism, a 'clean-green' and a 'planet safe partnership'. In addition, an important strategy to implement now was to diversify the tourism market place and offer complementary experiences to the reef. By 2070, respondents considered high adaptive strategies to the consequences of climate change to be to look at new opportunities as a result of change to the reef, use video-cameras on the reef relayed to a pristine area on land, and market what the region has to offer in terms of its climate compared to the rest of Australia.

All sectors of the industry considered the need for the tourism workforce to be trained and valued in a way that ensures they can offer tourists a rewarding experience and where we are known as a place where exceptional service is provided. This was a high priority for 2020 and 2070: 'This needs to start right now (before 2020) to ensure that there is enough capacity in the tourism sector to respond to future changes. At present there are critical shortfalls in entertainment, accommodation and wage and general conditions for tourism industry staff – a social change is required to move away from the casual staff approach with no benefits' (C).

Planning and policy

Many adaptation strategies for 2020 were based on better planning and policy implementation on the land. To this end, building and infrastructure that implements a low 'carbon' footprint and is designed to cope with sea level rise and extreme events, such as cyclone and storm surge, was considered a high priority. This was particularly so for the coast, where most of the tourist accommodation is situated.

The environment sector considered implementing green zones, planting trees and wildlife corridors as adaptation strategies and a reduction in emissions and work to keep CO_2 levels below 500 ppmv (mitigation strategy) as high priority areas with flow-on effects for the reef. A high priority area also considered by this sector was a vulnerability assessment of the reef that would provide practical information and research needs. Considerable progress on accessing the vulnerability of the GBR to climate change has already been achieved (Johnson and Marshall, 2007), suggesting that this knowledge needs to be communicated to the different sectors.

Several high priority strategies to support the community were identified. These included effective communication between different sectors, for example information transfer between the environment and community sectors, information transfer between researchers and operators, transfer of knowledge in a useful form to policy developers and interpretation of knowledge for the lay person. An effective means of influencing the government and policy is to have a well informed community. This needs to happen through good communication and information transfer (C, E).

Related to information transfer is the need to combat negative publicity. To this means an adaptation strategy considered for 2020 was to construct a separate organization to manage climate change and broker knowledge in the region. Politicians were not considered necessarily the most appropriate group to manage this as the parliamentary term is too short. However, a group discussion by all participants considered that no single agency or organization should coordinate the adaptation strategies. This should be more about working in partnerships both locally and regionally. It was noted that there was no current regional organization with a climate change department: 'Cairns Regional council is being restructured, but currently has no climate change or sustainability department – this lack of focus on resourcing (climate change) makes it difficult to implement adaptation strategies'.

Discussion

As a system the GBR is highly vulnerable to climate change, however, some parts may be less vulnerable and more resilient than others (Hughes *et al.*, 2003; Marshall and Johnson, 2007). Several eminent marine scientists consider that although the projected increase in CO_2 and temperature of the oceans over the next 50 years exceeds conditions in the past, the reefs will change rather than disappear entirely (Hughes *et al.*, 2003). Due to the size and unique position of the GBR it is possible that in the future it may be the only location on the globe for tourists to see a coral reef ecosystem.

The community and tourist industry recognize that there will be many challenges they will have to face in responding to climate change if they are to maintain a sustainable tourist industry in the region. Planning and implementation of many of the adaptation strategies needs to begin early and be in place by 2020. The general feeling was that tourism will survive in the Cairns region but the reef may not be the prime attraction by 2070. Many of the participants had difficulty thinking of adaptation strategies for tourism for 2070, which was seen as too far into the future.

Significant shortcomings in government acceptance of climate change risks and appropriate resourcing to overcome these risks was seen as a real limitation to many of the infrastructure and policy adaptation strategies identified. Planning in particular was seen as requiring more support – both in terms of human resources and funding. It was also noted that state-wide or regional building codes should be developed (with greater governmental regulatory power) to ensure that developments are sensitive and appropriate to regions in which they are proposed.

In particular, to cope with extreme events the region needs improved planning, evacuation procedures and building codes in place by 2020.

Limitations to the low footprint tourism approach were raised, especially given community suspicions relating to the large number of certification schemes and the fact that there is no legislative power associated with them. The opinion was stated that tourists do not yet respond to the 'clean and green' labelling that Cairns is trying to portray. Furthermore, the Cairns region is lagging behind destinations in Europe such as Holland and Germany in terms of being green (although it is a long way ahead of most places that have tropical rainforest and reef attractions). However, emission trading schemes, carbon offset programmes and green accreditations were viewed with a degree of scepticism by most tourists and industry members.

Positioning the region as 'green and clean' is not only environmentally desirable but also important if the region is to be competitive in the market place in the future. The limitations to implementing this identified by the community sector were: 'the need for a lot of time to turn the industry into a greener one' as well as the need for more local staff and resources to assess the 'green credentials' of businesses. This will also require the resolution of some policies and legislation.

The tourist industry in the Cairns region has adapted to change in the past and has consistently shown resilience to previous threats. It is recognized by most of the representatives in this study that climate change is another major change to which they have to respond. However, the industry is still coming to terms with the magnitude of the predicted changes and needs direction from government in how to respond and implement adaptation strategies. To achieve this it is vitally important that collaborative relationships are built across all components of the tourism sector (see Table 17.3) to ensure that adaptation strategies are broadly accepted and adopted.

Acknowledgements

This research was funded by the Sustainable Tourism Cooperative Research Centre and the Australian Government's Department of Resources, Energy and Tourism. We would like to thank the following colleagues for their ideas and stimulating discussions: David Simmons, Susanne Becken, Wade Hadwen and Brad Jorgensen. Finally, we are greatly indebted to the 24 VICE matrix members for generously giving their time by participating in semi-structured interviews and the social learning workshop.

References

Anderson-Berry, L. and King, D. (2005) Mitigation of the impact of tropical cyclones in northern Australia through community capacity enhancement. *Mitigation and Adaptation Strategies for Global Climate Change* 10, 367–392.

Anon. (2003) Zoning plan for the Great Barrier Marine Park. Regulatory impact statement, pp.1–51. Delivered to Parliament. RIS: 25-11-03.

Berkelmans, R. and van Oppen, M.J.H. (2006) The role of zooxanthellae in the thermal tolerance of corals: a 'nugget of hope' for coral reefs in an era of climate change. *The Proceedings of the Royal Society: B Biological Sciences* 273, 2305–2312.

Berkelmans, R., De'ath, G., Kininmonth, S. and Skirving, W.J. (2004) A comparison of the 1998 and 2002 coral bleaching events on the Great Barrier Reef: spatial correlation, patterns, and predictions. *Coral Reefs* 23, 74–83.

Brodie, J., Fabricius, K.E., De'ath, G. and Okajic, K. (2005) Are increased nutrient inputs responsible for more outbreaks of crown-of-thorns starfish? An appraisal of the evidence. *Marine Pollution Bulletin* 51, 266–278.

Bruno J.F., Selig, E.R., Casey, K.S., Page, C.A., Willis, B.L., Harvell, C.D., Sweatman, H. and Melendy, A.M. (2007) Thermal stress and coral cover as drivers of coral disease outbreaks. *PLoS Biol* 5, e124.

Cairns Chamber of Commerce (2007) *2007 Cairns Report*. Australian Tourist Publications, p.34.

Carpenter, K.E., Abrar, M., Aeby, G., Aronson, R.B., Banks, S., Bruckne, A., Chiriboga, A., Cortés, J., Delbeek, J.C., DeVantier, L., Edgar, G.J., Edwards, A.J., Fenner, D., Guzmán, H.M., Hoeksema, B.W., Hodgson, G., Johan, O., Licuanan, W.Y., Livingstone, S.R., Lovell, E.R., Moore, J.A., Obura, D.O., Ochavillo, D., Polidoro, B.A., Precht, W.F., Quibilan, M.C., Reboton, C., Richards, Z.T., Rogers, A.D., Sanciangco, J., Sheppard, A., Sheppard, C., Smith, J., Stuart, S., Turak, E., Veron, J.E.N., Wallace, C., Weil, E. and Wood, E. (2008) One-third of reef-building corals face elevated extinction risk from climate change and local impacts. *Science* 321(1588), 560–583.

Congdon, B.C., Erwin, C.A., Peck, D.R., Baker, G.B., Double, M.C. and O'Neil, P. (2007) Vulnerability of seabirds on the Great Barrier Reef to climate change. In: Johnson, C.N. and Marshall, P.A. (eds) *Climate Change and the Great Barrier Reef: a Vulnerability Assessment*. Great Barrier Reef Marine Park Authority, Townsville, pp.427–463.

De'ath, G., Lough, J.M. and Fabricius, K.E. (2009) Declining coral calcification on the Great Barrier Reef. *Science* 323, 116–119.

Dryden, J., Grech, A., Maloney, J. and Hamann, M. (2008) Rezoning of the Great Barrier Reef World Heritage Area: does it afford greater protection for marine turtles? *Wildlife Research* 35, 477–485.

Engelhardt, U., Hartcher, M., Taylor, N., Cruise, J., Engelhardt, D., Russell, M., Stevens, I., Thomas, G., Williamson, D. and Wiseman, D. (2001) Crown-of-thorns starfish (*Acanthaster planci*) in the central Great Barrier Reef region. Results of fine-scale surveys conducted in 1999–2000. CRC Reef Research Centre *Technical Report No. 32.*, Townsville, 100pp.

Fenton, M., Kelly, G., Vella, K. and Innes, J. (2007) Climate change and the Great Barrier Reef: industries and communities. In: Johnson, J.J. and Marshall, P.A. (eds) *Climate Change and the Great Barrier Reef. A Vulnerability Assessment.* Great Barrier Reef Marine Park Authority and Australian Greenhouse Office, Australia, Townsville, pp.745–771.

GBRMPA (Great Barrier Reef Marine Park Authority) (2007) *Great Barrier Reef Climate Change Action Plan 2007–2011*. GBRMPA, Townsville.

Hennessy, K., Fitzharris, B., Bates, B.C., Harvey, N., Howden, M., Hughes, L., Salinger, J. and Warrick, R. (2007) Australia and New Zealand. In: *Climate Change 2007: Impacts, Adaptation and Vulnerability.* Contribution of working Ggroup II to the Fourth Assessment Report of the Intergovernmental Panel on Climate Change (eds Parry, M.L., Canziani, O.F., Palutikof, J.P., van der Linden, P.L. and Hanson, C.E.). Cambridge University Press, Cambridge, UK, pp.507–540.

Hennessy, K., Webb, L., Kirono, D. and Ricketts, J. (2008) *Climate Change Projections for Five Australian Tourism Regions.* A report prepared for the Sustainable Tourism CRC. CSIRO Marine and Atmospheric Research, Aspendale, Victoria, 21pp.

Hoegh-Guldberg, O. (1999) Climate change, coral bleaching and the future of the world's coral reefs. *Marine and Freshwater Research* 50, 839–866.

Hughes, T.P., Baird, A.H., Bellwood, D., Card, M., Folke, C., Grosberg, R., Hoegh-Guldberg, O., Jackson, C.J., Kleypas, J.A., Lough, J.M., Marshall, P.A. and Nystrom, M. (2003) Climate change, human impact, and the resilience of coral reefs. *Science* 301, 929–933.

Jackson, J.B.C., Kirby, M.X., Berger, W.H., Bjorndal, K.A., Botsford, L.W., Bourque, B.J., Bradbury, R.H., Cooke, R., Erlandson, J., Estes, J.A., Hughes, T.P., Kidwell, S., Lange, C.B., Lenihan, H.S., Pandolfi, J.M., Peterson, C.H., Steneck, R.S., Tegner, M.J. and Warner, R.R. (2001) Historical overfishing and the recent collapse of coastal ecosystems. *Science* 293, 629–637.

Johnson, J.E. and Marshall, P.A. (2007) *Climate Change and the Great Barrier Reef. A Vulnerability Assessment.* Great Barrier Reef Marine Park Authority and Australian Greenhouse Office, Australia.

Kingsford, M.J. and Welch, D.J. (2007) Vulnerability of pelagic systems of the Great Barrier Reef to climate change. In: Johnson, J.E. and Marshall, P.A. (eds) *Climate Change and the Great Barrier Reef: a Vulnerability Assessment.* Great Barrier Reef Marine Park Authority and Australian Greenhouse Office, Townsville, pp.555–586.

Lewis, S.E., Sherman, B.S., Bainbridge, Z.T., Brodie, J.E. and Cooper, M. (2009) Modelling and monitoring the sediment trapping efficiency and sediment dynamics of the Burdekin Falls Dam, Queensland, Australia. 18th World IMACS/MODSIM Congress, Cairns, Australia 13–17 July 2009.

Lough, J.M. (2007) Climate and climate change on the Great Barrier Reef. In: Johnson, J.E. and Marshall, P.A. (eds) *Climate Change and the Great Barrier Reef: a Vulnerability Assessment.* Great Barrier Reef Marine Park Authority and Australian Greenhouse Office, Townsville, pp.15–50.

Lough, J.M. (2008) 10th Anniversary Review: a changing climate for coral reefs. *Journal of Environmental Monitoring* 10, 21–29.

Marshall, P.A. and Johnson, J.E. (2007) The Great Barrier Reef and climate change: vulnerability and management implications. In: Johnson, J.E. and Marshall, P.A. (eds) *Climate Change and the Great Barrier Reef: a Vulnerability Assessment.* Great Barrier Reef Marine Park Authority and Australian Greenhouse Office, Townsville, pp.773–801.

McCook, L.J., Folke, C., Hughes, T.P., Nystrom, M., Obura, D. and Salm, R. (2007a) Ecological resilience, climate change and the Great Barrier Reef. In: Johnson, J.E. and Marshall, P.A. (eds) *Climate Change and the Great Barrier Reef: a Vulnerability Assessment.* Great Barrier Reef Marine Park Authority and Australian Greenhouse Office, Townsville.

McCook, L.J., Folke, C., Hughes, T., Nystrom, M., Obura, D. and Salm, R. (2007b) Ecological resilience, climate change and the Great Barrier Reef. In: Johnson, J.E. and Marshall, P.A. (eds) *Climate Change and the Great Barrier Reef: a Vulnerability Assessment.* Great Barrier Reef Marine Park Authority and Australian Greenhouse Office, Townsville, pp.75–96.

Moscardo, G., Saltzer, R., Galletly, A., Burke, A. and Hildebrandt, A. (2003) Changing patterns of reef tourism. *CRC Reef Research Centre Technical Report No. 49.* CRC Reef Research Centre, Townsville.

Norris, A. and McCoy, A. (2003) Recreational use of the Great Barrier Reef Marine Park. In: *CRC Reef Research Centre Technical Report.* CRC Reef Research Centre, Townsville.

Norris, A. and Murphy, L. (2004) Understanding Great Barrier reef visitors: market segmentation by motivation. James Cook University, Townsville.

Orr, J.C., Fabry, V.J., Aumont, O., Bopp, L., *et al.* (2005) Anthropogenic ocean acidification over the twenty-first century and its impact on calcifying organisms. *Nature* 437, 681.

Prideaux, B., Falco-Mammone, F. and Thompson, M. (2006) Backpackers in the tropics: a review of the backpacker market in Cairns and their travel patterns within Australia. www.jcu.edu.au/ctth/idc/groups/public/documents/other/jcudev_006420.pdf (Accessed: September 2009).

Russ, G.R., Cheal, A.J., Dolman, A.M., Emslie, M.J., Evans, R.D., Miller, I. and Sweatman, H. (2008) Rapid increase in fish numbers follows creation of world's largest marine reserve network. *Current Biology* 18, 514–515.

Scott, D., Amelung, B., Becken, S., Ceron, J., Dubois, G., Gossling, S., Peeters, P. and Simpson, M. (2007) Climate change and tourism: responding to global challenges. Advanced Summary. www.unwto.org/media/news/en/pdf/davos_rep_advan_summ_26_09.pdf (Accessed: September 2009).

Shafer, C.S., Inglis, G.J., Johnson, V.J. and Marshall, N.A. (1998) Visitor experiences and perceived conditions on day trips to the Great Barrier Reef. Tehcnical Report No. 21. CRC Reef Research Centre Ltd, Townsville, 76pp.

Smithers, S.G., Harvey, N., Hopley, D. and Woodroffe, C.D. (2007) Vulnerability of geomorphological features in the great Barrier Reef to climate change. In: Johnson, J.E. and Marshall, P.A. (eds) *Climate Change and the Great Barrier Reef: a Vulnerability Assessment*. Great Barrier Reef Marine Park Authority and Australian Greenhouse Office, Townsville.

Steinberg, C. (2007) Impacts of climate change on the physical oceanography of the Great Barrier Reef. In: Johnson, J.E. and Marshall, P.A. (eds) *Climate Change and the Great Barrier Reef: a Vulnerability Assessment*. Great Barrier Reef Marine Park Authority and Australian Greenhouse Office, Townsville, pp.51–74.

UNESCO (2007) *Case Studies on Climate Change and World Heritage*. UNESCO World Heritage Centre (WHC), Paris, France.

UNESCO World Heritage Centre (WHC) (2007) World heritage: marine biodiversity. In: *Case Studies on Climate Change and World Heritage*. UNESCO World Heritage Centre Paris, France. Available at: http://unesdoc.unesco.org/images/0015/001506/150600e.pdf (Accessed: September 2009).

Veron, J.E.N. (2008) *A Reef in Time: the Great Barrier Reef from Beginning to End*. Harvard University Press, Cambridge, Massachusetts, USA.

Wachenfeld, D., Johnson, J.E., Skeat, A., Kenchington, R., Marshal, P.A. and Innes, J. (2007) Introduction to the Great Barrier Reef and climate change. In: Johnson, J.E. and Marshall, P.A. (eds) *Climate Change and the Great Barrier Reef: a Vulnerability Assessment*. Great Barrier Reef Marine Park Authority and Australian Greenhouse Office, Townsville, pp.1–13.

Webster, N. and Hill, R. (2007) Vulnerability of marine microbes on the Great Barrier Reef to climate change. In: Johnson, J.E. and Marshall, P.A. (eds) *Climate Change and the Great Barrier Reef: a Vulnerability Assessment*. Great Barrier Reef Marine Park Authority and Australian Greenhouse Office, Townsville, pp.97–115.

18 Disappearing Destinations: Recognizing Problems – Meeting Expectations – Delivering Solutions

Andrew Jones and Michael Phillips

Indicators and Lessons for the Future

The erosion of coastlines and beaches will undoubtedly pose a significant threat to both recreation and tourism and, consequently, the tourist economy of many destinations and regions in the future. There is still continuing uncertainty regarding climate change and the validity of current predictions but the fundamental question of whether coastal tourism destinations will have viable sustainable futures is a critical one facing many destinations today. It is clearly not an easy question to answer, but the evidence from not only the case studies contained in this book but also from evolving research elsewhere, shows that there are a number of indicators and lessons from which we can draw some emerging themes and assumptions. Critical themes emerging from the cases discussed in this book suggest that there are a number of growing complex interactive relationships evolving between several dynamic forces, which will ultimately determine the future sustainability of many coastal tourism destinations. These dynamic forces can be classified into seven key processes, which include a changing dynamic, cyclic relationship between:

1. The extent to which problems and threats are identified, hazards predicted and recognized.
2. The impact of the media on interpreting key issues and threats from climate change.
3. The role of local governance and public policy making vis-à-vis local and strategic planning actions in combating perceived and actual threats – ensuring forward and long term planning strategies.
4. Accountability between alternative funding options and the roles and responsibilities between public and private funding streams.
5. Predicting climate change hazards – making informed choices and decisions between ameliorative protective and/or adaptive measures: hard–soft–non-response alternatives in this context.

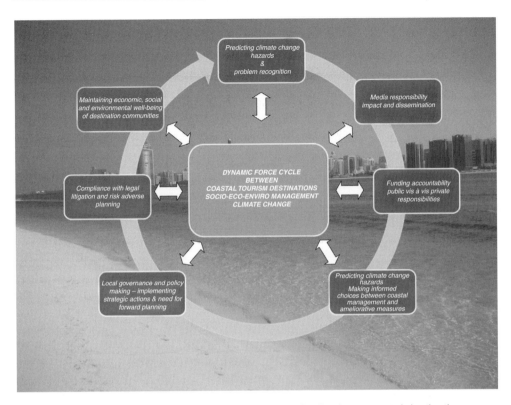

Fig. 18.1. The dynamic seven-force cycle for tourism destinations, coastal destination management and climate change.

6. Recognizing and ensuring compliance with growing legal frameworks, legal litigation threats, insurance hazard and risk adverse management strategies.

7. Maintaining the economic, social and environmental well-being of coastal tourism communities.

These issues are illustrated in Fig. 18.1.

Problem recognition: predicting climate change hazards

The consensus amongst coastal scientists and tourism managers is that there will be an increased incidence of storm surges and a general rise in sea level. As a result, erosion issues will become more prominent and coastal tourism managers and planners will increasingly have to use techniques that are best suited to the locality under specific threat. The cases discussed generally highlight an acceptance of the threats from climate change and present evidence from each sphere of the world. Such cases generally illustrate examples of threats, which largely relate to sea level rise, incidents of storm surges and storm damage particularly through flooding and high wind velocities, incidents of severe temperature rises, increased incidents of disease and resulting physical disruption as a consequence. These are issues illustrated for example by Hughes in her prediction of climate change impact on the Eastern Seaboard of the USA (Chapter 12). Despite such predictions, the main difficulty and concern that appears to emerge from the cases is not the general acceptance of potential climate change threats but the realities and ability to recognize time frames and the accuracy of current predictions at a specific destination.

These are sentiments that are widely expressed by a number of the authors of the case studies presented. Hughes again states that given the potential for change in societal attitudes and management policy, it is difficult to predict the impact of climate change on tourism. As another example, Moreno in his assessments of this problem on the Balearic Islands (Chapter 16) states that the island authorities and businesses should realize that current tourism management strategies will be insufficient to deal effectively with future climate change. He states that our lack of understanding of how tourism is affected by climate change is a major source of uncertainty and is thus a problem that urgently needs to be tackled. Michael Hall, in his review of the juxtaposition between climate change and tourism (Chapter 2), also reflects similar sentiments and says that it is clear that there are enormous knowledge gaps in understanding tourism and climate change relationships. He suggests that the greatest knowledge gaps exist between links that involve understanding the specific effects of climate change – tourism in particular locations and specific types of tourism activity. Cooper and Boyd's review using Ireland as an example (Chapter 10) provide evidence that predictions of the long term implications of climate change are likely to be highly damaging. In contrast, Jenkins (Chapter 5) highlights that the future is uncertain and change is inevitable. Jabour, on her assessments of Antarctic tourism (Chapter 13), raises the issue of commercial priorities, which tend to override and deflect arguments that might support more constructive recognition and reflections of climate change threats. She states that, for example, success will be complicated by the fact that the Antarctic tourism industry is, first and foremost, commercial in nature and secondly, that it is in competition with scientific research in locations that have the highest density of charismatic wildlife of the continent. Clearly, in this context, myopic objectives motivated by profit margins remain barriers to more responsible broader objectives that would enhance problem recognition. From a North American perspective, Meyer-Arendt (Chapter 15), although recognizing that climate change has already had severe consequences, for example on Grand Isle, suggests the future predictions and how to address them remain unclear. From Europe, Anfuso and Nachite, in their review of the Southern Mediterranean basin (Chapter 8), also stress that climate change has been largely neglected so far. Wilson and Turton (Chapter 17) look alternatively from a 'tourist gaze' at perceptual responses from tourists and provide some evidence from Australia that demonstrates that there is a obvious recognition problem from destination 'users and consumers' and that tourists do not yet respond to the 'clean and green' labelling initiatives that, in the long term, may offer some help with offsetting climate change threats. From a wider industry perspective, Jones, in his review of the UK (Chapter 14), advocates that professional opinion and management perceptions demonstrate some awareness of climate change threats but do not seem to promote effective mitigation or adaptive measures to confront them. He indicates that at best, professional attitudes to climate change and implications for coastal destination management are muddled.

The evidence is thus clear. From the cases discussed there remain critical recognition issues concerning the threats from climate change and predicted impacts at destinations. It can be seen that this lack of recognition spans across key stakeholder groups that include managers and planners at tourism destinations and the managers of tourism facilities and operations on the one hand and the users of tourism facilities, i.e. the tourists, on the other. Key to these difficulties can thus be attributed to: (i) limited professional and technical understanding or indeed full recognition of the problem; (ii) commercial priorities of tourism operations that tend to mask greater recognition of the problem; and (iii) general apathy and policy malaise from key policy makers, managers, consumers and users, which largely tend to ignore the problem or perceive it as a responsibility of others. Despite much global acclaim and reporting on such issues the problem of recognition at local level and empowering local people to act remains at best limited. Building professional capacity and empowerment would therefore appear to be important future tasks and priorities if such problematic issues are to be successfully addressed for destinations.

Media impact: dissemination and responsibilities

The juxtaposition between climate change, tourism and media reporting is a fairly recent phenomenon and remains largely in its infancy, particularly when tourism is considered. There has, however, been much awareness of global initiatives raised in the media with well documented events particularly associated with recent global climate change conferences, such as Kyoto and Copenhagen. This has also been augmented by preceding earlier reporting on events associated with, for example, the global earth summits. In this context responses from the media on climate change and its predicted impacts, particularly within tourism fields, have been inclined to be based on reporting that has tended to 'air' on the sensational, emphasizing critical concerns that often highlight perhaps, ambiguous, over-exaggerated or overstated issues. This has led in recent times to many legal and litigation issues arising, which Osborne and Jones have alluded to. As a consequence, media issues are now emerging as critical in ensuring and disseminating a rational argument that support the case for actions to address climate change and which in turn go some way to encourage responses and responsible actions for future policy.

In this respect, Burns and Bibbings, in their review of media challenges (Chapter 7), suggest at the very least, research in this area would deliver new knowledge in terms of identifying contradictions and challenges likely to confront policy makers and individuals as they seek change, and linked to this, clearer identification of attitudinal barriers to change and the provision of strategies for overcoming these. They add that such research would also provide much needed evidence for travel companies wishing to take a more socially responsible attitude towards the provision of travel products. In this respect the primary impact of such research could be on the academic community policy makers and lobbyists as insights into changing attitudes and behaviour towards climate change and air travel emerge. Plainly the use of media can assist with a greater understanding of the cultural dynamics that accompany social policies and anticipate attitudinal/ behavioural barriers to mitigation, and improved ways of framing communication to achieve better reception of key messages aimed at mitigation.

Clearly aspects of media presentations are impacting upon perceptions of climate change and how such impacts relate to tourism. There are undoubtedly positive and negative responses to such media representations, which emphasize the importance of ensuring both accurate and responsible media reporting. This will be increasingly critical if policy makers, planners and destination managers are to be encouraged to make or defend decisions that encourage informed responses to climate change and the future predicted impacts on tourist destinations.

Local governance and public policy making: focusing on forward and long-term planning strategies

The coastal tourism destinations have evolved from many natural and anthropo-centric factors and processes and within this often dynamic perspective it is logi-cal that management concepts, linked to governance and public policy, aim to be inherently integrated. It is this 'integrated' management concept that has been explored by several of the cases, which put forward notions, on the one hand, of the need to promote conservation and management of the coastal zone and on the other, of the need to ensure that recreational and tourism assets are pro-tected. How this is fully coordinated between organizations will bare heavily on achieving ultimate success in combating destination management challenges and tackling climate change predictions. As a consequence it is important to understand not only present day organization and decision-making processes but also processes linked to the coordination of public and private stakeholder organizations and how decisions concerning the management of destinations from a broad range of socio-economic and environmental stances are achieved. In addition to measures that enhance coordinated effort there is also a need to think with long term, lateral and strategic vision. Evidence from the cases largely demonstrates that current coastal and destination management practices tend to concentrate on immediate socio-economic and environmental responses, which often give little regard to longer term strategic coastal management concerns linked to long-term strategies that will address threats to coastal tourism destina-tions from climate change. In this respect it is becoming more critical that key stakeholders and appropriate policy implementation measures using institu-tional, legal, financial and technological frameworks not only aim to integrate more effectively but also aim to 'think' in longer term time frames.

These notions are explored by a number of the cases presented. Wilson and Turton (Chapter 17) suggest that this is one of the greatest challenges in achiev-ing climate change adaptation strategies and changing human behaviour. In this context they suggest that to achieve this it is vitally important that collaborative relationships are built across all components of the tourism sector to ensure that adaptation strategies are broadly accepted and adopted. Jones (Chapter 14) adds a proviso in this respect. His review of UK coastal destinations illustrates that professional awareness and in turn professional responses tend to be piece-meal and reflect a lack of strategic vision. He goes on to suggest that technical and professional understanding also remains minimal with little desire, or need, to initiate longer term policy or management responses to offset impacts. Jones consequently suggests that evidence shows that communications and actions between intra-governmental, national government, NGOs and municipal government will need to be strengthened in order to effect proper responses to ongoing and ultimately growing threats from climate change processes. Wilson and Turton's research also supports this general belief by suggesting that planning and implementation of many of the adaptation strategies needs to begin early and, in the context of their own case study, be in place by 2020. Jenkins (Chapter 5) puts it in more simplistic terms by implying that there is need for a new or a more efficient system to regulate tourism and manage growth. Hughes, using the North American Seaboard as an example (Chapter 12), concludes that little guidance was available from the federal government to steer either state-wide or local communities in the development of sustainable coastal tourism development and as a result concludes that there still remains a general lack of management policy, leading to the assumption that most organizations are not yet taking specific measures to prepare for rising sea levels. In this context, Hughes calls for actions that require a need to modify management policies that focus on preserving valuable coastal resources, which, she warns, ultimately support a billion-dollar tourist industry. Anfuso and Nachite (Chapter 8), in a similar vein, advocate that local planning staff must identify mitigation strategies from a regional, long-term perspective, this way providing a real foundation for cost-effective coastal erosion management.

Clearly, the case examples present a set of circumstances that suggests that it is becoming more critical that key stakeholders and appropriate policy implementation measures across all sectors, both horizontal and lateral, need to progressively change strategies in order to support future efforts and actions that combat threats to coastal tourism destinations from climate change. Thus recommendations are generally made for more integrated and long-term processes of problem recognition, planning, implementation and monitoring. Only by implementing such measures can more strategic approaches to the problems of coastal destination management be fully addressed. Ensuring such measures will go some way to make sure that: coastal environments are conserved; natural and anthropogenic factors and processes are integrated into the decision-making processes; coastal protection measures are fully evaluated; and selective strategies for future management of coastal tourism destinations prioritized. This will ensure the socio-economic and environmental well-being of such communities.

Roles and responsibilities between public and private funding streams

Tourism destinations are major sources of revenue for both local communities and broader national and global interests. This has been alluded to in some of the cases such as Williams' assessment of beach typologies and Hughes' and Jones' assessments in North America and the UK, respectively. The economic benefits of such destinations are thus now fairly widely recognized. What is questionable, however, is the clarity of financial and funding processes that underpin the well-being of such destinations. In this respect, the organizational and structural nature of financial governance and funding policy is increasingly at odds at a number of organizational levels. Consequently, the point at issue is one of how to balance and secure the funding for the protection and management of coastal destinations. This is particularly pertinent to ensure the economic well-being of the tourism industries and to secure adequate funding for the protection of such destinations from predicted climate change impacts. Critical to this are escalating concerns on climate change and mounting pressure to take effective ameliorative actions to fund hard and soft engineering responses, to fund managed retreat and develop funding strategies for the effective and sustainable management of tourism infrastructure. In this context the prime question is one which relates to who takes responsibility for enacting such measures and who pays or funds such actions. Such questions contribute to the increasing complex debate on these emerging funding issues, which are again a focus for discussion in a number of the cases presented.

Cooper and Boyd (Chapter 10) provide an interesting insight to such issues by using Ireland as a case. They suggest that coastal management requires an open-ended commitment if such resources are to be maintained and are thus usually confined to resorts whose economic situation depends on maintenance of the littoral fringe and associated infrastructures. In less developed areas they suggest that such options may perhaps be uneconomic and other solutions may prove both economically and environmentally more appropriate. Meyer-Arendt's case on the Southern USA (Chapter 15) suggests that maintenance can only be achieved in most cases through a generous infusion of federal funds, thus emphasizing the role of central government in taking responsible actions. He suggests that where local people are left to their own devices to defend and meet impacts from climate change, particularly storm damage, the long term sustainability of such effort, and indeed, such communities remains to be seen. Wilson and Turton (Chapter 17), using examples from Australia, indicate that planning in particular should be seen as requiring more support, both in terms of human resources and funding. Jones (Chapter 14) also advocates such sentiments. He states that the nature of funding arrangements vis-à-vis the relationships and responsibilities between locally based tourism industries, local government and central government are critical in ensuring effective long term funding strategies to meet needs for combating the effects of climate change.

Funding clearly remains a complex issue and the ability of coastal tourism destinations to secure effective strategies to finance long term measures or initiatives that will assist in defending destinations against predicted climate change impact are thus critical. Whether such initiatives are based upon local adaptation or mitigation measures or broader more strategic but less tangibles options are in essence individual choices for each destination. More significant, however, are the strategic mechanisms that are in place to help facilitate the funding of such options. Growing tensions between the private and public sectors are critical here and in this respect the key question tends to return to the fundamental issue of who has ultimate responsibility to ensure that funding and financial mechanisms are in place. At present the tourism industry, by its very nature fairly fragmented itself, is not in a position to coordinate such activities. Central governments with the assistance of local municipality input would appear to be the best options at present. Whether this direct funding can be sustained or whether it manifests itself into other forms of coordinated indirect funding through, for example, tourism taxes or user-pay principles remains to be seen. Funding, and how this is arranged to sustain coastal tourism destinations, will however remain critical in the foreseeable future.

Making informed choices and decisions between ameliorative protective and/or adaptive measures

Often policy choices for combating the impacts of climate change on coastal tourism destinations will invariably rely upon two alternative key strategies or of course a combination of the two strategies. These in essence will either focus upon direct adaptation of existing resources to address impacts or more broad mitigation measures to offset impact. Both contrasting strategies are widely seen and used as effective ameliorative measures that help reduce climate impact on local coastal destinations. Choices made between each of the measures available are of course largely dependent upon the nature and characteristics of the destination. Socio-economic, environmental, geopolitical influences are perhaps critical here in determining how decisions regarding ameliorative measures are taken and implemented. Indeed, correlation may exist between how proactive, how well organized, how politically vocal and how viable economically a destination is on the one hand and how its success is rated in securing effective and long term ameliorative measures on the other. In this respect the cases reveal that coastal destinations demonstrate a variety of alternative strategies and examples of feasible solutions. In this context several themes have emerged from the cases that raise issues and questions concerning the application and implementation of ameliorative measures. They relate in part to, for example, the 'art or science' of making informed choices and the degree to which technical knowledge is available, the availability of accurate data to support and enhance decision making and policy formulation, accepting the consequences and impact of the ameliorative choices made and tensions between long-term and short-term investment choices.

Hall (Chapter 2) expresses some of these tensions clearly in his case review by providing evidence that little research has been conducted specifically on climate change and its effects on tourism. This in turn, he advocates, makes it extremely difficult to understand the extent to which adaptation and mitigation processes can be effectively engaged in by the tourism sector or by government at various levels. Jenkins (Chapter 5) also supports such opinion and states that countries vary greatly in terms of their geography and climate and a more detailed construction is needed to explore the effects of climate change on the different regions of each country. Cooper and Boyd (Chapter 10), on their assessments of Ireland, provide an overview of some alternative management options that include several alternative strategies based upon accepting loss, creating compensatory habitat elsewhere, removing the sea defences and permitting the habitats to migrate. In this respect they qualify such actions as having important consequences for the natural habitats and associated tourism activity. As a consequence they infer that one particular challenge in Ireland is to maintain the coastal scenery by finding alternative approaches such as the proactive one of not permitting building in high risk zones and the responsive one of relocating threatened infrastructure. Dearden and Manopawitr (Chapter 11), in their assessment of specific tourism niches based on water sports in South-east Asia, also suggest there has been relatively little analysis of the knock-on effects of protective measures and works on such industries. In this respect they allude to a knowledge vacuum where much empirical work remains to be done in order to make accurate and informed decisions. Meyer-Arendt (Chapter 15), on his assessments on the Gulf Coast, proposes that coastal communities that face inundation due to climate change (e.g. rising sea level) have three options: protection, accommodation and retreat. In his case of Grand Isle he demonstrates that policy has shifted from a strategy of protection to one of accommodation. He proposes that hard and soft structural protection has proven to be stopgap at best, and although it may always remain a political priority, he concludes that its effectiveness cannot be guaranteed. Alternative policies based on accommodation via home-raising, roof-fastening and other defence mechanisms against water and wind, as well as rebuilding after every storm, are reviewed as the dominant adaptation strategies. He does qualify this, however, by questioning the sustainability of such options in the longer term. In addition to this, Wilson and Turton (Chapter 17), expressing issues from Australia, emphasize that many of the participants in their case had difficulty thinking of adaptation strategies for tourism for 2070, which was seen as too far into the future, thus again illustrating problems associated with long term thinking. Ultimately, however, their assessment of the greatest challenge in climate change adaptation strategies concerns the need to change human behaviour. Jones (Chapter 14) summarizes the problem as a need for technical understanding of, and the ability to differentiate between, mitigation and adaptation policies, which at best still remain somewhat ambiguous for managers and policy makers at a number of key destinations.

Clearly, the cases presented review a number of different strategies and measures that can be taken to offset climate impact at destinations, which are suited and 'fit' differently to different scenarios. Again there are a number of issues that have arisen as a consequence. The key to making choices between alternative ameliorative strategies would appear to be one that specifically relates to knowledge and knowledge gaps. In this context, making choices to ensure the effective amelioration of impacts will increasingly be dependent upon being 'well informed' with current data so that any decisions made on coastal tourism strategies and coastal defences remain appropriate to the sustainable management of the coastal destination. It is thus important, therefore, that research and monitoring of natural and man-made processes including the collection of primary data, is enhanced in order to ensure that accurate decisions are made. This, after all, remains the raw material for understanding the tourism industry and for evaluating protective measures for coastal destinations.

Compliance with growing legal frameworks, legal litigation threats, insurance hazard and risk-adverse strategies

The vocabulary of risk and associated legal issues is a fairly new phenomenon for coastal tourism destinations, particularly when considering the advent of climate change and its predicted impact. These are issues that still remain in their infancy and perhaps will require further exploration and research for the future. Nevertheless, risk and legal responsibility is an increasingly important issue that has been addressed by several of the cases. In essence, risk and legal frameworks are considered at a number of levels when addressing the issue of climate change and its impacts. Broadly it can refer to an assessment of risk predictions particularly in terms of a destination at risk. A number of insurance companies have alluded to this recently as suggested by Jones and Phillips in the introductory chapter. More specifically, risk can be applied at a more focused level by addressing risk assessments to specific actions or strategies at destinations and imply a more formal legal framework in this context. Increasingly, destinations, particularly managers of destinations, are having to address risk as a legal requirement of operating tourism facilities and activities. Although much analysis of climate predictions remains ambiguous there is nevertheless an underlying undercurrent of concern that relates to legal liability and potential litigious actions from consumers and users at destinations. As discussion and knowledge improve on climate predictions, legal responsibilities, particularly associated with 'duty of care', will become unavoidable operational concerns for tourism providers and destination managers. Issues associated with, for example flooding, storm damage, health, disease and heat, are predicted impacts from climate change and in turn pose potential risks and legal threats for both tourism providers and consumers. Where potential risks at a destination are perceived as high these may in turn have significant legal and operational consequences in the long term for the sustainability of coastal tourism destinations. Indeed, many destinations may have to significantly reduce their reliance on tourism not because of threats from the physical damage resulting from climate change but because of the threats induced from legal actions and litigation.

These are issues that are explored by Osborne (Chapter 6) in his review of legal frameworks for climate change. Other cases have also raised similar concerns. Jenkins (Chapter 5) implies that climate change is not new and is what the world has experienced for eons. He suggests the task ahead, however, is adaptation, to ensure that risk and hazard predictions are as accurate as humanly possible. He surmises that past prediction and forecasts have not been very accurate and therefore there is now an even greater urgency to ensure that new risk models of prediction are developed. In this context he advocates that the development of new climate prediction models relating to tourism impacts and risk are necessary and concludes that they require greater rigour than the current stochastic models. Jabour (Chapter 13), on her assessments of Antarctic tourism, illustrates that, for example, if ships are not ice-strengthened, as many are not presently, and if they continue to travel into poorly charted areas, risk will be exacerbated. In this context she predicts that localized extreme weather, especially during the summer cruising season, will make high latitude navigation increasingly dangerous when considered in combination with the presence of less predictable sea ice and icebergs and changing local weather conditions. Wilson and Turton (Chapter 17) foresee significant shortcomings in government acceptance of climate change risks and appropriate resourcing to overcome such risks and thus see barriers and limitations to securing many infrastructure and policy adaptation strategies as a consequence. As a side adage they comment that in their particular case of Australia a large number of control and certification schemes are on offer but with no legislative power associated with them. Moreno (Chapter 16), regarding his study of the Balearic Islands, proposes that to help increase the knowledge base on climate change impacts a vulnerability methodology needs to be more fully considered. In a similar vein Anfuso and Nachite (Chapter 8), in their assessment of the Mediterranean basin, add that despite concerns the regional government shows for the issue, little interest has been reflected in the provision of any legal document for tourism management. Jones (Chapter 14), in his assessments, provides a more frank view by suggesting that legal threats culminating from the physical effects of climate change will grow and insurance companies will increasingly determine where and when tourist can travel with, of course, severe consequences for many destinations that are significantly vulnerable to impacts.

Clearly legal liability and risk responsibility is a growing concern. The solutions are currently difficult to predict. However, as a consequence of such concerns raised, coastal tourism destinations will have to further develop risk adverse strategies in order to minimize, potentially expensive, legal actions. At a more strategic level clearly defined legal frameworks, roles and responsibilities will need to be defined in order for both users, consumers and managers to be more fully informed of their rights, roles and responsibilities. At best these still remain unclear and this emphasizes the urgency of the issue. The lesson may, however, be a severe one if such issues are not addressed. In such situations many destinations may be subject to the whims of insurance companies and tour operators who will ultimately decide whether the risks for visitors are too great to offset potentially damaging legal actions.

Maintaining the economic, social and environmental well-being of coastal tourism communities

Evidence highlighted from the cases presented demonstrates that coastal tourism destinations initiate a variety of actions that go some way to offset the predicted and actual effects of climate change or to manage expectation of such threats. These actions tend to differ according to the socio-economic, environmental, geographical and political contexts in which each of the destinations are located. In this respect the action taken by local and national organizations vary to quite a degree. Some destinations have a combination of both proactive adaptation and mitigation measures, others concentrate on adaptation, others mitigation and some offer limited responses to all but very basic measures. Each individual destination thus addresses problems associated with its own particular set of circumstances and needs and thus raises quite different sets of concerns. The cases do, however, illustrate that there are some positive moves in the right direction and a recognition that coastal destinations cannot pander to the status quo. Indeed most of the cases stress the economic, social and environmental importance of the destinations, particularly in the context of valued ecosystems, valued landscapes and dependent socio-economic systems particularly focused on the tourism industry. All these would appear to be interrelated and recognition from the cases illustrates that it will become increasingly important to enhance policy- and decision-making processes in order to sustain and protect such systems from climate change threats. Indeed, ensuring successful actions and outcomes in this context very much belie the future well-being of each destination. The cases clearly illustrate a set of emerging concerns and issues associated with such well-being. They include the need to make hard choices between economically sound and uneconomic destinations in terms of costs associated with protecting coastal resources. Several cases in this respect discuss options associated with not investing in protective measures and retreating to coastal hinterlands. Others discuss the concept of disappearing destinations in the context of the impact that climate change regulations may have. Carbon offset policies and the possible restrictions that these may impose on several destinations, particularly those that rely upon air transport, are a case in point. Calado *et al.* (Chapter 9), on their assessments of the Azores, especially stress this point. They state that climate change policies need to be tailored to a local scale in order for destinations, such as the Azores, to remain competitive. When considering the difficult mobility and accessibility conditions of such places, which have no alternative to air transportation, they stress that there will need to be a special exemption policy for each region. With no such exclusions or compensation mechanisms, they surmise that the increase in transportation prices will greatly aggravate accessibility and tourist mobility and thus, in turn, diminish such a destination's capacity to remain economic, with, of course, the negative repercussions for such tourist economies. As a result, Calado *et al.* conclude that places such as the Azores, though not a disappearing destination in terms of its touristic qualities based on preliminary climate change impact assessment, could however become a disappearing tourist destination due to undesirable travel cost as a result of climate change policies. Hughes suggests (Chapter 12), on her assessments of the US Eastern Seaboard, that there are perhaps limited options with little alternative but to invest. In this context she states that with the potential for dramatic land loss and ecosystem alteration on the East Coast as climate changes, it seems there is still a need to adapt management policies and preserve the valuable assets, which, she concludes, support a billion-dollar tourist industry. Meyer-Arendt (Chapter 15), in his review of Grand Isle, perhaps poses opposite sentiments by advocating retreat from non-viable locations and destinations. Jones (Chapter 14), in this context, may perhaps offer a compromise alternative. He stresses the continued need to integrate coastal tourism policies with tourism development policies linked to coastal hinterlands, which may go some way to help address specific problems and assist in relocating some tourism activities away from vulnerable coastal areas.

Clearly the socio-economic viability of coastal tourism destinations and climate change dynamics are sensitive political issues in the context of local, national and international politics. Whether economic sense will prevail, over-riding political sensitivities that include defending local and national interests remains a difficult issue to resolve. At best most tourism destinations will guard their economic interests and their social and environmental contexts, which in turn support their tourist economies. How some such destinations will continue to remain sustainable in the future is unanswerable. What will become increasingly important, however, is the need to balance decisions associated with climate change and the assessed socio-economic impacts these will have on specific tourism destinations. A 'one fits all' policy will clearly not be appropriate. Balanced decision making based upon protection of some areas and retreat in others will need to be made. The continued development of integrated tourism policies that encourage links to coastal hinterlands might also be an option to help offset vulnerability.

A Final Reflection

The loss or erosion of coastal destinations through predicted climate change impacts will undoubtedly pose a significant threat to both natural ecosystems and tourism infrastructures and consequently the tourist 'communities' at such destinations. Evidence from the cases reviewed illustrates that perceived and actual threats are indeed real although accurate predictions and current assessments remain at best ambiguous and at worst remain a guessing game. The cases present a variety and varied set of local destinations and experiences. In summary it seems fair to say that there remains uncertainty regarding climate change and the validity of current predictions. However, general perceptions amongst professional tourism managers demonstrate that there is recognition of increased incidence of storm surges and a general rise in sea level. Perceptions also recognize predicted erosion and loss issues, but mixed responses and knowledge of options for ameliorative actions appears to be a norm. In essence the cases have illustrated a complex relationship of concurrent processes or continuums that integrate at differing levels and stages of the tourism destination management cycle. These continuums address process associated with coastal tourism destination management, and associated dynamic processes of problem recognition, balancing strategies or meeting stakeholder expectations and providing solutions to the key issues, problems and threats at hand. These inter-relationships are illustrated in Fig. 18.2.

In essence, it is clear from the cases that there is still a need to think with long-term and lateral vision. Evidence shows that current coastal destination management practices tend to concentrate on immediate socio-economic and environmental issues, which often give little regard to longer term strategic destination management concerns. Again from the evidence it would appear that strategic longer term approaches to managing coastal tourism destinations based

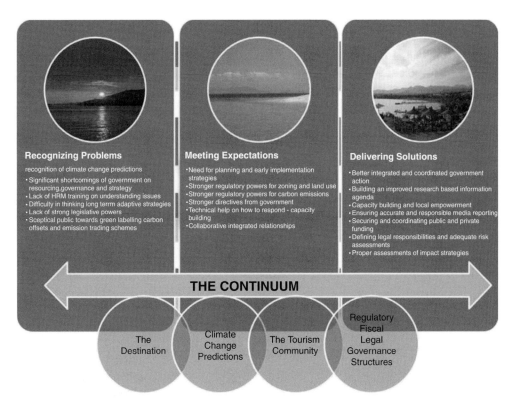

Fig. 18.2. Disappearing destinations – the coastal tourism destination management continuum: recognizing problems, meeting expectations and delivering solutions.

upon strategic governance, local empowerment and capacity building with more integrated legal and media processes are becoming critical. Evidence of good practice is demonstrated in many of the cases reviewed, however the examples are only a small illustration of the growing global threats that climate change can have on such destinations. In this respect the cases remain a 'patchwork' of lessons, which demonstrate pointers for how climate change is perceived, how destinations are managed and policy choices made. As such they cannot provide all the answers but nevertheless go someway to indicate a possible way forward in addressing specific threats. In an increasingly uncertain world where climate predictions are questioned and media hype appears to be the dominant conduit for presenting information, such cases are important in providing a rational base from which to assess and analyse current experiences and learn lessons. Despite remaining uncertainties, what is abundantly clear is that there is a need for all stakeholders, and this includes users, consumers, providers, administrators, planners and controllers, of the various processes operating within destinations to engage and integrate more fully with decision making and policy processes. Pertinent to this, is engagement with appropriate long term policy implementation measures that connect more closely with existing or perhaps newly created governmental, legal, financial and technological frameworks. In essence this means creating or ensuring structures for management and decision making that are fit for purpose. At present, evidence suggests that such structures and organizational structures remain lacking. In this respect the future success in managing coastal tourism destinations, particularly with the onslaught of climate change, will increasingly be dependent on effective measures that support a cyclic process of problem recognition, effective planning, proper implementation and controlled monitoring and research. Only then can appropriate responses to the complex problems associated with climate change, coastal erosion and the long term sustainability and management of coastal tourism destinations be fully addressed.

Index